£15

ANDREW
FLETCHER
OF SALTOUN

Fletcher

ANDREW FLETCHER
OF SALTOUN

His Life and Times

by

W. C. MACKENZIE

Edinburgh
THE PORPOISE PRESS

FIRST PUBLISHED IN 1935
BY THE PORPOISE PRESS
133A GEORGE STREET, EDINBURGH
LONDON : FABER AND FABER LIMITED
24 RUSSELL SQUARE, W.C. I
PRINTED IN SCOTLAND BY
R. MACLEHOSE AND COMPANY LIMITED
THE UNIVERSITY PRESS GLASGOW

CONTENTS

[*vii*]

Contents

PREFACE

A BIOGRAPHER wholly destitute of sympathy for his hero makes dull work," remarked Mr. Andrew Lang in the preface to his biography of Sir George Mackenzie of Rosehaugh. When writing my studies of Simon Fraser, Lord Lovat, and John Maitland, Duke of Lauderdale, I was conscious of the same kind of disability as that under which Mr. Lang had apparently laboured. But their *Lives* supplied a medium for presenting what I had mainly in view, namely, an account of the political relations between England and Scotland during a hundred years (between the middle of the seventeenth and the middle of the eighteenth century), and the present biography provides the necessary middle link; also it forms the last volume of the trilogy. Incidentally, it places a wholly honest man of simple character, between two men who were certainly not so honest, and quite as certainly not so ingenuous. The character of Andrew Fletcher needs no whitewashing, and from me it will receive no "debunking". Indeed, it is conceivable that I am laying myself open to the charge of allowing my admiration for him as a man to warp my critical sense of his shortcomings as a statesman and an economist. But my study of his career has led me to the conclusion that not only is the popular tradition of Fletcher in his native land as a sincere patriot—Fletcher *the* patriot is his usual cognomen—essentially sound, but that the originality of his views as a publicist, and his eminence as a writer, deserve greater attention than hitherto they have received. In England (I think I am right in saying) Fletcher's name, familiar of course to historical students, is known to the general public, when known at all, only as the author of an aphorism, usually misquoted, and sometimes attributed to Chatham, namely,

"If a man were permitted to make all the ballads, he need not care who should make the laws of a nation."

In the material (or lack of it) for a biography of Fletcher, there is involved a tragedy of lost papers. When George Keith, the tenth Earl Marischal of Scotland, who became Ambassador in

Paris and Madrid for Frederick the Great, was Governor of Neuchâtel, he struck up a friendship with Rousseau, then residing there. Keith urged Rousseau to write a biography of Fletcher, and obtained the necessary material from Scotland for the purpose. But the biography was never written, and the papers have been lost. The eleventh Earl of Buchan published in 1792 a rhapsodical sketch of Fletcher's career, based upon a manuscript now in the library of Edinburgh University, which was written by Madame Lally-Tallendal, granddaughter of Lord Milton, the "patriot's" nephew; but its informative value is slight. Fortunately, however, there is abundant contemporary material (as well as Fletcher's own writings), upon which to draw for a full account of Fletcher's career at home, and for an examination of his political philosophy, though there is a hiatus which must remain unfilled in respect of his adventurous life abroad.

In addition to an excellent sketch-biography of Fletcher, written in 1897 by Mr. G. W. T. Omond, for the *Famous Scots Series*, and a relatively valueless short *Life* published by Dr. R. Watson in 1798, articles on Fletcher have appeared in various publications. Those known to me are an article in the *Encyclopædia Britannica*, another in *The Retrospective Review*, Vol. IV (1821), by an anonymous writer; and a third in *The Scottish Review*, Vol. XXII (July 1893), by Mr. J. Ramsay MacDonald, the present Prime Minister, an ardent admirer of his subject. And, of course, there is the well-informed article by Mr. Espinasse in the *Dictionary of National Biography*.

The political reputation of Andrew Fletcher must necessarily stand or fall by his attitude towards the Parliamentary Union of England and Scotland, and I have devoted a substantial part of this biography, including excerpts from his speeches, towards elucidating his reasoned views on that all-important subject. Fletcher has been called Scotland's first Home Ruler, and in these times, when Nationalism in general, and Scottish Nationalism in particular is receiving increasingly growing attention, the opinions of their prototype cannot fail to be of interest to his present-day sympathisers.

A word about the portrait of Fletcher which forms the frontispiece of this book. It has been reproduced from the portrait in the

National Portrait Gallery in Edinburgh, which, in the view of Sir James L. Caw, is (like the portrait in Saltoun Hall) a copy of the original in the possession of the Earl of Stair. The artist's name (according to Sir James Caw) is uncertain. I have to acknowledge with thanks the kindness of the Curator of the National Portrait Gallery, in permitting me to have the copy photographed; it is a faithful reproduction of the original.

Also, my thanks are due to the officials of the National Library of Scotland, the Library of Edinburgh University, and the Register House in Edinburgh for the courtesy with which they have assisted my researches. Lastly, I have to offer my grateful acknowledgments to Mr. R. A. Scott Macfie, who, with Mr. E. Gordon Duff, has compiled a helpful bibliography of my subject. Mr. Macfie has kindly placed his valuable notebook at my disposal, and in other ways has assisted me with his expert advice on the authenticity, or otherwise, of works attributed to Fletcher. I have embodied Mr. Macfie's views in the notes at the end of the book, which include supplementary material of interest, more particularly, to historical students.

W. C. MACKENZIE.

St. Margarets-on-Thames.

Chapter I

THE PREPARATORY STAGE

PATRIOTISM was in the blood of Andrew Fletcher, "the patriot". For on his mother's side he was a descendant of King Robert Bruce, who successfully established the independence of Scotland. His mother, Catharine Bruce, was the daughter of Sir Henry Bruce of Clackmannan, who was descended from the third son of Robert Bruce, lord of Annandale, the grandfather of the hero of Bannockburn.

Andrew's father was Sir Robert Fletcher of Saltoun in Haddingtonshire, a son of Andrew, Lord Innerpeffer, a Senator of the College of Justice, whose title to historical fame consists in the fact that he was one of the seven Scots who protested against the delivery of Charles I by the Scottish Army at Newcastle, into the hands of the English Parliament (1).

Thus the subject of this biography, born in 1653, was, on one side, of Royal blood, and on the other side, of gentle and distinguished stock. Heredity might have predisposed him towards monarchy. Reflection, united to the possession of a judgment of marked individuality, made him, during the whole of his political life, an opponent of kings.

His studies during his youth turned his mind into a philosophic channel, and bent it in a direction which shaped his political career. And these studies were directed by one of the most remarkable men of his period, Gilbert Burnet, afterwards Bishop of Salisbury, and more particularly known to fame as the author of the great *History of His Own Time*. It is unfortunate that in his history, Burnet has told us so little about his old pupil; but the reason, as will be shown, is fairly obvious. He describes Fletcher as "a Scotch Gentleman of great parts and many virtues, but a most violent republican and extravagantly passionate". And Burnet was neither a "violent republican", nor was he "extravagantly passionate". It may be observed that in his unpublished MS. Burnet substitutes, for "a most violent republican", the words, "a most passionate and indiscreet assertor of public liberty" (2).

About the time that he attained his majority, Burnet was presented with the living of Saltoun by its patron, Sir Robert Fletcher, who in 1665 entrusted, on his deathbed, the education of his son, then twelve years of age, to the young clergyman. Any education Andrew Fletcher previously received, must have been at the hands of his parents, and possibly at the parish school, where, in those days, "gentles and simples" alike, without distinction of class, sent their children for the elements of learning. It has just been stated that in his history Burnet has said little about Andrew Fletcher. But a more amazing thing is that while his first published book was entitled *A discourse on the memory of that rare and truly virtuous person Sir Robert Fletcher, of Saltoun,* "written by a gentleman of his acquaintance", he achieved in this book the notable feat of saying practically nothing about his subject. The title of the book, indeed, is a character sketch in miniature of Sir Robert. But the biographer of Andrew Fletcher looks in vain for any detailed information not merely about Andrew, but about his father, the explanation being that Burnet's intention was to write a "sermon" with Sir Robert's character as the text, instead of a biographical memoir.

Young though he was, Burnet had seen something of the world before he became the incumbent of Saltoun. He had visited the English Universities, and had made the acquaintanceship of great English divines in London. Also, he had travelled on the Continent, and while in Holland, had rubbed shoulders with members of all the numerous religious sects of which that country, at the time, was so prolific. Having naturally an inquisitive turn of mind, and an acquired propensity for poking his nose into the affairs of other people, "Gibbie", we may be sure, made good use of his time while on his travels, and enjoyed a varied experience such as few, if any, contemporary Scottish clergymen of his years had reached. He was, indeed, a valuable acquisition to the parish of Saltoun, and Sir Robert Fletcher was justified in the confidence which he reposed in him, as an instructor for his son, when the mind of the latter was ripe for the impressions that last a lifetime.

[2]

Writing about his father's incumbency of Saltoun, Burnet's son says: "During the five years he remained at Saltoun he preached twice every Sunday, and once more during the week; he catechised three times during the same period, so as to examine every parishioner, old and young, thrice in the compass of a year: he went round his parish from house to house, instructing, reproving, or comforting the inhabitants, as occasion required; those who were sick he visited twice a day; he administered the Sacrament four times in the year, personally instructing all that gave notice they intended to receive it: all that remained above his own necessary subsistence, in which he was very frugal, he distributed in charity. A particular instance of his liberality was related by a person who then lived with him, and who afterwards was with him at Salisbury. One of his parishioners was distrained upon for rent, and came to our author (Burnet) for some small assistance, who inquired how much would again set him up in his trade. The debtor named the sum, which a servant was immediately advised to pay him. 'Sir,' said the domestic, 'it is all we have in the house.' 'Well, well,' replied Burnet, 'pay it to this poor man; you do not know the pleasure there is in making a man glad.' Thus, as he knew the concerns of his whole parish, treated them with tenderness and care, and set them a fair example of every article of that duty which he taught them, he soon gained their affection, not excepting the Presbyterians, although he was then the only man in Scotland that made use of the prayers in the English Church liturgy" (3).

An exemplary parish minister, and a good man: quite plainly so, after making due allowance for the partiality with which filial affection may have coloured this character-sketch. But what of his capabilities as a teacher and a mentor for young Andrew Fletcher? We do not know what course of studies Burnet set for his pupil; but it is permissible, by implication, to make a guess that is likely to be more or less accurate. Burnet, many years afterwards, was selected by William of Orange as the "preceptor" of the Duke of Gloucester, the only member of the Princess Anne's numerous progeny to survive childhood, but who died at the age of eleven. He was nine years of age when Burnet took him in hand, and he tells us what subjects he taught him, and his method of instruction. "I had read (he says) over the Psalms, Proverbs and Gospels with him, and had explained things that fell in my way very copiously. . . . I went through geography so often with him that he knew all the maps very particularly. I explained to him the forms of government in every country, with the interests and trade of that country, and what was both good and bad in it. I acquainted him with all the great revolutions that had been in the world, and gave him a copious account of the Greek and Roman histories, and of Plutarch's *Lives*, and the last thing I explained to him was the Gothic Constitution and the beneficiary and feudal laws. I talked of these things at different times nearly three hours a day: this was both easy and delighting to him" (4).

It is not assuming too much to suggest that we have here the subjects and the methods employed in Andrew Fletcher's education. Indeed, "the Greek and Roman histories" and "Plutarch's *Lives*" are written all over the face of his character. He had good reason to be thankful to his father for having provided him with a man like Burnet for his teacher, a teacher who was at once cultured, and (one may well believe) entertaining.

The (11th) Earl of Buchan (1742-1829), who had access to the family papers, tells us that from Burnet Fletcher received, as might have been expected, "a very pious and learned education and was strongly imbued with erudition and the principles of a free government, which were congenial to the family of Fletcher, and espoused by his mother and by those who had with her the charge of his nature" (5). Burnet describes his father as having been a very devout man, and, moreover, a man of culture who was interested in philosophy and science. But Andrew Fletcher himself attributed, in his later years, the formation of his character mainly to his mother, who seems to have been a remarkable woman. A pleasing story to that effect is related in the private family history.

"One day," so the story says, "after Andrew Fletcher had entertained his company with a concert of music and they were walking about in the hall at Saltoun, a gentleman friend fixed his eye on the picture of Katharine Bruce where the elegant pencil of Sir Peter Lely had blended the softness and grace that form the pleasing ornaments of the sex. 'That is my mother,' says Andrew, 'and if there is anything in my education and acquirements

[4]

during the early part of my life, I owe them entirely to that woman' " (6).

"When he had completed his course of elementary studies in Scotland under the care of his excellent preceptor (says Buchan), he was sent to travel on the Continent." This was the ordinary course to complete the education of a Scottish gentleman of good family, except that University studies usually lay between. The Register of the University of Edinburgh for 1668, says Mr. Omond, contains the name of "Andrew Fletcher". But a recent examination of the Register has failed to discover any such name. The culture and style of his writings certainly presuppose a University education, though cultured men have been known who have never been to a University, and University men have been known who have no knowledge of style. We have no record at all of the Continental centres visited by Fletcher on the "grand tour". It may, however, be surmised that Holland, which he was to know in later years very intimately, and whose varied interests Burnet had no doubt descanted upon, was one of them. But the countries usually visited by young Scotsmen, when making the tour, were France and Germany and Italy.

The year 1678 saw his entry into public life. In that year he was elected as one of the two Commissioners to represent his native shire in the Convention of Estates. It was an important year in the Parliamentary history of Scotland.

The Duke of Lauderdale, the "uncrowned King of Scotland", had his back to the wall in his struggle with the Opposition in the House of Commons, who were striving with might and main to overthrow him. His policy of repression in Scotland had to be justified in the eyes of the King, by whose favour alone he was able to stand on his feet. And for that policy money had to be found. Hence the summoning of the Convention of Estates in June 1678. Early in that year, the despatch of the "Highland Host" to put down an expected rising of the Covenanters (or to force a rebellion, as Burnet would have us believe), had brought the discontent with Lauderdale's administration to a head, and his enemies in Scotland were united with his English foes in their efforts to destroy him. The Convention was called, not to transact ordinary Parliamentary business, but for the sole purpose of granting a supply sufficient to maintain, for some years, "a competent force". The King's instructions to his High Commissioner (Lauderdale) were to raise a force to deal with "foreign invasion" or "intestine rebellion". A small minority of the Convention, headed by the Duke of Hamilton, made a fight for it, in opposing the Commissioner's proposals, but in view of the fact that Lauderdale carried "at least two third parts clear", they were powerless. The elections had been jerrymandered, and men had been elected who had no constitutional standing. And in any case, it needed strong Parliamentarians to stand up to an all-powerful dictator like Lauderdale. Among those who had the courage to oppose him was Andrew Fletcher. On his first appearance as a public man, he gave a foretaste of the independence of spirit and disregard of consequences in the discharge of what he conceived to be his duty, which characterized his whole career. During the session a striking incident occurred which serves as an illustration of his courage. His brother Henry, disregarding the order which barred admittance to Parliament House to all but members, had managed to evade the order. When discovered in the House, he was fined and sent to the Tolbooth for his pains. Next day his brother Andrew "pitched on little William Talmush as no member", and demanded his expulsion (Lauderdale's wife was the widow of Sir Lionel Tollemache of Helmingham in Suffolk); whereupon the Commissioner was compelled to explain apologetically that "little William" was one of his servants whom he was entitled to bring into the House. The youthful Fletcher was not one of the trucklers to the great man. He was soon to find an opportunity of showing his courage in a fresh direction (7).

The Convention was dissolved on 11th July, after voting a levy of £150,000 sterling by a land tax, to be spread over five years. Even the Duke of Hamilton "in this juncture" felt convinced "it was his duty" to vote for it. Only, he would have had the "privileges of the people untouched".

Just so. But were the privileges actually untouched? Lauderdale and Hamilton were polite enough to one another when they met, which was as infrequently as possible, for "these two dukes", says a caustic contemporary, "are like two buckets in a well; when one goes the other comes". But the enmity between them was too deep-seated to be eradicated by polite phrases. Hamilton posed as the people's tribune, whereas the policy of Lauderdale is epitomized succinctly and (I believe) justly, in the following words, by the shrewd observer who has just been quoted.

"The policy he follows is the point of absolute supremacy in his Majesty's person, and he values the clergy as little as the Presbytery when it comes in competition with that point, and I believe will live and die of this opinion" (8). Small room there for the "privileges of the people"!

Late in 1678, the Privy Council of Scotland was ordered to call out 5000 foot and 500 horse, being a quarter of the total authorized force of militia. This force of 22,000 men was constituted by an Act of 1663 for which Lauderdale was not responsible. But he was responsible for an Act passed by the Scottish Parliament of 1669-70, which, to use his own words, "ascertains and regulates" the militia. The object of this "regulation" was to place an army at the disposal of Charles II at a time when the King was at grips with the House of Commons: when he was treading the perilous path that led to the Treaty of Dover; and when red revolution, calling for repression by force of arms, seemed well within calculable distance. "If you command it," wrote Lauderdale to Charles in November 1669, "not only this Militia, but all the sensible men in Scotland shall march when and where you shall be pleased to command." And in a letter written to the King in October, he had declared that "those six regiments you may depend on to be ready to march when and whither you please" (9). The danger to Charles in 1669-70 had passed, for his people had remained in happy ignorance of the secrets of the Treaty of Dover. But in 1678 a portion of the militia was needed to suppress in Scotland itself a growing movement which was heading for revolution. On the 5500 men now called up, was to be imposed a special military oath, to be taken individually and not collectively, in addition to the oath of allegiance and supremacy.

In 1679 Shaftesbury's celebrated speech in the House of Lords made great play with the 22,000 Scots "ready to invade us on all occasions". It was a phantom army for the invasion of England; it never materialized; and if it had materialized, it would never have marched. But it was a different affair when this force, or a quarter of it, was to be called up for service in Scotland, where the Covenanters were formidable in numbers, and where their cause commanded, in the main, the sympathies of the Lowlands. That meant possibly civil war, and in the state of the religious atmosphere of that time, might have developed into that most horrible of all wars, a war of religious sects.

Scotsmen who looked at the portents without sectarian or political prejudice—and they were probably few in number—were gravely concerned for the welfare of their country. Among them was Andrew Fletcher. He recognized the danger inherent in converting a militia into what was, in effect, a standing army, controlled by a servile Privy Council, whose main concern was to obey the behests of a dictator pledged to carry out the wishes or the whims of his master. What was to become of Hamilton's "privileges of the people"?

But Fletcher and those who thought with him could do nothing. They could, indeed, place as many hindrances in the way of the "New Model" (such was the Cromwellian title given to the militia), as circumstances allowed. And so they did. Two hundred foot and forty-six horse were quartered upon Fletcher's shire of Haddington. "At Privy Council", says Sir John Lauder of Fountainhall, under date 29th July, 1680, "Fletcher of Saltoun, Sinclair of Stevenston, and Murray of Blackbarronie are pannelled for seditiously and factiously opposing, at least obstructing, his Majesty's service, in putting the Act of Privy Council to executions for levying the 5500 men out of the militia." "It was thought", says Fountainhall, that the Council would fine or imprison them, but (strangely enough, considering the sort of Privy Council they had to deal with), they were merely "rebuked". Charges of "horning" were, however, directed against all the "heritors" whom the Council "suspected" of recalcitrance, and they were ordered to meet and "stent themselves according to their several proportions of these 5500 men" (10).

Early in the following year a petition was presented to the Council, signed by "the Lord Yester, Salton, and the other gentlemen of East Lothian", complaining of the standing forces and their quartering upon them. "This bill was extremely resented, because it called quartering contrary to law, and seemed to derogate from the King's prerogative, and reflected on the Government"; which it certainly did (11).

All this tends to show the spirit of resistance that was being aroused in men like Fletcher to the arbitrary measures of the Government. It was the beginning of a lifelong fight by him against anything savouring of political or administrative tyranny.

The Government would fain have reduced to nullity men of his calibre who were not afraid to stand up to them. They had already punished Fletcher as a potential rebel, by quartering soldiers on him. Now, by means of an act of flagrant dishonesty on the part (it is said) of one of their creatures, Bishop Paterson of Edinburgh (a good type of what were practically Court officials, dignified by the name of bishops, who were imposed upon the Church of Scotland), they tried to keep him out of Parliament. With his colleague, Adam Cockburn of Ormiston, he was returned for Haddingtonshire, at the election of 1681, by the freeholders who were opposed to the Government. The Ministerial candidates were Hepburn of Humbie and Wedderburn of Gosford, who were also returned by their party. When the Committee on Disputed Elections met to resolve the election, the Chairman, Bishop Paterson, proposed that in order to "serve the King", the votes given to Fletcher should not be counted. He failed, however, to carry the Committee with him in this outrageous suggestion, and Fletcher and Cockburn were declared to be "more legally elected" than their opponents. Fletcher's services in the interests of liberty were soon to be needed in Parliament House (12).

Lauderdale was now definitely on the shelf. In October 1680, he resigned the Secretaryship for Scotland, after a career of which the piety and promise of his youth had been shattered by ambition and a woman. Seduced by glittering prizes, he had succumbed to them. His great gifts had been prostituted, against his truest convictions, to the service of a master who gave him his support so long as he promoted his interests, and who dropped him when he ceased to be serviceable to him. He died in 1682, some weeks after he had been heard to declare, "in Cardinal Wolsee's words", that if he had been as faithful to his God as he had been to the King, He would not have shaken him off in his old age, "as his Master and the Duke of York" had done.

The Duke of York reigned in his stead as High Commissioner in Scotland. As events proved, the change in respect of Scottish interests was definitely for the worse. For if Lauderdale had chastised his fellow-countrymen with whips, York, who was not a countryman of theirs (though he was a Duke of Albany), was now about to chastise them with scorpions.

At first the Duke, knowing the suspicion in which he was held on account of his religion, was wholly conciliatory. He held the zealous bishops in check; he made a great show of exploring and cleaning out the Augean stable of finance; and he proved himself a capable administrator in matters relating to trade. But it was not long before the cloven hoof showed itself. The Covenanters, the extreme section of whom had now been driven to open rebellion, were to experience the horrors of what is known in Scottish history as the "killing time". But it was by Parliamentary action that the Duke hoped to obtain the complete and permanent subjection of the nation to the will of the Crown.

When Parliament met in July 1681, with York as Commissioner, no time was lost in passing an Act securing to the Duke the succession to the Scottish Crown. According to Fountainhall, Andrew Fletcher had written privately and anonymously to some members of the Parliament, beseeching them to oppose the Succession Act (13). He was not in the least deceived by the Duke of York's policy of conciliation. He knew that the Duke, besides being a Roman Catholic, was fanatically attached to monarchial prerogatives, and he was convinced that a reign of tyranny would follow the death of Charles II, if his brother succeeded to the throne. But his voice and his vote were powerless against the crowd of sycophants of whom the Parliament was largely composed.

The Test Act was the second of the two measures that mainly occupied the attention of Parliament during that session. Following upon the Act of Succession, it was designed to give legislative sanction to what was, in effect, a surrender of the liberties of the nation, both civil and religious, into the hands of the Crown. Happily, there were a few members of that Parliament who saw clearly through the schemes of the Court party, with the Commissioner at its head; and no one saw more clearly than Fletcher.

"Mr. Fletcher of Saltoun," says Sir John Dalrymple, "after long opposing the bill with all the fire of ancient eloquence and of his own spirit, made a motion which the Court party could not, in decency, oppose, that the security of the Protestant religion should be made a part of the Test" (14).

That was the first challenge to the Duke of York, which the Duke did not think it prudent to accept. The bishops, his willing servants, could not "in decency" oppose a seemingly obvious provision which had somehow been overlooked, though if they had all been like Bishop Paterson (which they were not), it could scarcely have been deemed to be an important omission. For Burnet says, "And it was reported that Paterson, then Bishop of Edinburgh, said to the Duke that he thought the two religions, Popish and Protestant, were so equally stated in his mind, that a few grains of loyalty in which the Protestants had the better of the Papists turned the balance with him" (15).

The question naturally arose: what, for the purposes of the Act, was the "Protestant religion"? and how was it to be defined? The Lord President of the Court of Session, Sir James Dalrymple, had a ready answer. Presuming on the ignorance of his hearers (including the bishops), he proposed (and his proposal was accepted), that the standard for the interpretation of Protestantism should be the Scots Confession of Faith, authorized in 1560 by the Estates. "That was a book", says Burnet, "so worn out of use that scarcely anyone in the whole Parliament had ever read it; none of the bishops had, as appeared afterwards." For thirty years the Westminster Confession of Faith had been used in the Church of Scotland, with the grudging but politic assent of the bishops.

Now the Scots Confession of Faith happens to be a child of John Knox, prepared for the English Congregation at Geneva, of which he was minister. It contains theology which would have made the hair of the bishops in the Parliament of 1681 stand on end. And if the Duke of York had but known it, the same *Confession* strikes at the roots of the very principles which the Test Act sought to legalize, namely, non-resistance to the Crown of "any sort", or under "any pretence", and never to "endeavour any alteration in the Government, in Church or State". For the

Confession makes it obligatory upon its subscribers to "represse tyrannie", and to "defend the oppressed". How this obligation was interpreted by John Knox and the Reformed Kirk, which accepted the teaching of the *Confession* as its guide, the ecclesiastical history of Scotland amply testifies.

Here then was a condition in the Test Act which stultified the intentions of the Court. When the Act was printed, its implications caused a feeling of bewilderment. In spite of an attempt by the episcopate to explain away its difficulties and its dangers to their clergy (for the Church as well as the State was concerned), there was no means of avoiding the plain fact that the oath to be sworn was to be taken "in the literal sense of the words". The King's prerogative enabled him to do what he pleased. Anyone holding office in Church or State, all members of Parliament, and all electors of members had to swear not to oppose him in doing what he pleased. But the *Confession* incorporated in the Act obliged those who took the oath, to "represse tyrannie" and to "defend the oppressed". Sir James Dalrymple, the great lawyer, who proposed its incorporation, had a sardonic sense of humour (16).

The clause compelling electors, as well as members, on pain of forfeiting the franchise, to take an oath never to attempt to "bring about any change or alteration in Church or State as it is now established by the laws of this Kingdom", was strenuously resisted by Fletcher, who had the honour, in company with "the Laird of Grant", of being in a voting minority of two (17).

The Test Act drove out of the country a number of the best of the clergy who, after being treated by their bishops with "much contempt" (the words are Burnet's), resigned their livings. Some twenty of them went to England, where Burnet helped them; and England seems to have been the richer for their migration. But the most notable effect of the operation of the Act was exemplified in the case of the Earl of Argyll, whom the Duke of York had determined to destroy. The Duke, says Burnet categorically, "concluded it was necessary for him either to gain him or to ruin him". Failing to gain him, he ruined him.

Argyll, being a Privy Councillor and a Commissioner of the Treasury, was compelled to "declare himself". Lauderdale (of whose policy of non-resistance to the Crown, York's Test Act was the inevitable corollary) had a real friendship for Argyll. His past support of the Earl was one reason, among others, for York's dislike of Argyll. For York had thrown over his predecessor in the Commissionership, and had struck at him effectively by stopping the lucrative trade in bribes, in which Lauderdale's "rascally" brother, Lord Halton, and Lauderdale's avaricious wife had long been partners. But his main reason for planning Argyll's ruin was that he was "the Protestant Earl", and especially because, as York told the King, Argyll was "greater than it was fit for a subject to be". Shrewdly, also, he conceived that in humbling the Earl, he would have the sympathy of certain of Argyll's neighbours, who were jealous of his power and who accused him, not without justice, of being a notorious land-grabber.

So the Test Act provided the Duke of York with an excellent opportunity for eliminating Argyll. The latter duly took the Test oath, so far as it was "consistent with itself". His qualified acceptance of the oath had to be given in writing. It was wilfully misconstrued as treasonable, and the Earl was brought to trial. The result was a foregone conclusion, for the Duke of York had decided on his destruction. He was found guilty of high treason. "No sentence in our age", says Burnet, "was more universally cried out on than this. All people spoke of it, and of the Duke, who drove it on, with horror."

Argyll was lodged in Edinburgh Castle, but (remarks Burnet significantly) "rooms were also fitted for him in the common jail to which peers used to be removed a few days before their execution". Speaking after the event, the Duke of York strove to create the impression that he had not intended to take his life, but merely to limit his powers—and presumably to give him a good fright in advance. Efforts were made to save the Earl. Lauderdale "tried his whole strength with the King to preserve him"; but Lauderdale was now a spent force. Argyll's step-daughter solved the difficulty very cleverly. By "changing clothes with her footman and carrying up her train", her father passed out of the Castle "undiscovered by the guards", and escaped to Holland, after lurking for some months in London. Some of the Duke of York's sycophants on the Privy Council advised that the intrepid lady should be "publickly whipt through the streets of Edinburgh". But the Duke had the decency to reply that "they were not used to deal so cruelly with ladies in his country" (18).

Lesser men, like the youthful Andrew Fletcher, who had consistently opposed York's policy, could scarcely expect to escape his enmity when the big men like Argyll felt its full brunt. His Whig contemporary, Macky, says he "openly opposed the Arbitrary Designs of that prince" (York), "and the final Bill of Accession, which obliged him wisely to retire, first to England and then to Holland. The Duke of York", he adds, "could not forgive his behaviour in that Parliament" (1681) (19).

It was only a question of time and opportunity for him to leave the country if he wanted to save himself from ruin. Accordingly, like Argyll, he went to London, where they had many sympathizers among the Whigs. But before he left Scotland, he had, in 1682, one more tussle with the authorities. As a Commissioner of Supply for Haddingtonshire, he had certain duties to perform in settling prices and providing storehouses for provender for the horses of the troops. With some fellow-Commissioners, he was accused by the Lord Advocate of neglecting, or setting at naught, these duties. Probably there was considerable substance in the complaint made to the Privy Council, for Fletcher and other Commissioners for East Lothian were deliberately set upon thwarting the Government where and when they could (20). They gave in to the Government on this occasion, but continual friction of this sort could have only one end. And Fletcher, by his flight from Scotland, obviously concluded that the time had come when canny discretion should take the place of blind valour.

Thus ended the first chapter of his political career.

Chapter II

THE COUNCIL OF SIX

"AHITOPHEL" had fled to Holland for refuge, rejoicing in the fact that "Carthage", after all, had not been destroyed. "Absalom" remained at home, there to become a focus for the growing forces of rebellion in the kingdom. The spirit of revolt was not indeed directed wholly, or even mainly, against the "King David" of Dryden's Biblical analogy. Charles II, it is true, had been giving, in his later years, fuller evidence than at any previous period of his reign, of his determination to rule without the concurrence of his Parliament, and to crush ruthlessly all opposition to his will. But Charles, with all his faults, had the gift of inspiring popularity, which (so the Whigs may have reflected) might be proof against the ill-effects of arbitrary government, or even an exposure of his truckling with France. It was popularly believed that in him the country had a sure bulwark against Romanism, for it needed the imminence of death to reveal the fact that he was a Protestant for State reasons and a Romanist by conviction. But his brother, the Duke of York, apart from his open Romanism, lacked the gift of making himself popular. And it was believed with good reason by the Whigs, that his accession to the throne would stereotype and probably accentuate the absolutism of Charles. It was certain, as Charles himself shrewdly remarked, that no one would think of killing him to put his brother on the throne. But there was an alternative successor to Charles, namely "Absalom", his handsome, popular, and Protestant son by Lucy Walters: James, Duke of Monmouth. If he could be legitimated, well and good; if not, he would, at least, serve usefully as a centre for plots against the Royal brothers.

In 1682 the affairs of the malcontents in England were managed by what came to be called the "Council of Six", consisting of the Earl of Essex, Lords Grey, Howard, and Russell, and Mr. Hampden, besides Monmouth himself. On certain occasions conspirators of lesser importance but greater fierceness of temper, men such as

[*15*]

Armstrong, Ferguson, and Rumsey, were present. The meetings sometimes took place at Hampden's dwelling, but usually in Abchurch Lane at the house of a wine-merchant named Shephard, who had a good reputation on 'Change, and who was wholly in sympathy with the politics of the six councillors. Subordinate to the Council of Six were other "cabals" of the same political complexion, the members of which were more revolutionary in their aims and much less scrupulous in their means of attaining them. These clubs used to meet at the chambers in the Temple of a lawyer named West, or at various public-houses and taverns in and about London. They had their code of language designed to foil the attempts of eavesdroppers and informers to penetrate their secrets. The King (for example) was "the Churchwarden of Whitehall"; the Duke of York, "the Blackbird", "the Goldfinch", "the Captain", and "the Lieutenant". The intended insurrection was "the General Point", and the proposed assassination of the King and the Duke, "the Lopping Point", or "Striking at the Head"; and so forth. Among themselves, when in no danger of being overheard, their favourite toasts were: "To the man who first draws his sword against Popery and Slavery in defence of the Protestant religion", and "Confusion to the two brothers, Popery and Slavery": a neat reference to Charles and James (1).

By these lesser societies the scheme of killing both Charles and James and precipitating a revolutionary crisis was discussed and ultimately planned; Rumbold, a daring ex-Cromwellian soldier, volunteering to be a "marksman", and calling upon a fellow-conspirator, Robert Ferguson, an ex-clergyman, to "consecrate" the blunderbuss which he intended to use. Thus was hatched the "Rye House Plot", with the concoction and carrying out of which the Council of Six had nothing whatever to do. The high-minded men who composed the Council would have viewed with horror the proposals for the treacherous murder of the two brothers; not because the brothers were "hedged" by any "divinity", but because they were protected by a feeling of humanity against the plans of assassins. The political plots and the murder plots were thus unrelated, and, moreover, they were conceived, respectively, by men whose minds worked on a different plane when the question of lawful and unlawful methods of securing a common end had to be resolved. If, in the result, it suited the policy of the Court to refuse, as far as possible, to discriminate between the two sections of malcontents, and to sentence them accordingly to a common doom, the distinction was, none the less, clearly made by discerning men of their time.

The association of Andrew Fletcher with the Council of Six rests upon the authority of the family manuscript which Lord Buchan used in his fragmentary memoir; and upon a statement by Fletcher's contemporary, Fountainhall. Burnet, the old tutor of Fletcher, must have had some knowledge of this association, if it existed in fact. Yet Burnet does not include Fletcher's name in the list of Scotsmen, headed by Baillie of Jerviswood, who were co-operating with the Council in plotting against the brothers. But Burnet's reticence on so delicate a subject is understandable. He himself tells us that Hampden, knowing that Burnet was collecting material for a history of his own time, had offered, on several occasions, to provide material relating to the plot; but the offers were declined, pending the publication of an indemnity for all who had been engaged in the conspiracy. The canny Burnet thought it better to know nothing than to know all. He was resolved not to run the risk of being compelled either to reveal his knowledge or to commit perjury. At the Revolution it was intended that Hampden should supply Burnet with the inner history of the conspiracy, but by some mischance the information was never given. Thus Burnet may have known that Fletcher had worked with the Council of Six, but the knowledge may not have extended beyond that bare fact; and he may have deemed it prudent, when chronicling the fact, to suppress Fletcher's name entirely during the lifetime of the latter (2).

"In the year 1683", says Lord Buchan, "he (Fletcher) with Robert Baillie of Jerviswood, came into England in order to concert measures with the friends of freedom in that country, and they, I believe, were the only Scotsmen who were admitted into the secrets of Lord Russell's Council of Six. They were likewise the only persons in whom the Earl of Argyll confided in Holland the common measures of the two countries, which were then concerted with much secrecy and danger, for the recovery of the Constitution and liberties of the British Kingdom" (3).

B

That statement, based upon the family records, is sufficiently explicit, and I can see no valid reason to question its substantial accuracy. It is certain that Fletcher's sympathies were with the malcontents; that the danger to freedom in England and Scotland was identical; and that owing to his resistance to the exercise of tyrannical powers by the Administration in Scotland, he had made his native country too hot to hold him. What more likely than that he joined the small band of Scottish Whigs, who, with a view to co-ordinated action in both countries, held conferences in London with their English colleagues?

The latter had sent a man named Aaron Smith, who was *persona grata* with the Scottish Presbyterians, to arrange for a visit to London of certain of the Scottish Whigs. These consisted of Baillie of Jerviswood, Sir Hugh and Sir John Campbell (near relations of Argyll), Sir John Cochrane, and one Munro, who were appointed to act in concert with the English conspirators. A further Scottish contingent included Lord Melville, James Stewart, Sir Patrick Hume, Hugh Scott, William Carstares, "and some others". And among these "others", Andrew Fletcher was inferentially to be found. The Earl of Argyll, too, was lurking in London after his escape from Scotland, but whatever secret communications may have passed between him and the Council of Six, he took no active part in their deliberations (4).

These men (Argyll and Fletcher excepted) came from Scotland, ostensibly to discuss the affairs of the Scottish colony founded in Carolina during the previous year, but really, as it would appear, to discuss the prospects of an insurrection in England and Scotland. If all the members of the Scottish delegation were men like Baillie of Jerviswood and Fletcher, they were a group of earnest patriots, concerned only for the future of their country and desirous only of preserving her religion and her liberties. They had no sympathy whatever with the Rye House plotters. The only Scotsman among that clique was the notorious Robert Ferguson, who, in an age of plotters, had well earned the distinctive title of "Ferguson the Plotter". There was no political plot of major importance in the late seventeenth and early eighteenth centuries with which he was not connected, either directly or indirectly. "Of all the conspirators, whether English or Scotch", says one report, "the deepest man (next to Shaftesbury and Argyll) was Robert Ferguson, a Scotchman living in England" (5).

Originally a Presbyterian clergyman, he had been thrust out of that discerning body, and had then ingratiated himself with the Independents. "He had been divers years a fierce Independent preacher in the City of London, and had long exercised his virulent pen against the Government, in which he had a peculiar talent, and by means of a fluent tongue, a subtile head, and invincible" (by which "brazen" is probably meant) "spirit, he animated the whole, and moreover excited and actuated the blackest part of the contrivance" (the Rye House Plot). He had tried, says Burnet, to make advances to him as a "brither Scot" who could be useful to him. But Burnet was too careful of his own reputation to have anything to do with him. Ferguson was, in short, an arrant scoundrel (Burnet calls him a "profligate knave"), who was ready to sell his wretched soul for money; or alternatively, scheming was so ingrained in the texture of his mind that he plotted incessantly because he could not help plotting (6).

Fountainhall supplies the missing link in the account given by Lord Buchan of Fletcher's association with the Council of Six. He states that Fletcher was living in exile in Brussels; that the Duke of York requested the Spanish Governor there to have him arrested; and that Fletcher, realizing his danger, came over secretly to London and joined the Monmouth group. That he succeeded in gaining admittance to, and sharing in, the counsels of the inner circle of those who were plotting against Charles and James, while he kept the authorities in total ignorance of his presence in London, is proof alike of his resourcefulness and his courage. His life would not have been worth a bodle had he been discovered (7).

That Fletcher was strongly suspected by the Government of having had intimate relations with the Council of Six, is clear from the efforts that were fruitlessly made to procure damnatory evidence against him, after the discovery of the plots. Baillie of Jerviswood, a sick man, who was hurried to execution after a trial that outraged all sense of justice, and who was spared no cruelties that malignancy could suggest to break down his fortitude, courageously refused to listen to all suggestions to give

[19]

Fletcher away. On no consideration, not even to save his life, would he offer evidence against his friends who had shared with him the attempt (which the conspirators made no effort to conceal) to bring about an insurrection. "They who make such a proposal", was his notable reply, "neither know me nor my country" (8).

But clearly, after the discovery of the Rye House Plot, neither England nor Scotland was a safe place for Baillie's friends; and those of them who were able to escape to the Continent hastened thither with all speed. Among them was Fletcher, who seems to have renewed his acquaintance with some of the places he had visited during his "grand tour". The Government continued to keep an eye on him, as may be judged by the fact that, in October 1683, Viscount Preston, the Envoy Extraordinary from the English Court, reported from Paris that "one Fletcher, Laird of Saltoun, was in Paris, lately come from Scotland. He is an ingenious, but a very dangerous fanatic, and doubtless has some commissions, for I hear he is very busy and very virulent" (9).

Holland became the only safe refuge of the fugitives from the vengeance of Charles and James. There the exiles, English and Scottish alike, held continual consultations for their common safety and for their future policy. The main links between them and the Dutch were their common Protestantism, and, within certain limits, their common political ideals. Also, Holland possessed in the Prince of Orange the future ruler of their hopes, and a present helper in their troubles. Monmouth, the darling of his father, who saved him from the fate that would otherwise have befallen him, found a home in hospitable Holland. There, too, the Earl of Argyll breathed in safety after English adventures as "Mr. Hope". The Scots discovered a Scottish colony in Rotterdam, where a flourishing Scottish congregation served to stimulate their patriotism and preserve their Presbyterianism. In Rotterdam, plans were discussed by Monmouth and Argyll with their English and Scottish colleagues. Amsterdam then became their headquarters, and there they waited anxiously for something to turn up. And that "something" turned up with the death of Charles II.

Meantime, for the young, pleasure-loving, indolent Monmouth, life in Holland was comparatively free from care. His indulgent father, who on his death-bed was anxious that "poor Nellie" should not starve, was also careful that his boy by Lucy Walters should not lack bread. Nor did he lack amusement, for he was a familiar figure at the race-courses and the balls of the capital. He was liked by the Dutch, and he was even favoured by the critical Scots, who remembered his clemency after Bothwell Bridge, and who remembered, too, that he was the Duke of Buccleuch, as well as the Duke of Monmouth. They must, indeed, have regarded with strong disapproval his association with the Countess of Wentworth, that charming woman who loved him so recklessly that she followed him to Holland. His marriage with the Countess of Buccleuch had been unhappy: it had been a marriage entirely of convenience; and it had turned out a failure. He regarded Lady Wentworth as his wife, and she regarded him as her husband (10).

In these pleasant surroundings Monmouth was well content to remain for an indefinite period; and if a timely gesture had just then been made to him by his father and uncle, it seems not improbable that there might have been no Monmouth rising, and that the young Duke might have lived possibly to a good old age after a quiet life in which politics found no place.

But the death of his father immediately changed everything. No sooner had the Duke of York become James II, than he seemed to detect a potential danger in the presence of Monmouth in Holland. He sent an envoy to his son-in-law, the Prince of Orange, desiring him no longer to offer an asylum to the Duke; and he stirred up the Spanish Court to prevent his taking refuge in the Spanish Netherlands.

Something had to be done by the exiles, and without delay. Monmouth himself was averse from a premature trial of strength with his uncle. He wished to retire to Sweden, and there await a favourable conjunction of events for his effort. But the eager men around him, who were straining their eyes across the North Sea, persuaded themselves that they saw convincing signs that the time was ripe for action. Two men, and two only, looking at the situation with the detached eyes of the cool observer, opposed that view. One of these was Andrew Fletcher, and the other was Captain Matthews. As an adviser, Fletcher possessed a great advantage over the others, in the fact that he was totally devoid of personal ambition, and was therefore capable of reaching unprejudiced and sound conclusions, having as their aim the common good, and the common good only. Monmouth, indeed, placed such reliance on his judgment, that he had sent a special messenger to Brussels, where Fletcher was then residing, desiring him to come to see him (11).

The English visionaries saw things in the light of their hopes, and not in the light of the facts. The Duke of York, they argued, had made himself so obnoxious to the nation that his dethronement by a popular movement headed by the popular Monmouth could scarcely fail to succeed. The West of England would follow the Duke to a man. The Whiggish City of London, which had felt the heavy hand of Charles, would give its support to the removal of a king who was not in the least likely to be an improvement on his brother. Monmouth's eager advisers, among whom Lord Grey and a Taunton goldsmith named Dare were prominent, urged him to cross the sea at once and take the land which the Lord had given to him. Ferguson the Plotter, too, seems to have used his oily tongue to persuade the Duke to venture, though, characteristically, he denied after the event having taken that line.

All this talk sounded to Fletcher like the prattling of children. "How", he asked scornfully, "are you going to conquer England with less than a hundred men?" "Henry the Seventh", replied the egregious Lord Grey, "landed with a smaller force and succeeded." "Ay," retorted Fletcher, "but Henry the Seventh made sure beforehand of the support of the nobility, who were little princes in those days" (12).

The fact was that, as Fletcher clearly perceived, unless the ground had been carefully prepared in England, and the adherence of influential men secured, a rising could have no reasonable hope of succeeding. He knew, and Monmouth as a soldier knew, that a badly-armed, insufficiently disciplined, and unskilfully led mob of peasants and tradesmen could stand no chance against well-armed and well-drilled troops. They might, indeed, achieve temporary successes, but even these would be of no permanent value unless the direction of the revolt resided in the hands of men of real influence in the nation. And of influential forces in England, waiting to throw themselves into the arms of an invading body of adventurers, there were no signs whatsoever. But the talkers continued to talk, and the Duke continued to listen and to hesitate.

While these discussions were going on, the Scottish exiles were making plans of their own. At their head was the Earl of Argyll, by far the most important of Monmouth's friends. As MacCailein Mór, he could command the broadswords of five thousand fighting Campbells. He was the most influential of the Scottish Whig peers. By heredity he was the most powerful layman of the Church of Scotland. And his Presbyterianism, suspect, with justice, in his younger days, seems to have caught fire by contact with Scottish enthusiasts at Rotterdam. He, if anybody, was capable of leading an insurrection in Scotland, for his courage was undoubted, and his cause was the cause of the people. He believed, quite honestly, that if provided with the necessary money for arms and ammunition, he could sail for Scotland forthwith, and quickly secure control of the administrative power in that country. A rich widow found the money; and the arms and ammunition (ostensibly purchased for the Venetian Republic) were soon at his disposal. All was now ready for his share in the adventure (13).

Andrew Fletcher refused to have anything to do with Argyll's expedition. With the prescient eye of the statesman, he foresaw its failure. We do not know the precise reasons he gave for not joining the Earl and his Scottish friends. But they may be surmised.

It is easy to be wise after the event; but it is also easy to detect beforehand fundamental weaknesses in some calculations. And to a man like Fletcher, who knew his countrymen intimately, and whose power of critical detachment had not been vitiated by contact with ambitious adventurers, Argyll's plan may have seemed from its inherent weakness foredoomed to failure. Argyll was, indeed, master of thousands of Campbells. But his scope of influence as a Highland chief was confined to his own clan. The mere fact of the Campbells being on one side would incline the neighbouring clans to range themselves on the other. For the traditional attitude of the Western clans, such as the MacDonalds and the Macleans and the Camerons, towards the Campbells, was an attitude of hostility. The Campbells were numerically the most powerful of the clans, and were consequently feared by the less powerful. They were regarded, and with some justice, as oppressors of their neighbours. They were Whigs and Protestants; and the bitterness of religious and political differences was, in some instances, added to traditional antagonism on other grounds.

There were other arguments against success which must have presented themselves to Fletcher's mind. The natural leaders of the Scottish people were either in exile, avowed enemies of the Crown; or were at home in comfortable Government posts; or were too cowed in spirit to risk their lives and fortunes for abstract notions of liberty or (possibly mistaken) fears of religious persecution. Also, Argyll's chief companions were Sir Patrick Hume of Polwarth, a maker of phrases rather than a man of action, and Sir John Cochrane, son of the Earl of Dundonald, whose sphere of influence, in each case, lay outside Argyll's territory. These two men represented Lowland and Covenanting interests, as distinguished from the Highland and moderate Presbyterian connexions of the Earl. As the event showed, they performed the paralysing functions of an advisory committee which insists upon its advice being followed against the wishes of the man in supreme command. That was the sort of interference by committee which played into Cromwell's hands at the battle of Dunbar; and its Dutch counterpart, in the early years of the next century, was to hamper seriously Marlborough's operations in his Continental campaigns. Argyll's character was masterful rather than yielding, and in submitting to dictation by a committee, he must have believed himself capable of imposing his will as leader of the expedition upon his subordinates. He had two capable English officers, Ayloffe and Rumbold (of Rye House fame), under his command, and on these he could rely to carry out his orders with skill and resourcefulness. But Cochrane and Hume had their own strong views on the plan of campaign, and after their arrival in Scotland, Argyll found himself hopelessly at variance with them. He had exacted a promise from Monmouth to sail for England six days after his own departure for Scotland. Partly (it may be supposed) because he was awaiting news of Monmouth's landing, and partly with the hope (perhaps an unjustified hope) of adding to the disappointing number of recruits who obeyed his call to arms, Argyll lingered in his own Highland country while his colleagues insisted upon dividing his force, with one portion of which they made an unavailing demonstration in the Covenanting West. But two things are sufficiently clear: the ground had been far from adequately prepared beforehand; and a leader whose subordinates opposed his plans could scarcely expect to succeed in an enterprise which was, at best, a gamble.

It is probable that Fletcher's objections to Argyll's plans sprang mainly from the same root as his disapproval of Monmouth's similar adventure, namely, that there was no reasonable prospect that it would receive the support of the influential men of the country invaded. Lacking that support, it would lack all the essentials of permanent success. Argyll did not so misjudge the situation as to believe that his action in Scotland, even if successful, could possibly effect the common end of Monmouth and himself, unless co-ordinated with similar action in England. Hence his agreement with Monmouth that six days after the Earl's departure for Scotland, the Duke would set sail for England. The honourable fulfilment of that promise proved highly embarrassing to Monmouth, who, there is reason to believe, might very well have postponed his enterprise indefinitely, had it not been for his pledged word to Argyll (14).

It would appear that James II had sound information, from a "bottle companion of Monmouth" and other sources, of what was going on in Holland. His envoy at the Hague was instructed to press for the detention of Argyll's three vessels, which, however, were allowed by the Dutch Admiralty to leave without hindrance on 2nd May, 1685. The same thing happened when Monmouth's vessels lay at the Texel, when the Dutch Admiralty declared that they had not adequate means of detaining them. Whether or not the Prince of Orange was behind these obvious attempts to evade the necessity of detaining the adventurers, it is impossible to say, though there is what appears to be reliable evidence that he kept his father-in-law informed of their sailing. And Andrew Fletcher, protesting against the adventure, but refusing from chivalrous motives to desert Monmouth in his hour of need, was one of the passengers to England who sailed by the *Helderenberg* in 1685.

Argyll's adventure did not contain even the element of surprise which alone could have given it a chance of success. Time was given for preparations to be made against the invaders. Many of

Argyll's influential clansmen (also his wife, one of his sons, and his step-daughter) were kept safely in Edinburgh, where they could harm neither themselves nor the Administration. Consequently, less than half the full strength of the Campbells joined their Chief, and that number was subsequently reduced by desertions. Divided counsels, and plans that went astray, fatally impaired the effectiveness of the force. And when, finally, the arms which had been stored in a castle at Loch Ridden for safety were captured by a Government ship, Argyll lost hope and courage, and the enterprise was doomed. By his capture, soon afterwards, when trying to escape in disguise, he entered the path to the scaffold which he trod like his father before him. And like his father before him, he died with quiet and dignified heroism. He was sentenced on the charge of treason which had caused his flight from Scotland (15).

Chapter III

THE MONMOUTH RISING

BEFORE his execution Argyll complained bitterly of Monmouth's failure to set out upon his adventure on the date agreed between them. He should have sailed on 8th May: he did not leave Amsterdam until 24th, and the expedition did not sail from the Texel until about a week later. What was the cause of the delay?

There was one obvious reason why the adventure should be held up, if not, indeed, ultimately abandoned: and that was the lack of money. Arms and ammunition had to be found; tonnage had to be chartered; current expenses had to be met. Where was the money to come from? That, indeed, was a problem, and a very serious problem. So serious did it become that Monmouth's infatuated mistress, Lady Wentworth, had to come to the rescue with her jewels; and the Duke himself was compelled to pawn the gems that had been given to him by his father. But at length the necessary means had been scraped together; a frigate loaded with arms and ammunition (ostensibly for Bilbao) was chartered; and everything was ready for the departure.

Neither Argyll nor Monmouth had made sufficient allowance for the vagaries of the weather. Monmouth and his party of thirty left Amsterdam in a lighter to join the vessels at the Texel, where they found about fifty adherents awaiting them; but conditions in the Zuider Zee were so bad that the short journey to the Texel took nearly a week. That is a measure of the foulness of the weather which, there is every reason to believe, was the true reason why Monmouth failed to synchronize his adventure in England with Argyll's invasion of Scotland. The bad weather continued during the passage from the Texel, and it was not until 11th June that the frigate *Helderenberg*, with two tenders (one of the three tenders originally attached to the frigate had been seized by the Dutch authorities at the Texel, as a feeble sort of demonstration), dropped anchor off Lyme in Dorsetshire.

Why Lyme? The answer is probably provided by the fact that one of the most vociferous of the eager partisans who urged Monmouth on his enterprise, was Heywood Dare, the goldsmith of Taunton, who, before his exile, had been an alderman of that town, then a relatively more important place than it is now. He professed to have considerable influence in Taunton and its neighbourhood; and there appears to have been some substance in his boastfulness. He seems to have been an ill-mannered, loud-voiced, overbearing sort of individual, the type from which gentle, sensitive natures like that of Monmouth shrink, but the type which in the active affairs of life generally succeeds in getting its own way. He had apparently the influence over Monmouth that a strong character exerts over a weak one; and thus we find (what might otherwise need explanation) that he acted as Monmouth's secretary, and afterwards as his paymaster.

This was the man, indeed, on whom Monmouth mainly relied to bring the first batch of recruits to his standard. There were only two representatives of English or Scottish aristocracy in his party, namely, Lord Grey and Andrew Fletcher, and it was on these two men that his hopes were set as leaders; it was on Dare and his like that he depended for the men to be led.

Dare was put ashore at Seaton, west of Lyme, with the object of bringing the news of Monmouth's imminent arrival to the knowledge of those he could trust with the secret.

On Thursday, 11th June, a band of eighty-one adventurers landed at Lyme and set up the standard of revolt. Realizing that he was appearing in his rôle of the "Protestant Duke", Monmouth caused his following, on reaching the shore, to kneel in thanksgiving for a safe voyage, and in prayer for Divine help in their struggle for religious and political liberty. Then, drawing his sword, he bade his company go forward.

The first thing to be done was to publish a manifesto setting forth the aims of the adventurers. This was a task suited to the genius of that wordy schemer, Robert Ferguson, Shaftesbury's ex-chaplain, who, though apt to be carried away by the exuberance of his entangled rhetoric, lacked none of the arts, common to all times, of the demagogue seeking to influence public feeling. Some of the charges made in the declaration were disgracefully

[28]

blatant, and wholly incapable of proof. One of these extravagant statements was that the King had poisoned his brother, a charge the truth of which was certainly believed by some who were blinded by political rancour. By permitting the publication of this manifesto, Monmouth erected a scaffold for himself in the event of failure. Indeed, when he was a suppliant for his life at the feet of James, after the rising had been quelled, the latter might conceivably have pardoned him but for two things: the charge of poisoning Charles, and Monmouth's assumption (later) of the title of King (1).

The commencement of the rising was completely favourable. The villagers of Lyme gathered round the blue flag, and cheered for the popular "Monmouth and the Protestant religion". Recruits flocked rapidly to his call. But they needed drilling, and Bristol, the key of the West, slipped from Monmouth's grasp as the result of the delay that drilling entailed.

The leaders, who lodged in the George Inn at Lyme and held frequent consultations there, knew well that an anxious time lay immediately ahead of them. Of these leaders, Fletcher was in an anomalous position. As we have seen, he had declared against the wisdom of the rising, to the surprise, indeed, of those who knew him most intimately. Writing about the preparations for the adventure, Burnet says that "Fletcher, a Scotch gentleman of great parts, . . . was now much in favour. I that bred Fletcher should have expected that he should have driven him (Monmouth) on to the mad attempt he made, but I know the contrary." For Fletcher, being the most chivalrous of men, had decided to venture all rather than desert his leader. As Burnet puts it, "So Fletcher told him (Monmouth) he would run fortunes with him, though he could not hope for great matters" (2). Imposed upon him at Lyme was the invidious task of influencing decisions for a campaign which he regarded as hopeless before it started. But the dice had now been thrown. Monmouth had unsheathed the sword, and flung away the scabbard. Not merely rhetorically, but literally, his followers had to conquer or die.

Here it may be convenient to pause, to consider a curious point that seems to need elucidation. Contemporary and later historians are agreed that Fletcher was the only member of the party who had any military experience or competence. Sir John Dalrymple says Fletcher was "the only soldier" in his (Monmouth's) army (3). Ferguson testifies to his "courage and military skill" (4). Old-mixon, who, as a boy, saw Monmouth ride out to Sedgemoor, states that it had been intended to give Fletcher the joint command of the horse with Lord Grey (5). Lingard, among later historians, says: "The intrepidity of Fletcher had been proved in several en-counters: the superiority of his military knowledge was univers-ally acknowledged." (6).

The question at once arises: where, and at what time, had he acquired this military experience and soldierly skill: I can find in contemporary evidence only one statement that seems to explain the puzzle. All other sources state that he went to Hungary, where he fought against the Turks, *after* the Monmouth rising; and there is no mention of any previous visit to that country. But Macky, the Secret Service man, who prepared a special report on his contemporaries for Princess Sophia, tells us that before he came over with Monmouth, Fletcher had "retired to Hungary and served several campaigns with the Duke of Lorraine" (7).

It is clear that he had had no military experience in Scotland. Although, as appears by his writings, he had studied military matters closely, especially in relation to standing armies and militias, and although he may have served in the Haddington militia, before an attempt was made to convert the militia into a standing army, no opportunity for active service had been given him in his native country. But that he was believed by some of his contemporaries to be a capable soldier is beyond doubt.

It will have been observed that Burnet, who knew his unde-veloped character more intimately probably than anyone else, says that he was "very hot and violent". He was, in short, a typical example of the fiery Scot of the sixteenth and seventeenth cen-turies as seen by Continental eyes. "He is a Scot: he has pepper in his nose," was a French saying. Fletcher was very decidedly a peppery individual: no Scot ever better personified the national motto.

A curious example of this trait may be given, as the prelude of a description of the tragic incident that darkened his whole career. It is a story that was believed to refer to Andrew Fletcher. But it was written forty years after Fletcher's death: a fact that makes the identity of the subject of the story a little doubtful.

"They tell a story", says Mrs. John Calderwood, "of old Fletcher of Salton and a skipper. Salton could not endure the smoak of toback, and as he was in a night scoot, the skipper and he fell out about his forbidding him to smoak. Salton finding he could not hinder him, went up and sat on the ridge of the boat which bows like an arch. The skipper was so contentious that he followed him, and on whatever side Salton sat, he put his pipe in the cheek next him and whiffed it in his face. Salton went down severall times and brought up stones in his pocket from the ballast, and slipt them into the skipper's pocket that was next the water, and when he found he had loadened him as much as would sink him, he gives him a shove, so that over he hirsled. The boat went on and Salton came down amongst the rest of the passengers who probably were asleep, and fell asleep among the rest. In a little time bump comes the scoot against the side, on which they all damned the skipper. But, behold, when they called, there was no skipper, which would breed no great amasement in a Dutch company" (8).

One is inclined to say that Mrs. Calderwood should have told that story to the "marines", for frankly it is unbelievable of Andrew Fletcher. One is prepared to agree that probably he did not like some Dutchmen, and that probably he detested tobacco. Also, if told that, when goaded to fury by the bad manners of the Dutch skipper, and his evident desire to pick a quarrel, Fletcher had taken him by the scruff of the neck and hove him overboard (and afterwards rescued him), one could believe that as the most likely thing to happen. But that is a very different thing from the cold-blooded, deliberate method described by the authoress, who, by the way, tells the whole story as a good joke! It serves, however, to throw some light upon what is known as the Dare incident in the Monmouth rising.

We have seen that Dare was Monmouth's mainstay in Taunton and its vicinity. As a first instalment to the cause, Dare brought in to Lyme, on 13th June, forty horsemen. He himself had a magnificent mount, which was said to have come from the seat of Mr. Prideaux of Ford Abbey. As it so happened, Fletcher was dining that day with Monmouth, and conferring with him on the immediate steps to be taken. The alarm had been given to the authorities, and the County militia were assembling at Bridport, near Lyme. It was decided to attack them, and attack that very day. Monmouth's horse was to be under the joint command of Lord Grey and Fletcher. But Fletcher was without a suitable mount. Remembering the fine horse on which Dare had entered Lyme, with his forty recruits, that morning, and seeing the horse ready equipped for his master, Fletcher took possession of it and mounted, Dare being apparently absent at the time. It is clear that Fletcher thought that Dare would have behaved in the matter as he would have behaved himself: he would have made no objection to his act, on the ground that they were all out for a common cause, and that the horse was to be used for the common service. The horses were all what Fountainhall calls "robbed horses", and the question of private property did not arise. But Dare was far from thinking that way. He thought that Fletcher had acted in a high-handed manner. He was, perhaps, entitled to take that view, and had he remonstrated with the offender politely, the incident would probably have led to no serious consequences. But Dare, whom Oldmixon describes as a "rough, ill-bred man", did not remonstrate politely. He ordered Fletcher to dismount; apparently called him names; and to crown his insults, threatened to cane him (one report says he actually applied his whip to him), if he refused.

Consider the situation. Here was a rough, bullying English tradesman, swollen with a sense of self-importance, threatening to horsewhip in public a proud, quick-tempered, Scottish aristocrat (and Monmouth's chief adviser), unless he meekly dismounted; and that, too, after launching at his head a shower of insults. The insults were borne with dignity, but the point was reached when Fletcher's irascible temper could no longer be controlled. He whipped out his pistol, and shot Dare dead.

An interesting point of view, as illustrating the notions then current on the question of defended honour, is presented by Dalrymple's comments on the incident. Dalrymple states that Dare gave Fletcher "opprobrious language, shook his cane, and attempted to strike Fletcher; though rigid in the duties of morality, yet having been accustomed to foreign services both by sea and land" (a statement that seems to confirm Macky), "in which he had acquired high ideas of the honour of a soldier and a gentleman, and of the affront of a cane, (Fletcher) pulled out his pistol and shot him dead on the spot. The action was unpopular in countries where such refinements were not understood."

Certainly, Dare's friends completely failed to "understand" such "refinements".

Ferguson the Plotter (who, with calculated secretiveness, when relating the incident, omits Fletcher's name, and refers to him as a "gentleman") seeks to convey the impression that Fletcher drew his pistol to defend himself from Dare's assault with a cane, and that it went off accidentally. But the evidence for deliberate shooting is altogether too strong for that story. Ferguson avers that Dare's death "was occasioned by his own intemperate and unruly passion"; which is not incorrect as far as it goes. But when he adds that the act was "beyond the intention of the gentleman whose misfortune it was to do it", he appears in the capacity of special pleader. What is completely credible, however, is Ferguson's further statement about Fletcher, namely, that the tragedy caused him "inconceivable grief". We need not question the accuracy of Ferguson's considered remarks on the results of the tragedy. "Nor was our loss", he says, "confined to him that fell, tho' therein we sustained considerable prejudice by being deprived of a person whose acquaintance and esteem in that part of the Kingdom rendered him useful to us above many others: and the Duke, upon this deplorable accident, thought it necessary" (in order) "to prevent murmuring among some of ourselves, as well as to remove occasion of resentment in the inhabitants of Taunton, where he promised himself a hearty welcome and considerable supplies, to advise the other gentleman for a time to withdraw; but under a desire and command to return and meet him at a place which he named, where alas! we never had the happiness to arrive. And tho' the damage that befell us by the dismissing of that gentleman cannot easily be imagined or expressed; yet this I may say towards giving an idea of it: that as he was a person who, by his courage, military skill, civil prudence, application to business, and the interest he had in the Duke, would have contributed much to the conduct of our whole affairs, and have promoted the embracing of all opportunities for action, attended with any probable success, so he would have done everything that could have been expected from a person of character and worth in a decisive engagement" (9).

Ferguson's long-winded estimate of the results of the shooting of Dare may indeed be substantially correct, as appears from more reliable evidence provided by other eye-witnesses. Not only was the Duke deprived of the services of his most capable adviser— "with Fletcher" (says Dalrymple) "all Monmouth's chances of success in war left him"—but he lost the assistance of Dare, whose undoubtedly forceful character and the extent of whose local influence made his death peculiarly inopportune for Monmouth.

The unfortunate incident had its immediate repercussion upon events. Dare's son and his friends demanded that Fletcher should be given up to their vengeance. Monmouth was placed in a delicate predicament. Immediately after firing the fatal shot, Fletcher seems to have gone to the Duke in an agony of remorse, and told him what had happened. So Monmouth was compelled to choose between disobliging the Taunton folk, from whom he expected so much, or handing over to certain death a man for whom he had the highest esteem, and whose explanation of the circumstances had doubtless satisfied him that Dare had only himself to blame for his tragic end. Whatever he did, it was plain that Fletcher could no longer continue in his service (10).

In the circumstances, the Duke did the best thing possible to meet the situation. He hurried Fletcher on board the *Helderenberg* and ordered him to set sail for Bilbao, the ship's papers being made out for that port. As one historian puts it, "Monmouth was under the necessity of dismissing an officer who had courage, and continuing to employ one who had none" (Grey) (11).

Ferguson's statement that Monmouth arranged for Fletcher to return to him after the Dare affair had blown over, may be correct; it seems quite probable. But Lord Buchan's statement that Fletcher had told George Keith, the Earl Marischal, later in life, that he left Monmouth because the latter, contrary to his promise, had declared himself King, is certainly incorrect (12). For

Fletcher left England on 13th June, and the Duke was not proclaimed King at Taunton until 20th June. There has been some misunderstanding of Fletcher's narrative, possibly due to the fact that he was known to hold strong views on Monmouth's assumption of the title. Probably his statement to Keith was, that *had he been* in Taunton when Monmouth was proclaimed, he would at once have left his standard. Argyll, it will be remembered, complained bitterly of Monmouth not having sailed in accordance with their agreed programme. He complained no less bitterly of the proclamation of his kingship at Taunton, after his promise not to commit that folly. For both Argyll and Fletcher knew that it was folly. Argyll was firmly bound to the principle of monarchy by the ties of tradition. Fletcher, to say the least, held these ties conspicuously loosely. But both were aware that the acceptance of Lucy Walter's bastard as their King by the English people, or, at any rate, by the English nobility and gentry, was in the highest degree improbable.

Monmouth himself, as he afterwards pleaded to James, was talked into the declaration chiefly by "that bloody villain, Ferguson". And Oldmixon declares that the Duke "never thought of it till after he landed, and was put upon it by that Arch-Traytor and Villain, Ferguson, whose treasonable Practices since may very well make us suspect he was a spy upon him and a secret agent for the King" (13). It is probable, indeed, that Monmouth's declaration was not of his own volition, though his vanity was doubtless tickled by the suggestion. The argument for calling himself King was superficially plausible: the declaration, it was stated, was desirable in order to invest his adventure with the authority that was needed; and many people would gladly believe the legitimacy which was embodied in the declaration. Ferguson, who was Monmouth's evil genius, was looking after himself and his future. He tells us that, on the voyage from Holland to England, he sounded the Duke on his intentions in the event of success. One day, he relates, he struck an attitude calculated to catch Monmouth's eye. "What are you thinking of?" asked the Duke. "I am thinking", was the jocular reply, "to beg a particular favour of you: when you are King of England that I may be your Prime Minister." "I cannot do that," was the quick and unthinking reply, "for that post must be given to Lord . . ." "By which", says Echard, "Ferguson, as he said afterwards, made a double discovery" (14). But Ferguson's unsupported statements of fact are probably of small historical value.

The end soon came to Monmouth's spirited attempt. On the day following the Fletcher-Dare incident, the Duke was made to realize very forcibly what Fletcher's loss to him entailed, and as the campaign proceeded, the magnitude of his loss was made still more apparent. Lord Grey was sent with a small party of horse to observe the movements of the militia at Bridport. When they stumbled across some militia, Grey incontinently bolted, "but his men stood", and came back in good order after a warm skirmish with the militia, whom they forced into Bridport. His colleague, Ferguson, calls Grey "an unworthy man and a cowardly Poltrone". "What shall I do with him?" asked Monmouth despairingly of Matthews. "There is not a general in Europe who would ask such a question but yourself," was the reply (15).

It was the horse, too, that failed in the final clash at Sedgemoor. The night attack which had been planned was a sound conception, but (says Oldmixon) "the guide got confused with the importance of the occasion", and missed the ford of the ditch behind which the troopers were encamped; "otherwise, so far as can humanly be judged, an easy victory awaited the Duke's attack on the sleeping camp". The "traitorous discharge of a pistol" alarmed Dumbarton's regiment; the drums beat to arms; and although the regulars were thrown into temporary confusion by the unexpectedness of the attack, the discipline of a fine regiment quickly asserted itself; and thenceforward all the advantages lay with the King's troops. Monmouth's yokels and tradesmen put up a wonderful resistance, "but their horse", commanded by Grey, "miserably failed", and Grey "again played the poltroon" (16). Deserted by the horse and short of ammunition, mowed down by the artillery, and left without leadership, the foot finally gave ground and fled; and the slaughter then commenced on the field which was continued on the gallows by Jeffreys. Feversham and Churchill had an easy task.

"Grey," says the same contemporary historian, "after his capture, was treated like a milch cow. He was preserved until the Authorities had sucked him dry of money (he had a great estate) and information" (17). And Monmouth? Well had it been for him, perhaps, had he died on the field with the poor, brave men who fell in his cause; and certainly, well had it been for his honour had he been spared, after his capture, his painful grovelling before the relentless James in a hopeless effort to save his life. Not thus had Argyll met his doom, though, at the end, Monmouth, like Argyll, showed the fortitude that was expected of him. King James no doubt found ample excuse for his contemptuous treatment of the Duke, in his professed belief that he was not a son of Charles at all. "All the knowing world," he declared some years later, " as well as myself, had many convincing reasons to think the contrary (that he was not his brother's son), and that he was Rob. Sidney's" (18).

Whoever Monmouth's father was, he, himself, was capable of inspiring affection, and even devotion, in those who were associated with him. Fletcher, among others, was drawn towards him, and nothing but his personal attachment to the Duke can explain his resolve to "run fortunes with him". But Monmouth, the amiable, handsome Monmouth, had not the qualities that were demanded by a successful issue to a desperate enterprise. Like Bonnie Prince Charlie, whom he resembled in many ways, he was wholly admirable when the sun of prosperity blazed on him. But (again like Charles Edward) in the darkness of adversity, his latent weaknesses of character could not be concealed. He carried charms for good luck, but they failed to work. The only charm that was of any value was his personal charm (17).

Chapter IV

CONDEMNED TO DEATH

WE left Fletcher on board the *Helderenberg*, a fugitive from the fury of the Taunton men. We next find him in a Spanish prison, in company with the master and pilot of the frigate.

Exactly what his adventures were during the interval between his imprisonment in Spain and his reappearance in Holland, in time to join the Dutch "Deliverer" before he embarked for England, it has been found impossible to ascertain. The only record extant consists of reminiscences of conversation between Fletcher and George Keith, one of the two famous Scottish brothers, the elder of whom (George) became a Prussian Ambassador, and the younger (James) a Prussian Field-Marshal. George Keith's story about Fletcher's adventures in Spain (as given in the family MS.) is so remarkable that nothing less than a verbatim relation can be adequate. Fletcher was incapable of romancing. Whatever may seem fantastic in the following account, must be attributed to the Earl Marischal's indistinct recollection of what Fletcher had told him many years previously. Keith, who was born about 1693, must have been quite a young man when he met Fletcher.

The latter informed Keith "that soon after his landing" (in Spain), "he was committed to prison, and on the application of the English Minister at Madrid, he was ordered to be delivered up, and transmitted to London in a Spanish vessel which was named for that purpose. That one morning, as he was looking pensively through the bars of his dungeon, he was accosted by a venerable person who made signs to speak to him. Fletcher looking if any passage could be found for his escape, discovered a door open, at which he was met by his deliverer, with whom he passed unmolested through three groups of soldiers, who were fast asleep; and without being permitted to return thanks to his guide, he prosecuted his escape, with the aid of a person who seemed to have been sent for that purpose, concerning whom he never could obtain any information. That, disguised, he proceeded in safety through Spain, where, when he found himself out of all apparent danger, he lingered and amused himself with the view of the country, and with study in the conventual libraries; and having privately obtained credit by bills upon Amsterdam, he bought many rare and curious books, some of which are preserved in the library at Saltoun in the county of Haddington. That he had several very narrow escapes of being detected and seized in the course of his peregrinations through Spain, particularly in the neighbourhood of a town (the name of which Lord Marshall had forgotten), where he intended to have passed the night; but in the skirts of a wood a few miles distant from thence, upon entering a road to the right, he was warned by a woman of a very respectable appearance, to take the left-hand road, as there would be danger in the other direction. Upon his arrival, he found the citizens alarmed by the news of a robbery and murder on the road against which he had been cautioned. Some time after this escape, Fletcher's active genius led him to serve as a volunteer in the Hungarian war, where he distinguished himself by his gallantry and military talents. But the glory which he might have acquired in arms, had he served long enough to have obtained a command, he cheerfully sacrificed to the safety of his country" (1).

It is quite credible that Fletcher's friends exerted themselves in secret to save him from his inevitable fate if he were given up to the vengeance of James, and that arrangements towards that end, of which his escape was the outcome, were accordingly made by them. It seems certain that he fought in Hungary after leaving Spain, and apparently won distinction there on the battlefield. But with that general statement we must remain content; also with the statement, on the authority of the family papers, that he went to Holland when the prospect of an invasion of England by William of Orange offered to him, as to other Englishmen and Scotsmen, exiled from their homes, a chance of repatriation (2).

Meanwhile, what was happening to the Scots who took part in the Monmouth rebellion?

Ferguson, the slippery Ferguson, made his escape without difficulty; in fact, so easily as to arouse in some quarters the suspicion of Government connivance. He was fated to live to plot and to go on plotting, and, in the end, to escape the gallows which he so justly deserved. At the Revolution he got a comfortable post, but he soon commenced plotting in the Jacobite interest. He was the vainest of men, and was never happy unless he was notorious. Monmouth himself, who, by virtue of his property as Duke of Buccleuch, was amenable to Scottish law, had paid the penalty of his rebellion before the legal machinery had been set in motion in Scotland. But that did not prevent his citation (quite legally) along with his widow and children, to answer the charge of treason. And simultaneously with the citation of Monmouth, Andrew Fletcher and Sir James Dalrymple, the celebrated jurist, were also called upon to appear to answer a similar charge.

The specific charge against these men was that they had taken part in the Whig Plot and the Rye House Plot (for it was the policy of the Court to conjoin the two); and in Fletcher's case, that he had "landed" with Monmouth; that he "rode up and down the country with him, and was in great esteem with him for two or three days; and continued in open rebellion with him till, having killed one Dare, an English goldsmith, who was likewise with them in the said rebellion, he was forced to fly in the frigates in which they came and make his escape".

The case was in the hands of the Lord Advocate, Sir George Mackenzie (the "Bluidy Mackenzie" of Covenanting tradition), perhaps the ablest lawyer in Scotland at that time. It came on in the High Court of Justiciary on 21st December 1685. Forty-five jurymen had been summoned but only thirteen attended; and an adjournment to 4th January was therefore necessary. But in the interval it had become clear that the charge against Fletcher of complicity in the Whig and Rye House conspiracies could not be sustained. This charge was consequently dropped. The charge of taking part in the Monmouth rebellion alone remained; and it was enough.

Andrew Fletcher had displayed for years extreme cleverness in throwing off the scent the Court bloodhounds that were on his track. On 21st November 1684 he had been cited on criminal letters "at the market-cross of Edinburgh and pier and shore of Leith" (the common form of citation), to answer the charge of "conversing with Argyle and other rebels abroad". Again, in January 1685, his name appears in a list of twenty-two "fugitive rebels who were abroad" and who were cited to appear before Parliament on 26th March on a process of treason. But before his execution, Argyll had "purged" Fletcher, declaring that he had written him several times without getting an answer. So the charge of "conversing" with Argyll had also to be dropped.

In August 1685 two witnesses arrived at Leith from London in the King's yacht, to give evidence against Fletcher. One of them was named Anthony Busse (or Buyse), "the German" (he was a Brandenburger), and the other was a Captain Bruce.

When the case was heard in January 1686, it was found that the German was useless as a witness, for he could only speak from hearsay. He had sailed in the same ship as Monmouth, where he saw "a gentleman who was called Fletcher of Saltoun", who, he "heard", was "a Scots gentleman of good estate". Also, he had seen this Fletcher "flee to the ship" after Dare had been shot. But except that the person called Fletcher was "a little man who had a brown periwig, of a lean face, pock-marked", the witness knew nothing further about him.

Bruce, however, who had also sailed in the Monmouth ship, knew Fletcher personally, and his evidence of identification was deemed satisfactory by the Court. His testimony was supported by the declaration of "one Mr. William Williams, the Duke of Monmouth's servant, lying in Newgate", stating that Fletcher "came over to Lyme with Monmouth and was very familiar with him, and was to have been a Lieutenant-Colonel of Horse, but was forced to flee by his killing Dare the goldsmith". Three or four of the jurymen thought that "there was only one probative witness" (Bruce). But the majority held that the proof of identification was complete, and that Andrew Fletcher of Saltoun was consequently guilty of treason (3).

It will be seen that Fletcher had, by his wariness, compelled the Crown, for lack of evidence, to abandon their charges against him for complicity in the Whig Plot and in Argyll's conspiracy. The King and his advisers were probably aware that Fletcher was concerned in both, but they were unable, with any show of legality, to bring the charges home to him. So, unless they could convict him of treason for his share in the Monmouth rebellion, he would escape out of their clutches altogether. And, had a majority of the Scottish jurymen decided that the proof of identification was incomplete, the charge of treason might very well have fallen to the ground entirely, although everybody knew that Fletcher had taken part in the Monmouth adventure. One wonders how the resourceful mind of "Bluidy Mackenzie" would have met that impasse.

The jury, which was composed of well-known peers and commoners, with the Earl of Lauderdale (ominous name!) as foreman, having returned the verdict of "guilty", the Court, on 4th January 1686, pronounced its sentence. Fletcher was attainted as a traitor with all the implications of that sentence. His life was forfeit; his estates passed to the Crown; his name and memory were declared extinct; his blood tainted; and his descendants disabled from holding any places or honours. The sentence was pronounced "with all the formalities of sound of trumpet, tearing his arms, reversing them on the cross, etc." His brother, Henry, was one of those who had been clapped into jail when Argyll invaded Scotland. Clearly Henry was suspected by the authorities of sympathy with Andrew's politics, and his brother's estates, which were valuable in relation to those of the average laird, were reserved for someone who had served the King. The recipient of the grant proved to be the Earl of Dumbarton, a brother of the Duke of Hamilton, the drums of whose regiment had sounded the alarm when the rebels made their night attack at Sedgemoor. Dumbarton appointed his brother to act as his agent for the Saltoun estates. Fletcher was fated to make close contacts with the House of Hamilton at every stage of his career. He honoured the Duke of Hamilton not because of his well-grounded pretensions to the Scottish Crown, but as the head of the aristocracy of Scotland. At the time he was found guilty of treason, Fletcher was justly regarded by the aristocracy of his own country as a man who feared God, but who did not honour the King. The same aristocracy, said King James himself in later years, were "very loyal and monarchical". Loyal, yes; but to which monarch? Whatever respect Fletcher had for monarchy was based upon the personality of the monarch. The principle of heredity meant nothing to him; and in that view he was in agreement with Sidney and Halifax. In conversation with Dr. Pitcairn on one occasion, allusion was made by Fletcher to a man who was "hereditary Professor of Divinity" at Hamburg. "Hereditary Professor!" laughed Pitcairn scornfully. "Yes, Doctor," repeated Fletcher quietly, "hereditary Professor of Divinity. What think you of an hereditary king?" Lord Buchan remarks, "Fletcher used to say with Cromwell and Milton that the trappings of a monarchy and a great aristocracy would patch up a very clever little Commonwealth" (4). "A dangerous fellow," thought King James, who knew Fletcher of old, when, as Duke of York and Administrator of Scotland, he found himself opposed by a young man who was known to his neighbours as the bold laird of Saltoun.

There was a chance in 1686 of Fletcher being able to return home in safety if he so wished. For in April of that year James endeavoured to make a bargain with the Scottish Estates. He wanted toleration in Scotland for his co-religionists: a proposal that no Scottish Parliament of that day could venture for a moment to accept. As a bait, James offered free trade with England, and "a full and ample indemnity for all crimes against our Royal person and authority". But the Estates would not go further than agree that they would do as much for the relief of Roman Catholics as their consciences would permit: and that, in effect, meant nothing at all. Presbyterians and Episcopalians alike were opposed to any toleration of Romanism. There were individual members of Parliament, no doubt, who, in advance of their time, were ready to grant some modified form of toleration; but they were as voices crying in the wilderness of religious suspicion and hate. Negligent of popular opinion in secular matters the Estates might be, and often were, but in religious matters their ears were always laid close to the ground. And so the Royal indemnity was not granted, and Fletcher, with the other political exiles, was not allowed to return, a pardoned man, to his native land.

Failing to obtain by cajolery the toleration for his fellow-Catholics on which he had set his heart, the King set in motion, for securing his ends, the machinery of absolutism, which led straight to the Revolution. But, as a last effort to placate his enemies—an effort that came too late to save him—James issued, in October 1688, his declaration of a general pardon. Yet, with the narrow spitefulness that was in subsequent years to injure his

[43]

cause by its manifestations, he excluded certain persons from his pardon. Among them was Andrew Fletcher. When it is considered that names like those of Fletcher and Burnet were placed in the same category as the names of men like Titus Oates and Robert Ferguson, we have the measure of James's mentality (5).

Fletcher was at this time at the Hague, actively employed in the preparations that were being made for the invasion of England by William of Orange. The circumstances were vastly different from those which existed when, three years previously, he had tried to dissuade Monmouth from his ill-advised gamble, or (more accurately) to protect him against the advice of those who were urging him to venture. That was an attempt by one who had no legitimate title to the throne, and one who represented only a faction, and a faction of doubtful importance. This was an attempt, not, indeed, by the nearest legitimate heir to the throne, but the husband and the representative of her who stood in that relation. That was an attempt by a man who was not a statesman, and whose sole qualifications for leadership were his popularity and his convenience as a focus of disaffection. This was an attempt by a man whose statesmanlike qualities and whose military abilities were admitted even by his enemies. Above all, Monmouth's attempt was in response to no national call; and its support by the nation was desperately doubtful. The attempt by the Prince of Orange coincided with the peak of the national discontent, and although by no means assured beforehand of being militarily successful, was correctly gauged to possess the sympathy of the majority of the people of England and Scotland.

It can be readily believed, too, that in the conversations which must have taken place at the Hague between Burnet and his old pupil, William of Orange lost nothing in magnitude of character by Burnet's eulogies of him to Fletcher. It must have been with a heart full of hope for the future of his beloved Scotland, therefore, that Andrew Fletcher stepped aboard the ship that was to carry him to Torbay; thence, in due course, to repair to his native land, "none daring to make him afraid" (6).

Chapter V

THE CLUB AND ITS ENVIRONMENT

"TELL King William from me", said Andrew Fletcher to the Duke of Hamilton, "that he has not as good a right to his Crown as I have to my estate." "Devil take me", replied the Duke, "if it is not true" (1).

These bold words were spoken by Fletcher as a comment upon the delay which had occurred in the formal removal of his forfeiture and the restoration of his property. Argyll, the son and successor of the forfeited ninth Earl, had been restored to his estates without delay after his return from exile. Why not Fletcher and others similarly situated? The latter deputed Fletcher to act on their joint behalf, and as the result of his representations an Act was passed on 30th June 1690, by which Saltoun was returned to him, and his former privileges were restored. He had sturdily refused "to return to his estate by any law but his own " (2).

In the meantime a Convention of the Three Estates had been summoned by circular letter from the Prince of Orange. The usual method of summoning by proclamation was not employed, because the Convention was not a Parliament. Andrew Fletcher's indignation at not being a member of that Convention may be measured by his remarks to the Duke of Hamilton. His interest in the political situation was intense. We find him writing to his old friend Sir Patrick Hume, on 18th September 1689, urging the "assertion" of the Claim of Right (then engaging the attention of the Convention) in its most "considerable" Article, namely, "that against a Popish king". With the future of the nation hanging in the balance, his exclusion from such a superlatively important Convention must have chafed his ardent spirit sorely. Yet it was possible to be an active participator in politics outside the Convention; and so, in fact, he became, for "no man" was "busier than Saltoun" in the affairs of the association of politicians which was known specifically by the name of "The Club".

The affairs that led up to the formation of the Club must be briefly described.

Upon the flight of James II, Scotland, as well as England, was left without a king. But whereas England, by offering the Crown to William and Mary, soon settled her future without civil or ecclesiastical disorder, the sister country, an independent nation with an independent Parliament, was plunged into a state of confusion. The ecclesiastical polity imposed by law was Episcopacy, which claimed as its adherents a majority of the nobility and gentry, of whom a substantial number were indifferent to Episcopacy and Presbyterianism alike. The number of professed Roman Catholics, at any rate in the South, was relatively negligible. Presbyterianism found its main strength among the common people, and its vitality may be gauged by the sacrifices these people were prepared to make, and had, in fact, made, for their opinions during the reigns of Charles II and James II. Even among moderate Presbyterians tenacity of belief in their ecclesiastical system was remarkably strong, while the extreme Covenanters clung to their opinions with a bitter rigidity that was blind to any merits in the polity that they comprehensively denounced by the word "prelatical".

When, therefore, it was realized that their Roman Catholic persecutor had left the country, and that a Deliverer had arrived, whose ecclesiastical viewpoint approached their own, the Scottish Presbyterians felt that their night of oppression had fled, and that their year of jubilee was come. A reaction of feeling was unavoidable. And it took the form of "rabbling" the Episcopal clergy, who were contemptuously termed "the curates". A rough element in any community, by whatever label it may be named, is found everywhere and at all times. And it was the rough element among the Presbyterians that unceremoniously turned 200 "curates" out of their livings, and left them to fend for themselves. In view of the fact that resentment against the Stewarts and their friends had been pent up in the Scottish Presbyterian breast for a generation, it is scarcely surprising that when the dam burst, the waters did some damage. Yet, unlike the experience of the Presbyterians when they were the "under-dogs" themselves, no loss of life occurred. The blind fury of the mob was visited upon comparatively harmless men. But it was directed, in fact, against a system, the hatefulness of which to the people concerned now received concrete proof. And yet, strange to say, the whole machinery of Presbyterianism—Kirk Sessions, Presbyteries, and Synods —had remained intact all the time that bishops had ruled an alien Church as Court officials, and (their main purpose) had emasculated the virility of the General Assemblies.

On civil life these ecclesiastical and irreconcilable elements had their baneful repercussions. The religious cleavages left gaping wounds in the civil structure which could only be healed by a revolutionary cure. Parliamentary representation had withered at its roots by the operation of the Test Act of 1681. For the Act virtually disenfranchised the Presbyterians of the country, and not merely the Presbyterians, but all who refused to acknowledge as just an iniquitous Statute. Even at its freest, the Scottish Parliamentary system could by no stretch of the imagination be regarded as democratic. There was small room for the voice of the common people in a system by which the three Estates—bishops, barons, and burghs—were generally more concerned for the privileges of their respective orders than for the welfare of the nation. With the bishops having one eye on their Church (and occasionally directed towards the Church of England), and the other on the Court; with the great nobles influencing the county elections of the lesser barons; and with self-elected magistrates settling the elections for the Royal burghs, democracy was more or less a helpless spectator of the laws made by the upper classes for its weal or for its woe. Only in the General Assembly of the Church did the common people find their spokesmen. Hence the Court hatred of General Assemblies, which, in time, led to the appointment of bishops to curb them. But the General Assemblies, democratic though they were, and courageous though they were, could scarcely be expected to be invariably statesmanlike in their attitude towards national affairs, or conciliatory in their mien towards either Parliament House or the Crown. As a fact, there were occasions when they were neither one nor the other. But they were always a bulwark of the common people; and the people knew it.

Such, then, was the national situation at the time of the Revolution. The group of noblemen and gentry who went to London and asked King William to undertake provisionally the administration of Scottish affairs, may have acted without a national mandate, but they tried to act in the national interest. Also, the dispensing power set in motion by William, which freed the elections in Scotland from the operation of the Test Act of 1681, may have been unconstitutional, but it was necessary; and necessity has no law. The result of the elections, after allowing for unavoidable pressure by popular excitement, showed clearly the trend of national opinion. The Convention of Estates was overwhelmingly Whig and Presbyterian in composition. At the outset, therefore, of their proceedings, the Estates, by a majority, were predisposed in William's favour. The adherents of James were depressed by a letter from him which was read at the Convention. It showed that the Bourbon traits of forgetting nothing and learning nothing, were too strong in him to be resisted. Inspired by the Earl of Melfort, one of the Drummond brothers (the other being the Earl of Perth), who were renegades from their religious faith to become unhelpfully bigoted advisers of the Stewart dynasty, this letter did the fugitive King the greatest possible disservice. There was a heavy fall in Stewart stock soon after the Estates met.

But the Estates, notwithstanding, did not fall precipitately into the arms of the cool, self-reliant, watchful Dutchman, who was waiting in London for developments in Edinburgh. A considerable and influential section of the members was inclined towards caution. Of the two men, William of Orange and James Stewart, William was their obviously preferential choice. But surely they were not going to accept him unconditionally. Such an excellent opportunity of squaring up accounts with England should not be allowed to pass without being utilized in Scotland's interests. Scotland, as an independent nation, was in no way bound to accept England's King. Long-concealed grievances came to the surface. Ever since the Union of the Crowns, the smaller country had received scurvy treatment from her Kings, because they were bound to consider the interests of England first. Disabilities, political and economic, had been imposed upon the poorer country, just because she was poorer, and was therefore of less importance than her southern neighbour. Cromwell alone had been fair to her in trading and other matters; and he was despised as a usurper, and hated as a conqueror. But he had ruled Scotland justly, and had given her Parliamentary representation, as well as trading privileges that were substantial, and Courts of Justice that were impartial. Why not demand a restoration of these privileges, or an enlargement of them, before settling the Crown on any James or any William? Why not, indeed, have complete unity between the two nations on a basis that should be fair to both?

That was the train of reasoning which influenced the dissentient Whigs from hasty action in settling the Crown upon William. And that, essentially, was the position of Andrew Fletcher at this juncture in the affairs of his native country.

There were obvious objections on the English side to the negotiation of a treaty of union while the question of the Scottish Crown was still unsettled. So long as the Scottish throne was vacant, Scotland must inevitably remain the back-door to England, which England's enemies had for centuries striven to keep open. From the Scottish point of view, the opening or the closing of the back-door constituted a bargaining weapon of prime importance. From the English standpoint, to have it open or even ajar, constituted a potential and ever-present danger, and therefore the sooner it was closed the better. Consequently, the English reply to the proposals for union was that their consideration must be postponed, because the settlement of the Crown brooked no delay. In Scotland, the advocates of union included some of the Jacobites, who naturally wished to do what they could to retard a settlement, and who saw in the union proposals elements of probable friction from which party advantage could be reaped.

It seemed certain that the negotiations for union would be protracted, and might result in failure, as they did in the years 1604 and 1670. Yet it was freely recognized that the Scots had now a better chance than ever before of obtaining their desires on equitable terms. As for the views of King William himself, it seems obvious that, in principle, the complete union of the two kingdoms was always favoured by him, though it can well be supposed that in 1689, he was averse from having a Crown offered to him that was hedged by prickly limitations.

In the end, the Convention of Estates, with the Duke of Hamilton as its President, agreed to offer the Crown to William and Mary, after declaring that James, by his misrule, had forfeited all right to it. The offer was conditioned by a Claim of Right, which, as we shall see later, was cited in 1706 as opposing a barrier to an incorporating union with England. The Claim of Right purported to be declaratory of the law as it then stood; but some of its supplementary clauses stipulated, in effect, for the abolition of Episcopacy as a national grievance. It was the prelatic element of Episcopacy that was odious to the people. The acceptance of William and Mary as sovereigns of Scotland was accompanied by the appointment of commissioners to treat for an entire and complete union between the two kingdoms. Alas! it was soon all too evident that once the danger of a vacant Scottish throne was over, the English Parliament had no intention of negotiating any union with Scotland that removed the grievances of that country. And it became no less clear that the fears entertained by Fletcher and his friends that Scotland had been too precipitate in accepting William as her King, without safeguarding her rights adequately, were only too well justified. But the alarm caused by the Jacobite rising under Viscount Dundee may have been partly responsible for that precipitation.

In due course, William and Mary were proclaimed at Edinburgh, and a deputation from the Estates—consisting of the Earl of Argyll for the peers of Scotland; Sir James Montgomery for the Commissioners of the Shires; and Sir John Dalrymple of Stair for the Commissioners of the Burghs—proceeded to London, armed with the authority of the Estates to administer the oath of office to William after the Scottish fashion (3). That ceremony over (William making it plain that in religious matters he would be no persecutor), a scramble for office by the favourites of the King ensued. In Scottish affairs, William had always by his side, as trusted advisers, Fletcher's old tutor, Burnet, now high in favour at Court, and especially "Cardinal" Carstares, a Presbyterian who had suffered for his faith and his politics under the old régime, and who was rightly believed to be a level-headed man and a shrewd adviser in political affairs. It was important for ambitious Scots to be on good terms with their fellow-countrymen, Burnet and Carstares; in Scottish affairs, they had the King's ear. For of these affairs William had the most profound ignorance; an ignorance which, unfortunately for Scotland, he never took pains to correct. The Scottish Episcopalians thought that Burnet, the future Bishop of Salisbury, might have done more than he did to help them. But Burnet was too much of a Scot not to have Presbyterian leanings hidden away in the recesses of his Episcopal being (his mother was a sister of Lord Warriston, a fanatical Presbyterian, and his first wife was Lady Mary Kennedy, a strong-minded member of the Kirk). Also, he held moderate views on ecclesiastical polity, and Whig views in political affairs, while most of his co-religionists in Scotland held neither the one nor the other. And, of course, his influence was balanced by that of Carstares. Ultimately, after William had been pushed first one way by Presbyterian pressure, and then the other way by a combination of Scottish-Episcopal and Anglican representations, Presbyterianism, in 1690 (the year, also, in which the Convention was made a Parliament), was re-established as the national form of Church government, and has so remained to the present day. As already emphasized, ever since the Presbyterian machinery was set up, mainly by Andrew Melville's initiative, in 1581, and legalized by Parliament in 1592, it had continued to be the ecclesiastical framework of the Scottish Church, even under the rule of the bishops; so there was no violent change in polity to prevent an amicable settlement of differences. But what was called "prelatry" had by this time got such a bad name in Scotland, owing to its association with the horrors of the last régime, that in the view of what was believed to be a majority of the people, the total abolition of Episcopacy as a national institution was necessary. And, of course, as a corollary of that view, bishops were no longer allowed to form one of the Estates of Parliament.

The new King would gladly have seen the two bodies settle down together with complete toleration of one another. But the sores inflicted by the Stewarts were still festering; neither side knew what true toleration was; and the attempt made to arrange a comprehensive scheme proved unsuccessful. The material spoils remained to the Church as by law established.

In the domain of civil affairs exciting events were occurring. When the guns of Edinburgh Castle threatened the Convention with Jacobite shot, a body of sturdy Covenanters from the West offered its services to the Convention to protect it from violence. That danger to the Convention passed; yet when "the bonnets o' Bonnie Dundee" looked like winning, the Convention and the settlement with William were alike momentarily imperilled. But that danger also passed, with the fall of Dundee at Killiecrankie in the hour of victory; with the failure of his successor to use effectively the fine fighting material bequeathed to him by Graham; with the dour resistance of the Cameronians at Dunkeld to the attacks of the Highlanders; with the dispersal of the baffled Jacobites to their native hills; and finally, with the complete collapse of open resistance to the *de facto* King (4).

Now, in the light of these events, we get back to the Club. We left Sir James Montgomery in London officiating at the administration of the oath to the new sovereigns. We soon find him reappearing in Edinburgh as President of the Club. He was, no doubt, a disappointed place-hunter. He had expected the Secretaryship for Scotland, the most influential post in the Administration. In the days of Charles II, Lauderdale, his Scottish Secretary, living as he did in London, had the King's ear, and while exploiting, as circumstances dictated, the King's name in support of his measures, was himself virtually the King of Scotland. That was the post for an ambitious man, and Montgomery, endowed with great political ability and eloquence of speech, was an ambitious man. But he had been a Covenanter, and in that capacity had been fined and imprisoned, and almost forced into exile under the Stewarts. It was feared, perhaps with some reason, that the great power he would exercise as Secretary might be employed vengefully upon "prelatists". A more moderate Presbyterian, the Earl of Melville, was therefore selected for the post of Secretary. Montgomery was offered the post of Justice-Clerk to console him for his disappointment. But he refused to be consoled. He became a bitter opponent of the Administration, and with other leading Whigs, formed the Club, the *raison d'être* of which was to force the political views of its principal members on the Government. The Club became the focus of Whig discontent, while the Jacobites looked on with ill-concealed enjoyment of the spectacle presented by the division of Whig strength.

The membership of the Club grew in size as the discontent swelled in volume. Its headquarters became the meeting-place of disappointed place-hunters, equally with disinterested patriots. Discordant elements such as these could scarcely be expected to harmonize for any length of time, and the eventual disappearance of the Club was certain. Meantime, however, it was a power behind the Parliament, and gradually its main work emerged as being that of a highly efficient watchdog against Court manœuvres.

Macaulay says that "the Scotchmen of that generation who made a figure in the Parliament House and in the Council Chamber were the most dishonest and unblushing time-servers that the world has ever seen". That statement is a rhetorical exaggeration. As long as Parliaments and Council Chambers have existed, so long have time-servers flourished. It does not call for extraordinary powers of detection to discover their presence at all periods, though in varying numbers, among the great men of "the Parliament House and in the Council Chamber" of England, as well as Scotland. And the English type was perhaps as little afflicted by a tendency to blush, and as careless of the laws of honesty, as its Scottish contemporary. But, broadly speaking, it is quite true that the Scottish Parliament evolved by the Revolution included among its prominent members, men whose political convictions showed whatever elasticity was necessary to make them stretch a point (or many points) to gain office with its emoluments.

Successful place-hunters in office, and disappointed place-hunters out of office, the latter being disgruntled members of a political club who agreed only in their common desire to embarrass the Administration: such is the picture that presents itself to us in outline soon after William of Orange became King of Scotland. Against this background stand the figures of those members of the Club who were actuated by patriotism alone. And pre-eminent among the latter, by reason of his activities as a member of the Club, and still more by reason of his character as a politician, was Andrew Fletcher.

"While others", says Lord Buchan, "whether Whigs or Tories, were endeavouring to turn the Revolution in Britain to their own selfish purposes, Fletcher neither asked nor obtained any emolument from the Court . . . he was continually attentive to the interest and honour of Scotland" (5). The Court, indeed, could scarcely be expected to look with favour on so unpliant a politician. For disillusionment had soon fallen on Fletcher's hopes of the Revolution. "William of Orange", says the Tory Lockhart, "was not many months in England till he (Fletcher) saw his designs and left him, and ever thereafter hated and appeared as much against him as any in the Kingdom " (6). Yet when danger threatened the established Government from Jacobite intrigues and the imminence of a French invasion, Fletcher immediately ranged himself on the side of those who, he believed, were relatively safer guardians of the liberties of Scotland. "When", says Buchan, "an attempt was made in 1692 to bring about a counter-revolution, Fletcher's ruling principle (though dissatisfied with King William) was the good of his country. He used all his influence with the Duke of Hamilton to forget the causes of his disgust, and to co-operate with his friends of a free constitution " (7).

For the Duke of Hamilton, though he had been appointed Lord High Commissioner, after the settlement of the Crown, was always probably a lukewarm Williamite. When Melville superseded him, he retired from public life (8). Sulking in his tent, he was unresponsive to the call for the suppression of personal grievances when the national ranks needed closing, in face of the French invasion that threatened the country. It was in those circumstances that Fletcher, who was a believer in Hamilton's innate patriotism and political honesty, addressed the following letter to him:

EDINBURGH: *29th of April* 1692

May it please your Grace,

I know you will be surprised to receive a letter from me; but my writing to you in such an exigence, shows the high esteem I must have of you, and of the true love you bear your religion and country. If, laying aside all other considerations, you do not come in presently, and assist in council, all things will go into confusion; and your presence there will easily retrieve all. The Castle (of Edinburgh) has been very nearly surprised, and an advertisement which Secretary Johnston had from France and wrote hither, has saved it. When things are any ways composed, you may return to your former measures, for I do approve of them. I do advise your Grace to the most honourable thing you can do, and without which your country must perish.

Your Grace's most humble servant.

(Signed)   A. FLETCHER (9).

Whether as the result of this letter or not, it is certain that the Duke made his peace with the Court, returned to public life, and in 1693 was presiding, as formerly, in Parliament House. The victory of the English fleet at La Hogue in May 1692 removed the danger of invasion, but the implied rebuke administered by Fletcher was not lost on the rough outspoken Hamilton; and he sulked no more. Macaulay's strictures on him as being "fickle, false, and greedy" mean nothing more than that he was never the consistently humble, obedient servant of the historian's hero, William of Orange.

It was in acts such as his intervention to arouse Hamilton's patriotism, that Fletcher's influence and example told heavily. He exerted it mainly by his membership of what Macaulay calls "the powerful and vindictive Club".

The Club, in its early days, had practically ruled the Convention. Its policy was mainly directed by Montgomery, the Earl of Annandale, and Lord Ross, who kept open the wounds caused by national grievances, and thus influenced the blocking of legislation and the withholding of supplies. Its leaders had what King William regarded as the temerity to wait upon him in London, with a list of national grievances to be remedied. The remedial measures impinged upon the King's prerogative, and the "Deliverer" was slow to abandon any of the privileges which the Revolution retained for the Crown. The leaders of the Club were trying, in effect, to obtain, after the accession of William, what should have been stipulated for before he was crowned; and the failure to make a timely bargain was brought home to them and to the nation, in striking ways, before the end of William's reign. Fletcher's attitude towards the prerogative of the throne was one of uncompromising and sustained hostility. His political philosophy during the whole of his career was based upon the conception of a monarchy, strictly limited in its powers by the legislative body of the nation. If the nation must have a monarchy, it should be a strictly constitutional monarchy. "He believed", says Macky, "that all Princes are made by and for the good of the people, and thinks that Princes should have no power but that of doing good" (a strange doctrine in his time, though sufficiently commonplace now) (10). Therefore, the King's prerogative, which placed the real power in the personal hands of the monarch, was anathema to him. The reason why he opposed William's measures was that he saw in them the cloven hoof of the prerogative: that principle, which, as he had known to his cost, had wrought incalculable mischief during the last two reigns.

Such being his views, he could scarcely be expected to co-operate with Montgomery and the other leaders of the Club when, failing to receive a sympathetic response from William to their manifesto of grievances, they commenced forthwith to coquet with the fugitive James and his supporters. Lockhart, himself a Jacobite, is quite clear on Fletcher's attitude towards his party. He states that, in his later career, Fletcher's "aversion" to the English (Buchan rightly explains this by saying that he "disliked England merely because he loved Scotland to excess") and the Union was so great, "in revenge to them he'd have sided with the Royal Family" (the Stewarts), "but as that was a subject not to be entered upon with him, this is only conjecture from some innuendoes I heard him make" (11).

Fletcher's attitude towards contemporary politics cannot be understood unless the fact is firmly grasped (a fact as to which there is no possible room for a divergence of opinion), that his actions were completely selfless, and just as completely divorced from party interests. He was ready to act with any party, always provided that the measures in which he was invited to co-operate would, in his opinion, benefit, not a person only, not a party only, and especially not a king only, but his native country first and last. If that assumption be conceded, all the stages of his political career fall within a consistent whole.

He did not think it accorded with his country's interests that the Stewarts should be restored. He believed that the despotic principle was so deeply ingrained in their nature, that it would emerge in political action sooner or later, no matter what pledges might be given by the representatives of that dynasty. Also, they were Romanists: and he was a sturdy Protestant (12). On political and religious grounds, therefore, when some of his colleagues who directed the policy of the Club began to trade in the Jacobite market, he did not follow them. He saw them drifting apart from their friends, who adhered to Whig principles; and when, finally, the Club lost its political power and prestige, and passed out of existence, by the rifts in its ranks, he had no cause for regret. Its work was done when it forced attention upon the disabilities under which Scotland suffered; its policy was accomplished when it curbed, in some degree, the Royal prerogative.

But before its dissolution, it was the means of effecting one reform which alone would have justified its existence: it forced Melville, the High Commissioner, to obtain from the reluctant King his consent to abolish the Lords of the Articles. And that was a measure which must have had Andrew Fletcher's whole-hearted approval.

The Lords of the Articles may be briefly described as the dictators of Parliament. Originally a Committee of Parliament instituted for the convenient preparation of legislation to be discussed and settled by Parliament, it became, in its later phases, virtually a contrivance to force Court measures on the Estates. The Lords of the Articles prepared legislation in secret, and presented it, cut-and-dried, to Parliament, which then mechanically passed it into law. Debate by the Estates was reduced to a minimum. Scores of measures might be (and sometimes were) rushed through Parliament in one day. The Scottish Estates met in one Chamber, and there was no House of Lords or Second Chamber of any kind to revise ill-digested or positively pernicious legislation. The method of election of the Lords of the Articles was deliberately designed to impose the will of the Court upon Parliament, and to destroy the initiative of the Estates. There were usually forty members on this Committee—eight bishops, eight peers, eight shire members, and eight burgh members, with eight Officers of State to represent the Crown. The bishops, who were invariably at the Court's disposal, chose eight peers who, they knew, would vote to please the Court. These peers then chose eight bishops, whose votes were similarly safe for the Court. Then the eight peers and eight bishops, so chosen, together elected the county and burgh members, whose votes they held in their lawn-sleeves and their pockets. And of course, the eight State officials were there to see that the King's will should prevail. The Lords of the Articles were, in short, the "forty thieves" who stole the people's liberties.

This institution, by its composition and its method of procedure, was the gravest defect in the Scottish Parliamentary Constitution. It was responsible for the iniquitous legislation affecting the rights of the people which had been passed by servile Parliaments during the reigns of Charles II and James II. It is true that it was also responsible for some useful laws which regulated the daily life of the people. But its larger measures, which vitally affected the national life, were inspired by the never-relaxed aim of maintaining and increasing the King's supremacy in the domains alike of Church and State. In the reign of Charles II, Lauderdale, the Scottish dictator, had found the Lords of the Articles "a very present help in time of trouble", as he, who could quote Scripture with any living man, would have expressed it. "Nothing", he once declared, "can pass in Articles but what is warranted by his Majesty, so that the King is absolute master in Parliament both of the negative and affirmative" (13).

In May 1690 the Committee of Articles was dissolved, and thenceforward, until the Union, Scotland had a free Parliament. The Estates were now at liberty to elect whatever committees they pleased, subject to the condition that the Crown was represented on those committees; but the State officials were not to be allowed to vote. The results were soon apparent in the course of the debates in the House, as well as in the character of the legislation that was enacted. Independent views, long silenced, again found a voice and a vote, and a new school of Parliamentarians arose, endowed with an unexampled brilliancy of debating power, which attained its climax just before the "auld sang" reached its end. And of these polished debaters, Andrew Fletcher was, for stateliness of diction, and soundness of reasoning, easily first.

The Parliamentary machinery was not made perfect by the

abolition of the Lords of the Articles. Hasty legislation was still possible, though a later enactment, compelling a second reading of all measures introduced to the House, was a safeguard. But it was now an essentially different Parliament from its predecessors, under the dictatorship of the "forty thieves".

Chapter VI

GLENCOE AND DARIEN

THE thirteenth of February 1692, an ominous date, and an unlucky number! For it is the date of the Massacre of Glencoe, an event which had political results that overshadowed the treacherous slaughter of two score Highlanders.

At the end of the seventeenth century, the Highlands of Scotland were foreign country, not merely to Englishmen but to Lowland Scots as well. And the Highlanders themselves, with their Gaelic language, their strange customs, their quarrelsome temper, their mixed religions, and their racial aloofness, were as sharply divided from their Lowland neighbours as were the Lowland plains from the Highland hills. Their foreign speech and their quaint garb were known in the cattle markets of Crieff and Falkirk, which the Highland drovers periodically frequented, or in distant Glasgow, to which market the West Coast Highlanders, after an arduous journey, brought their plaidings, their dried hides, their goatskins, and their deerskins for sale. But their reputation did not rest upon their contact with the South as peaceful traders. To the Kirk and its adherents they revived painful memories of the Montrose scourge which had swept the country, and destroyed Covenanting army after Covenanting army. To the farmers of Ayrshire they brought reminiscences of the Highland Host, the engine employed by Lauderdale for bringing recalcitrant dissenters to their knees. And to the whole body of Lowland Whigs, they were the impudent rogues who, quite recently, under Dundee, had well-nigh succeeded in effecting a counter-revolution, and bringing Jacobite predominance on the nation. Forgotten by the whole of the Lowlands were the occasions when the ancestors of these same Highlanders had stood shoulder to shoulder with their Lowland fellow-countrymen in defence of the nation against the "auld enemy", from Bannockburn to Flodden, and from Flodden to Worcester. Forgotten, too, (if ever realized) was the fact that, as Scottish toponomy plainly

[60]

teaches, the two peoples at one time mainly formed one race, though the racial kinship had since been obliterated by differences acquired by the Lowlanders in language, customs, and religion.

In the seventeenth century the Lowland prejudice against the Highlanders was ineradicable. Their perennial clan feuds; their occasional raids on their Lowland neighbours; their complete aversion, so it was believed, from habits of industry and honest toil; their supposed devotion to fighting and thieving as their normal occupations: these were the characteristics by which mainly the people of the hills were known to the people of the plains (2). Even so enlightened a Lowlander as Andrew Fletcher shared in this Lowland antipathy towards the Highlander, as may be seen by his writings. "The Highlands", he said, "were possessed by a People, who are all gentlemen only because they will not work. . . . For the most part they live upon robbery" (3). Had he known better, he would have judged better. But there is nothing to suggest that he placed a gulf of racialism between the Highlanders and the Lowlanders. Had he done so, his ideals of nationalism would have been seriously compromised by a false ethnological distinction. He would have stood for a "little Scotland", instead of a Scotland stretching from Thurso to the Tweed. Macaulay, with his encyclopædic knowledge, had less excuse for his picture of the Highlands and the Highlanders in the reign of King William, which has coloured the views of many subsequent historians. They presented an excellent medium for the use of his favourite antitheses to get his effects, and the broad sweep of his brilliant brush obliterated many underlying virtues that had an existence in fact. Had he given more attention to a work, for example, like that of Martin Martin, a Skye man, written at the end of the seventeenth century, and less to Captain Burt, an Englishman, who wrote nearly a generation later, he could have told his readers that, in the most remote island of the Hebrides (the island that gave birth to his own ancestors, and where some of his own forebears were then residing) a state of society existed that was widely different from the Lowland and English conception of it. He could have justly pictured a well-ordered community, not of savages, as, in effect—mistaking a part for the whole—he described the Highlanders indiscriminately, but a society of hardy, law-abiding and industrious people, to whom warfare, tribal or national, was an interruption in the normal pursuits of their daily life. He could have pictured a community imbued with the same likes and dislikes as their Lowland fellow-countrymen, practising customs and superstitions which had lingered in the villages of the Isles after they had died out in Glasgow and Perth. He could have pictured a community of Highlanders of the same flesh and blood as their neighbours, and he could have urged that Shylock's plea for the Jew might have been appropriately employed as a defence of the Highlander (4).

The truth is that the whole body of Highlanders of that period, and later, have had the misfortune to have ascribed to them, as normal habits of life, what were regional, abnormal, and only spasmodically recurring episodes of conduct. It is true that some of their leaders were frequently swaggering bullies, whose hands were ever on the hilts of their swords, and impecunious chiefs, at once pugnacious and proud, whose overmastering emotions were revenge for affronts and suspicion of the Sassenach not unmixed with contempt. Yet Lowland Scotland had been just as quarrelsome, and as predatory in the Border country, a century earlier. For fierceness of temper and ruthlessness of action, the Lowland noble of the sixteenth century was certainly the peer of the Highland chief of the seventeenth. Yet neither can be said to have been representative of the contemporary community.

These observations concerning the Highlands have a bearing upon the Glencoe murders and their after-effects. For the attitude of the Estates towards the crime, and especially the attitude of King William, was coloured by the views they entertained, in common with the rest of the Lowlands and England, concerning the victims of the tragedy and the race from which they sprang. Had the inhabitants of a village in the Lowlands been wiped out in the unspeakably treacherous fashion in which the MacIans of Glencoe were slaughtered, it is inconceivable that the perpetrators would have escaped punishment. Yet the criminals of the Glencoe massacre all got off. Campbell of Glenlyon, the leader of the actual murderers, who in February 1692, like the other officers concerned, was faced by the choice between resigning his commission or becoming an assassin, and who, like them, elected to be an assassin; that old fox, the Earl of Breadalbane who "double-crossed" alike the Highland Jacobites and the Government Whigs; Sir John Dalrymple, the Master of Stair (his learned father, Sir James, was now Viscount Stair), the able, eloquent, but malignantly ruthless Secretary, who planned the massacre like a master; and lastly, William of Orange himself who signed the fatal order, either as carelessly or as callously as he might have signed an order to shoot pigeons: all of them were responsible in varying degrees of culpability for the tragedy. But the chief culprit, as the responsible Secretary of State, was Stair, and the decision of the King in merely depriving him of his office, without bringing him to trial for his life, was the first of the two big blunders committed by William in Scottish affairs. In whatever degree of antipathy the Lowlanders held a Highland tribe, like the MacIans, who were regarded in the Lowlands as a pack of thieves deserving of punishment, or by men like Stair as vermin that should be exterminated, the people of Scotland were not going to condone an atrocious act of this kind, no matter against whom committed; for, after all, the MacIans were Scotsmen like themselves. The Dalrymples were not liked either by the Whigs or the Jacobites, and that was another factor which added to the unpopularity of the King's inaction, for which no excuse save a guilty conscience can be found.

Andrew Fletcher was among those who abominated the crime, and who thought that Stair should have been brought to trial. Years afterwards, during a debate in Parliament on Fletcher's famous "limitations", which provided that no pardon should be granted by the Crown for an offence without the consent of Parliament, Stair, then Earl of Stair, sneered at the provision. "It is no wonder", said Fletcher hotly, "that his lordship is against this, for had there been such a law, he would have been hanged long ago for the advice he gave King James, and (for) the murder of Glencoe, and his whole conduct since the Revolution" (5). Plain speaking, to be sure, but it hit the right nail on the head.

If the King's attitude towards the Glencoe affair was his first big blunder in Scottish administrative policy, his next, and a bigger blunder, related to the Darien affair. He was completely out of touch with Scottish sentiment, in spite of Carstares and Burnet being at his elbow, because he knew nothing and cared nothing about his northern kingdom. He was so engrossed with European politics that he forgot that Scotland formed part of Europe, and sometimes seemed to forget that it did not form part of England. His attitude is well epitomized by his petulant exclamation on one occasion, that he wished Scotland was "a thousand miles away, with the Duke of Hamilton as her King": he would then, he said, "be rid of them both". Beyond doubt, it was this cold-blooded indifference that inflamed the patriotic ardour of Fletcher against William of Orange. Yet he blamed his advisers, i.e. Stair, more than he blamed William himself, for the "bad counsel" that had been given the King in "that Glencoe murder".

The initiation, progress, and failure of the Darien scheme is a familiar story. We are concerned with it here because it was a project the success of which Fletcher had very much at heart. In fact, it has been stated, but the statement lacks contemporary confirmation, that the scheme took its origin in a discussion between Fletcher and William Paterson in London in 1690. According to this statement, Fletcher brought Paterson to his home at Saltoun, and there introduced him to the Marquis of Tweeddale, who was the Lord High Commissioner, and therefore the Minister who touched with the sceptre the Acts of the Scottish Parliament. "Fletcher", says this authority, "with that power which a vehement spirit always possesses over a diffident one, persuaded the Marquis, by arguments of public good, and by the honour which would redound to his administration, to adopt the scheme" (6). Whatever passed between Fletcher and Paterson in 1690, and between both and the High Commissioner, it seems certain that at this stage no one except Paterson had Darien in view as the likeliest field for Scottish enterprise. What concerned Paterson and Fletcher, and Tweeddale as well, at that time, was the initiation of whatever steps were needful to encourage and promote the foreign trade of Scotland.

A big Corporation for trading far afield was a new thing for that country. Scottish efforts in that direction had, in the past, been confined, more or less, to individual enterprise. The seventeenth century had, indeed, witnessed Scottish settlements, not merely in Northern Ireland, but in Nova Scotia, New Jersey, and

Carolina, whence radiated Scottish commercial influence to a
limited extent. Her small merchants, or Scots pedlars, abounded
not only in England but on the Continent, where, too, her mercenary soldiers were held in high esteem. And her trade with
France and Holland had, for a long period, been a trade of substantial dimensions relatively with her population. But that Scotland, a country of unimportant traders compared with England,
should venture, all of a sudden, to originate a national scheme
which gave promise of seriously disturbing the monopolies of
the great East India Company and the African Company, was a
development for which England was completely unprepared.

In the latter part of the sixteenth and nearly the whole of the
seventeenth century, Scotland was engrossed in questions of
theology and politics and war. Why this sudden change in the
direction of the national aspirations? Why this desire to become
colonists, instead of soldiers; to become traders instead of theo-
logians? When discussing this question, Fletcher, writing in
1698, says that by an "unforeseen and unexpected change of
the genius of this nation, all their thoughts and inclinations, as
if united and directed by a Higher Power, seemed to have turned
upon trade, and to conspire together for its advancement, which
is the only means to recover us from our present miserable and
despicable condition" (7). He was writing at a time of great
dearth in the land, and it will be observed that the urge towards
trade had his whole-hearted approval. An unidentified pamphleteer, writing in 1696, comments on this change in the Scottish
attitude, "for", he says, "the Bias of their people seems generally
to be another way . . . yet that is merely the effect of custom and
not of nature, and as it would not have been difficult at any time
heretofore to have diverted and turned their inclinations and
humours from souldiering to commerce, so it is not to be doubted
but that upon their being once brought to apply unto it, they
would be found as ingenious and diligent in Trade as they have
had the character to be skilful and brave in War" (8).

As the succeeding centuries have amply demonstrated, this
prophecy turned out to be accurate. But it will be observed that
while Fletcher offers no solution of his own to account for the
change in the Scottish outlook, and while his contemporary

E   [65]

simply notes that the nation had turned from soldiering to trading, neither of these writers suggests what, at this distance of time, would appear to have been the likeliest reason for the change.

Dominated by ecclesiastical and theological questions through-out the century to an extent for which history offers no exact parallel, the Scottish nation was now permanently freed, as it too prematurely thought it was, by the Revolution Settlement from the anxieties and bitterness which those questions had per-ennially entailed. The thoughts of the nation were turned into a new channel when the old channel was blocked by the medium of legislation. The question of providing daily bread for the country became the dominant consideration under the stimulus of an economic situation of uncommon stringency. If the English nation had become prosperous by trading, why not the Scottish nation also? This was the question that was asked by all thinking men north of the Tweed. The answers were provided by an Act of Parliament, passed in 1693, for the encouragement of Foreign Trade, and, as its corollary, an Act passed in 1695, constituting "The Company of Scotland trading to Africa and the Indies".

These, then, were the circumstances under which Scotland developed, at this point in her history, a hitherto unparalleled keenness for overseas trading. But, in point of fact, the change of attitude had probably been more gradual than would appear to be suggested by contemporary pamphleteers. It had been develop-ing throughout the seventeenth century, though it reached its greatest intensity at the end of the century. During the Crom-wellian Incorporating Union, some knowledge of the advantages accruing to England by her plantation trade had been acquired by the Northern Kingdom, and the equality of trade then bestowed upon Scotland had enabled the poorer country to participate in those advantages. With the Restoration came a free Scotland and a national Parliament in name, but an enslaved Scotland and a shackled Parliament in reality. Chief among the shackles were the English Navigation Acts, which, after the Restoration, had a paralysing effect upon Scottish commerce. Thenceforward, for Scotland, the English plantations were closed markets, except by evasion of the Acts, by which evasion, the Scots became expert smugglers. In the reign of Charles II, during the Commissioner-

ship in Scotland of the Duke of York, afterwards James II, trade
questions emerged which, to give James his due, were handled
by him with ability and fairness. Thus in 1681 conferences between the Duke and Scottish merchants resulted in legislation
which attracted attention to the possibilities latent in a well-
devised encouragement by Parliament of manufactures and trade.
And five years later, the destruction by the Spaniards of a Scottish
Covenanting settlement at Stuart's Town, South Carolina, caused
renewed attention to be paid to colonial enterprise. In 1691, at
the instigation of some Glasgow merchants, the Convention of
Royal Burghs gave consideration to the question of colonial
settlements, but it was not until 1693 that a real stride forward was
taken. The Committee of Trade of the Estates decided to recommend to Parliament that, with the approval and co-operation of
the Crown officials, immediate action should be taken to legalize
the promotion of foreign plantations.

The great East India Company, with its monopolies and privileges, had long been the envy of those English merchants who
had been shut out of the profitable trade in which the Company
had been engaged since the reign of Queen Elizabeth. The Company had been the target of strong criticism in later years. How
to break the monopoly had been the subject of unremitting consideration by the Company's rivals, or "interlopers" as they were
unfairly called. It was not easy. It is never easy to invade successfully long-established interests, if these are conducted with prudence and skill. The Company, despite its blunders, and despite a
record that was by no means blameless, was, on the whole, a
national asset of great value. It had considerable influence; it could
bribe heavily; and it possessed the inestimable advantage of long
and hard-earned experience. But the fortress of its trade was not
regarded as impregnable, and towards the end of the seventeenth
century plans were taking shape for a vigorous attack by skilful
rivals. The latter formed themselves into what was called the
"New" East India Company, and in spite of the bitter opposition
of the old Company, got their charter in 1698. But before that
stage was reached, much spade-work had to be done.

In 1693 a frontal attack on the old Company was not thought
feasible. But why not attack (it was apparently thought) through

England's "back-door" in the North, and secure, by means of
the Scottish Parliament and in co-operation with Scottish colleagues, trading privileges which it would be hopeless to expect
from the English legislature, where the influence of the old
Company was irresistible?

There were thus two main factors to account for the genesis of
the Company of Scotland. The ground was ready for the sowing
of the seed; and the sowers of the seed were ready for the ground.
In Edinburgh there was a group of merchants eager to secure for
their country a share of the wealth of the East, and in London
there was another group of merchants, some of them Scots, ready
to co-operate with any agency that promised to undermine the
position of the East India Company. And the Act that was touched
with the sceptre in 1695, investing the Company of Scotland with
valuable trading privileges, seemed likely to have that effect,
ultimately if not immediately. For its scope was so wide, and its
benefits so substantial—they included freedom from all duties
for twenty-one years—that success seemed assured for the new
venture.

The first meeting of the "Company of Scotland trading to
Africa and the Indies" was held in London in November 1695.
Three directors from Scotland attended the meeting; two of them,
James Balfour and Robert Blackwood, being the real founders
of the Company; the third director from Scotland, Lord Belhaven,
a Hamilton, presided at the meeting (10). One-half of the total
capital of £600,000 was issued in London, and in a few days the
whole of the £300,000 was subscribed, and a quarter of that sum
paid up. So far it had been roses all the way for the new concern;
the thistles had not yet made their appearance.

Then the blow fell. The terms of the Act constituting the Company having been made public, there was immediately a great
outcry in England. The House of Commons appointed a Committee in December 1695 to inquire into the circumstances of the
passing of the Act. The House of Lords also appointed a Committee to take evidence. The old East India Company wildly
shrieked, "Ichabod". The new East India Company sat tight.
London merchants, other than the "interlopers", fulminated on
'Change against the impudence of the beggarly Scots. At Garra-

way's, where (the quotation is from a Scots pamphleteer) "the mob to whom God hath given riches for denying them understanding and good nature" forgathered to hear the news, the threatened competition of a neighbour, hitherto despised commercially, was discussed with alarm. The Scottish fat was fairly in the fire of English criticism.

All this may have been anticipated by the Scottish promoters of the Act, for they could scarcely have expected the London merchants—least of all the old East India Company—to accept meekly this threat to their monopoly. But the Scots had their Act of Parliament as a sheet-anchor; and they believed, reasonably enough, that it would enable them to weather the storm. Besides, were they not inviting English traders to share in whatever good fortune might be awaiting them? The furious opposition of the old East India Company was intelligible: already the anticipated results of the new rivalry had caused a severe slump in their stock. But, as the author of a remarkable memorial wrote in his spirited defence of the later Darien scheme: "it must certainly be better for the Kingdom in general that everyone who has occasion for muslin or Indian silks etc. should have so many shillings per yard a piece in their pockets, than that some two or three merchants should once in an age get money enough to make a Daughter or two a Countess or Duchess. . . . How can it be denied" (he goes on to say) "but it is better for England that Housekeepers in general should save that money to buy Provisions for their Families which consume our own Product, than that a dozen of merchants should be enabled by the extravagant prices of those commodities to keep their Coaches." Sound political economy, the soundness of which, in these latter days, has been demonstrated over and over again.

But at the end of the seventeenth century arguments such as these were not agreeable to commercial England. It was an age of monopolies; an age of privileges; an age of farming duties; an age, in short, of favouring the few at the expense of the many. The Parliamentary Committees were not going to stand any nonsense with this new-fangled Scottish concern. Indeed, they took so high a hand that at one time the directors of the Scottish Company were in imminent peril of being impeached for a misdemeanour.

The misdemeanour apparently was that they had had the impudence to invite the English public to share in their good fortune.

The King found himself in a difficult position. When he gave his consent to the passing of the Act (its implications were at the time pointed out to him by Johnston, his Secretary for Scotland), he did so in the hope, apparently, that it would soothe Scottish feelings, which had been severely wounded by his handling of the Glencoe affair. Now he had to choose between offending his English subjects by backing up his Scottish Commissioner, or offending his Scottish subjects by throwing him over. He chose the line of least resistance. Burnet defends him by stating that his Commissioner in Scotland ignored the reservation for the protection of English trade which the King had intended should be embodied in the Act (11). The defence is not convincing. A clearly expressed instruction would have been obeyed by the Commissioner as a matter of course. Probably this is another instance of carelessness in the affairs of a despised part of his dominions by a harassed King, who had the main burden of the whole of Europe on his shoulders.

Tweeddale, the Commissioner, and Johnston, the Secretary, were dismissed, their master alleging, in reply to the English remonstrances which poured in on him, that he had been "ill served in Scotland". He hoped, however, that "remedies" would be found to prevent the ill-consequences of the Act that were anticipated in England (12). As events showed, the remedies were drastic.

Meanwhile the London subscribers to the capital of the Scottish Company, taking alarm, withdrew their subscriptions. Of the two hundred subscribers only four remained faithful to their engagements.

When the London news reached Scotland, the whole country was aflame with resentment, which the Jacobites naturally did their best to intensify. The ground had previously been carefully prepared for the issue of capital in Scotland, and the affront to the nation, as it was considered, by the English Parliament, was utilized by the promoters to stimulate the flow of subscriptions. It became a point of honour to put money into the concern. All the monied ranks of society, from the highest downwards, eagerly subscribed to what was regarded as a national undertaking. The maximum subscription for any one applicant was fixed at £3000 stock, and the minimum at £100. "The Scottish nation", says Burnet, "fancied nothing but mountains of gold, and national subscriptions flowed in beyond what any believed the wealth of that kingdom could have furnished" (13). But Burnet tells only half the story. He fails to make it clear that these subscriptions were for the African and East Indian trade, before Darien and its "mountains of gold" were ever heard of in public. The enthusiasm that swept the country—resembling in its intensity the enthusiasm that accompanied the signing of the National Covenant sixty years earlier—was different in kind from the excitement that impelled the frantic rush into a financial morass, which disturbed England so seriously in 1720. The South Sea Bubble burst on a nation of deluded gamblers, all of them intent on getting something for nothing. The subscribers to the Scottish Company's capital were inspired only partially by a desire to get rich effortlessly as individuals. The main ingredients in the application for stock were national pride, touched to the quick by what was regarded as scurvy treatment by a sister nation, and national ambition clamouring for "a place in the sun". Certainly these were the motives that impelled Andrew Fletcher to subscribe (a thousand pounds), and others like him whose patriotism had been aroused by the venture. "Fletcher", says Dalrymple concerning the scheme, "had nothing to hope for and nothing to fear because he had a good estate and no children, and he was indifferent who had the honour of doing good provided it was done" (14).

Within six months of the lists being opened in Edinburgh and Glasgow, the whole of the £400,000 issued (half the total original capital, with an additional £100,000) was cheerfully subscribed by a nation normally poor and suffering at that time from two bad harvests in succession, the effects of which were driving crowds of famishing emigrants over to Ireland. It was a stupendous effort for the impoverished Scotland of 1696, and but for the patriotic impulse at the back of it, a hopeless effort it would probably have proved to be. But when the call of patriotism is sufficiently loud and its notes sufficiently clear, the Scottish people have never been slow to respond to it; and have never shrunk from the sacrifices which the response may have entailed.

Chapter VII

THE DARIEN SCHEME: THE NEXT STAGE

ENGLAND having cold-shouldered the Scottish trading venture, recourse was had to the Continent. Amsterdam, where the Company had placed some shipbuilding orders, was sounded for the balance of the capital, £200,000. But the Dutch had their own East India trade to develop and protect, besides being the native country of William, Prince of Orange, whose disapproval of the Company's activities was known. So Holland proved as unresponsive as might have been expected to the proposals. Vessels were also being built in the Hamburg dockyards for the Company, and Hamburg looked like a promising place—as, indeed, it was—for raising the additional capital. So Hamburg was tried. The free burghers of Hamburg were not proof against the manifest advantages which the Company offered. Protected as it was by an Act of Parliament and by a charter of incorporation conveying the trading privileges conferred by legislation, the Company seemed likely to have a prosperous career. The prospects looked so attractive to the merchants of Hamburg, that had it not been for something that happened, the capital needed would have been quickly subscribed unconditionally, and the Company's subsequent financial troubles would not have arisen.

What happened was that once more an English spoke was put in the Scottish wheel. Sir Paul Rycaut, the English Resident at Hamburg, in September 1696 was blustering: "I hope with God's grace and help so to manage this businesse that the businesse of the Scotch East India Co. shall get no footing in my province." And he was later declaring quite candidly that "it shall be my business to decry it as much as I am able". Nor did he stop there. In April 1697, when negotiations were still proceeding, he addressed a memorial to the Hamburg Senate, which informed the members that the King of England would regard as "an affront" to his Royal authority, which he would not fail to "resent", any agreement made by the City of Hamburg with the Company. And the "friendship and good correspondence" which England desired to cultivate between herself and the City of Hamburg, would be endangered by Hamburg giving any countenance to the Scottish venture.

As the result of these representations, the considerable sums which the Hamburg merchants subscribed, were offered subject to the condition that the King of England, who was also incidentally King of Scotland, could be prevailed upon to issue a declaration securing the subscribers against the penalties threatened in Rycaut's bellicose memorial.

It is impossible to believe that Rycaut acted on his own initiative in this matter. Neither national animosity against the Scots, nor the bribery of the old East India Company (if, as was suspected, influential people in London were plied with it), can account in full, though it may in part, for his extraordinary memorial to the Hamburg Senate. Rycaut must have had the King's authority, if not his positive instructions, to present it. Writing in October 1696 to Secretary Trumbull, he refers to "the commands of His Majestie touching the danger of the Scotch East India Companies in these parts, how and in what manner I was to act against them, to pervert their actings so prejudiciall to our East India Companies and the whole realme of England" (1).

That seems clearly enough to throw the responsibility on the shoulders of the King. But the public did not know whether or not Rycaut had exceeded his instructions, nor did the directors of the Company of Scotland. Neither the Scottish Estates nor the directors of the Company could believe it possible that William would consent to what was virtually a repudiation of an Act of Parliament, passed by his own authority. They addressed the King, praying him to correct the disconcerting attitude of his Resident in Hamburg. William said he would look into the matter, and in the meantime would order Rycaut not to use his authority in obstructing the interests of the Company. But Rycaut professed to have received no such orders. The directors then complained to the King that his Resident continued "contumacious", and petitioned that he would order him to follow his master's instructions. The King, through his Secretary, replied that he had already given orders to Rycaut to "conform to his previous letter". And so the correspondence went on in this evasively unsatisfactory fashion, until finally the Hamburgers, perceiving that there was no hope left of their embarking capital in the Company without running the grave risk of England making trade reprisals, withdrew their money altogether. The Scottish directors who had been negotiating the deal, were compelled to return empty-handed to their own country (2).

The evasiveness of William can be readily understood. He must have known that he was shuffling in this business, and must have felt ashamed of having to play so unkingly a part. It was bad enough to freeze English capital when it was sought by the Scottish Company. It was worse to scare away, in this deliberately unfriendly fashion, neutral capital when it was offered by Hamburg. But the King's relations with his English Parliament were not so easy that he could afford to disregard the views of its members on this Scottish business. These views, swayed as they were by powerful commercial interests, were unmistakably hostile. The pressure of opinion was too great to be resisted by the King; and, as usual, the smaller, the poorer, the less politically important country, had to suffer. It was a sorry episode in the commercial history of England.

Nothing in the consistently hostile acts of England, or, to be more precise, the trading interests of England, against the smaller country's efforts to establish herself in world commerce, was ·so hotly resented in Scotland as the Hamburg affair. Excuses have usually been offered for England's attitude towards the Darien venture, in view of the delicate relations then existing between her and the Spanish Empire. But the Hamburg snub happened before the Darien venture was made public. No excuse, indeed, can be found for the incident, unless it is provided by trade jealousy, unreasoning fears, and national enmity. A memorial of 1699 makes the point just stated. "The present juncture of affairs", it says, "obliges the Kingdom of England to carry fair with Spain, thus providing some excuse for English opposition. But the questioning our Act of Parliament first, and then hindering our subscriptions at Hamburg afterwards, before ever they knew what our design was, make that excuse of little weight."

William Paterson declared that it had been his great desire to unite the English and Scottish East India Companies. But on the failure of this scheme, and when the Scottish nation "was vilified and esteemed as a Company of Beggars, their people were so provoked by this contempt and scorne that they were resolved to let the world see that they could stand upon their own leggs". Alas, their own "leggs" proved shaky (3).

Paterson himself was the Cecil Rhodes of his day in conception, though not in achievement. His mind was filled with big schemes, not for his personal benefit only, but for the benefit of his native country. And not for his native country alone, for the establishment of the Bank of England was Paterson's conception. When the conception fructified, the credit of the achievement was appropriated by others, and Paterson profited little by it. Burnet, who seems, for some reason, probably political, to have been prejudiced against his fellow-Scot, says that he was a man of no education, but "grand notions, which, as was generally said, he had learned from the buccaneers with whom he had consorted for some time" (4). There was a good deal to be learned from the buccaneers of his time. Buccaneering, though it had now passed its zenith, was not generally regarded as a particularly disreputable trade. Morgan had acted as Governor of Jamaica after a long spell of buccaneering. Dampier, who comes on the scene presently, was esteemed by his fellow-countrymen as an intrepid sailor and a gallant fellow. There were, of course, buccaneers and buccaneers. There were buccaneers between whom and pirates no line, however thin, could be drawn. But there were others who disclaimed, and disclaimed justly, the Jolly Roger as their flag. They were mercenaries with all the implications of the term. Their services were available to any nation that paid them sufficiently well. They stormed forts and took towns. The capture of a Spanish treasure ship was at once a profitable and a praiseworthy job. The looting of a Spanish settlement was a legitimate act of war against hereditary foes. Hitherto English and French buccaneers had acted more or less in concert in the Spanish Main. But in the time of King William, the bond of common predation that had united them in the past, was now loosening under the pressure of national jealousy.

Few of these buccaneers, at this time, were other than treacher-

Andrew Fletcher of Saltoun

ous and lecherous ruffians, who would have been strung up in a jiffy if their crimes had been committed in England. But the charms of distance, and tropical romance, and glittering gold, and desperate adventure invested these desperadoes with an interest which ensured for them a popular meed of respect, if not of hero-worship.

To suppose that William Paterson belonged to this crew is to suppose what is almost unbelievable. He knew the Spanish Main intimately, and he must have had more than a passing acquaint-ance with the buccaneers who swarmed on it. But that he was ever a buccaneer himself (he was also believed to have been a missionary), is in the highest degree unlikely. Dalrymple tells us that Paterson formed a friendship with Fletcher, for "ingenious men draw to each other like iron and the loadstone" (5). "A friend of Andrew Fletcher" is an excellent certificate for the character of any contemporary of his.

It was this man, then, who was mainly responsible for the Darien scheme. For years it had been a favourite project of his, which was not put into execution only for lack of opportunity. The opportunity had now arrived. To the directors of the Scottish Company, it was now clear as noonday that to enter into direct competition with the East India Company, or the new Company that was about to take its place, was to court loss of capital and loss of national prestige. The English traders simply would not suffer any disturbance of their East Indian monopoly; nor would their Parliament permit them to join the Scottish venture, even if they were willing to become partners with the Scots.

The directors were therefore quite ready to listen to Paterson when he unfolded his extraordinarily bold plan for starting Scot-land on a dazzling career of commercial opulence. This was not to be an affair of humdrum prospecting in the Isthmus of Darien, and of building up a trade there staidly, painfully, and precariously. No, it was to be a veritable New Caledonia; another Nova Scotia in the Caribbean Sea. A steady stream of emigrants was to pour out of the Mother Country and people this new land with a hardy race of settlers, who would in course of time secure the recognition of Scottish influence, if not indeed of Scottish predominance, in the Spanish Main. The situation of Darien admirably fitted it for materializing Paterson's glowing vision of a great entrepôt, which would attract to itself the riches of the East equally with the riches of the West. This great centre of trade, in a land so peculiarly adapted geographically and otherwise to be an emporium of commerce, and itself so prolific in tropical produce for which a ready market could be found; a land, too, in which the promise of gold would ever beckon to enterprise and stimulate immigration; a land planted in the midst of dominions that had yielded vast treasure to Spain in the past: this centre of trading in such a land could not fail to secure, at last, for poor distressed Scotland, the place in the commerce of the world which had been denied to her in the past.

These were Paterson's golden dreams; and they were not, as is frequently supposed, the dreams of a visionary. The ideas latent in the plan were evolved from the imagination not of a feckless politician made of words, but a hard-headed man of experience, who had worked out the scheme with the same care for practicability as he had devoted to his plan for founding the Bank of England.

Andrew Fletcher was infected with Paterson's enthusiasm for the prospective Eldorado. According to Dalrymple, it was he "who persuaded Paterson to trust the fate of his project to his own countrymen alone, and to let them have the sole benefit, glory and danger of it, for in its danger Fletcher deemed some of its glory to consist" (6). That is an interesting sidelight on an aspect of Fletcher's character. To use a cant phrase, he loved to live dangerously. The supposed national trait of caution was not prominent in his mental equipment. If he believed a thing to be right and needful, he did not pause to consider whether its advocacy entailed risk. If an enterprise was surrounded by danger, it was, for that reason, all the more attractive to him. If his country could be made prosperous and happy (which was all he cared for) by means of this project, "Then, in Heaven's name," he said in effect, "let us get on with it, let the consequences be what they may."

The Darien plan had his blessing and his hearty co-operation. Indeed, if Dalrymple is to be believed (his account of this business, like Burnet's, is strangely incomplete and in some ways misleading), "the character of Fletcher" was one of the positive assets of

Paterson's scheme, ranking with the "Act of Parliament and Royal charter" as an element in the confidence with which he "threw his project boldly upon the public" (7).

It was not made public with any degree of haste. On the contrary, it remained a close secret long after it had been proposed by Paterson. The directors did not place complete confidence in Paterson's optimism. They took the advice of others who knew more about Darien than he did, for although his knowledge of the Spanish Main generally was extensive, he had never been in Darien. Of the Darien experts, the two most important were Captain William Dampier and, particularly, Lionel Wafer, ex-surgeon and ex-buccaneer.

A year previously these men, "the buccaneer seaman and the buccaneer surgeon", as they were described, had been invited to attend a conference at Whitehall of the Commissioners of Trade (one of whom was John Locke, and another the Earl of Tankerville, the pusillanimous Lord Grey of the Monmouth rebellion). The object of this summons was to obtain information about Darien, for hints of a possible diversion in that direction of Scottish interests had reached the English Government, and they wished to be prepared against the contingency. The Darien scheme was, indeed, a reversion by the Scots to their original idea of planting a great colony in some tropical or sub-tropical region, and for that reason, Paterson's proposals had received an impetus which otherwise they would have lacked. Dampier and Wafer told the Commission that if the goodwill of the natives could be secured, 500 or even 250 determined men could hold Darien against anything that the Spaniards could do against them by land. That was quite true, as events proved; but defence against Spanish sea-power, as events also showed, was a different affair altogether. Defencelessness at sea and lack of provisions proved, in the end, to be the undoing of the Scottish settlement. Both Dampier and Wafer were strong advocates of a settlement in Darien, if not by the English, then by the Scots. They prepared a paper for the Commissioners of Trade, descriptive of Darien and its relation to the Spanish settlements by which it was surrounded. If England had been at war with Spain, instead of being anxious, above all things in her foreign policy, to keep friendly with her in view of the Spanish Succession, it seems not unlikely that she might at that time have forestalled Scotland by taking possession of Darien herself as, indeed, she seems to have intended, later on, to do. But the political situation just then forbade such a course, and in the view of King William, it forbade also his approval, as King of Scotland, of a Scottish settlement on the isthmus.

That was the position when Dampier and Wafer found themselves objects of interest to the directors of the Scottish Company. Would they supply the directors with information about Darien? They would—or, at any rate, Wafer would—for a consideration. Wafer, according to Dampier, was the greatest authority in the country on Darien. Also, he could write a neat report, and was even then preparing a book on "the Isthmus of America".

The directors of the Scottish Company eagerly embraced the opportunity of getting first-hand information about Darien from an intelligent man who knew the place intimately. The introduction to Wafer was secured by means of Fletcher, who had a meeting with the surgeon in a London coffee-house, together with one Captain Pennycook; the latter had been appointed Commodore of the Company's fleet, which was to sail in summer (1698). As the outcome of this meeting, a Dr. John Munro was sent by the directors to London, with instructions to engage Wafer, late "Chyrurgeon to Captain Dampier", on certain terms. He was to have £750, serve the Company for two years, and in the meantime proceed to Scotland to give the Secret Committee of the Company, and the Committee of Trade, whatever information they might desire about Darien. Wafer agreed to these terms, and set out for Edinburgh, under the assumed name of "Brown", armed with the report (with some unimportant modifications) which he and Dampier had prepared for the English Commissioners. The arrangement was that he was to go secretly to Fletcher's house at Saltoun, where he would receive instructions about his further movements. No one was to know anything about his mission, especially Paterson, without whose knowledge all these negotiations were being conducted. No doubt the object of the directors was to check Paterson's statements, compare them with those of Wafer, and thus arrive at the truth about a part of the world concerning which the directors themselves were profoundly ignorant. Also, Paterson was rather in disgrace at the time, owing to his having been the innocent but too confiding means of the Company losing, through a swindling broker in London, a sum of over £8,000. Wafer ("Brown") was met at Haddington by Captain Pennycook (also a surgeon), who took him secretly to Fletcher's house at Saltoun, where he remained several days. During his stay there, certain of the directors of the Company (those of them who knew what was going on) came to interview him and listen to what he had to say. And he had a good deal to say. In the manner of his kind, who are always with us, he expatiated upon the wonders of the new land that was going to make the fortunes of them all, and (this for Fletcher's benefit) of the country. Especially valuable was the asset represented by fragrant Nicaraguan wood, which, of itself, would, when cut down and sold, pay for the whole of the expenses of the expedition.

Wafer seems to have been a plausible fellow, who had the knack of getting people to believe anything he told them until they had had time to think things over. And he certainly seems to have impressed his Saltoun hearers with the reliability of his statements. From Saltoun he went, again secretly, to Edinburgh, where lodgings in a small room, high up in one of the "lands", were found for him, and where he was visited by some of the directors. But by this time, in spite of all the secrecy observed, the news was getting abroad that a Scottish expedition was about to sail to Darien. The English Government had actually warned Admiral Benbow to be prepared to intercept the ships when they sailed. Apparently from the first the directors feared English intervention, *vis-à-vis* Spanish displeasure, and wished to have other strings to their bow. Did Wafer know anything about the Amazon, or Rio de la Plata, and could he help them if they sent an expedition there? No, Wafer could not help them there at all.

Ultimately the directors informed Wafer that he could add nothing to the knowledge they already possessed. He was conducted from Edinburgh by a Dumbarton man named Herries, a brother surgeon (surgeons were adventurous fellows in those days), who actually sailed with the expedition, and afterwards wrote a bitterly critical account of it. In that account Herries accuses the directors of having pumped Wafer dry, and having then found an excuse to get rid of him. Possibly they had come to the conclusion that they had wanted a statistician, and had discovered a romancer. At any rate, Wafer returned to his study and the compilation of his Journal, perhaps a sadder and certainly a wiser man, but with his sorrow tempered by the satisfactory fact that, when negotiating terms with Scots directors, he had succeeded in extracting from them, in advance, £50 cash down.

According to Herries, it was Fletcher who conducted the negotiations with Wafer, and made the final agreement with him for £750. But Herries acquits Fletcher in handsome terms of any intention to take advantage of Wafer. When the directors finally dismissed Wafer, he was released from his undertaking (for which he received a gratuity of twenty guineas) to delay publishing for a month the book which he was then writing (8).

Chapter VIII

ON UNEMPLOYMENT

IN the year of the expedition to Darien (1698), after the ships had sailed, Andrew Fletcher published anonymously the first of his political works. They were distinguished from the common rut of political tracts by clarity of reasoning, purity of style, and moderation of tone. The writer at once made his mark as a controversialist in Scottish and foreign affairs, whose ability was unequalled in his native land. The domestic conditions of Scotland and the political conditions abroad engaged his attention; and it is clear that it was in the light of these conditions that he had given his whole-hearted support to the Darien adventure.

Domestic matters are discussed in *Two Discourses on the affairs of Scotland*, and foreign matters in an essay, written in Italian and published ostensibly in Naples, which is entitled *Discorso delle cose di Spagna*. Also, in the same year, he published an essay on militias. For the moment we are concerned with the two domestic discourses, in the first of which he explains that he has entered the controversial field because he was constrained by feelings of patriotism "and the circumstances of my affairs not allowing me to be otherwise serviceable to my country" (an obvious reference to the fact that he was not a member of the Convention).

He commences his *First Discourse* by congratulating the country on being "no more under those tyrannical reigns in which it was a crime to speak of publick affairs or to say that the King had received bad counsel in anything". He then attacks vigorously the farming of the Customs to the burghs. He declares " corruption is the blackest of crimes", and adds, "when I name any guilty of it I name a very odious criminal". This sentiment, incidentally, uttered by most politicians of his time, would be justly regarded as a Pecksniffian platitude, but the incorruptible Andrew Fletcher, as even his enemies were forced to admit, had a moral right to preach to his generation. He enlarges upon political corruption, by showing how the waters, if tainted at their source, spread in ascending degrees of criminality from private individuals to judges; from judges to legislators; ultimately embracing an entire estate of the realm, to wit, the burghs. The results were standing armies, oppressive taxes, and slavery. He thinks that Parliament should sweep away every trace of this corruption before proceeding to any further business. For he believed that the burghs were bribed by the Customs farm to secure their votes.

The next matter that should engage the attention of Parliament is the business of the African and Indian Company. It is, he says, "a greater venture at sea than at any time since we have been a nation". Supplies should be incessantly provided for the settlers, who may have to suffer great hardships by delay whilst "our standing forces are living at ease". And he adds these words, prophetic as they seemed to him and certainly true in relation to his own generation: the nation, he says, "has so great a concern in this enterprise that I will say all our hopes of ever being any other than a poor and inconsiderable people are embarked with them" (the colonists).

He then proceeds to show how necessary for the economic salvation of Scotland was this Darien venture. Partly through the fault of Scotsmen themselves, and partly by the removal of her native Kings to England, the country, notwithstanding its natural advantages for trading and fishing, had fallen so low that "we are despised by all our neighbours and made incapable to repel an injury if any should be offered". Indeed, the national motto might well be inverted, "and all may not only provoke but safely trample upon us". What then are we to do? The answer is to "become a nation of traders", as being the only means "to remove us from our present miserable and despicable condition". The harbours, seas, and lochs of Scotland, hitherto unprofitable, might be employed to advantage. "No care has been taken to set the poor at work, and multitudes of families, for want of employment by trade and manufacture, go yearly out of the Kingdom without any intention to return."

It may be argued, he says, that King William, being King of England and Stadtholder of Holland, must do nothing calculated to prejudice the trade of those nations. But Scotland has offered both nations a share in the trading advantages she obtained, by

Act of Parliament, for herself: to England, indeed, an equal share. Would the King break the laws and violate his oath by Scotland's destruction? Surely not. There had been underhand dealings, though presumably without the King's knowledge, in opposing Scottish plans (witness, for example, "the affair of Hamborough"), and the King's Ministers abroad were no longer to be looked upon as Ministers for the Crown of Scotland. But since England and Scotland are separate Kingdoms, and have separate Ministers at home, Scotland ought to have separate Ministers abroad also. In the past, Scotsmen had reposed too much faith in the impartiality of British Ministers abroad for the protection of Scottish interests, and "now we are undeceived". At the late treaty (Ryswick) Scottish interests had been shamefully neglected.

"These gentlemen" (the English Court party) "would persuade us to pay almost as many forces in time of peace as war", and, "like Pharaoh's taxmasters, would have us make brick without allowing us straw." And all this, forsooth, that these forces and the regiment which, "to the consuming of our people", we Scots recruit in Holland, may be employed, in the event of a rupture abroad, in the defence of English or Dutch trade! Instead of taxing our people for such purposes, we ought to raise revenue by taxation for carrying on our own trade, and should levy a twelve-months' cess for the support of it. In return, when the Darien Company earns a dividend, "it should go to the easing of the nation from publick burdens". Having been baulked (by the English) of foreign money, it is only reasonable that the Company should look to Parliament "for the capital it needs".

Here, indeed, was an advocacy of State Socialism, long before the theory became a party label.

The Scottish Parliament, he proceeds, should also petition the King that the three small frigates, lately built at the expense of the Scottish nation, should be allowed to convoy the next ships sent out to Darien by the Company.

Supplies and a naval force! Fletcher had placed his finger unerringly on the two main needs of the young colony, if it was to maintain itself until firmly established; and for lack of which it perished dismally (2).

The Scottish nation, Fletcher goes on to say, had been exhausted of money by the three years' scarcity, "next to a famine". How long this may continue, "God only knows" (it lasted five years longer). The recent long and tedious war had cost Scotland much blood. Her money contributions had been necessarily small, owing to her poverty. But "seven or eight thousand of her seamen were on board the English Fleet; two or three thousand in that of Holland; we had twenty Battalions of Foot, and six Squadrons of Dragoons here and in Flanders. Besides, I am credibly informed that every fifth man in the English Forces was either of this nation or Scots-Irish, who are a people of the same blood with us" (probably Fletcher means here Ulstermen, whom elsewhere he calls "the Scots of the North"): altogether, by a modest computation, perhaps thirty thousand men. He mentions these facts merely to answer the reproaches of those "who vilify us as an inconsiderable people, and set a mean value on the share we have borne in this war". And a poor return they have had for it all!

Fletcher's *Second Discourse* was of a more general and philosophical character than the *First*. He is at close grips with the state of poverty touched upon in his *First Discourse*, and his plan for dealing with unemployment, caused by the bad seasons and the absence of trade, is one of the most strikingly original that has ever been offered by a responsible publicist. But before this *Discourse* is analysed, it may be well to give a brief account of the main features of Scotland's social and economic life, as it was at the close of the seventeenth and the beginning of the eighteenth century.

The economic condition of the people was truly appalling. At the time Fletcher wrote his *Discourses*, the country was well on in the seven years of blight and famine which commenced in 1696. Sunless summers with drenching rains, snow and frost in autumn, and mists from the east known as "haars", had combined to ruin the harvests. Cattle and sheep perished by thousands; prices of the necessities of life rose to heights which placed them beyond the means of the poor; the struggle for existence crushed all natural feelings and made beasts of human beings; men and women literally fought for their food; children were sold into slavery on the plantations to provide the means of existence; and in some cases, even the dead were left to bury themselves. It is a grim picture.

Out of Scotland's population of little over a million, it is estimated that during the seven hungry years thousands died of actual starvation, and thousands more took refuge in emigration. And still the population was too large for the means of subsistence (3).

Palliatives were applied by the Privy Council. Foreign grain was allowed to enter the country free of duty. Forestallers were denounced from the pulpit and punished by the law. Maximum prices were fixed, and hidden stores were exposed for sale. But of what use were these measures to the starving poor who had no money to buy even at the regulated prices? The Kirk instituted fasts and days of humiliation for woes which were attributed to Divine wrath for national sins. But the Kirk also strove to stimulate liberality by those who could give to those who needed their gifts so desperately. All classes were suffering—the lairds, with their depleted incomes, equally with their dependents who had nothing at all. It was a terrible time of trial for the unhappy country.

Is it surprising that patriots like Andrew Fletcher, with their hearts wrung by the misery which they saw around them, should welcome any enterprise, however risky? They knew that the plight of the country was due in some measure to circumstances that were not beyond the control of the people. They knew that the system of agriculture was hopelessly archaic. They knew that by her superiority in farming England had escaped the worst effects of bad seasons, though she was also favoured by a better climate and a richer soil. And as we shall see, Fletcher in later years showed his fellow-countrymen in a practical fashion how their lot could be improved by a departure from primitive methods and the adoption of aids to successful farming. But improvements of that description could not be improvised, and time was needed for their development. Trade as a foundation for prosperity was an immediate possibility; and trade alone could save the country from its most pressing calamities.

In his *Second Discourse* Fletcher proposes that Parliament should take into consideration "the condition of so many thousands of our people who are this day dying for want of bread". The famine, he fears, may be followed by plague, when a state of affairs would arise which no one could contemplate without horror. "What man is there in this nation," he asks, "if he have any compassion, who must not grudge himself every nice bit and every delicate morsel he puts in his mouth when he considers that so many were already dead and so many, at this minute, struggling with death. . . . And must not every unnecessary branch of our expence, or the least finery in our houses, clothes or equipages, reproach us with our barbarity so long as people born with natural endowments perhaps not inferior to our own, and fellow-citizens, perish for want of things absolutely necessary to life?" How was the position to be met?

Public workhouses for such a vast number of poor were impracticable. Only one country, Holland, could afford them. The Hollanders, "by reason of the steadiness of their temper, as well as of their Government being a Commonwealth", could probably remain constant to this method, for Holland was "the richest of any nation in the world's trade". Even France could not keep vast workhouses going except perhaps spasmodically. For the old and infirm and helpless such institutions might be necessary, and should indeed be provided at the public cost. But what of the able-bodied work-shy who roamed the country from the Highlands to the Borders? "In spite of restraining laws", he says, "this country has always swarmed with such numbers of idle vagabonds as no laws could ever restrain."

These he divides into two classes: the dangerous ruffians and the harmless vagrants. Besides the poor families supported by Church contributions, there were in Scotland, he estimated, no fewer than two hundred thousand people begging from door to door, and even in normal times the number reached one hundred thousand. The criminal beggars he comprehensively describes as "incestuous, murderous ruffians", many of them perpetually drunk: "a cursing, blaspheming, and fighting" crowd. These men were the terror of cottagers living in lonely districts, and the drunken disturbers of the peace at markets, weddings, and funerals. He would have no mercy on them. "Sell them to the plantations," or pack them off to Venice, "to fight against the Turks". Such was his remedy for ridding the country of her dangerous pests.

The real problem was, however, how to bring the harmless

beggars and honest work together. And here Fletcher tries to get down to the fundamentals of unemployment. He reviews the relations of the Church in the past towards slavery, and comes to the conclusion that the attitude of the Church on this question had been the main cause of unemployment throughout Christendom right down the ages.

He argues that when Christianity was first established publicly, the Church recommended the masters of slaves to set at liberty those slaves who embraced the Christian religion. He quotes St. Paul as recommending (by *his* interpretation of St. Paul's words) those Christians who were slaves to be content with their lot, and thus show to the world that they were not what are nowadays sometimes cynically called "rice" Christians (4). St. Paul, he remarks, offered this advice, partly because even in his day a doctrine was being preached that slavery was inconsistent with Christianity, and such a doctrine impeded the spread of the new religion. As the result of the attitude of the Church, the cities of the Empire found themselves in time burdened with an infinite number of men "who had no other estate but their liberty, of which the greater part would not work, and the rest had been bred to no profession". This state of matters compelled the Emperor Constantine to make edicts in favour of beggars, and from that time, at the request of the bishops, hospitals and almshouses not formerly known in the world began to be established. But the Mahomedan religion arose, to which proselytes were attracted by the freeing of all slaves who professed that faith. The Christians were so harassed by the rebellions that became so frequent among their slaves, that they also freed them all. This step was apparently thought necessary for the salvation of their own souls and the preservation of their religion; and as its result, the problem of unemployment became increasingly more and more difficult to solve.

In ancient times, so the argument continues, when a man was the property of another, he was provided, in his master's own interest, with meat, clothes, and lodgings; and not only himself, but his wife and children as well. But the provision made for the poor by hospitals, almshouses, and the contributions of churches or parishes, has been found by experience to increase the number of those that live by them. And the liberty every idle and lazy person has of burdening the society in which he lives with his maintenance, has increased their numbers to the weakening and impoverishing of that society, for "he needs only to say that he cannot get work, and then he must be maintained by charity".

The only remedy is to use compulsion in the absorption of the unemployed. "Back to servitude," should be the cry, but it should be a punishable offence to call these men "slaves". " A slave, properly, is one who is absolutely subjected to the will of another man without any remedy;" whereas the servitude he had in view would be subjection only "under certain limitations, and upon certain accounts necessary for the good of the Commonwealth." In practice, the only difference between his "slaves" and ordinary servants would be that their masters would have power to sell them to other employers who could give them work when they themselves for any reason had no work for them to do, and thus, "the profit is permanent to the society".

He does not shirk the charge of inconsistency. "Would I", he seems to hear his critics say, "thus bring back slavery into the world? Shall men of immortal souls and by nature equal to any be sold as beasts?" Shall they and their posterity "be for ever subjected to the most miserable of all conditions, the inhuman barbarity of masters who may beat, mutilate, torture, starve, or kill so great a number of mankind at pleasure? Shall the far greater number of the Commonwealth be slaves, not that the rest may be free, but tyrants over them? With what face can we oppose the tyranny of princes, and recommend such opposition as the highest virtue, if we make ourselves tyrants over the greater part of mankind? Can any man from whom such a thing has once escaped ever offer to speak for liberty?"

"They must pardon me", he replies to all this, "if I tell them that I regard not names but things;" a characteristic phrase. " We are told", he continues, "that there is not a slave in France". "I say there is not a free man in France." The King of France is the absolute ruler; he can do what he pleases with a man's property, and there is no remedy. Similarly, the Turks say they have no slaves, except Jews or Christians. But they are all slaves to the Grand Seignior. The fact is that real slavery has been confounded with the type of servitude which he is proposing; but the two have nothing in common. "We are all", he concludes, "subject to the laws; and the easier or harder conditions imposed by them upon the several ranks of men in any society make not the distinction that is between a freeman and a slave."

In Fletcher's day servile conditions in certain industries were in active operation in Scotland. An Act of Parliament in 1606 legalized the enslavement of colliers and salters as "necessary servants". They were compelled to work in many of the mines and at all the saltpans (e.g., at Prestonpans near Saltoun) during the whole of their lives without hope of freedom. If the property were sold, they passed with it to the new proprietor. If they ran away or offered their services elsewhere, they were prosecuted for theft, i.e., the miner or the salter had stolen himself! They became a hereditary caste of serfs, born into thraldom and (never knowing the joys of freedom) reconciled, it would appear, to their miserable lot. Their wages were relatively fair enough, and their masters were bound to keep them in sickness and in health, and, at the end, to provide them with a coffin. It was not until 1775 that any attempt was made to abolish this abominable system of perpetual bondage. And the abolition was followed by consequences resembling in some of its aspects those which flowed from the emancipation of slaves in America. It was not until the last year of the eighteenth century that complete and unconditional freedom was granted to the whole of these serfs, who then became merged in the general community. But they bore the marks, in their own lineaments and those of their descendants, of the bestial characteristics which centuries of hopeless servitude had impressed upon them.

That certainly was not the type of serfship which Fletcher had in view as a solvent of unemployment.

It will be observed that his proposals were based upon the assumption—presumably well-grounded—that a contributory cause of Scotland's poverty, apart from the reasons already assigned, was the incorrigible aversion from work of a large proportion of the labouring classes. Of the lazy beggars he had in mind (for begging was their profession), those of them who were not dangerous, and for that reason exportable, ruffians, would become useful members of the community, if compelled to work; and by their labour would add to the wealth of the nation instead of increasing its poverty by sponging on their neighbours. It was of no use to set the wheels of industry in motion unless the necessary labour for keeping the wheels moving was made available. Thus the proposals were complementary: a vast extension of trade abroad and a vast compulsory addition of labour at home.

Whatever else may be said for it, Fletcher's plan was a conception of remarkable courage. He risked his reputation as a lover of liberty by proposing what was difficult to distinguish from a system of domestic slavery. He himself was as little a slave to words as he was to any other master. "Will it work?" That was the question that concerned him, and in the light of that question he was content to ignore his reputation for consistency. Once he was satisfied that a certain course of action would be for the permanent benefit of his native country, he waived aside all other considerations as being of relatively small consequence (5).

As a step further in the proposed regeneration of Scotland, he suggested that rents should be reduced all round. Rents that were too high constituted an important element in the causes of the prevailing poverty. All classes of the community were affected. The tenants could not afford to pay wages to their labourers, and the labourers could not afford to buy from the village tradesmen and shopkeepers. And not only must rents be reduced, but by Act of Parliament no man should be allowed to possess more land than he and his servants could cultivate. This, he believed, would make for better cultivation, and would provide more employment for the workless. "In a few years", he says optimistically, "the country will be everywhere enclosed and improved to the greatest height, the plough being everywhere in the hand of the possessor." He propounds a scheme for dealing with land under the value of £200 sterling ("clear profit" annually), the object of which was to force the land into the hands of men of substance, who would pay their men well; and thus "all servants, day labourers, tradesmen and all sorts of merchants" would benefit. Owners of these lands were to be compelled by law to sell, at twenty years' purchase, half the annual profit derived from their properties (6).

The lesser tenants or heritors (those who may be called the

"lairdies" in relation to the lairds) were showing, in Fletcher's opinion, too great a tendency to ape their superiors, to be compatible with good farming. Their lands were no better cultivated than those of "beggarly tenants", and their servants were "wretched and half starved". They would suffer no injustice if they were compelled to relinquish half their annual revenue, for they would receive full value for the rent they gave up. Besides, urges Fletcher quaintly, it will "put them in mind not to live after the manner of men of great estates, but as husbandmen, which will be in no way derogatory to their quality, however antient their quality may be". A Scots farmer, in short, could remain a gentleman, even if he worked hard.

The grazing industry of the country, while its plight was not quite so bad as that of tillage (the agricultural tenant paid rent in kind: an obnoxious system, Fletcher believed), was by no means in a satisfactory state. No adequate provision was made for the cattle and the sheep in winter. They had neither hay nor straw, nor any enclosure to shelter them or the grass from the cold easterly winds in spring. The beasts were in a dying condition, and the grass was consumed by those winds until summer brought relief.

It was not surprising that men of substance in Scotland would have nothing to do with farming. How were these men to be attracted to the land? There must, he concluded, be compulsory legislation. "It is next to an impossibility", he argues, "to alter a general bad custom in any nation without a general regulation." Also, "alterations that are not countenanced by the Public Authority proceed slowly."

So, once more, compulsion must be applied by the State in order to drive capital into land. By what method was this to be done?

Fletcher's plan has, at least, the merit of simplicity. "Abolish interest for money," he said, in effect, "and the thing is done." He had no medieval notions about the immorality of accepting interest for money. All he wanted was that money should be made to serve another purpose. Let it be enacted, so he suggested, that the interest for money shall fall next year from 6 per cent. to 5 per cent., and go on falling every year by 1 per cent., until it is finally extinguished altogether. This "inevitability of gradualness" could not conceal the revolutionary nature of the proposal. It was feasible, of course, if any Scottish Government could be found daring enough to risk it. Nor can it be denied that had it been put into force, farming would have received a remarkable fillip from the diversion of capital. Land needed fertilizing by capital, and here was the fertilizer. In Fletcher's day, a "flight of capital" abroad, when the timorous get scared, was not the easy remedy for confiscatory measures at home, or for State interference with the channels of investment, that it is to-day. The Scottish financial sky would scarcely have fallen had his plan been adopted by Parliament; nor, indeed, in view of the economic gymnastics in which the world has exercised itself in recent months, would it be esteemed to-day as the horrifying heresy of a generation ago. Fletcher was not concerned with charges of heresy. His reputation among his contemporaries was that of an honest but misguided man, with a swarm of bees in his Scots bonnet. He was generations ahead of his time.

Indeed, he himself says: "I know these proposals, by some men who aim at nothing but private interest, will be looked upon as visionary." His sole concern was with the public interest; and he was convinced that it was in the public interest that the land should be put to the best use of which it was capable. "It is the interest of all good Governments", he declares with conviction, " at least to encourage a good sort of husbandry." His brain teemed with constructive ideas, some of which, regarded askance by his contemporaries, have since been proved to have had the root of the matter in them. A contemporary named Sir John Clerk (whose type of mind is exemplified by the fact that he was the man who worked out the 'Equivalent' to shillings, when the terms of the Union were arranged) tells us that Fletcher's schemes had "very little credit", and that he was always changing them himself, though, of course, adds the unctuous Clerk, he was "a very worthy man".

One wonders what sort of Scotland Fletcher would have produced under, say, a Five Years Plan, with Andrew Fletcher as sole dictator (an impossible supposition) for that period. He had the courage necessary for the post; the self-assurance for assuming its responsibilities (if he had believed in dictatorships, which he did not); and the fertility of imagination necessary for working out its problems. But Scotland's Cato was not destined to be Scotland's Mussolini.

On the subject of education, Fletcher was, of course, on the side of the angels. The better education of the youth of Scotland was declared to be absolutely necessary. "I must confess", he mournfully remarks, "I know no part of the world where education is upon any tolerable foot." His efforts towards better education may well have stimulated the legislation in 1696, which settled schools and schoolmasters throughout all the parishes of Scotland: an ideal visualized long before by John Knox. Whoever conceived that Act of Parliament did more for the true prosperity of his country in the generation which followed the enactment of the measure, than any political result which flowed from the union of the two Parliaments.

And even on such a matter as the most convenient site for the capital of Scotland, Fletcher had decided views. He suggested that as "the happy situation of London has been the principal cause of the glory and riches of England", so the "bad situation" of Edinburgh has been one great occasion of "the poverty and uncleanliness in which the greater part of the people of Scotland live". An Edinburgh man himself (practically), Fletcher was, nevertheless, not prevented by sentimentality, or his sense of the picturesque, from viewing the question from a commercial standpoint. Therefore he advocated a change for the seat of government, but to what alternative site, he did not suggest.

Andrew Fletcher was a practical man of affairs, and not a theorist only. Even his revolutionary method of curing unemployment has its imitators. We are seeing to-day, in different European countries, a tendency to adopt schemes of "obligatory labour service" which, essentially, are only modifications of his plan for Scotland (7).

Chapter IX

ON THE BALANCE OF POWER

ANDREW FLETCHER cannot, with any degree of justice, be described as a man with a parochial mind. On the contrary, his political vision stretched far beyond the confines of his native land. He had studied with care the literature of Greece and Rome. He had travelled widely on the Continent. He had acquired the languages, and read the histories, of the countries he had visited. He had sought on foreign soil answers to foreign political questions. He had thought deeply on the means by which the peace of Europe could be preserved, and he had weighed in the balance of a sagacious judgment the States of Europe, in their relations towards the principles of liberty that lay at the root of the whole body of his speculations.

It is probable that he was better equipped with a knowledge of foreign politics than any other man in the Scottish Parliament. It is doubtful if he was inferior in that respect to any member of the House of Commons. It is certain that, in comparison with his understanding of foreign politics, the talk of the average country gentlemen who voted on foreign issues in the English Parliament was as the babbling of babes to the speech of a full-grown man.

In 1698 Europe was in a state of tension, all because of a sickly imbecile King who had relapses and recoveries which excited hopes and fears alternately. Charles II, the King of Spain, ruled over a vast Empire. On his death, without issue, it was certain that there was going to be a scramble for his Crown unless European agreement was reached beforehand. There were only three possible claimants to the Spanish dominions; and these were France, Austria, and Bavaria. How then was Great Britain interested? Why the feverish anxiety of William of Orange to effect an agreement before the death of Charles of Spain; or, failing agreement, to have forces sufficiently strong to face all consequences with equanimity? The answer is given by that perennial bugbear of Europe, the balance of power.

The balance of power lay at the centre of Fletcher's *Discourse* on the Spanish Succession, published, in Italian, in 1698 (1). At the time he wrote, the claimants, like alert vultures, were hovering round the sickbed of the dying King, awaiting the hour to strike for them to plunge their hungry beaks in the decaying carcase of his far-flung Empire. It was a time of crisis for Europe. The possibilities of war were ever present, and unless a treaty could be negotiated, war, in which the whole of the European Powers might be involved, was more than likely.

It was with that contingency in view that Fletcher prepared his *Discourse*, dealing with the situation from every angle that presented itself to his fertile mind. It was a remarkable example of his self-assurance that he did not hesitate to instruct the European nations in their duty at this crisis. In effect, his conclusion was, that at all costs, in order to prevent the certain domination of the world by an arrogant Power, France must be shut out of the Succession.

He commences his *Discourse* with the thesis that the monarchy of Spain afforded a "proper foundation" for "erecting on it the Empire of the World". And he develops his thesis by the argument that the decay of the Spanish Empire can be arrested if certain steps are taken, chief among which are the rearrangement, by exchange, of her dominions. The dead wood, in effect, must be cut out. Especially must Spain relinquish her hold of the Low Countries: "the cancer of Flanders", as he calls it. The wars in the Low Countries were the most apparent cause of the downfall of Spain, "as they continue to be of its weakness at this day". "For through the seventeen provinces as through a fistulous wound, all the aliment that ought to have nourished the Empire of Spain has continually distilled."

The main causes of the decay of the Spanish Monarchy have been the want of good order within its Government; also the fact that "the most vigorous and flourishing Kingdom of France, its perpetual enemy," lies between its disjoined dominions. He suggests methods for repeopling Spain and her Indian dominions, and inducing their inhabitants to apply themselves to "agriculture, the mechanical arts and commerce". An increased population would stimulate improvement in these fields of effort, and the

Spaniards would be cured of "that strong propensity to sloth and idleness which has been one of the chief causes of their weakness". But failing this remedy, "the most rigorous laws and regulations must be added to it as for the cure of an obstinate evil". To attract strangers, measures must be taken to make justice prevail even in the most remote province, and it must be speedy and inexpensive. The cruelties that are secretly committed in the Spanish colonies must be punished with the utmost severity, and an endeavour must be made "to correct that fantastic pride which is so incompatible with all good Government". Also, religious toleration must be established as a permanent principle.

So much for the internal reforms of the Spanish Empire. But in what way did it form the basis of World Empire? Spain herself is geographically well situated as the focus of this imperialism. Egypt would form a convenient seat of universal empire, were it not for the "barren countries and vast deserts" that block it in on two of its sides, and almost sever it, except by sea, from the rest of the world. The strategic importance of Gibraltar is stressed. "The Straits of Gibraltar, being as it were the centre of meetings amongst those seas that embrace all the countries of the world," furnish "the greatest conveniency for transporting armies and military stores with the utmost care and expedition". Well, why not make Lisbon or Carthagena or Seville or Cadiz or Tangier (for the shelter of its bay and the fertile country around it) the centre for the residence of the Spanish Sovereign and for the conquest of the world? A union between Spain and Portugal would be desirable, with, in that event, a removal of the Spanish Court to Lisbon. As the result of this union, the Spanish dominions in America would be enlarged by the accession of Brazil, and the whole world would rejoice "to see France fallen from her hopes of succeeding to the Spanish monarchy". All this from the Spanish standpoint, but not, of course, from the standpoint of the rest of Europe.

If France succeeds to the monarchy, there will be no hope for Europe. "Truly", he says, "the power of the Most Christian King has in our time become so formidable that if he intends to seize any part of the Spanish Monarchy, he must lay his account with having the whole world combined against him, excepting perhaps a few princes whom he can tempt to a share in the spoil." (For the Most Christian King, read the Kaiser, and the analogy between 1698 and 1914 is by no means remote.)

No nation could aspire to World Empire without command of the sea. If France succeeded to the Spanish throne and the Spanish dominions in South America, she could easily attain to World Empire owing to her power at sea. Europe, as a whole, would prefer any prince to one of the House of Austria or of Bourbon, and Europe's choice, if free to choose, would be the Electoral Prince of Bavaria, certainly the most innocuous of the three. The whole world would combine against the pretensions of the Dauphin. France has tried to lull suspicion of her intentions by "fine gilded words" and by "gilding the soporific pill". He (Fletcher) foresees her course of action. She will propose that the King of Great Britain and the Republic of Holland shall be her joint guarantors, and thus save Europe from "a most consuming war". Being financially exhausted by the recent war, these countries can regain prosperity only by means of peaceful commerce, and they ought therefore "to endeavour by all means to preserve the peace of Europe". But, says Fletcher, these artful arguments would soon be destroyed, and the guarantee, if given, would be nullified by the intrigues of King Louis, to "set England and Holland by the ears", or by means of fomenting internal dissensions in England, "things by no means hard to accomplish". Also, it would seem that there is some "hidden venom" working in England and Holland, which, "corrupting all their affairs, must at last precipitate them into utter ruin." Therefore it was quite possible that "in this most profligate age, amidst such prodigious degeneracy of every rank of man, who allow themselves to be deluded, not from want of knowledge but of virtue", the "gross imposition" of France might succeed. This was all the more conceivable because "the people of Europe are so much impoverished and tired with war". If France does not spare her money to courtiers and her promises to princes, "to assist them in robbing their subjects and neighbours of their liberty, and in banishing it out of the world", she will probably succeed in her object. If France fails in her attempt to fool England and Holland in this fashion, she may resort to force, making rapid conquests to prevent the Germans from effective opposition, while "amusing" the English and Dutch by a defensive war in the Low Countries. Having thus stabilized his position, Louis will commence to arrange an adjustment of territories in Italy, wherewith to buy allies. Bavarian friendship will be detached from the House of Austria, "and the Germans, having no sea power, could do nothing to oppose the French armies in Spain".

If the French should become masters of Spain and her dominions, the commerce of the English and the Dutch will assuredly be hurt. Thenceforward, "declining daily, these nations will, in a few years, be driven entirely out of the sea by the superior strength" of the fleets of France. The manning of the French ships could be reinforced by the sailors whom the commerce of the Indies and the Mediterranean would bring to their flag. Besides, the wealth of France would be greatly increased by the new avenues of commerce opened up to her, and by her acquisition of the mines of Peru.

What, then, should Great Britain do if faced by the threat of French domination? The King of Great Britain has a "vast power at sea", enabling him, by means of the combined fleets of England and Holland, not only to obstruct France in the conquest of America, but to paralyse any hostile action directed against Spain herself, by protecting the Spanish coast against French naval attack. It is incredible, indeed, that King William can allow a prince of France to succeed to the throne of Spain, "without reaping some great advantage from it to his own subjects and the Dutch". This can be nothing less than surrendering the whole of North America to the English (where already they have many colonies), and withdrawing all French settlers from that continent. And the Dutch should be recompensed for their acquiescence, by receiving a grant of the dominions of Spain in the East Indies, "together with the part she still retains of the Low Countries". If it should be objected that these conditions are intolerable, "I answer that Louis, by grasping at all the Spanish dominions, would lose them all". These concessions to the King of Great Britain, who cannot accept lower terms, if he would not have the English and the Dutch driven off the sea, would make things easy for Louis, "who would still retain enough". For if France possessed Spain and South

America, Louis might in time easily make himself master of the world.

Suppose, now, that a claimant other than France succeeds to the throne of Spain. Leaving the Elector of Bavaria out of account (his son was the candidate), there is the Archduke of Austria, son of the Emperor Leopold. He would be "a very fit successor", being of the same family as the feeble King of Spain. Also (an important consideration), he would be very useful for "balancing the excessive power of France". It would be "a capital point" to have the goodwill of the Spaniards themselves, and, indeed, it would be a good thing if the King of Spain were to nominate his successor himself. The Hapsburgs would probably have many partisans in Spain; the Bourbons few. So it is probable that the Spaniards, "their interests concurring with their inclinations", may make an offer to the Emperor to accept the King of the Romans (the eldest Archduke), on condition of his hereditary dominions being joined to the Crown of Spain. This would give "great jealousy" to the Germans, and might cost the House of Austria the imperial dignity; but there would be sufficient compensation.

Suppose, further, that a Power other than France obtained the Succession, how would she proceed to consolidate her position? First and foremost, by acquiring a strong naval force, which the geographical situation of Spain would facilitate. Then she would have to reform her land forces by restoring discipline, where needed; by imitating the methods of the military masters, the Romans, "in their battles, marches, and encampments"; and those of the French in the conduct of sieges. These foundations laid, there would only be one thing lacking for the conquest of the world, and that is "the Empire of the Sea". Without that the Power acquiring the Spanish Empire would quickly find herself in trouble with the Naval Powers, France, England, and Holland. Her policy would then be to ally herself with one against the other two. That would keep the Naval Powers busy, while she was exterminating the fleets and colonies of her enemies in the Indies, Africa, and the Mediterranean. She would keep on good terms with her ally until, her enemies being driven from the seas, she could deal with her at leisure. The "strongest possible efforts" should be made for the empire of the sea. Having once surmounted that difficulty, the victorious king "leaves the world in chains to his successor".

The empire of the sea being gained, the remaining colonies in the world would easily fall into the hands of the new King of Spain. The last enemy, to be attacked in due time after the command of the sea had been won, would be France, a France now seriously weakened by the expulsion of the sturdy Calvinists. Having by this time lost Louis, and the results of his policy, having by reason of the great miseries of her people, neither horses fit for war, nor indeed men, except the nobility, France would be in no condition to make a prolonged resistance.

As for the English and the Dutch, after losing their strength at sea, they "will become poor and inconsiderable". Italy will be "sunk in effeminacy". Germany will not be able to "hold out long". The Empire of the Turks will be "an easy prey". The Empires of Persia, Muscovy, the Mogul, Tartary, China, and Japan "as so many empty names will vanish before so great a Power, serving only by the strange variety and riches of the arms and dresses of their feeble inhabitants to adorn trophies: in all which, the name of the restorer of the Empire will shine above every other." The Emperor, in short (for it was he that Fletcher had in view), who had already threatened to make himself master of the world, could do so by easy stages, if only the sovereignty of Spain came into his hands.

"Do what you may," Fletcher seems to say to England, "you will find it difficult to avoid great danger over this Succession question." He envisages a World Dictator as its probable outcome, ultimately if not immediately. He seems to suggest that England's wisest policy on behalf of herself and Holland might be to come to terms with France, acquiescing in her Spanish aims but only in exchange for adequate compensations to both countries.

Fletcher published his *Discourse* in 1698 at a time when negotiations for the first Partition Treaty were proceeding (and incidentally when the Darien expedition was setting out). Subsequent events showed how accurately he had gauged the situation, and his prescience seems to justify the suggestion that his mind was that of a statesman of first-rate calibre. William of Orange, upon whose "good European" shoulders rested the main burden of protecting the general interests of Europe, had reason to congratulate himself upon overcoming (temporarily, as it proved) the difficulties of coming to an arrangement with His Most Christian Majesty of France. Louis relinquished, in favour of the young son of the Elector of Bavaria, the claim of the Dauphin to the Spanish Crown, in consideration of territorial adjustments in Italy between himself and the Emperor. But the death of the Bavarian Prince in the spring of 1699 made a fresh shuffle of the diplomatic cards needful. A new Partition Treaty was arranged, the fresh deal giving better cards to the astute Louis. The Emperor's second son, the Archduke Charles, was to receive the Spanish Crown, the Spanish Netherlands, and the Indies. But the whole of the Spanish territories in Italy were to be handed over to France. This arrangement was not satisfactory to Austria, but, lacking a navy, she could only protest ineffectively. Nor can it have been satisfactory to England and Holland, for the "compensations" offered to them were far short of the minimum requirements suggested by Fletcher. But England had no army, and her navy was hopelessly undermanned. Meanwhile the poor imbecile at Madrid showed an exasperating unwillingness to die: and his resiliency complicated still further a tangled situation. The proud Spaniards chafed under the proposed dismemberment of their monarchy by the Powers, whom they regarded, not unjustly, as a gang of bandits. They advised their wretched king, torn this way and that (in so far as he was capable of understanding the questions at issue), by the intrigues of the French and the Austrian partisans at his Court, to settle his Crown himself, one way or the other, before he died. He did so by making a will which embodied a complete victory for French diplomacy. The will bequeathed the whole of the Spanish Monarchy to the Duke of Anjou, the second son of the Dauphin.

Louis, as William bitterly remarked, "preferred the Will to the Treaty". But William was unable to carry his country with him in his resentment. England was sick of war, and war undertaken to maintain the balance of power, by turning out of Spain a young French prince who might one day become more Spanish than the Spaniards themselves, could not fail to be unpopular. France skilfully intrigued to divide the English politicians, as Fletcher had foreseen she would do; and by lavish expenditure in England of French gold, as Fletcher had also predicted, she succeeded in warding off Parliamentary antagonism to French policy. Also, France had in contemplation a second "Treaty of Dover" (which Fletcher had hinted at as a possibility), if the circumstances and prospects of success should warrant such a proposal. It needed, indeed, the undiplomatic, if generous, recognition by Louis of the son of James II as the King of Great Britain, so to inflame England against France as to provide the necessary atmosphere of popular indignation which made a declaration of war against France possible.

Fletcher was too confident in his prediction that if the Spanish Succession fell to France, nothing could prevent the domination by that Power of the whole world. But it needed twelve years of bloody war, the amazing military genius of Marlborough, and the whole naval strength of Great Britain and Holland combined (it will be remembered how Fletcher stressed the importance of sea-power), to prevent the realization of that ambition.

The maintenance of the balance of power has always been, and will always continue to be, a terrifying nightmare for European statesmen, until physical force yields to moral compulsion, and fear yields to mutual confidence, as the main factors in preserving the peace. In Fletcher's day such a solution was beyond the purview of the statesmen of Europe.

In April 1701 an anonymous tract was published, entitled *A Speech upon the state of the nation*, which is always included (and rightly included) in the body of Fletcher's writings, though doubts have been cast on the propriety of the inclusion. In the first place, it is a speech which was never delivered. In the second place, it falls into its proper position as a sequel to Fletcher's *Discourse* on the balance of power, published three years previously. Political events in Europe had developed since that *Discourse* was written, and the speech is a reflection of these developments.

In the *Speech*, the people of Britain are warned against their apathy in face of the dangers which surround them. Formerly they were convinced that the French King was "a dangerous neighbour, powerful and vigilant; that there was no end to his designs; no relying on his treaties". Now, however, "you concur with the designs of France and the Court in everything". Yet France "has seized the whole Spanish monarchy, and if suffered to enjoy it quietly, he who previously was able to oppose may here-after trample on the rest of mankind".

The *Speech* then goes on to suggest plainly that a bargain had been struck between King William and King Louis. And yet no notice is taken of so portentous an event. The people of the country are so much engaged in their personal pursuits, their gaming, and their stock-jobbing, and their politicians in their party interests, that they have no time to watch the liberties of the nation. Having so much business at home, they can hardly attend to what is going on abroad. Yet from the first appearance of the Partition Treaty, it was clear to the most ordinary capacity that it would inevitably throw the whole Spanish Monarchy into the hands of the House of Bourbon. The letter of the treaty pretends that the dismemberment of the Spanish Monarchy was necessary for the peace of Europe. But the spirit of it "throws it entire into the family of Bourbon, entails an endless war upon Christendom, breaks the balance which has preserved its liberties for two hun-dred years, and will consequently banish all remains of freedom, both civil and religious, from among men." "This treaty," he goes on to say, "like an alarum bell (is) rung over Europe. Pray God it may not prove to you a passing bell." Poor, helpless Spain! rather than divide the child, she had chosen to give it entire to the harlot to whom it did not belong. And she has got it, for the Solomon "who commanded to divide the child did it not in order to do justice".

As those who are marked out for ruin are first bereft of under-standing, so the people of this country "see nothing but sham upon sham" played upon them, and seem to be altogether in-capable of seeing through the shams. Yet it is plain that those who have the direction of their affairs have "broken the balance of Europe and delivered a great part of the world into the hands of France". But it has not dawned upon the people that in all this there has been an ulterior end in view.

He has found the secret of the treaty which had seemed so

puzzling. His explanation of what would otherwise be inexplicable is, that William had acquiesced in the French hegemony of Spain, knowing that in the end it would ruin France, on the understanding that France would assist him "to establish himself here and in Holland". Perhaps indeed the agreement may be "to unite the whole seventeen Provinces to the Crown of England, and in lieu of these to give his Kingdom of Portugal to Spain". What a glorious government would the three Kingdoms and the seventeen Provinces be! Might they not, when united under "one able and absolute prince . . . bid defiance not only to France but to the World?" Might they not for ever establish in themselves "the Empire of the Sea with an entire monopoly of trade"? "Is there, after all, a better way of resisting the power of France? Is it not, indeed, the only way of saving us and our religion; which is our main concern?" These were the arguments that would be used in defence of this line of policy.

And that was the "secret" which Fletcher claimed to have discovered in the Treaty of Partition. He wanted to warn the country of the danger which threatened, of their liberties being filched from them, though, indeed, he feared that "jealousy for public liberty is vanished", and that "the English nation have not now anything remaining but the outward appearance and carcase, as I may call it, of their ancient Constitution. The spirit and soul is fled." Shortly expressed, his suggestion was that William's aim was to control the foreign policy of Great Britain and Holland, "not subject to the storms of a House of Commons, or the caprices of a free people little conversant in foreign affairs" (2).

In that diagnosis he was certainly correct, though the actual existence of the Machiavellian policy which he attributes to William is more open to doubt.

In less than a year afterwards King William was dead, and the ruler of Great Britain was Queen Anne.

Chapter X

A SHATTERED DREAM

THE laird of Saltoun had followed the Darien scheme with the utmost interest when preparations were being made, and with the gravest concern when the crisis in its affairs was approaching. Like the directors of the Company, he had never anticipated the calamitous collapse, at an early stage of its existence, of this great and national undertaking. On the contrary, he had visualized complete ultimate success, however much initial troubles might threaten to overwhelm the venture. He could not know that his fellow-countrymen in Darien had laid themselves open to the charge of having deserted their post at a time of difficulty and danger. Nor could he know that the description he had received of Darien: its illimitable potentialities, its salubrious climate and its comprehensive desirability, existed, as an accurate picture, in the minds of Wafer and other romancers, rather than in the world of stern reality. He was not a director of the Company of Scotland, and had no responsibility of any kind for the administration of its affairs. Probably he assumed, as he was bound to assume, that the business of the Company had been managed with ordinary prudence and skill. Yet his was the only public voice raised, in 1698, urging the necessity of providing "an incessant supply" for the settlers in New Caledonia, "who may have to suffer great hardships by delay". He had put his finger on the obviously weak spot in the arrangements for ensuring, not merely the comfort but the lives of the colonists. His own contribution to the success of the undertaking had been his subscription to its shareholding. But the larger aspects of the venture, its bearing upon international relationships, the political complexities which it created, the national suspicions which it was bound to arouse: these considerations were present to his mind in a way that could not be expected of the majority of his fellow-shareholders. Difficulties with Spain, difficulties, perhaps, with France, and certainly difficulties with England: all these had to be faced. An official protest from Spain was soon forthcoming. On

3rd May 1699, the Spanish Ambassador in London handed in a note which protested against the occupation of Darien as an insult to his Spanish Majesty, who proposed "to take such measures as he thinks convenient". In his view, the Darien settlement constituted "a rupture of the alliance between Spain and Great Britain" (1).

That was a document the truth of the allegations in which the English Council of Trade and Plantations was instructed to investigate. Apparently the Company of Scotland was called upon to defend its action, which it did by a memorial that came under review by the Council of Trade. In this memorial it was sought to place upon the Spaniards the onus of proving their title to Darien. The Council of Trade was charged with a difficult task, which it performed with due regard to the political questions involved, and the urgent necessity for extricating King William from an admittedly delicate situation.

Uneasy lies the head that wears a crown. And doubly uneasy if it wears two crowns. William the Third of England was faced by the problem of justifying himself to William the Second of Scotland.

The two horns of the dilemma stood out clearly and menacingly. For at the very time that the Spanish protest was officially lodged, William was in the midst of delicate negotiations for the second Treaty of Partition with France, rendered necessary by the recent death of the Prince of Bavaria. To quarrel with Spain at that particular juncture was singularly inopportune. But if, on the other hand, he were to repudiate the Scottish occupation of Darien, he would be stultifying his own Act of Parliament* and throwing over the interests of his "own ancient Crown and Kingdom". Yet, stay; was there not a way out of the dilemma?

If, in fact, the occupation infringed the Act of Parliament, he would no longer be bound to implement its provisions. That condition would be met, if it could be shown that the Spanish claim to the possession of the Isthmus was good in law and substance. So the English Council of Trade and Plantations set to work to justify William in placing the Scots in Darien outside the pale of his protection.

* The Act permitted the Company to operate in any part of Asia, Africa, or America.

"The whole weight of the argument", declared the Council, turned upon the question whether or not the Isthmus was a Spanish possession. If it was a Spanish possession, then "the descent made by the Scots" was "not only a manifest contravention of the patent, but also an open violation of the Treaty betwixt England and Spain. 1670: Art VII. & VIII". It was not sufficient for the Scots to allege that the natives had invited them. The Scottish memorial had challenged Spain to prove her claim. But such a proposal, said the Council, would be offensive to the Spaniards, who claimed the supreme sovereignty of the whole country. Spain, the Council concluded, has "an indisputable and uncontravened right" to Darien, "grounded upon near 200 years prescription" (2).

That was a sufficiently definite conclusion, which, on the face of it, seemed to charge the Scots with acting illegally and in opposition to the terms of their charter, which had for its foundation the Act touched by the King's sceptre.

It was not disputed that nearly 200 years previously the Isthmus had been occupied for a few years by Spaniards. Acla, where the Scots had landed, was founded by Gabriel de Rojas in 1514, and fortified in 1516 by Pedrarias Dávila, who abandoned it sixteen years later for Panama. It was Balboa's base of supplies from Cuba, when he planned to colonize on the Pacific side of the Isthmus, of which he had been put in charge. Also, it was the scene of his "judicial murder" by Dávila (3). And it was an undoubted fact that the Scots had planted themselves midway between Porto Bello and Cartagena, Spain's principal strongholds in that region. But all this left untouched the basic argument that the Scots occupied Darien by consent of, and in alliance with, the natives (quite a modern standpoint, by the way), the Cuna Indians, who had never recognized the sovereignty of Spain over the Isthmus. No doubt Darien was included in the Papal general grant to Spain, for by medieval law the Pope had the right to dispose of newly-found and unoccupied lands. These grants had, in the past, given rise to considerable rivalry and numerous disputes between the colonizing nations of Europe. The Portuguese, for example (with a population much about the same as that of Scotland in 1700), had been charged by Spain with "insolence" for the same reason as the Scots were now arraigned. But a Papal grant could receive no recognition at the hands of a Protestant country like Great Britain. Nor was it quite reasonable to expect the Scots to recognize a prescriptive right that had been in complete abeyance for nearly two centuries.

The Spanish claim was held by the English Council to be good, because they wanted it to be good. Had the circumstances been different, it would doubtless have been ignored by England as it was ignored about 1680. And it was futile to attempt to base the English opposition to the Scots on the sanctity of treaty obligations with Spain. Months before the Spanish protest had been lodged—to be precise on 2nd January 1699—the English Government had instructed the Colonial Governors to issue a proclamation forbidding them to give assistance of any kind (arms, ammunition, provisions, "or any other necessaries whatsoever") to the Darien colonists (4). Indeed, Captain Rupert Long had been sent by the English Government to Darien to spy the land, and, if necessary, to forestall the Scots in the occupation of the Isthmus. He arrived too late for that pleasant act of neighbourliness. But had he reached Darien before the Scots, he would presumably have claimed the country for England. What, then, becomes of the plea that the English opposition to the Scots was caused by a sense of fairness to Spain, or was the expression of a desire to conform with treaty engagements?

The truth was that trade jealousy was at the root of the opposition, and King William felt compelled to bow to the sentiment; all the more readily, no doubt, because the Darien affair was cutting athwart his foreign policy. And for him his foreign policy was of greater importance than trade disputes between England and Scotland. This trade jealousy shows itself in the despatches of the Colonial Governors. Governor Beeston of Jamaica—a colonial possession from which the Scottish colonists had a right to expect sympathy—told the Council of Trade on 5th December 1698, that the Scots fleet had arrived at Darien. "If they settle there", he adds, "and are healthy, the noise of gold will carry away all our debtors, servants, and ordinary people, in the hope of mending their fortunes, and will much weaken whatever strength we have." And Governor Basse of the Jerseys (East and West

New Jersey) told the Council that the trade of the Jerseys and Pennsylvania "seems to be much in the hands of that people (the Scots), several of them being our principal dealers, and their number yearly increasing whilst the interest of our nation seems so much declining. Certain I am their prosperity in the Plantation cannot but extremely prejudice the general interest of our own nation, impair His Majesty's Revenue, and in time give no mean fears of their subjection to their so-much-applauded Caledonia, which I cannot but say seems by nature and situation to pretend in time to be the emporium of trade and riches in America if it meet with encouragement and be suffered to grow, (so) that (it) may in time collect to it riches of the Eastern and Western Indians: the one safely transported through the famous South Seas, over the Isthmus of Darien, and the other from the two adjoining empires of Peru and Mexico" (5).

So here we have a contemporary English Governor, a man of wide colonial experience and close knowledge of local conditions, confirming the practicability of Paterson's proposals: the proposals which most modern historians, in their superior wisdom, have condemned as being hopelessly unsound. Also, both Governors show clearly their fear of Scottish traders. These, it is obvious, were displaying a disconcerting aptitude which, under the blighting influences that in Scotland clogged enterprise, was not too conspicuous at home. It is a chastening thought that the Scots in Darien were eager for English co-operation on equal terms with themselves, and were denied that partnership with contempt. And the dictates of humanity were not allowed by the colonial authorities, acting on instructions from home, to interfere with the complete boycott of their fellow-subjects in Darien, even when the plight of the unfortunate Scots there had become pitiful in the extreme.

The "much applauded Caledonia" was, in fact, not allowed to "meet with encouragement" nor was it "suffered to grow". On the contrary, nothing was omitted that was calculated to bring about its complete and disastrous collapse. The climate does not seem to have been a primary cause of the failure. The Spaniards had left Darien for Panama, alleging "the unhealthiness of the air". Yet we find one of the Darien colonists writing to a friend in Boston that "the country is healthful to a wonder, insomuch that our sick that were many when we arrived are now generally cured" (6). Of the three hundred members of the first expedition who died in Darien, and the four hundred famishing wretches who were buried at sea during the dreadful voyage between Darien and Jamaica and New York, it is probable that the greater number succumbed to privations rather than to the effects of the climate, though seasonal sicknesses could scarcely have been avoided. The death-roll was the indirect result, mainly, of the callous boycott of the colony by the English Government.

Nor did the English attitude towards the Scottish settlers relieve the English themselves from the suspicious jealousy of the Spaniards, and especially of the French. The treasures of Peru were carried over the South Sea to Panama, and thence overland, by the Province of Darien, to Porto Bello; and the Spaniards were bound to view with hostility any settlement that threatened the safety of this transport, inasmuch as it would "touch them in the most sensible and vital part". They would not permit the English even to cut logwood in Yucatan, and they had broken up an English settlement at Port Royal, killing some of the settlers and carrying others to Mexico, "where they kept them working in chanes upon the fortifications". And the French, who, for their own reasons, had officiously offered their assistance to the Spaniards to drive the Scots out of Darien, were now trying to persuade the Spaniards that the English boycott of the Darien settlement was all "a blind", and that "the English and the Scotch are all one people". Thus the English and the Scots were involved in one common odium. But the Spaniards feared the French, "bringing gifts". They knew that they were a greater source of danger to themselves than either the English or the Scots. But they could not help being influenced by the French, who regarded themselves as the prospective heirs of the Spanish Empire, and acted accordingly. To the English, so reported Governor Beeston of Jamaica, the French refused "all civility", or even "common respect"; and they called them "ill names", because of the Darien settlement, which they would not believe was "without the King's consent, or connivance at least, though I have written to all the Governors to assure them to the contrary."

This attitude of the French towards the English may be compared with the English attitude towards the Darien colonists. "None", so the English order ran, were to "go near the Scotch, nor trade with them, nor assist them with provisions, nor anything else." The English were boycotting the Scots because they were rivals; and the French were boycotting the English because they were hypocrites (7).

Thus, while the English Government pleased the English traders by opposing the Scottish settlement, King William was not so successful in pleasing the Spaniards, and still less successful in pleasing the French. The King's policy did not prevent the War of the Spanish Succession, nor did that war achieve its ostensible purpose of preserving Europe against an increase of Bourbon ascendancy.

Perhaps it was not altogether by a coincidence that Fletcher wrote his treatise upon economic conditions in Scotland and upon the European balance of power, about the time that the first Darien expedition sailed from Leith, in July 1698. Superficially these subjects and Darien were not correlated. But a closer examination suggests that Fletcher's intention may have been to survey the whole field of economics and politics as a justification for his countrymen's new enterprise. The implications which his views on these subjects carry would seem to warrant the conclusion that he was seeking to prepare the ground for the reappearance of Scotland as a factor to be reckoned with in European affairs, as she had been before the Union of the Crowns.

The story of the Darien venture has been told so frequently that there is no need, except by a brief recapitulation, to repeat it. What strikes a business man more particularly is the ineptitude displayed by the directors of the Company. Instead of sending out competent and trustworthy agents to examine minutely, and report carefully upon, the whole of the conditions in the Isthmus before plunging the country into the venture by appeals to patriotism and individual cupidity, they seem to have relied upon the "yarns" of men like Wafer and Dampier, and upon the enthusiasm of Paterson, for their confidence in a successful plantation. They honestly believed that they were offering an Eldorado to their fellow-countrymen. But it does not seem to have occurred to them as matter for surprise that this Eldorado had remained so long unappreciated, or at any rate, unappropriated by other nations with greater resources and more powerful means of protecting their interests than Scotland could command. Yet, after all, the same argument might have been used against the chances of some colonial enterprises, which, since the days of Darien, have more than fulfilled the glowing hopes of their promoters.

When the venture had been finally launched, insufficient care (if, indeed, any) was taken in the choice of the colonists. The shareholding of the Company was widely spread among Scots people of the upper and middle classes, and the shareholders seem to have freely exercised whatever privileges they may have possessed of nominating settlers. The result was that the twelve hundred men (the applicants far exceeded that number) who sailed from Leith in the three patriotically named ships, were a heterogeneous crowd. Clearly, many of them were "misfits". The appeal of the speculation was primarily to the adventurous, of which class Scotland was peculiarly prolific. But other qualifications were needed. Inevitably, in view of the slackness of the directors in sifting the applicants for adventure, a large proportion of the twelve hundred who sailed from Leith had not the stuff of pioneers in them, particularly the qualities of patience and endurance. The promises held out by the adventure were alluring to the man who had wasted his substance in riotous living, and the gambler who was eager to stake his all on a chance. When such people discovered that they were not going to pick up an easy fortune without working for it; when they found that their toil would be arduous and unremitting, and their reward distant and uncertain; when, instead of the bracing air of their native land, they had to suffer the discomforts of a tropical and not conspicuously healthy climate; when their food ran short and the English colonists refused to feed them at any price; when the Spaniards openly showed their hostility; when, in fact, the testing time for pioneers came, they proved themselves lamentably unequal to the task of facing their troubles like men.

Included in the first twelve hundred emigrants were three hundred "gentlemen", so we are told. What the expedition sadly needed was not three hundred "gentlemen", but one man—a real

H   [*113*]

man capable of enforcing discipline and imposing his will upon the insubordinate elements of which the settlers were largely composed. Such a man might have saved the situation. Paterson might have proved to be that man, had he not fallen out of favour with the directors. He travelled with the expedition as a volunteer, and although he was subsequently co-opted on the Council of Seven appointed by the Company to manage its affairs, he never possessed the requisite authority for repressing the discords that ensued between his colleagues. When he recommended an overhauling of the stores, which turned out to be partly rotten in quality, and wholly inadequate in quantity, he was told, in effect, to mind his own business. If he had minded his own business, and not that of his country, he would, one thinks, have given his fellow-councillors a wide berth.

Small details serve as indices to the mentality of the directors in their administration of the Company's affairs. Fifteen hundred Bibles, printed in English, were of little use to the Gaelic-speaking Highlanders who formed a substantial proportion of the emigrants, and of still less use to the natives of Darien, for whom they were primarily intended. The toys which accompanied the Bibles might, indeed, amuse the simple Indians (as they did, in fact), for they were useful for "trading", just as the Jews' harps, which, over a generation ago, formed part of the regular "trade" of the Queensland schooners engaged in recruiting labour for the sugar plantations from the South Sea Islands, amused the Kanakas.

Toys for the Cuna Indians, yes. But four hundred periwigs! And not a man of the twelve hundred emigrants who could speak Spanish!

Also, if the colony was to have a fair chance of establishing itself as a permanent settlement, it was clearly the duty of the Company's directors to keep it well supplied with necessary stores (as Fletcher publicly urged), until it should become self-supporting. But, until too late, this the directors failed to do, either directly or by means of credits to their agents in the English colonies of America, though, to be sure (according to Herries), the Company's credit was "not worth twopence". Embargo or no embargo, means could certainly have been found for sending stores to Darien from the English colonies if the credits, which could have been negotiated, had been there in time. After the first patriotic scramble for shares in the Company, Scotland, as the directors discovered, was drained dry of ready money. But that was surely no secret in July 1698, when the first expedition sailed. Quite certainly there had been a lack of prevision on the part of the directors.

When they despatched a relief expedition of two vessels, carrying three hundred men, the directors appear to have thought that they had done everything necessary to ensure adequate supplies for the settlers. That might have been the fact if their Councillors, who had sworn allegiance to the Company, had been men of sufficient vision, and if the rank and file had been men of sufficient grit to hold on. But, as events showed, they were not the stuff of which heroes are made, and the directors seem to have expected them to behave like heroes. When the relief party arrived at Darien, they found awaiting them, not the flourishing colony that they had expected, but a deserted settlement and a number of buildings in ruins. These were the memorials of the Darien venture, the only tangible relics left of the first colony to show that their fellow-countrymen had planned a settlement in the Caribbean Sea, and had hurriedly scrapped their plans. They were now looking upon a body from which the soul had fled. What a chilling prospect for optimistic colonists! And what a bitter reflection, that they had only just missed saving the settlement!

Even then it was not too late to make a fresh start, for the main party of the second expedition sailed from the Clyde in September 1699. But the relief party that preceded this body were dogged by misfortune, while the main expedition proved to be "misfits" like their predecessors.

The first group of colonists were in Darien less than eight months: their successors less than five months. And that was the total duration of this remarkable settlement, of which the names "Caledonia Bay" and "Point Escosces" are the sole memorials of a historic tragedy.

The Councillors of the first batch of emigrants seemed to be more concerned with enunciating high-sounding principles than

with taking practical steps to put the colony on a sound footing
with the least possible delay. On arrival at Darien, the Council
issued a proclamation full of goodwill towards all men, including
even Spaniards and Englishmen. The Councillors actually drew
up a Constitution, by which Parliamentary government, on a
popular basis, was established. And the Parliament met. In one
session it enacted thirty-four laws, embodying principles so
exalted in their idealism and uncompromising in their Puritanism
as to compel comparison with the legislation favoured by the
Cromwellian Commonwealth. But as one of the Councillors was
mournfully obliged to confess, the people for whose benefit these
laws were primarily intended, were not worthy of them. They had
not, he said, "the true notion of liberty". The colonists were indeed happy in having good laws, even if prematurely enacted. But
what is the use of good laws if they cannot be enforced?

The seafaring men on the Council were quite happy so long as
they could get "their pipe and their glass"; and the landsmen on
the Council showed small capacity for anything except quarrelling
among themselves and planning impossible Utopias.

The second group of colonists, during their short stay, were, if
anything, less united than the first. Indeed the chief concern of
some members of the Council—and the more vocal section—was
to get away from Darien as quickly as possible. As for the rank
and file, the following report by the chief of their ministers (a
"hind let loose" among hungry dogs) attests their quality sufficiently cogently to warrant the conclusion that many of them were
of a different breed from the Covenanting stock in Scotland,
which, whatever its faults, was never lacking either in ethical
correctness or in physical pluck. "Our meetings amongst ourselves", wrote the Rev. Alexander Shields, "are in the woods,
where the chattering of parrots, mourning of pelicans, and din
of monkeys, is more pleasant than the hellish language of our
countrymen in their hutts and tents of Kedar, and our conversation with the Indians, though with dumb signs, is more satisfying
than with the most part of our own people. Several of them came
to our meetings for worship, and we have exercised in their
families when travelling among them, where they have behaved
themselves very reverently, but we have neither language nor

interpreter." (The same minister later on had to communicate with the Spaniards in Latin.) "But our people doe scandalize them both by stealing from them and teaching them to swear and drink" (8).

The picture is not enticing: and it prepares one for the speedy evacuation of the settlement before it had a chance of proving its possibilities. When the Spaniards, after the hesitation caused by a fear of strong resistance, at length attacked by land, they were driven back by a force of two hundred resolute men (the colonists were not all made of poor stuff), led by Captain Alexander Campbell of Finab, a capable soldier of experience. But the Spaniards soon afterwards blockaded the port with a fleet which had been despatched from Spain to operate against the colony (the Spanish Government subsequently tried to recover the costs from the Scottish Company), and the blockade forced the capitulation, on honourable terms, of the garrison in Fort St. Andrew, as the Darien fort was named. And that was the end of the Darien adventure.

The names New Caledonia, New Edinburgh, Fort St. Andrew —all symbols of a great national failure—have been mercifully expunged from the topography of the Caribbean Sea, for they serve as reminders of a venture in which few of the Scots engaged showed the national characteristics, as Empire-builders, of dogged persistence and patient endurance, which, in later years, their countrymen in every quarter of the world have proved themselves, in no common degree, to possess. Of all the factors that contributed to the failure, Spanish hostility, English jealousy, and Scottish mismanagement, perhaps the last was the most potent, for the others, though deadly, were not necessarily mortal.

But, of course, the storm burst upon the head of "the auld enemy" alone. The national fury in Scotland against her kind neighbour was such, that little was needed to set alight the firesticks that were ready to blaze into a war which would have been disastrous to both nations. It is idle to speculate what Fletcher would have done had he been a member of the Convention, and the dominating figure in the Parliament which he was a few years later. Would the fiery little man have thrown down the gauntlet of defiance and urged his hearers to challenge the might of England? Or would he have kept a cool head, and played the part of the statesman that he always played except when the ardour of his patriotism exceeded the soundness of his judgment? Anyhow, he was not a member of the Convention in the opening year of the eighteenth century, when the word "Darien" was on the indignant lips of every Scot; and the Convention in Edinburgh, seething with wrath though it was, sent up no cries for vengeance that were meant to be translated into concrete action.

King William had made his second big blunder in dealing with his Scottish people. But he stubbornly refused to retrace his steps. His interest had to be jogged by his Minister, the Earl of Seafield, even in securing the pardon of an unfortunate ship's company from Darien, who had been seized by the Spaniards. They were on their way to the Barbadoes for provisions when their ship sprang a leak, and they had to take refuge in Cartagena. The Governor sent them to Seville, where they were sentenced to death as pirates, a monstrous sentence against which William could not but protest. But he refused point-blank to sanction an Act of Parliament asserting the rights of the colonists in Darien. The Scottish Government urged his consent, hoping thereby to divide the Opposition in Parliament, who were raging furiously against the English for their handling of the Darien business. William's unpopularity in Scotland was only removed by his death, when his virtues as a British Deliverer were remembered as an offset against his shortcomings as a Scottish King.

And England, too—no, not England, but the English Government, backed by the greed of the merchants of London and Bristol—had shown none of her accustomed sense of justice and fair play, national characteristics by which she was distinguished, then as now. Far from being generous, she had been vindictive.

But "jobbing backwards" is always an unprofitable occupation. It is no less true of nations than of individuals: the people who never made a mistake never made anything. Scotland had to buy her experience very dearly. She bought it, and she paid for it. But England's mistake would almost certainly have precipitated a war between the two countries if only the Stewart exile in France had just then again turned his ecclesiastical coat and become a Protestant!

The word "Darien" was branded on the national consciousness

of Scotland, just as the word "Calais" was traditionally imprinted on the heart of "Bloody Mary". Had there been no Darien, there might have been no Union. And had there been no Union, many things in the relations between England and Scotland would bear a different aspect today.

From first to last, the Darien adventure cost Scotland nearly two thousand lives and some £200,000 (an incredibly large sum for that country in 1700) in dissipated capital. The loss in terms of money might be made good to the shareholders (in fact, it was made good by the terms of the Union); and the wrecked and derelict ships could be replaced. But the loss of life, much of it avoidable, was irreparable; the blow to the national prestige was unforgettable; and the shock to the national confidence had so paralysing an effect that when Paterson in 1701 (he was one of the few survivors who found their way back to Scotland) attempted to organize a fresh expedition to Darien, he could get no one to listen to him. Of the fact that he was a man of vision, the Bank of England and the Panama Canal, which he thought quite feasible, are concrete proofs. But the run of the cards was against him (9).

Thus, by a succession of crushing blows, was shattered a national dream of easily acquired wealth. It was a pleasant dream while it lasted. It envisaged a nation once economically comfortable and now sunk in a mire of poverty and distress, being rescued from the morass and rendered commercially prosperous by means of a bold national scheme that was to make the silent ports of Scotland alive with shipping designed to link the Clyde with the Caribbean Sea; to cure her unemployment; and, in fine, to make everybody happy. A different tale, alas, had to be told. Had the colony been a success—and it might well have been a success—we should today be glorifying the shrewdness of the foresight and the brilliance of the strategy which added Darien to the British Crown in the first year of the eighteenth century, and diverted the trade of the world to the British Isles. But as it was a failure—and its failure was complete—historians, English and Scottish alike, have contemptuously dismissed the brave enterprise as "fantastic", "chimerical", and what not. It is indeed a true, if trite saying, that nothing succeeds like success. Also, nothing fails like failure.

After 1700 the Scottish people had ample leisure to attempt to work out the economic salvation of their country afresh, for it was not until well-nigh fifty years afterwards that they found their commercial feet at last. And they found their feet, partly by legislative union with the country that had blocked their path at Darien, and partly (perhaps mainly, as already suggested) owing to the superiority of the system of national education introduced into Scotland by the Act of Parliament passed in 1696.

A few survivors of the unhappy Caribbean expedition prospered in Jamaica and other English colonies, and some of their descendants may be there to this day. In Darien itself the office of the Company of Scotland was turned into a "home for paupers", while the Company's warehouse became "an asylum for lunatics" (10).

Chapter XI

ON STANDING ARMIES AND MILITIAS

ANYONE who has studied the relations of William of Orange with the English Parliament in the later part of his reign, cannot fail to have observed the feeling aroused on both sides by the question of standing armies. It was the rock of offence on which the King and his Commons split. When William's Dutch soldiers were sent back from their English quarters, it seemed highly probable at one time that the King would follow them to the Holland he loved so well, and would not return to the England that was never his spiritual home. But the difficulty passed and William remained. He had to bow to the will of his people's representatives, but his view that their attitude towards standing armies was profoundly mistaken underwent no change.

In the England of King William's day there was a growing feeling against the employment of mercenaries. Order at home and protection from invasion, it was thought, could be secured by means of well-trained militias and a strong navy. And as for foreign adventures, the less England had to do with them the better.

In a remarkable work, published in 1698,* on the relative merits of standing armies and militias, instigated doubtless by the widely spread interest on the subject, Andrew Fletcher discusses the matter exhaustively in all its bearings. And, as usual, he is not content simply to theorize. He has a cut-and-dried original plan of his own which he offers for the consideration of the English as well as the Scottish nation.

He commences with a characteristic reflection on the fact that while great pains were taken by mankind to instruct themselves in the arts and sciences, very few applied themselves to consider the nature of government, "an enquiry so useful and necessary both to magistrates and people". If men would only bestow a small part of the time and application which they throw away on "curious but useless studies" or "endless gaming", upon the

* The title is *A discourse of government with relation to militias.*

"excellent rules and examples of government" handed down by the ancients, they would be enabled to discover all the more readily such "abuses and corruptions as tend to the ruin of public societies". "It is very strange", he says, that "the noblest and most useful of all applications, the art of government, should be so much neglected". As one of the results, "the generality of all ranks are cheated by words and names."

Next, he reviews the course of history which led up to the alteration in government that happened in most European countries about 1500. Under the feudal system a standing army was unnecessary, for when the defence of a country needed the raising of an army, the king summoned the barons to his standard, and they obeyed the call with their vassals. Thus the sword was placed in the hands of the subject, and the liberties of the people were preserved. But when princes got possession of the sword, by maintaining mercenary forces in times of peace, the government changed from monarchies to tyrannies. For not only is that government tyrannical which is tyrannically exercised, but all governments are tyrannical which have not in their Constitution an adequate security against the arbitrary power of the prince. He does not deny that the limited monarchies which existed when the barons were so powerful had their defects. "I know few governments free from them." But a balance was maintained which made for steadiness, and there was an effectual provision against the encroachments of the Crown. But a return to those conditions was now impossible.

The principles of government were affected by the Renaissance, by the invention of printing, by the general pursuit of pleasure, and, more than anything else, by the discovery of "the needle". The improvement in navigation opened a passage by sea to the East Indies and spread the luxuries of Asia and America before the eyes of Europe. A total change of living had resulted from the discovery. That age of luxury coincided, it is true, with a great increase in knowledge, and men imagined themselves to be gainers in every way. But they forgot the evils which are inseparable from an expensive way of living. These expenses fell mainly on the barons, many of whom got into debt and had to sell or alienate their lands, or otherwise find money in exchange for military service. Their vassals, no longer holding their lands on the old easy terms, were not obliged to perform complementary military service, and became tenants only. Thus armies which in former times were always composed of men such as these, ceased to exist, "and the sword fell out of the hands of the barons". But the country had to be defended all the same, so princes were allowed to raise armies of volunteers and mercenaries. And the people who had grown rich by trade, and were incapable of defending themselves, had to maintain these armies by taxes. When the occasion for raising such armies passed away, they were disbanded. But princes soon found excuses for making these armies perpetual. The methods of warfare had changed, mainly owing to the invention of gunpowder, and frontier towns and fortresses had to be garrisoned by mercenaries, who, depending on the prince, "as the former militias did upon the barons", looked to him alone as their master. Thus the power of the sword was transferred from the subject to the king, and "war grew a constant trade to live by". Indeed, many barons, reduced to poverty themselves, took command of these mercenaries, and continuing to be hereditary members of "diets and other assemblies of State", after the loss of their vassals, whom formerly they had represented, were now the readiest of all to load the people with heavy taxes. Such taxes were employed to increase the princes' military power by means of guards, armies, and citadels beyond bounds or remedy.

And "wise" princes (really "cunning and able" princes) were more dangerous than those less able, in relation to standing armies, inasmuch as they were more capable of using them for the attainment of arbitrary power. Louis XI was a case in point.

Subsidies were often given by Parliaments, Diets, etc., and sums were raised by edicts of princes for maintaining wars. But these were small, and in no way sufficient for the upkeep of such numerous armies as those of the barons' militias. Likewise, mercenary troops were sometimes entertained by the princes who aimed at arbitrary power, also by some Commonwealths in times of war for their own defence. But these troops were only strangers, and their numbers were small. They bore no resemblance to "those vast armies of mercenaries which the change has fixed upon Europe to her ruin".

All this applies to Europe generally. Now to consider the situation in Great Britain. In that country the employment of mercenary troops had not yet become an established practice, the reason being that England had lost her French conquests before the change, Calais alone excepted; and Calais was taken before the change had become complete. So the Kings of England had no excuse to keep standing forces in garrisons or in frontiers towards France. Nor could the frontiers towards Scotland lend colour to the excuse for raising mercenary forces, since the Kings of Scotland had none, and Scotland could not afford the luxury. True, the example of France had induced Mary of Guise to propose a tax for mercenary soldiers for the defence of the frontiers of Scotland. But three hundred of the lesser barons protested against the employment of mercenaries, arguing that if the country needed defence, as in the past, so in the future, it would be provided by the Scots themselves. Mary, Queen of Scots, too, found an excuse for the employment of guards, but they were soon disbanded.

How, then, did standing armies first find a foothold in England? The practice had crept into being in an insidious fashion. "Charles I. attempted to seize the purse before he was master of the sword". But "very wise men have been of opinion that if he had been possessed of as numerous guards as those which were afterwards raised, he might easily have succeeded in his enterprise." In the reign of Charles II the Country Party were prevented by these guards from bringing about the revolution afterwards compassed by a foreign Power. James II had provoked his people, and made his own game as hard as possible, not only by invading the civil liberties of his people, but likewise by endeavouring to change the established religion for another which the people abhorred. Yet, after all, Britain "stood in need of a foreign force to save it, and how dangerous a remedy that is, the histories of all ages can witness".

What, in fact, is the situation at the time of writing? After a long and expensive war, the country is much impoverished, and England, by means of her former riches and present poverty, "has fallen into all the corruptions which these great enemies of virtue, want and excess of riches, can produce". There are large numbers of mercenaries at home and abroad, whose officers have no other means of subsistence. They are commanded by a wise and active king, who has at his disposal "the formidable land and sea forces of a neighbouring nation, the great rival of our trade": a king, who, by various ties, has for his friends and allies Austria, most of the German princes, and potentates of the North; who, indeed, whatever interest he may join with, can do what he thinks fit in Europe. What security, therefore, can there be for British liberties if a mercenary standing army is to be kept up, the first of that kind (except those of "the usurper Cromwell" and King James) that Britain had seen for thirteen hundred years? It is to be hoped that those who are under the mistaken impression that in advocating standing armies and advancing the prerogative, they are reverting to ancient usage, "will see what sort of patriots they are". To the argument that only perpetual standing armies of mercenaries can defend the country from France, the reply is, that there is no security that these standing armies will not, at one time or another, be used in the suppression of the liberties of the people, "though not in this king's time, to whom we owe their preservation". It is an evasion for people to argue that they are not in favour of standing armies, but only for an army raised from year to year, or until the militia can be usefully employed. There is nothing to be feared from France, at any rate until she has had a breathing space and recovers from her exhaustion. Before then, the militia will be "in order". And meantime there is the fleet. "The French King is old and diseased and was never willing to hazard much by any bold attempt." If he, or, after his decease, the Dauphin, may be suspected of any further designs, these must be on the Spanish Monarchy on the death of the King of Spain. What if he attacks? Well, our strength at sea will account for him.

See what happened to Carthage when mercenary forces were employed by her! The Romans, on the other hand, pursued the wise course of changing their men after a period of service. The men went from the armies straight into civilian life. If we had followed the example of Rome in the last war, we could now have thrice as many trained men as at present.

Mercenary standing forces in times of peace, if not employed to do mischief, soon become like those of Holland "in '72", "fit only to lose forty strong places in forty days". There are hardly any sort of men who are less men of honour than the officers of mercenaries, "and indeed honour has now no other signification among them than courage". But he would be willing to recommend to "the bounty of both Parliaments" all officers and men (over forty) of a standing army before disbandment, for, after all, they had faithfully served their employers.

He cannot see why mercenaries were employed in the British Isles. England and Scotland are nations that were formerly very jealous of liberty. It was to be hoped that they would now preserve the rights and privileges they had gained by the Revolution. "I shall not say how readily the regiments that were in the service of Holland came over against the Duke of Monmouth; he was a rebel and did not succeed." But they all knew how quickly Irish mercenaries were brought to Britain to oppose the Prince of Orange, "in that glorious enterprise for our deliverance". Formerly the subjects had a real security for their liberty "by having the sword in their own hands". That security, which is the greatest of all securities, is now lost, and not only so, but the sword is put into the hand of the king by his power over the militia. Also, we have standing armies of mercenaries "who, for the most part, have no other way to subsist, and consequently are capable to execute any commands".

The only security, indeed, that remains, is that it has been contrary to English law for standing armies to be allowed in times of peace. It was one of the Scottish grievances that standing armies had been kept up in Scotland, and, in the forfeiture of King James, one of the articles described them as a grievance. If the monarchy having control over a standing army is a limited monarchy, then, as there are conditions, so there ought to be securities, on both sides. To give a monarch standing armies gives him uncontrolled power, and consequently makes him absolute. And, "whoever is for making the king's power too great or too little, is an enemy to the monarchy". If the people had any real security with standing armies in times of peace, there might be some ground for demanding them. But if their only remaining security be taken away from the people, "we have destroyed these monarchies".

No pretence of danger from abroad can be regarded as a sound argument for keeping up standing armies or mercenary forces. If that plea were accepted, we should be "saving our lives by the loss of our liberties". It may be taken as a certainty that standing armies and absolute power have become complementary.

But what of militias? Here Fletcher, as usual, traces the subject from its beginnings. He shows how, after the barons had lost the military service of their vassals, militias of some sort were established in most parts of Europe. But the prince had the power of naming and promoting the officers, so the former balance was not maintained. The essential feature of the militias he has in view, is that the officers should be named and promoted, "and as well they and the soldiers paid, by the people that set them out". So if princes look upon the present militias as incapable of defending a nation against foreign armies, the people have still reason to entrust them with the defence of their liberties. Princes had tried to discredit militias, preferring standing armies "that had no other interest in the Commonwealth than their pay". They had succeeded only too well in this design, for the greater part of the world had been fooled into the belief that a militia cannot be made really serviceable.

He knows the prejudice and ignorance of the world concerning the art of war, "as it was practised by the ancients, though what remains of that knowledge in their writings be sufficient to give a mean opinion of the modern discipline". And then he sets out to elaborate a thesis that was completely opposed to all prevailing notions in his time, namely, that militia officers might well be preferable to those bred in foreign wars. Take, he says, the great Montrose for example. His actions may be compared, "all circumstances considered, with those of Caesar, as well for the military skill as the bad tendency of them." Montrose had "never served abroad nor seen any action before the six victories which, with numbers much inferior to those of his enemies, he obtained in one year", and the most considerable of them were chiefly gained by the assistance of "the tenants and vassals of the family of Gordon".

Again, look at the battle of Naseby, which was usually regarded as the decisive battle of the Civil War. The number of forces engaged on both sides was about equal; (2) there was no advantage of ground; nor was there any "extraordinary accident" during the fight to give any considerable advantage to either side. In the Parliamentary army only nine of the officers had served abroad, and most of the soldiers were apprentices drawn out of London only two months previously. In the King's army, on the other hand, there were over a thousand officers who had served in foreign parts (3). Yet the King's army was "routed and broken" by the newly-raised levies, who were obedient in command and brave in combat all through the campaign.

"The people of these nations are not a dastardly crew like those born in misery, under oppression and slavery, who must have time to rub off that fear, cowardice, and stupidity which they bring from home." Though officers seem to stand more in need of experience than private soldiers, yet it was seen in the Civil War that the "sobriety and principle" of the officers on the side of the Parliament prevailed over the "experience" of the officers on the King's side.

It was well known that certain regiments of the British army lately in Flanders had never been in action; not one half of them more than thrice; and none of them more than five times during the whole war. Yes, was the obvious reply, but they have been under discipline during the whole time, and become accustomed to obedience. But is there any reason why militiamen should not be similarly trained? They had had to deal with an enemy on the Continent who has plenty of excellent officers, "yet never dares to fight without a visible advantage". Is such an enemy likely to invade Great Britain? For "he must win or starve in ten days".

A good militia is of such importance to a nation that it should form the chief part of the Constitution of any free government. A good militia will always preserve the public liberty. "The militia of ancient Rome, the best that ever was in any government, made her Mistress of the World. But standing armies enslaved that great people, and their excellent militia and freedom perished together. The Lacedemonians continued eight hundred years free and in great honour, because they had a good militia.

The Swisses at this day are the freest, happiest, and the people of all Europe who can best defend themselves because they have the best militia."

The whole free people of any nation ought to be exercised in arms. Their own ancestors, as seen by their Acts of Parliament, and the wisest governments among the ancients, had shown them a good example in that respect. In countries where husbandry, trade, manufactures, and other mechanical arts are carried on even in times of war, "the impediments of war are so many and so various that unless the whole people be exercised, no considerable number of men can be drawn out without disturbing those employments which are the vitals of the political body". Besides, in times of extreme calamities, "every nation stands in need of all the people, as the ancients sometimes did of their slaves". Why, indeed, should arms be denied to any man who is not a slave, "since they are the only true badges of liberty"? They ought never, except in times of emergency, be put into the hands of mercenaries or slaves. And if a man be put in possession of arms, he should be taught the use of them.

By the constitution of the existing militias in England and Scotland, only a small number of able-bodied men are exercised, and "men of quality and estate" are allowed to send "any wretched servant" in their place. They themselves had become disused to handling arms, and they will not learn because they are ashamed of their ignorance. So the militias are composed only of servants, and this makes the nation unfit to defend itself and standing forces necessary. Can it be supposed that servants will fight for the defence of their masters' estates if the masters only look on? Or that the smaller freeholders, who mainly officer the militias, should expose their lives for the bigger men without receiving any assistance from them? No bodies of military men can be of any force or value "unless many officers of quality or education be among them". And such men should blush to think of excusing themselves from serving their country, at least for some years, in a military capacity, if they consider that every Roman was obliged to spend fifteen years of his life in their armies. Shame on these modern slackers! Some trouble and some expense were needful to put a country in a posture of defence. Better, much better, to incur both than risk the possible consequences of slackness.

But where are the men to be found who are capable of training recruits in so many different places of the country simultaneously? The nobility and gentry are useless. Mercenaries, it is true, can be found for the purpose. But that would be a dangerous expedient, and in any case their employment would be fatal to the scheme he has in view, the main principle of which would be to breed "men of quality to command, and the others to obey".

Fletcher now propounds his plan, which, as he rightly claimed for it, was something quite novel.

He would have four camps, one in Scotland and three in England, into which all the young men of the respective countries shall enter "on the first day of his two & twentieth year of their age", and remain in camp for two years if they can support themselves; if not, for one year only at the public expense (4). They should be taught the use of all sorts of arms, with the necessary evolutions: also "wrestling, leaping, swimming, and the like exercises". He who could afford to keep a horse should be obliged to do so, and to learn how to ride.

The camp should not be more than eight days in any one place, but should remove "from heath to heath", not merely because health and cleanliness demanded it, but in order to teach the youth how to fortify a camp and how to march; also, in order to accustom them "to carry as much in their march as ever Roman soldiers did" (the weaklings, of course, excepted), such as tents, provisions, arms, armour, utensils, and the "palisadoes" of their camp. They should be taught to forage, and compelled to deal justly with the countrymen in their bargains. The food should be the same for all. For bread they should use wheat only, to be ground by their own handmills. Salt was to be allowed, and beeves at certain times of the year. For drink, water only. But it might be "sometimes tempered with a proportion of brandy, and at other times with —vinegar". The clothing of the men should be plain, coarse, and suitable for camp life.

For all these things those who could afford to pay should be compelled to pay. The others would be maintained at the public cost.

The camp should be divided sometimes into two parts, situated many miles from each other, in order to give the officers the opportunity of learning strategy and tactics, and the men practice in endurance in marching and general efficiency. Persons of quality or estate should be instructed in fortification work, gunnery, and all things "belonging to the duty of an engineer". Forts should sometimes be built by the whole camp, "where all the arts of attacking and defending places should be practised".

The youths, having been taught to read at schools, "should be obliged to read at spare hours some excellent histories, but chiefly those in which military actions are best described, with the books that have been best written concerning the military art". Speeches exhorting to military and virtuous actions should be often composed and pronounced publicly by such of the youths as were by education and natural talents qualified for the task. There being none but military men allowed within the camp, and "no churchmen being of that number", the youths who were "fit to exhort the rest to all Christian and moral duties, chiefly to humility, modesty, chastity, and the pardoning of private injuries" (was Fletcher thinking of Dare, the Taunton goldsmith?), "should be chosen to do it every Sunday, and the rest of that day spent on reading books and in conversation directed to the same end".

The severest discipline was to be exercised, attended by rewards and punishments rigorously bestowed by the officers. The rewards to be honorary and to be suited to the quality of the youths on whom they were bestowed. Punishments to be "much more rigorous than those inflicted for the same crimes by the law of the land". There should be punishments for some things not liable to any by the common law, such as, "immodest and insolent words or actions, gaming and the like". No woman to be suffered to come within the camp, and self-abuse to be punished by death.

All these things would be judged by the Councils of War attached to the camps, by means of Articles drawn up by them and approved by their Parliaments.

The instructors should be experts who would be encouraged to come from all parts of Europe, due care being taken that they should not infect the youths with "foreign manners". Afterwards they should be chosen from men of quality or fortune, who had spent two years in camp and since then had "improved themselves in the wars". It would be no hard matter for men who had passed through the camp discipline to retain it after returning home. An excellent general training could be attained, if, under the expert instruction of such men, the townsmen and villagers, "with those of the adjacent habitations", were obliged to meet fifty times a year "on convenient days", and exercise four hours every time. A camp might be formed yearly in the summer time if "some thousands of the nearest neighbours" were brought together for a week, to perform those exercises which cannot be performed in any other place. Every man of a certain estate should be obliged to keep a horse fit for war.

By this means it would be easy on any occasion, great or small, to bring together such numbers of soldiers and officers as the exigency demanded; that was the custom in ancient Rome. By that method, if once established, it would be unnecessary to keep up a militia formed into regiments of foot and horse in times of peace.

If it were sought to improve the quality of the militia still further, it might be desirable to have a small number of forces employed in a foreign country, in order to gain experience, a fourth part of such forces to be changed every year. Such forces might be dispersed, as a stiffening element, among the regiments of any army that the defence of the country might call for.

The scheme could be carried out at a minimum of expense, for it would only involve the provision of clothing and provisions for those who could not maintain themselves. The only additional expense would be for arms, a small team of artillery, and "what is fair for the encouragement of the first officers and masters".

A militia on such a footing would have none of the disadvantages of bringing together a few men who live at a great distance from one another, to exercise away from home for several days, and of finding instructors to train raw recruits in different places, and mostly at the same time. Besides, there would be none of the inconveniences and expense of forming militias into regiments of foot and horse in times of peace.

The youths would learn how to use a musket, with a few evolutions, which is all that men in ordinary militias pretend to: "the least part of the duties of a soldier". Besides physical exercises, the youths would learn to fence, ride, manage a horse for war, forage, live in a camp, fortify, attack, defend a place, and undergo the greatest toils, and give obedience to the severest orders. Such a militia, if sent overseas to relieve the professional soldiers from time to time, would enable us to assist our allies more effectively than we could ever do by means of standing armies.

Beginning early, "when like wax they may be moulded into any shape," the youth of the country would place their greatest honour in the performance of these exercises, which would "inspire them with the fires of military glory" to which the age is so much inclined; and the inspiration would be lifelong. Such a camp would be "as great a school of virtue as of military discipline, in which the youth would learn to stand in need of few things; to be content with that small allowance which nature requires; to suffer as well as to act; to be modest as well as brave: to be as much ashamed of doing anything insolent as injurious." They would learn to "forgive injuries done to themselves," but to embrace with joy "the occasion of dying to revenge those done to their country, and virtue imbibed in younger years would cast a flavour to the utmost periods of life. In a word, they would learn greater and better things than the military art, and more necessary too, if anything can be more necessary than the defence of our country".

Such a militia would be sufficient to defend the country "if the fleet of England, to which Scotland furnished, during the late war, seven or eight thousand seamen", were in such a condition as it ought to be.

If our fleet only were employed to maintain the balance of power, and the money needed for its equipment and upkeep spent among ourselves, our trade would at once be preserved, and our enemies driven off the sea. This course should have been followed in the recent war. The balance of Europe can be maintained by our fleet. But if we send forces overseas, they ought to be part of our militia. The weaker part of the Continent ought to accept our assistance in whatever way we may choose to give it.

"The sea is the only empire that can naturally belong to us.

Conquest is not our interest, much less to consume our people and treasure in conquering for others."

"To conclude: if we seriously consider the happy condition of those nations who have lived so long under the blessings of liberty, we cannot but be affected with the most tender compassion to think that the Scots, who have for so many ages, with such resolution, defended their liberty against the Picts, Britons, Romans, Saxons, Danes, Irish, Normans and English, as well as against the violence and tyranny of so many of their own princes; that the English, who, whatever revolutions their country has been subject to, have still maintained their rights and liberties against all attempts; who possess a country everywhere cultivated and improved by the industry of rich husbandmen; her rivers and harbours filled with ships; her cities, towns and villages enriched with manufactures; where men of vast estates live in secure possession of them, and where merchants live in as great splendour as the nobility of other nations; that Scotland which has gentry born to excel in arts and arms; that England which has a commonalty not only surpassing all those of that degree which the world can now boast of, but also those of all former ages, in courage, honesty, good sense, industry, and generosity of temper; in whose very looks there are such visible marks of a free and liberal education, which advantages cannot be imputed to the climate or to any other cause but the freedom of the government under which they live—I say it cannot but make the hearts of all honest men bleed to think that in their days, the felicities and liberties of such countries must come to a period if the Parliaments do not prevent it, and his Majesty be not prevailed upon to lay aside the thoughts of mercenary armies which, if once established, will inevitably produce those fatal consequences that have always attended such forces in the other kingdoms of Europe: violation of property, decay of trade, oppression of the country by heavy taxes and quarters, the utmost misery and slavery of the poorer sort, the ruin of the nobility by their expenses on Court and army, deceit and treachery in all ranks of men, occasioned by want and necessity.

"Then shall we see the gentry of Scotland ignorant through want of education, and cowardly by being oppressed. Then shall we see the once happy commonalty of England become base and abject by being continually exposed to the brutal insolence of the soldiers; the women debauched by their lust; ugly and nasty through poverty and the want of things necessary to preserve their natural beauty. Then shall we see that great city, the pride and glory, not only of our island but of the world, subjected to the excessive impositions Paris now lies under, and reduced to a pedling trade, serving only to foment the luxury of a Court. Then will Britain know what obligation she has to those who are for mercenary armies."

And that was Fletcher's scheme for the defence of the country, and for preserving the liberties of Europe. It was based upon an idealism to which he could scarcely have expected that practical expression could have been given without large modifications; unless, indeed, his optimism exceeded his sense of realities. For the Spartan régime which was to be imposed upon the youth of the country made small allowance for the frailties of human nature, and especially of human nature in Great Britain, at the beginning of the eighteenth century. But in the person of Fletcher the fire of the crusader was added to the austerity of the Puritan. His plan needed for its acceptance a generation imbued with the high-souled ideas with which he had made himself familiar, and inspired by the intense patriotism which was the passion of his life. In our own day we have seen movements like that of the Boy Scouts and similar organizations, which embody, in some degree, his aim of forming character by means of properly directed camp discipline; and we have seen, too, in this country, his ideal of a citizen army (without the element of compulsion) capable of defending the country, and, when necessary, serving overseas, realized by the creation of the Territorial forces. In some of the smaller countries of Europe, such as Norway and Switzerland, the main principles of his plan are in active practice; while in other countries, such as Germany, the rigour of his disciplinary methods would appear to be emulated, in the spirit if not in the letter. It will be seen that he was not free from the thirst, universal in his time, for military glory; but it was glory in defending one's own country and not in wars of aggression. In his case, it was sublimated by the higher desire to build up character, to breed a generation of

young men avid to serve their country and die for it if necessary,
fitting themselves by rigorous training to accomplish that end in
the most effective manner; finding, in the pursuit of that aspiration, no burden too heavy, and no sacrifice too great; leading
clean, even ascetic lives; fearing God and nothing else except dis-
honour. His model for discipline might well have been Cromwell's Model Army. But he who was a child when Cromwell ruled
his native country with a rod of iron, would be little inclined to
admire, in other respects, a military system which became an
engine in the suppression of liberty. For, from first to last, the
maintenance of national and individual freedom—and not for his
own country only—was the mainspring of his actions, the motive
force of his life. He wanted a thoroughly efficient militia, not to
threaten liberty anywhere, but to defend it if attacked from any
quarter whatsoever. He wanted it as a bulwark of defence against
tyranny from any side, foreign or domestic, and from any party,
Royalist or Republican.

It will be seen that he was no admirer of the Dugald Dalgettys
of whom, in the seventeenth century, his native country was so
prolific. But he was well aware that it was the poverty of Scotland,
as well as their inherited pugnacity, that drove these "bonnie
fighters" in shoals to the Continent, where they offered their
swords to the highest bidders (Protestants preferred), and where
their military prowess was held in the highest esteem. It was the
same cause that sent Scottish pedlars swarming over the Border
and overseas, where the pack took the place of the sword, and
keenness in driving a bargain impetuosity in storming a fort.
It was this poverty which, as we have seen, it was one of his
most earnest wishes to remove; and to remove, if at all possible,
by agreement with England.

That he was influenced by any animosity towards England as a
nation—he always drew a sharp distinction between the nation
and its rulers—is negatived by the noble and eloquent tribute to
the character of the English people which I have just quoted in
full. It is an example of his more rhetorical style, and a statement
of his sentiments towards a people of whom, as a nation, he was
a consistently warm admirer. It confirms the view already
noticed, which he held strongly and tenaciously, namely, that full

co-operation between his own country and England, with due regard to the national welfare and the historic rights of both, was a consummation devoutly to be wished. He had no desire to erase the Tweed, but to bridge it by a sympathetic community of feeling, and by a full and mutual recognition of common interests (5).

Chapter XII

THE PRELUDE TO THE UNION

SIR JOHN DALRYMPLE suggests, in his *Memoirs*, that in 1702 an attempt was made to throw political dust in the eyes of the Scottish nation by the benevolence of the Ministerial attitude towards Jacobites and Episcopalians alike. "But", he goes on to say, "those arts could not deceive Fletcher of Saltoun, to whose opinion his countrymen looked up, because they knew he had no good but his country, and who said that most Kings were bad, but a Woman King was the worst" (1). (Was it not his fellow-countryman, John Knox, who wrote about the "monstrous regiment of women"?)

Fletcher, says Dalrymple, contrived and presented to the Scottish Ministry the draft of an Act of Security ("afterwards so famous"), "to make Scotland independent forever of England and English Counsellors. The Ministers, however, considered his proposals to be both too bold and too refined" (2).

That can be easily understood. The Ministry tried to carry things with a high hand after the death of William of Orange. They summoned a meeting of the Estates, and, in doing so, were guilty of the constitutional error of delaying the summons later than the time prescribed by law. The Opposition, headed by the Duke of Hamilton (the fourth Duke: his father died in 1694), wished to force a General Election, the results of which, in view of the Darien disaster, were not in the least likely, as the Ministers foresaw, to be favourable to them.

At the Meeting of the Estates, which Hamilton refused to acknowledge as a Parliament (urging that by the ancient Constitution of Scotland Parliaments were annual, and were, by law, dissolved by the death of the Sovereign), the Country or National Party and the Jacobites refused to take part in the proceedings. On their joint behalf Hamilton made a formal protest, declaring the Convention to be illegal, and, having made his protest, left the building, accompanied by "80 peers and Commoners, who were the greatest number in the House, and of the best families, estates and characters in the nation." Moreover, they refused to pay any taxes levied by what was contemptuously termed "The Rump".

The Whig Members who were left, got to work, and before they separated, they had taken an important step. They came to the decision that the only way to escape from the difficulties with England which were now ominously threatening, was to initiate negotiations for a union between the two nations.

In the previous year the Act of Settlement had been passed by the English Parliament. By that Act the Succession to the English Crown was definitely settled on the House of Hanover. Before the Act was passed, the English Ministers did not consult the Scottish Parliament: they ignored that body completely, the inference being that it was a matter with which Scotland had no direct concern. That was a precedent which the Scottish Estates did not neglect to follow, when the question of the Succession to the Scottish Crown came, in turn, to be considered. Yet the English Parliament felt aggrieved when the sister nation asserted its right to make whatever stipulations it chose in settling the Succession to the Scottish Crown.

Nothing could more clearly exemplify the one-sided attitude of English politicians towards the lesser nation. It was this attitude which was at the root of all the ill-feeling that poisoned the relations between the two countries. English public men had never accustomed themselves to the idea of Scotland being a Sovereign State, with inherent rights of self-determination. Since the Union of the Crowns it had become increasingly the practice for successive English Ministers to dictate Scottish policy, as if Scotland were, in fact, a province of England.

It needed some courage for the "Rump" Parliament to initiate by an Act of Parliament, negotiations for union. The "affair of Caledonia" was still rankling deeply in the Scottish memory; indeed, to the excited imagination of the country, it seemed to be the culmination of numerous acts of studied un-neighbourliness and irritating arrogance. "What! unite with the supercilious English, who sneer at our poverty and scoff at our pride? Certainly not." "What! unite with the beggarly Scots who rob us when they can, and hate us when they can't? Assuredly not!" It is no exaggeration to say that the mutual sentiments then prevailing may be thus expressed. When the two sets of Commissioners, both appointed by the Queen, met to consider the terms of the proposed union, it was soon seen that the time was not ripe. The Scottish Commissioners would not dare to put a merging treaty before their Parliament for ratification that did not yield tangible benefits to Scotland. And the English Commissioners would not dare to risk an explosion in their Parliament by agreeing to remove the trade disabilities under which Scotland suffered, and by which English merchants profited. In principle, yes; but in practice, no. Certainly, they agreed, Scotland should have equal privileges with England if the Parliaments were united. But when it came to the translation of these generous sentiments into specific acts of concession, they found it convenient to postpone future discussions until a more convenient time. The same old stumbling-block which had prevented union in the reigns of James I and Charles II had again got in the way. Once more, the union negotiations were fruitless.

Yet both sides realized that something must be done to relieve the tension which prevailed in Scotland. A spark might set the heather afire at any moment. The Jacobites might precipitate a sudden crisis. For everything was in their favour. The English felt that this back-door for their enemies must be closed somehow. The Scots felt that they must do something for the desperate state of their trade, and those who were not Jacobites felt, too, that the uncertainty about the Succession was harmful to their own as well as the English nation. What was to be done?

The Scottish Parliament that was to settle this question met in 1703. Its composition was by no means to the liking of the Court party. They saw clearly that trouble was ahead; and they were not wrong.

Among the new members, one of the four representatives of Haddingtonshire attracted the notice that was reserved for men of special distinction, who were expected to take a leading part in the debates. He was a short, thin man, with a brown complexion, whose physical appearance would have been unimpressive but for his eyes. His eyes were "piercing", and no one who observed their flash as he listened to some insincerity or fatuity, would care to take liberties with Andrew Fletcher. Such was the outward appearance of the Laird of Saltoun, the newly elected member for the shire of Haddington.

It is now possible to examine at closer view the dominating principles which guided the man who was about to be the centre of attraction in the new Parliament, and the most inspiring figure in the passionate debates by which the Union was preluded.

Nowadays, to call a man a "politician" is to fasten on him a term of reproach. To the person who prides himself on his aloofness from contemporary politics, the word connotes the insincerity of the platform and the tyranny of the Whips. But Fletcher's conception of politics was something quite different. The art of government was to him, as we have seen, a noble art, for was it not concerned with the well-being of his fellow-countrymen? His political philosophy covered so wide a range that it touched human effort at all points. Such catholicity in politics was a rare thing in his day; rare in England, though exemplified by some outstanding personalities, and much rarer in Scotland. But for the narrow scope of party politics and its mechanical gibberish, Fletcher had no flair whatever. His only party was his country, and his only allegiance was to his country's interests. He was, in fact, an impossible Parliamentarian, entirely lacking in conciliation, a foe to compromise, and a stranger to intrigue. There were times, indeed, when he showed that he could turn the tables on his opponents with considerable adroitness. But political strategy was alien to his nature. And as an opportunist—which is supposed to be the main occupation of a politician—he was the despair of all political parties alike. He took himself so seriously as a politician, that he regarded the use of his vote in the House as a sacred trust, to be misused at his peril. On one occasion he earnestly charged his fellow-members to exercise their independent judgment instead of slavishly following their neighbours. Every member, he solemnly assured the House, "must account for his own actions to his great Lord and Master": a novel viewpoint for hardened Parliamentarians, both in the eighteenth and the twentieth century.

Taking his duties as he did in that spirit, he had little patience with those who regarded politics as a game, and still less with those who used politics as a lever for their own advancement. Indeed, his lack of patience, his extreme irritability with those who took views opposed to his own, were serious flaws in his character. He was a Scot with an unusual amount of "pepper in his nose". As we shall see, this quickness of temper embroiled him in quarrels which there was no need to engage upon, and squabbles which affected his dignity prejudicially. But he was uncontrollably irascible only when a question of honour was concerned, and on questions of honour his touchiness was so sensitive that sometimes he seemed to go out of his way to discover insults that were not intended. Yet it would be a mistake to suppose that Fletcher had no sense of humour. He had humour in abundance, of rather a grim quality.

The extreme tenacity with which he held his views was well known to his contemporaries. These views were not lightly formed, and being formed only after mature consideration, became the rigid things that opinions so formed usually are. That was, no doubt, what Dean Swift meant when he said of him (but anything Dean Swift said about Scots must be taken in a Swiftian sense) that he was "a most arrogant, conceited pedant; cannot endure the least contradiction in any of his visions or paradoxes". Certainly Fletcher had less inclination than any other great man of action of whom I have any knowledge, to "suffer fools gladly"; and when he spoke in Parliament, his manner must have impressed his hearers with the conviction that they were listening to a man who was saying to himself, "I'm not arguing with you; I'm telling you."

But though in essentials he was adamant, his sense of proportion protected him from equal rigidity in things which, in his view, did not matter. He was all for toleration, or, better still, complete concord in ecclesiastical matters. Indeed, when an Act of Toleration for Episcopalians was discussed in the House, he desired to substitute the principle of comprehension for that of toleration. He was not interested in ecclesiastical squabbles. He recognized, like Amiel, that they never consoled a heart nor edified a conscience. Differences in ecclesiastical polity, in his view, had their secondary uses, but they did not touch fundamentals. Fletcher was neither a good Presbyterian nor a good Episcopalian, but (what was better than either) he was a good Christian. He did not, like some statesmen of his own day and later days, regard Christianity merely as useful material for social and moral cement; for to him it was a live coal of burning conviction. Of all his contemporaries, he was, perhaps, the least capable of "speaking through his nose": but his belief in Christianity as the firmest basis of morality for the community, and the surest anchor of hope for the individual, was invariably exhibited on occasions which called for a confession of his faith (3).

He attacked tyranny wherever he found it, and under whatever political or ecclesiastical guise it concealed itself. In a speech dealing with arbitrary government in Scotland, he asserted (what was historically correct) that it took its rise after the Union of the Crowns. He said that the overthrow of the Constitution and the establishment of the Crown prerogative was due chiefly to "the prelatical party, tho' the peevish, imprudent and detestable conduct of the Presbyterians who opposed these principles only in others, drove many into them, and gave them greater force and rooted them more deeply in the nation". And in another part of the same speech, he made pointed allusion to "the uncharitable and insupportable humours and ridiculous conduct of bigots of any sort". In still another passage he exhorted his fellow-members as follows, "Let us not then tread in the steps of mean and fawning Priests of any sort." He hated priestcraft and all that it connoted, whether attired in lawn sleeves or Geneva gowns.

He truckled to no political party: he feared no Church ban. He turned the searchlight of sincerity on all parties and all sects to discover their true motives. He detested tyranny over the conscience in the Church as heartily as he abhorred the suppression of liberty in the State.

Listen to the words of a prominent fellow-member of the Parliament of 1703, George Lockhart of Carnwath, an ardent Jacobite but, their political differences notwithstanding, a warm admirer of the character of the member for Haddington.

"Being elected a Parliament man in the year 1703, he (Fletcher), showed a sincere and honest inclination towards the honour and interest of his country. The thought of England's domineering over Scotland was what his generous soul could not away with.

The indignities and oppressions Scotland lay under galled him to the heart so that in his learned and elaborate discourses he exposed them with undaunted courage and pathetic eloquence. He was blessed with a soul that hated and despised whatever was mean and unbecoming a gentleman, and was so stubborn to what he thought right that no hazard nor advantage, no, not the universal empire nor the gold of America could tempt him to yield or desert it. And I may affirm that in all my life he never once pursued a measure with the prospect of any by-end to himself, nor further than he judged it for the common benefit and advantage of his country. He was master of the English, Latin, Greek, French, and Italian languages, and well versed in history, the civil law and all kinds of learning. And as he was universally accomplished, he employed his talents for the good of mankind. He was a strict and nice observer of all the points of honour, and his word sacred; as brave as his sword: and had some experience in the art of war, having in his younger days been some time a volunteer in both the land and sea service. In his travels he had studied and come to understand the respective interests of the several princes and States of Europe. In his private conversation, affable to his friends (but could not endure to converse with those he thought enemies of their country), and free of all manner of vice. He had a penetrating, clear, and lively apprehension, but so extremely wedded to his own opinions that there were few (and these must be his beloved friends and of whom he had a good opinion) he could endure to reason against him, and did, for the most part, so closely and unalterably adhere to what he advanced (which was frequently very irregular), that he'd break with his party before he'd alter the least jot of his scheme and maxims; and therefore it was impossible for any set of men that did not give up themselves to be absolutely directed by him, to please him so as to carry him along in all points. And thence it came to pass that he often in Parliament acted a part by himself, tho' in the main he stuck close to the Country party and was their Cicero" (4).

This, then, was the sort of man, as described by an acute observer, whose contributions to the debates in 1703 reached, in elegance of form and weightiness of matter, the high-water mark of Scottish Parliamentary eloquence. Indeed, as already stated, and now emphasized, it was a Parliament that was distinguished by an extraordinary wealth of oratory, evoked, doubtless, by the gravity of the issues which were discussed. In the opinion of his contemporaries, Viscount (afterwards the Earl of) Stair, of Glencoe infamy, was the most powerful orator in the House, but we have no means of judging for ourselves whether that view commends itself to us. Fletcher's speeches, however, are still with us, to be read and admired as models of calm reasoning, passionate appeal, and impeccable English.

Let us see what happened on the opening day, 6th May 1703, of that eventful Parliament.

The House assembled with the full ceremonial that Edinburgh loved, the ceremony of "riding the Parliament". It was an elaborate ceremony, and had the citizens of Edinburgh known that the "riding" of 1703 was the last they were ever to see (at any rate until the present time), the elaboration would have lost none of its impressiveness. Some of the older onlookers may have remembered the "riding" over thirty years before, when Lauderdale, then at the height of his power, was the Commissioner. They may have remembered the bulky form, the red sensual face, of the man who, himself a pious Covenanter in his youth, had employed all the engines of force and conciliation to bring the Covenanters to their knees. They may have recalled the hatred and fear which he had inspired, tempered, it is true, by patriotic pride in a Scot who had avenged Flodden by spoiling the victors! They may have remembered, also, seated by his side, his beautiful duchess, the "greedy cormorant", as a contemporary styled her, who, the daughter of Will Murray, the whipping-boy of Charles I, and the grand-daughter of a humble Fifeshire minister, had swayed statesmen by her feminine arts, and, it was spitefully said, had overcome the austerity of Oliver Cromwell himself.

During the generation that had passed, the sceptre had been wielded by less imperious, but no less tenacious hands. The Queen's High Commissioner in 1703 was James, second Duke of Queensberry, a suave statesman, a dignified Douglas, a pleasant companion, and a dangerous foe. To his patience, his accommodating disposition, his skilful management, his unwearied pertinacity, and his unwavering devotion to the interests of the

Court, was due, equally with any other individual factor, the ultimate success of the Union negotiations. As King William's Commissioner (he was Lockhart's "proto-rebel"), he had managed things so well for his master, with the help of Argyll, as to obtain a majority for the Government when sorely pressed over the Darien disaster. He was now to prove himself equally serviceable to William's successor. He was the chief figure in the "riding" of Parliament in 1703 (5).

As High Commissioner, Queensberry occupied, as was customary, the royal apartments in Holyrood Palace, where, on the day before the opening of Parliament, he received formally from the Treasury Officers the "Honours Three" of Scotland, to wit, the Crown, the Sceptre, and the Sword, which were kept in Edinburgh Castle. These had an important place in the procession of the morrow from Holyrood to Parliament House. Preceded by the Lyon King-of-Arms, they were borne each by a nobleman whose privilege it was to carry them.

On the morning of the "riding", the Commissioners held a levee at which the three Estates of Parliament were present, thereafter taking their appointed places in the procession as determined by the Lyon King. The procession was headed by a troop of grenadiers. They were followed by the representatives of the burghs, riding two abreast, their horses' trappings, appropriately, sober black. The Commissioners for the shires came after them, followed by certain officers of State, who were not peers. Then came the most spectacular section of the procession: the barons, the viscounts and the earls, in their brilliant scarlet robes, their horses led by servants who wore their appropriate liveries, the number of the servants varying with the rank of their masters. The Lyon King, carrying his official baton, and accompanied by his pursuivants and trumpeters, next rode in state, followed by the "Honours".

As with the Lord Mayor's Show in London, interest culminates in the heavily-gilded lumbering coach of the newly-elected Chief of the City Corporation, so with the Edinburgh "riding" of 1703, popular attention was now riveted on the genial, smiling face of the Crown Commissioner as he rode up the High Street, surrounded by his pages and the gentlemen of his household. And

last of all came the guard of honour, a squadron of the Royal
Horse Guards, led by Archibald, Duke of Argyll, whose son,
"Red John of the Battles", had already won his spurs in war, and
was soon to win them in politics as well.

And now the cavalcade has arrived at Parliament House. In the
earlier part of the seventeenth century, the Estates were housed in
the old Tolbooth, near the north-west corner of Parliament
Square (Parliament Close). But a building more fitting the dignity
of Parliament was deemed necessary, and in 1641 it was occupied
for the first time; it is now the great entrance hall of the Court of
Session, where brisk young advocates daily perambulate. There
is little in its present appearance to recall the excited scenes of the
Union debates, but the fine hammer-beam roof under which these
impassioned speeches were delivered, remains unaltered. The
Scottish Estates met in one Chamber. The three Estates—the
clergy as an Estate had ceased to exist in 1693 and their place as
a separate Estate was taken by the lesser barons, or shire representatives, who had previously been included with the peers or
greater barons—had their allotted places in the Chamber, and
every member of each Estate had his own allotted seat. This
disposition made it impossible for the Scottish Parliament to
arrange itself in the party divisions of the English Houses of
Parliament.

At the south end of the Hall, under the great window, stood
the throne. On its steps were the officers of State. Below them sat
the readmitted eldest sons of the nobility. Benches in tiers at
the right and left of the throne were reserved for the nobles themselves. At some distance down the Hall, the Lords of Session sat
at a table allotted to them. At the further end of the table, remote
from the throne, were seated, on forms, the Commissioners for the
shires and for the burghs. And the space behind the bar at the
north end was allocated to privileged members of the public who
were admitted to the debates. The table reserved for the Clerk
Register and his deputies stood in front of, and below the throne.
The "Honours" were on the table facing the throne: symbols of
Scottish sovereignty which had a special significance in this
Parliament above all others.

The House was in full session twice daily, except on Saturdays and Mondays. Morning and evening prayers were read, and every Sunday the members listened to a sermon preached by a minister of the Church of Scotland (6).

This description of the Parliament Hall and its grouping of members makes it easy to visualize the exciting Session of 1703, as the members took their places to listen to the speech from the throne of the High Commissioner. Every member of that assembly must have realized that he was about to play his part in a drama which was fraught with far-reaching significance to his native country. And there, among the representatives of the counties, says Professor Trevelyan, "observed and courted by all, sat Scotland's Cato, the Republican Fletcher of Saltoun" (7), to which one would like to add that to describe Fletcher as a Republican in principle may be accurate, but that the accuracy is subject to reservations.

Chapter XIII

A NOTABLE SESSION

IN the year 1704 was published anonymously "An account of the proceedings of the Parliament of Scotland which met at Edinburgh May 6, 1703". Its author was George Ridpath, an active and acute Whig controversialist (1). It is prefaced by "a true list of the lords, barons and burgesses" who composed this historic Parliament, and it includes among the lords those who were minors, "Papists", holders of extinct peerages, and English subjects, one of whom, it is interesting to observe, was "John Churchill, Lord Eyemouth, now Duke of Marlburrough". From this list it would appear that there were 153 lords, including those disabled from taking their seats, 85 lesser barons or Commissioners for shires, and 67 Commissioners for the burghs: from which it would seem that the Constitution provided for the maintenance of a balance in numbers between the peers on the one side, and a combination of the lesser barons and the burghs on the other.

Coinciding with the opening of this Parliament, the publication of a book entitled *An Historical account of the antient Rights and Power of the Parliament of Scotland* attracted considerable attention. Efforts were made by the Government to suppress its circulation, for it contained doctrine that was by no means palatable to the Court party. Published anonymously, this book is, for some reason, always included in the body of Fletcher's writings. He may have inspired the book, but certainly he did not write it. Indeed, the preface alludes to him as "a very learned gentleman of our own country, a great Patron of Liberty and happy in a Polite Pen", who had "written a Discourse of Government with relation to Militias". One can only suppose that it has found its way into the *corpus* of his works because the author, like himself, was the possessor of a "Polite Pen" in promulgating opinions common to both. The author was, in fact, George Ridpath.

The treatise, which contains "A short introduction upon

government in general", reviews the rights and power of Scottish Parliaments in the past, and shows by concrete examples how severely the prerogatives of the Kings were curbed by Parliament. In effect, the writer's thesis is, that previous to the Union of the Crowns of England and Scotland, Scottish kingship was a strictly limited monarchy, the real sovereignty, in the last resort, resting with Parliament. The treatise is "humbly offered to the consideration of the Estates when they come to settle limitations for the next successor". Beyond doubt it was prepared for the instruction of the Estates in relation to the Parliamentary fight on the Succession, which everybody could see was to be the main business of the first session of the new Parliament. And it can be well believed that its influence on the views of the members was not negligible: Fletcher himself alludes to the treatise in one of his Parliamentary speeches.

The composition of the Ministry in the new Parliament was admirable in its blend of personal qualities and political sympathies. For this Ministry was designed to be a Ministry of conciliation. The Queen had issued an indemnity which enabled the exiled adherents of James to return to their native land and take part in its political life. These immigrants were deftly used to smash the Country party in the elections, and they received their reward in the appointments that were made of declared or suspected Jacobites to fill certain offices in the Government. The Duke of Queensberry, Secretary and High Commissioner, was an impeccable Whig; but in this mixed Ministry he had to find his way in strange company. Almost ostentatiously, the more pronounced Whigs in the recent Convention of Estates were dropped to make way for the Tory newcomers. The new colleague of Queensberry in the Secretaryship was Sir George Mackenzie, Viscount Tarbat; and Tarbat's brother became Lord Justice-Clerk. The Earl of Tullibardine was appointed Privy Seal, and the Chancellorship went to the Earl of Seafield. To balance these Tory or semi-Tory appointments, the Marquis of Annandale was made President of the Privy Council.

These newcomers were expected to bring an accession of strength to the Courtiers, in view of the following and voting power which they commanded. But it was not long before

Queensberry was made to realize that in politics there is no such thing as gratitude, and that what appeared to be strength turned out, in the end, to be a source of real weakness.

Tarbat, like Queensberry himself, was "the pleasantest companion in the world", and a man who had "a great deal of wit" (a useful qualification for a Secretary of State). Moreover, he was "a great master in philosophy, and much esteemed by the Royal Society in London" (which, one fears, were Secretarial qualifications not deemed essential for success). Also, this handsome elderly man was one of the astutest politicians of his time, and, by his opponents was (of course) regarded as being hopelessly unstable. He was a trimmer beyond any doubt.

The new Lord Privy Seal, John Murray, Earl of Tullibardine, now, by his father's death (on 6th May 1703), Marquis of Atholl, had six thousand Highland broadswords at his disposal, and for that reason, if for no other, was courted by both Jacobites and Hanoverians alike. He had, however, qualifications of his own, apart from his fighting clansmen. He had courage and assiduity, and a sense of duty to his country. He suffered under the disability of a temper of unusual violence—"he choaks himself with passion," says a contemporary (2)—and his haughty demeanour impaired his popularity even with his friends.

James Ogilvie, Earl of Seafield, was the victim of a consistent belief that under no conceivable circumstances could the Chancellor's chair be adequately filled by anyone but himself. He was the "Vicar of Bray" of Scottish politics, and, indeed, the success with which he clung to office proves not merely his adaptability but his capability. His good looks, his soft tongue, his smiling countenance, and his conciliatory attitude, were excellent attributes for the successful performance of the duties of a Chancellor (Speaker) in an unruly Parliament such as that of 1703-7. He was a firm believer in the efficacy of private conversations for swaying the views and the votes (it was the votes he wanted) of hesitating members of Parliament, and in his exercise of plausible persuasiveness he seems to have had no rival. It was said of him that he was "a blank sheet of paper which the Court might fill up with what they pleased"; (3) and judging by his own letters to Godolphin, this description of his pliancy does not seem to be altogether unfair. He had made himself unpopular in Scotland during the Darien discussions by his subservience to William of Orange; and the strength of his devotion to Queen Anne (and his own interests) was still less in doubt.

The Marquis of Annandale, an old member of "the Club", had "good sense", which he used to form independent judgments of his own. For that reason, and in consequence of his being an indifferent party man, he was not altogether *persona grata* with the Whigs; indeed, Lockhart's view of him was that "even those of the Revolution party only employed him as the Indians worshipped the devil, out of fear". Certainly, his colleagues found him a difficult man to work with.

The ranks of the Opposition looked unanimously to one man as their natural head: namely, James Hamilton, the premier duke of Scotland.

The Duke of Hamilton was a well-made man, "of a coarse black complexion", with a "brisk look" (he is not easily recognizable as Thackeray's Hamilton in *Esmond*). He had a baffling personality which easily deluded the Scottish people into the belief that he was a sound patriot and a great man. He might have been both, but for temperamental infirmities and unpropitious circumstances. He was physically brave, as became a Hamilton. But his moral courage was not impeccable. He never ran away from any man. But he often ran away from decisive action. In Parliament House he piped patriotic pibrochs with Hamiltonian skill; but when the time came to act, he preferred to stay at home to nurse his toothache. His hesitations, his oscillations, his vacillations, and finally, his repudiations, were the despair of his friends and the jest of his foes. As the leader of a party, his consistency was affected by three disabilities, which explain, if they do not excuse, his political gymnastics. He was heavily in debt; he had large, if burdened, estates in England, perilously liable, in those critical times, to forfeiture; and, above all, he had what was clearly a legitimate, if distant, claim to the Crown of Scotland, which, in certain circumstances, might easily be pressed with some prospect of success. Naturally he was opposed to union with England, for that would be an end to all his hopes. Quite as naturally, the triumph of Jacobitism on the one hand, or the adoption of the

Hanoverian Succession on the other, would rule out his dynastic aspirations. These irreconcilable factors swayed his policy this way and that. They made of him the most impenetrable man of mystery in Scottish politics, and caused a paralysis of effort which was finally detrimental to the interests of his country. It is permissible to believe that at the height of his popularity, this proud patrician, who personified (at any rate to the Edinburgh mob) the national cause more than any other man, might have found himself carried to the throne by a gust of patriotic enthusiasm, had he possessed the adventurous spirit necessary for the encouragement of that decisive step. Yet, when he reached the crest of this wave of popularity—at a time when anti-English feeling was at its height—he continued to show the same infirmity of purpose as before. His public utterances were brave enough, but his acts—now truckling with the Jacobites, then leaning towards the English Court—were certainly not those of a resolute claimant to a throne. Hamilton was not a Cromwell; he was not even a Monmouth. He was too cautious a politician to take risks.

The most effective debaters in the House were a remarkable group of young noblemen, all belonging to the sadly attenuated Country party, who occupied a share in the Parliamentary proceedings which was greatly out of proportion to their numerical strength. They were the Earl, afterwards Duke, of Roxburgh; the Earl of Rothes; his brother, the Earl of Haddington; and the Marquis of Montrose. The leader of the party was John Hay, Marquis of Tweeddale, a man of whom everyone spoke well, for he had "good sense", was "very modest" and "much a man of honour". But his force of character was unequal to the difficulties of his position, and compared with the gifted young men whose titular leader he was, he played an undistinguished part in the Parliamentary proceedings. He suffered the usual fate of politicians of whom everybody speaks well.

Of these young men, John Ker, Earl of Roxburgh, was easily the most brilliant and the most purposeful. His accomplishments and his personal charm were acknowledged by all ("perhaps", says Lockhart, "he was the best accomplished young man of quality in Europe"). But he was ambitious (for which he can scarcely be blamed), and is charged by his political opponents with letting nothing stand in the way of the attainment of his personal aspirations and his political designs.

Of the Earl of Rothes, Lockhart (Tory) has nothing good to say; he accuses him of being destitute of a single good quality to recommend him. But Macky (Whig) says that both Rothes and Haddington were "in great esteem" in their country, which could scarcely be claimed for persons without a redeeming trait of character.

James Graham was a great-grandson of the "glorious" Marquis of Montrose. He showed, says Macky, "sweetness of behaviour" and was "very beautiful in his person" (which, by the way, was a characteristic ascribed by Macky to several members of this re-markable Parliament). Lockhart says he was a weak man who was "led by his nose" by others; also, he accuses him of "insincerity and falseness". It is, indeed, a nice task for the impartial historian to make a just estimate of the value of these character-sketches, and to strike a correct balance between Whig and Tory prejudices.

Another outstanding nobleman, whose attachment to the Country party was relatively loose, was John Hamilton, Lord Belhaven, who has the distinction of being the author of what has been called the " greatest" speech that was delivered during the Union debates. Macky, who does not seem to have liked him, describes him as " a rough, fat, black, noisy man, more like a butcher than a lord, who loves to make long speeches in Parliament and hath the vanity to print them". But Boyer calls him " steady in his principles", and a man with a "graceful manly presence". His portrait is certainly more prepossessing than unattractive. It is true that he liked making long speeches, for he was an accomplished rhetorician, though the quality of his orations was on an entirely different plane from Fletcher's addresses. Also, he was inclined to parade his knowledge of Scottish history in the House, though not without considerable aptness. His record is, on the whole, that of a patriot, though, like his neighbours, he showed a keen appreciation of the sweets of office. And if he liked to hear his own voice in the House, and if he printed his speeches: well, what member of Parliament, conscious of the possession of uncommon oratorical powers, ever willingly refrained from making long speeches, or of printing them, if anybody could be got to read them? There are, of course, speeches which read well, and speeches which read not so well. Fletcher's were well worth printing as contributions to current literature, if for nothing else. But that can scarcely be said of Belhaven's speeches, though, as moving oratorical efforts, they must have been extraordinarily effective when delivered.

To this group of young noblemen was added the steadying influence of George Baillie of Jerviswood, whom Lockhart, a political opponent, describes as " having a profound, solid judgment, and by far the most significant man of all his party, to whom he was a kind of dictator". That the Country party's influence in the Session of 1703 was so disproportionately greater than its numerical strength, is explained by the quality of its personnel.

There was another party in this Parliament: a party of one, and its name was Andrew Fletcher. He was with the Country party, but not of it. In the Session of 1703 he was ready to offer that party his counsel and, on most occasions, his support. But his complete detachment from party ties, and his consistent independence of judgment, he maintained throughout the whole course of the Union Parliament. During no phase of his career was the individualism, which was so marked a trait of his character, more frequently exemplified than in the heated discussions of the Session of 1703. "In the main, he stuck close to the Country party and was their Cicero;" but only as long as the Country party stuck closely to him.

The Session opened quietly, with officially correct speeches by the Commissioner and the Chancellor. On these two men rested the management of the House in the interests of the Court. Both were suave in their manner and dexterous in their methods. Both knew that their majority was precarious and their policy unpopular. Both were adepts in the handling of men. They could, indeed, strike, and strike hard, when necessary, though normally the dangerous claws were concealed in the softest of pads. But the wild men from France whom they had manœuvred into the House to act as a counterpoise to the Country party, could not be expected to remain attached to their interests by the ties of gratitude while dissevered from their sympathies by the claims of political antagonism. They could not depend even upon their own colleagues. The Lord Privy Seal lay under the suspicion of corresponding with St. Germains. Tarbat, Queensberry's co-Secretary, was notoriously unreliable in his political attachment. The time came when the " beautiful" Seafield detached himself from the perplexed Commissioner, who was left to fight a lone hand for Godolphin and the Court. But the rifts in the solidarity of the Government were gradual, and its majority, at the beginning of the Session, was apparently not in doubt.

The primary business of the Session was to pass an Act recognizing Anne's title to the Crown of Scotland, and the first reading was moved by the Duke of Hamilton. But whereas, on the first and second reading, Hamilton based the validity of her title on the Claim of Right, by virtue of which William of Orange was offered and accepted the Scottish Crown, the clause actually added to the statutory part of the Act, moved by the Lord Advocate, made short work of constitutional quibbles by rendering treasonable any questioning whatever of the Queen's title or of her exercise of the government of Scotland from her actual entry thereon. The Country party refused to recognise the validity of the tender of the Crown to the Queen by a few members of the nobility and gentry, instead of by an Act of a properly constituted Parliament; and they refused to acknowledge the validity of the Convention of 1702 as a Parliament. The Jacobites, of course, had their own views about Anne's title. But both parties were forced to acknowledge the logic of facts, and the majority agreed that the method adopted by the House for confirming the Queen's title and validating, as a Parliament, the Convention of 1702, was the only practical way of settling the difficulty. An important constitutional point was involved; and, in view of what actually happened during the Session of 1703, Hamilton's action must be regarded as the preliminary step in the sequence of events which led up to the famous Act of Security, passed in 1703. For, if the title to the Scottish Crown was based upon the Claim of Right, it followed that the holder of the title was bound to regulate the administration of Scottish affairs by the conditions of that Claim; whereas if the Succession was merely by virtue of Anne's being the next Protestant heir, the House of Hanover, by the same inherent right, would succeed automatically to the throne, without any new Act being necessary for their Succession, or for their method of governing Scotland. And in the Session of 1703, only a minority of the members, if indeed any, could acquiesce in that solution of the constitutional problem.

After a few days spent in deciding disputed elections, the House settled down to its legislative work. The first act of the Cavaliers (the Tories) was to authorize their leader, the Earl of Home, to give in the draft of an Act of Supply; and that was the greatest service they could have offered their benefactors. For it was a Vote of Supply that the Commissioner was desperately anxious to obtain, before any other business was transacted. And he could carry it only with the help of the Cavaliers. Once Supply was voted, he could easily manage any awkward matters that were raised for debate. The weapon of adjournment was always at his disposal to be used when danger threatened. But money for the services he must have, and the Cavaliers must help him to obtain it.

The very day on which the Earl of Home submitted his Act of Supply, the Marquis of Tweeddale, the leader of the Country party, presented an Overture (4) from which flowed results that upset Queensberry's plans like a pack of cards, and left him, in the end, virtually helpless. This Overture was for a resolve by the House "that before all other business the Parliament might proceed to make such conditions of government and regulations in the Constitution of this Kingdom to take place after the decease of Her Majesty and the heirs of her body as shall be necessary for the preservation of our religion and liberty".

The battle had commenced. But Queensberry was sure of his majority—unless the Cavaliers deserted him. What has just been described occurred on 14th May. Until the 26th the attention of the House was engaged upon the settlement of contraverted elections, one of which affected Fletcher; for, much to his satisfaction, the result gave him a valued colleague in John Cockburn, younger of Ormiston, in the representation of Haddingtonshire. On 26th May, Home's Act for Supply and Tweeddale's Overture came before the House for consideration, and the debate was adjourned until 28th May, when it was resolved "that the Parliament will proceed to make such Acts as are necessary or fit for securing our religion, liberty, and trade before any Act of Supply or any other business whatsoever".

This was a complete victory for the Country party. What had happened to cause the desertion of the Government by the Cavaliers upon whose support they had relied?

It is difficult to answer that question, though Lockhart, the apologist for the Cavaliers, affirms that it was the result of Queensberry's coquetting with the Whigs to "dish" his Tory allies. It is probable that during the interval between the introduction by the leader of the Cavaliers of the Act of Supply, and the decision of the House to keep it dangling like a bait before the eyes of the Commissioner, the Cavaliers found that they had made themselves unpopular in the country by their espousal of the Act of Supply, and had reconsidered their position in relation to the Government. Also, speeches had been made in Parliament which conduced towards their change of front. Of these the most remarkable was by Andrew Fletcher.

"Mr. Fletcher of Saltoun", says the Marquis of Atholl, writing to Godolphin on 20th May, 1703, "offered (on 26th May) a resolve to the House, vizt:—that before all other business whatsomever, they should pass all Acts for security, liberty, and trade, which was understood both as to the limitations of the Succession and during the Queen's reign. This was opposed all that could be, and after spending 7 or 8 hours in debate, or rather wrangling, the Commissioner and the rest of the Queen's servants yielded to proceed upon any particular Acts for religion, liberty and trade, but then the opposite party, finding their strength, nothing would satisfy but this resolve. At length, about nine at night, the Commissioner adjourned the Parliament" (5).

Who would suppose from this letter that Atholl himself had already submitted to the House the nucleus of what was to become the Act of Security: an action on Atholl's part which, it is to be presumed, would have been as displeasing to Godolphin as it was embarrassing to the Queen's Commissioner? Nor is it easy from the evidence to accept the accuracy of the suggestion that Fletcher intended, at any rate in May 1703, that any Act of Security which might be passed should take effect during Anne's lifetime. But Atholl was angling for the dukedom which had been promised to his father (6). It is not ungenerous to suggest that he had to appear in his correspondence with Godolphin as a loyal servant of the Court, while in Parliament he wished to stand well with the Cavaliers.

The Cavaliers were now fairly committed to the patriotic side, and thenceforward Queensberry knew that his majority was gone. Therefore, in order to get a Vote of Supply, he was compelled to make concessions where they were unavoidable, and to put his trust in a break-up of the coalition between the Cavaliers and the Countrymen, now united for tactical purposes under the leadership of Hamilton. The Whig supporters of the Government did their best for the Ministers by trying to divide the Opposition. They introduced matter for debate calculated to set by the ears the Episcopalians and the Presbyterians comprehended in Hamilton's followers. But these manœuvres failed to achieve their object, for the whole of the Hamiltonians had concentrated upon one object before granting Supply, namely, to adjust once for all the unsatisfactory relations between England and Scotland before Queen Anne's successor was offered the Scottish Crown. Indeed, the Whig attempt to divide the Opposition served only to isolate the Commissioner, for it drove Atholl, Tarbat, his brother the Justice-Clerk, and, worst of all, the supple Seafield, if not into the arms of Hamilton, at any rate an appreciable distance away from Queensberry's throne.

The Act of Security was now a foregone conclusion: it became entirely a question of terms. On these, the House, as might be expected, found itself sharply divided. The debates on this Act, during the Session, were of extraordinary vivacity. "At times", says the Whig, Sir John Clerk, "we were often in the form of a Polish diet with our swords in our hands, or, at least, our hands on our swords" (7).

From the 9th of June to the end of the month, little was done in Parliament except discussions of the clauses for the Act of Security: the passing of the Act was now tacitly agreed in principle, whatever its ultimate fate might be when it came to be touched by the Commissioner's sceptre. On 22nd June no fewer than four Overtures in the form of Acts were presented, read, and ordered to be printed. But "that which was most taken notice of and came nearest to the Act that the House agreed to, was the draught given in by Mr. Fletcher of Salton" (8).

Fletcher's draft Act contained the famous limitations with which his name is always associated. These limitations stated with complete precision the conditions of government upon which Fletcher proposed that the Estates should receive the Successor to the Scottish Crown, "in the case only of our being under the same King with England". Briefly stated, his limitations, twelve in number, were as follow:

(1) Annual elections; (2) increased representation for the shires, corresponding with the last increase in the creation of peerages; and, in future, for every fresh creation of a peer, a shire representative to be added to Parliament; (3) the vote in Parliament to be confined to noblemen and elected members; (4) the King, or his representative in the House, to give his sanction to all laws offered by the Estates; (5) during the intervals between Parliaments, a Committee, appointed by and responsible to the Estates, to have, under the King, the administration of government, with power to summon Parliament in extraordinary circumstances, and the voting by this Committee, acting as the King's Council, to be by ballot; (6) the King to have no power of making peace and war or treaties without the consent of Parliament; (7) all places and offices, civil and military, and all pensions formerly in the hands of the King, to be given by Parliament; (8) no regiment or company of horse, foot, or dragoons, to be kept on foot in peace or war but by the consent of Parliament; (9) all the fencible men of the nation, between sixty and sixteen, to be armed with all diligence and kept supplied with arms (bayonets and firelocks, all of a calibre) and ammunition; (10) no general indemnity or pardon for any transgression against the public to be valid without the consent of Parliament; (11) the Senators of the College of Justice to be incapable of being members of Parliament or of holding any other office or pension; the office of President to be in three of their number to be named by Parliament; no extraordinary Lords; and the Lords of the Justice-Court to be distinguished from the Lords of Session, but to be under the same restrictions; and (12) if the King break in upon any of these conditions of government, he shall by the Estates be declared to have forfeited the Crown (9).

Chapter XIV

THE LIMITATIONS

THE limitations proposed by Fletcher in Parliament were supported by him with every weapon of argument in his well-stored armoury. His case was that "they are not limitations upon any Prince who shall be only King of Scotland, nor do any way tend to separate us from England, but calculated merely to this end, that so long as we continue to be under the same Prince with our neighbour nation, we may be free from the influence of English Councils and Ministers; that the nation may not be impoverished by an expensive attendance at Court; and that the force and exercise of our government may be, as far as is possible, within ourselves. By which means, trade, manufacture, and husbandry will flourish, and the affairs of the nation be no longer neglected as they have been hitherto" (1).

An opportunity had now arrived of remedying the country's grievances.

"We have this day an opportunity in our hands, which if we manage to the advantage of the nation we have the honour to represent, we may, so far as the vicissitude and uncertainty of human affairs will permit, be for many ages easy and happy. But if we despise or neglect this occasion, we have voted our perpetual dependence on another nation."

The adoption of the limitations would ultimately prove to be in the best interest of both nations.

"The best and wisest men in England will be glad to hear that these limitations are settled by us. For though the ambition of Courtiers lead them to desire an uncontrollable power at any rate, yet wiser men will consider that when two nations live under the same Prince, the condition of the one cannot be made intolerable but a separation must inevitably follow which will be dangerous, if not destructive, to both. . . . For my own part, my Lord Chancellor, before I will consent to continue in our present miserable and languishing condition, after the decease of Her Majesty, and heirs of her body failing, I shall rather give my vote for a separation from England. . . . Would we rather court an English Minister for a place than a Parliament of Scotland? Are we afraid of being taken out of the hands of English Courtiers and left to govern ourselves? And do we doubt whether an English Ministry or a Scots Parliament will be most for the interest of Scotland?"

". . . Now since I hope I have shown that those who are for the prerogative of the Kings of Scotland, and all those who are possessed of places at this time, together with the whole English nation, as well as a King of Great Britain, have cause to be satisfied with these regulations of government, I would know what difficulty can remain, unless that being accustomed to live in a dependency, and unacquainted with liberty, we know not so much as the meaning of the word."

He appeals to history:

"That our ancestors did enjoy the most essential liberties contained in the Act I have proposed, and though some few of less moment are among them which they had not, yet they were in possession of others not contained in these articles; that they enjoyed these privileges when they were separated from England, had their Princes living among them, and consequently stood not in so great need of these limitations"—these were facts which he deemed to be incontrovertible.

"The heart of every honest man", he goes on to say, "must bleed daily to see the misery in which our commons and even many of our gentry live, which has no other cause but the ill constitution of our government and our bad government; no other root but our dependence upon the Court of England. If our Kings lived among us, 'twould not be strange to find these limitations rejected. 'Tis not the prerogative of a King of Scotland I would diminish, but the prerogative of English Ministers over this nation."

The acceptance or refusal of his proposals would, in his view, be a test of patriotism.

"He who refuses his consent to them, whatever he may be by birth, cannot sure be a Scotsman by affection. This will be a true test to distinguish, not Whig from Tory, Presbyterian from Episcopal, Hanover from St. Germains, nor yet a Courtier from a man out of place, but a proper test to distinguish a friend from an enemy to his country. And, indeed, we are split into so many parties, and cover ourselves with so many false pretexts, that such a test seems necessary to bring us into the light and show every man in his own colours. In a word, my Lord Chancellor, we are to consider that though we suffer under many grievances, yet our dependence upon the Court of England is the cause of all, comprehends them all, and is the band that ties up the bundle. If we break this, they will all drop and fall to the ground; if not, this band will straiten us more and more, till we shall be no longer a people."

The significance of Fletcher's limitations can only be fully gauged if it is understood that, although Scotland had a Parliament that was nominally free, the real seat of power in Scottish affairs was in London. The "hidden hand" there was not a thing of fiction, but an actuality that effectively directed the course of political affairs in the northern kingdom. Scotland was, in fact, controlled from London very much as nowadays a subsidiary Company is governed by a big controlling Corporation. The analogy, indeed, seems to be fairly close. The Corporation that has a majority shareholding and vote in a subsidiary Company, can, if it wishes, so direct the policy of the subsidiary as to suit its own immediate interests. Shareholders in the subsidiary may be blandly assured by its smooth-tongued Chairman (what a model Chairman of a modern City Company meeting the insinuating Queensberry, or the suave Seafield, would have made!) that their Company is totally independent of its big brother, and does not allow its policy to be deflected by any extraneous influences. But the critical shareholders would be still more critical did they know, as their Chairman and the more sophisticated shareholders know, that most or all of the directors of the subsidiary, are nominees of the controlling Corporation, and that they are sometimes charged with the difficult task of reconciling the interests of the Company that pays them, with the interests of the Corporation that appointed them.

So it was at the beginning of the eighteenth century, with England the big controlling concern, and Scotland the relatively small subsidiary. For the bigger country had to deal with a nation whose leading figures in the world of politics were subjected, from the nature of their circumstances, to the strain of a peculiarly insidious temptation. They were poor; and pensions meant much to them. They were ambitious; and places were like fruit hanging attractively from boughs that were well within the reach of all of them. But for the pensions and for the places, the price had to be paid. And the price was subservience to the wishes of the Ministers in London. Thus the needs of the Scottish noblemen were the opportunities of the English statesmen.

Fletcher was very well aware of the temptations to which the Hamiltons, the Seafields, the Queensberrys, and even the Roxburghs, were only too liable to succumb. Pensions and places had succeeded the "Articles" as the secret and far more subtle method of making the freedom of the Scots Parliament a delusion, and its independence a sham. Rightly he perceived that the only means of making the freedom a fact, and the independence a reality, was to sweep away, root and branch, the whole system of appointments from London, and to vest them in the Scots Parliament itself, if both nations were to be under the same Sovereign. There was no certainty that if this were done, the result would be a succession of Administrations purely patriotic and austerely incorruptible. Indeed, there was a distinct possibility that, in view of the traditional Scottish tendency to split into cliques, the narrowness of the framework in which the interests of most of the Scottish politicians were confined, and the jealousies to which the distribution of the plums of office would inevitably give rise, the transference of the right of making appointments from London to Edinburgh might conceivably set up, not the selfless nationalism which was Fletcher's ideal, but a condition of positively increased political corruption and a state of greater national disunity than before. Inevitably that was a risk which was inherent in Fletcher's proposals. But if a representative institution like the Scots Parliament could not be trusted to create Administrations that would subordinate all other interests to the national welfare, then farewell to every vision of a united, a prosperous, and a happy Scotland. His assumption—surely a naïve assumption—was that all the ills of his native country were due to her dependence on another nation, and that these ills would disappear if the dependence ceased. He was willing to stake everything on the soundness of his thesis. What he wanted was that his country should be allowed to work out either her own salvation or her own damnation. Under English supervision she was damned already, because her interests were always made subservient to those of another nation. He believed she could save herself, if left to herself. If she failed, she would be no worse off than she was already; and a domestic failure would have none of the spiritual bitterness caused by the ills imposed by an outside agency. Rather than submit to that imposition in perpetuity, he would "vote for a separation from England", even although he fully recognized that it would be "dangerous if not destructive to both" countries.

In his arguments respecting the ancient rights of Scottish Parliaments, Fletcher followed closely the Ridpath book, the authorship of which, as we have seen, is sometimes erroneously attributed to himself. This book shows clearly enough the extent of the powers nominally vested in the Sovereign, but really possessed by the Parliament, before the Union of the Crowns. The emphasis is strongly laid upon the acts of the King being with the advice and consent of his Estates; and concrete instances are given of acts that indicate the supremacy of Parliament, even after the King had attained his majority (2).

Originally, it seems certain that all barons and freeholders of the Crown had the right to attend Parliament, based upon the ownership of land. But it was a privilege which, owing to the expense involved by the attendance, was not always appreciated; and in time, following the precedent set up by the burghs, the practice (stabilized by an Act of 1587) grew of sending representatives from the shires in lieu of personal attendance. But this method of delegation was of gradual growth. It was not until the seventeenth century that it fully matured; and it reached its maximum efficiency and influence just when the Parliament was nearing its extinction (3).

When, after the Revolution, the clergy ceased to be one of the three Estates of the Scots Parliament, and the representatives of the shires (the "lesser" barons) became a separate Estate, the latter developed into an increasingly influential constituent element of Parliament. On the whole it was the soundest, and in practice probably the most democratic, of the three elements. For the burghs were chiefly concerned with questions of trade, and were relatively indifferent to the wider and more intangible aspects of nationalism; while the nobility, although probably the most intelligent class in the country, were morbidly jealous for the privileges of their order; and it would be hardly unfair to suggest that, as a body, they were devoted more to caste than country. Only by means of the members for the shires—corresponding socially with the English squires—could the fundamental and permanent interests of the nation, and particularly the agricultural part of the community (the nation's backbone), receive from Parliament the attention which was their due. For although the shire members were far from being the mouthpieces of democracy, as democracy is understood in these days, they were, as a body, probably the least susceptible to self-interest of the three Estates. Besides, their interests as country gentry were inevitably bound up with those of their tenantry. When, as frequently happened, owing to a variety of reasons, agricultural distress prevailed, gentry and tenantry suffered alike; and when agriculture flourished, the peasants prospered with the lairds. This was the class—the gentry class—to which Fletcher belonged, and the community of interests which he believed to exist between them and their dependents is clearly seen in his writings. It was the class which he relied upon to maintain in Parliament the balance which he deemed necessary, to prevent the predominance of any one Estate over the others. And it was from the representatives of the shires that he hoped to get the main support for his proposals. He saw clearly that, as a body, the nobles, who were the main recipients of places and pensions, would probably scrutinize his limitations with a wary eye, having regard to their effect upon their own personal prospects. Also, the representatives of the burghs would, in all likelihood, examine them from the narrow standpoint of trade alone, which was only one item of his programme.

All three Estates were unanimously ready to agree to platitudinous resolutions about preserving the liberties of the nation. The vaguer the resolutions, the better they pleased the Government, for the Ministers could the more easily obtain Supply at the smallest cost. But Fletcher would have none of this highfaluting verbiage. He was determined to pin the House down to precisely worded conditions, which, by his inimitably clear phrasing, were completely shorn of all dubiety or ambiguity.

By so doing he risked the active or latent antagonism of every member in the House who was not, in the last resort, ready, in effect, to "cut the painter". The concrete precision of his proposals showed that if, as some of his fellow-members believed, Fletcher's head was in the clouds, his feet were on the ground. The opposition of the placemen to his proposals could be taken for granted. The Whigs, as a party, favoured an Act of Security (with more or less nebulous clauses), to signify their traditional rôle as the guardians of their country's liberties. But they were desperately anxious to secure the Protestant Succession, and they deprecated any proposals that seemed to contain the germ of a rupture with England. The Cavaliers, on the other hand, were ready to support any proposals, which, in their judgment, would probably be rejected by England, and would thus raise a barrier against Hanover, while opening a door to St. Germains. But how, consistently with their Tory principles, could they support limitations that seemed to interfere with the sacredness of the Royal prerogative (although, as Fletcher pointed out, the interference would only take effect if both countries had the same monarch)? There remained the Country party, the patriotic party, whose support might surely be counted upon. But they were numerically so weak that their vote, even if cast unanimously in favour of the limitations, could easily be swamped.

Fletcher was completely indifferent to dynastic considerations. Whether Hanover or St. Germains succeeded to the Scottish throne after the death of Queen Anne, was all the same to him, if the safeguards provided for the country's civil and religious liberties were adequate and impregnable. In one of his speeches he taunted the Jacobites with their inconsistency. They were "so absurd as to provoke England and yet resolve to continue slaves of that Court. This country must be made a field of blood in order to advance a Papist to the throne of Great Britain. If we fail, we shall be slaves by right of conquest; if we prevail, have the happiness to continue in our former slavish dependence. . . . For

[*167*]

my own part, I think that even the most zealous Protestant in the nation, if he have a true regard for country, ought rather to wish (were it consistent with our Claim of Right) that a Papist should succeed to the throne of Great Britain under such limitations as would render this nation free and independent, than the most Protestant and best Prince without any. If we may live free, I little value who is King: 'tis indifferent to me, provided the limitations be enacted, to name or not name Hanover, St. Germains, or whom you will."

"Whom you will", if his power be strictly defined, and the ultimate authority rest with the Parliament! Not with Ministers "who frequently mistake former bad practices for good precedents" (a neat phrase), but with a body representative of the nation. Personal dictatorship of any kind was completely repugnant to Fletcher's passion for liberty. He knew human nature too well to put his trust in Princes or Presidents endowed with power unrestricted by national safeguards.

He failed to carry his limitations, which were rejected by twenty-six votes. Yet during practically the whole of the Session of 1703, the House was infected by their spirit, and the Act of Security, as finally passed, was inoculated by their content, where it did not actually incorporate their meaning. By general agreement, some sort of security was going to be insisted upon before Supplies were granted, and certainly before any measure assimilating England's Act of Succession could find a hearing. Early in the Session, Fletcher had poured scorn upon the practice which had grown up of securing Supplies prior to legislative work. "Experience might teach us", he said, "that such Acts should be the last of every Session, or lie upon the table till all other great affairs of the nation be finished, and then only granted. 'Tis a strange proposition which is usually made in this House: that if we will give money to the Crown, then the Crown will give us good laws; as if we were to buy good laws of the Crown and pay money to our Princes that they may do their duty and comply with their Coronation Oath."

The essential feature of the Act of Security, in its final form, was the provision it made for the successorship to the Crown of Scotland, "upon the death of Her Majesty without heirs of her

body:" a Successor "lawfully designed or appointed" by the
Queen, and also by the Estates. It stipulated that the Successor to
the Crown of Scotland ("the said Successor and the heirs of the
Successor's body being always of the Royal Line of Scotland, and
of the true Protestant religion") shall not be the Successor to the
Crown of England, "unless that in this present Session of Parliament, and any other Session of this or any other ensuing Parliament during Her Majesty's reign, there be such conditions of
government settled and enacted as may secure the honour and
sovereignty of the Crown and the Kingdom, the freedom, frequency, and power of Parliaments, the religion, liberty, and trade
of the nation, from English or any foreign influence. . . . Nor shall
the same person be capable, in any extent, to be King or Queen of
both realms, unless a free communication of trade and the freedom
of navigation and the liberty of the plantations be fully agreed to,
and established by, the Parliament and Kingdom of England to
the Kingdom and subjects of Scotland, at the sight, and to the
satisfaction of, this or any ensuing Parliament of Scotland."

Also, provision was made for the procedure to be followed
during the hiatus between the Queen's death and the taking of the
Coronation Oath, the underlying idea being to prevent the predominance of English interest.

Also, provision was made for "the whole Protestant heritors
and all the burghs" to "forthwith provide themselves with fire-
arms for all the fencible men who are Protestants within their
separate bounds"; and they were empowered and ordained to
"discipline and exercise their said fencible men once in the month
at least".

Also, it was enacted that upon the death of the Queen, or of any
of her heirs or successors, the commissions of all officers of the
standing forces, "above a captain", shall immediately become
"null and void" (4).

The Act thus painfully built up, clause by clause, during many
weeks of tense discussion, turbulent scenes, and eloquent speeches,
was, in effect, a compromise between the drastic Act originally
drafted by Fletcher and the moderating amendments of the whole
House. One of Fletcher's twelve proposals, namely, that war and
peace were to be made by Scotland, only by consent of the Scots

Parliament, was moved by the Earl of Rothes as a clause of the Act, and was, of course, supported by Fletcher in "a long harangue persuading to the making of this law" (5). The report proceeds:

"The Commissioner said he was ready to consent to anything for the good of the nation that the Queen had under her view when he came from her; but as to this, he thought it was not under her consideration. Salton had said that our Kings, since the Union of the Crowns, were under the influence of English counsels, and it appeared to be so from what the Commissioner had spoke.

"Upon this, those about the Throne got up and said he (Salton) deserved to be censured. Others cried: 'To the bar!' The Duke of Hamilton and a great many cried, 'What! was this the liberty of Parliament? Had not members freedom to speak out?' So there was a great hubbub for some time. And then the question was moved: If any limitations should be brought into this Act, or not? Carried *not*" (6).

The discussions on the Act of Security had gradually become focussed on the character of the demands which were to be made upon England: participation by Scotland in trading privileges, or renunciation by England of political domination. In a sense, it was a choice between trade and independence, between material aims and idealistic aspirations. Fletcher, it is true, contended that these were inter-penetrative: that political freedom involved economic prosperity, for there was no more eager advocate of parity of economic opportunity, as between the two countries, than himself. And by a happy if unusual opportunism, he so out-manœuvred the Ministers that he compelled them, much against their will, to combine both aims and incorporate them in the Act of Security.

The Government were eager to divert the attention of the House from dangerous constitutional problems into more innocuous channels. The country, as they were aware, was still smarting under the recollection of the Darien disaster, and the humiliation it had to suffer at the hands of England throughout the history of that miserable episode. They knew that the people were longing for an opportunity of squaring accounts with their southern neighbours; and that they were watching, with intense interest, the proceedings in the Edinburgh Chamber. "Trade in exchange for an Act of Succession" seemed an excellent conjunction of complementary issues to secure a popular reception in Scotland and polite consideration in London. To be sure (as Fletcher fully recognized), it was easy enough to grant trade concessions, in order to avoid disagreeable political consequences. But what of the guarantees for the permanency of these concessions, once the political occasion for them had passed? With this question, however, Queensberry and his colleagues were not immediately concerned. They aimed at the impossible feat of straddling on two horses, with legs as widely apart as Edinburgh and London. That they fell between the horses might have been foreseen by them.

It was with dismay that they heard the Earl of Roxburgh proposing to add a clause to the Act of Security, that the Successor to the Crown of Scotland was not to be the Successor to the Crown of England "unless that in this Session of Parliament, there be such conditions of government settled and enacted as may secure the honour and independency of the Crown of this Kingdom, the freedom, frequency, and power of the Parliament, and the religion, liberty, and trade of the nation, from the English or any foreign influence".

This clause contained the essence of Fletcher's limitations—much vaguer and easier of evasion, yet deadly in its implications. What were the Ministers to do? The acceptance of the clause would ruin their reputations in London, and, indeed, might lead to a serious rupture between the two countries.

A long debate ensued. "Salton moved it might be put to the vote 'add the clause or not', and as he was speaking, the Chancellor told it was late, and therefore the Commissioner adjourned the Parliament. . . . Great cry and hubbub" (7).

There was a "scene" in the House. Fletcher immediately drew up a protest against the adjournment. Hamilton and Fletcher prepared to draw up an address to present to the Queen, but the Duke thought better of it, and followed the Ministers out of the House. The address was prepared notwithstanding, and was signed by "above seventy" members the same night. On the following day the suavity of the Chancellor saved the situation for

the Government. The Ministry, he declared, had no wish to interfere with the privileges of members. The only reason why he had
adjourned the House on the previous day was the lateness of the
hour (in these 1703 debates, candles had sometimes to be brought
in). Thus the storm was quelled by the Chancellor's tact. But how
to counter Roxburgh's clause?

The Government had concocted a crafty plan overnight. In
accordance with their design to "dish" the Nationalists, they put
up the Lord Advocate, Sir James Stewart, to propose that, instead of the clause moved by Roxburgh, the House should adopt a
clause debarring the Successor to the Crown of England from
succeeding to the Scottish Crown, unless England agreed to free
trade with Scotland, and allowed her to share in England's
colonial trade. Fletcher at once sprang to his feet to congratulate
the Ministers on framing so acceptable a clause. He joyfully moved
that their clause, jointly with Roxburgh's, should be added to the
Act. Fletcher could be an adroit Parliamentarian when he chose,
as well as a constructive statesman. By his motion he placed the
Government in an obvious dilemma. They were, in fact, hoist
with their own petard. For they perceived that, if pressed to a
vote, his motion would carry. Once more they had recourse to the
weapon of adjournment as a temporary relief from their embarrass-
ment (8).

Clearly, the opinion of the House was gradually hardening in
the direction of Fletcher's views. And when, ultimately, the two
clauses were actually joined, and carried, on 26th July, by a
majority of seventy-two votes (the conjunction of the clauses
served party as well as patriotic ends), it was evident that all
Ministerial manœuvring against this manifestation of party and
national feeling in the House was futile. Queensberry and Seafield were beaten (9).

They had now to face, not merely the antagonism of a Parliamentary majority, but the displeasure of London. For Godolphin
disapproved, not only of Roxburgh's clause, but of the Government's additions as well, inasmuch as both tended in the direction of separation. And what Godolphin desired more than anything else was agreement on the Succession. The Queen, he declared, would never agree to any legislation of the Scots Parlia-

ment that established a Succession for Scotland different from that of England.

Meanwhile the Act of Security was nearing finality in Edinburgh. In the month of August there was a great debate on the vital clauses, carried against the Government, which ordained the arming of the country, and placed the standing forces under Parliamentary control on the death of the Queen. These were clauses, significant in their implications, which aroused more resentment in England than any of the others; indeed, they were probably the direct incentive to the retaliatory measures that followed their enactment. They embodied two of Fletcher's limitations, and therefore, as might be expected, received his hearty support.

"To rely upon any law without such a security", he declared, on the question of arming, "is to lean upon a shadow." He uttered some aphorisms on the subject, such as: "The possession of arms is the distinction of a freeman from a slave. He who has nothing and belongs to another, must be defended by him and needs no arms. But he who thinks he is his own master and has anything he may call his own, ought to have arms to defend himself and what he possesses, or else he lives precariously or at discretion. . . . If we are not rich enough to pay a sufficient number of standing forces, we have at least this advantage, that arms in our hands serve no less to maintain our liberty at home than to defend us from enemies abroad. . . . To continue still unarmed when by this very Act now under deliberation we have put a case, which happening, may separate us from England, would be the grossest of all follies. And if we do not provide for arming the Kingdom in such an exigency, we shall become a jest and a proverb to all the world."

He was ready to face, if need be, separation as a calamitous necessity. But he was not so foolhardy as to face the inevitable consequences, without the preparations that were obviously imperative, unless all prudence was to be thrown to the winds. Doubtless, also, he took full account of the probable reception by England of the clauses.

The Act of Security was finally passed, after two months' heated debate, by a majority of sixty (Ridpath says fifty-nine) votes. Then the members had a period of suspense. Queensberry was urged to touch the Act forthwith, but it was soon evident that he would do nothing until he had taken counsel with London. What would be the reception of the Act there? Would the Commissioner be authorized to touch it with the sceptre? Or would it be flung back in the face of the Estates? It was not until the 10th of September that the suspense was ended by Queensberry's announcement, that he had been instructed to touch all the Acts which had been passed during the Session *except* the Act of Security. And the Act of Security was by far the most important Act of the Session, if not indeed, the most important Act ever passed by a Scots Parliament.

This decision at once raised the question of the prerogative in an acute form. Fletcher made three speeches after the passing of the Act, in all of which he touched upon what was generally recognized to be an exceedingly difficult question.

"I know", he said, in one of his speeches, "'tis the undoubted prerogative of Her Majesty that no Act of this House shall have the force of a law without the Royal Assent. And as I am confident His Grace the High Commissioner is sufficiently instructed to give that Assent to every Act which shall be laid before him, so more particularly to the Act of Security of the Kingdom which has already passed this House: an Act that preserves us from anarchy; an Act that arms a defenceless people; an Act that has cost the representatives of this Kingdom much time and labour to frame, and the nation a very great expense; an Act that has passed by a great majority; and, above all, an Act that contains a caution of the highest importance for the amendment of our Constitution."

In another of the three speeches, he had something to say concerning "the delay of giving the Royal Assent to Acts passed in this House, for which I could never hear a good reason except that a Commissioner was not sufficiently instructed." But that could not be the reason for the delay in touching the Act of Security. Those who "speak freely" could only assume that the delay was caused in order that certain other Acts "may pass in a thin House", while "the Acts that concern the welfare and perhaps the very being of the nation remain untouched".

In his third speech, he came to close quarters with the question of the exercise of the prerogative.

"The questions concerning the King's prerogative and the people's privileges", he said, "are nice and difficult. . . . By the Constitution of this Kingdom, no Act of the Estates has the force of a law unless touched by the King's sceptre, which was his undoubted prerogative. The touch of his sceptre gave authority to our laws as his stamp did a currency to our coin. But he has no right to refuse or withhold either." The Act passed in the reign of Charles II for the assertion of the Royal prerogative was intended to "abolish and rescind" the unlawful usurpation of the prerogative by the Scots Parliament during the Civil War. "But a practice introduced in arbitrary times can deserve no consideration. For my own part, I am far from pushing things to extremity on either hand . . . and therefore those who have the honour to advise Her Majesty should beware of inducing her to a refusal of the Royal Assent to the Act for the Security of the Kingdom, because the unwarrantable custom of rejecting Acts was introduced in arbitrary times."

It was a moderately worded warning against raising a question of far-reaching implications, and conceivably it may have influenced Godolphin in his subsequent decision to advise the Queen to give her Assent to the Act. Fletcher made out an excellent case for his contention that by the ancient constitutional practice of Scotland, Acts passed by Parliament were confirmed as laws by the touch of the sceptre, without the King having a negative voice. He wished to guard jealously the prerogative rights inherent in the Scottish Constitution.

In another of his speeches, however—a lengthy speech on the freedom and frequency of Parliaments—he admits that "it is the Queen's undoubted prerogative to give or refuse" her Assent to the passing of Acts of Parliament. "But it is also true, it is the undoubted right of the people to grant or refuse subsidies". If, by "pernicious influence", the Queen refuses her Assent, "there remains no other remedy but . . . by a generous and bold refusal of a subsidy to force these our selfish neighbours, either to suffer our gracious Scots Queen to gratify her Scots nation in these Acts which stood them in so much expense of time, labour, and money, or otherwise to pay our subsidies out of their own pockets". His general observations at the end of this speech are notable for the vigour of their appeal.

"We have hitherto, my Lord, been prisoners at large; our keepers had no jealousy that we were sensible of our own slavery. But this late effort hath undeceived them, and must inevitably terminate in one of the two: either we must give the finishing stroke to the honour and power of our Queen, and to the liberty and trade of our nation by the Acts here proposed, or we must resolve to return into close prison under the chains of our irritated jailers, unpitied and mocked without any hopes of redemption."

In only one of these speeches did he advocate separation from England. It was a cry of despair, after he had reviewed all the circumstances, and decided that the Queen's refusal to give her Assent to the Act of Security pointed to a determination on the part of her English counsellors never to remove the shackles by which his country was bound. It was clear, he said, that the Queen's decision proceeded from English advice. And he proceeded to lash his subservient compatriots with whips of scorn.

"Nothing has been more common", he said, "than to see Scotsmen of the several parties addressing themselves to English Ministers about Scots affairs, and even to some ladies, whom for the respect I bear to their relations I shall not name.... No man in this House is more convinced of the great advantage of that peace which both nations enjoy, by living under one Prince. But as on the one hand, some men for private ends, and in order to get into office, have either neglected or betrayed the interest of this nation by a mean compliance with the English Court, so on the other side, it cannot be denied that we have been but indifferently used by the English nation". Here he quotes examples in support of his charges, including the "affair of Darien", and the cavalier fashion in which the Succession had been settled by England, "an affair of the highest importance and, one would think, of common concernment to both Kingdoms", without the concurrence of Scotland. Was not this a plain intimation of their neighbours' contempt for the sister Kingdom? And now, from the same source, comes the refusal to permit any limitations on a Successor, and the hint that we need not expect to receive the Queen's consent at any future time. Well, we must protect ourselves in the only way that is open to us. "'Tis my opinion that the House comes to a resolution that, after the decease of Her Majesty, heirs of her body failing, we will separate our Crown from that of England."

There was no other man in the Scots Parliament bold enough to express that opinion. It may not have been without its effect on the other side of the Border.

Other important Acts, besides the Act of Security, were passed in the latter part of this busy Session; one of which, the Act of Peace and War, passed in September 1703, was originally one of Fletcher's limitations; it will be remembered that it was refused incorporation as a clause in the main measure. Probably it was not seriously intended to be put into force unless certain contingencies arose; indeed, Fletcher admitted in one of his speeches that his aim was to provide a guarantee against England withdrawing from any trade agreement entered into between the two countries. "If", he said, "we were possessed of an Act lodging the power of peace and war in the hands of our Prince and Parliament, our neighbours of England must either be obliged and overawed to continue to us our communication of trade, thereby to engage us in their quarrel; or otherwise, if they should rob us of our communication of trade, we shall stand neuters in the war and shall thereby reap a vast advantage." The Act was a threat without using the language of menace. It could only become effective in the event of a final breakdown of any Succession negotiations that might be initiated: and it may be doubted whether at this stage, that outcome was seriously contemplated on either side of the Border except by the Jacobites. The Act received the Royal Assent, mainly, as it was supposed, in the hope "to have obtained a subsidy for the Army".

But if that was the expectation, it was doomed to disappointment. The Government were indeed in desperate straits for Supplies, and to that fact alone can be attributed their astonishing introduction of an Act permitting the importation of "all wines and foreign liquors". For this Act directly favoured a country with which Great Britain was then actually at war, and its introduction elicited a vigorous protest from the Cavaliers and the Country

M
[*177*]

party, together with some burgh representatives who detached themselves from their colleagues. Fletcher inveighed against the Act in two weighty speeches. He pointed out that though the proposal did not involve direct trading with the enemy, yet the French wines bought from neutrals were not needed in exchange for Scottish exports. Why not buy from the neutrals their own commodities which Scotland needed, instead of French wines? Could not wines be obtained from Portugal or Italy? "But it seems no wine will please us but that of a country against which we are in actual war, and which uses us ill both in peace and war." Trading with Portugal and Italy would involve the employment of Scottish tonnage, for the goods would be carried in Scots vessels, "not in Swedes, Danes, and Hamburgers to the ruin of our navigation. For if they drive" (i.e., carry) "our trade for us, we may indeed burn our ships and plow our towns." But there was a larger question involved. "No man in this House can be ignorant that this Act will not only open a trade and correspondence with France, contrary to the Declaration of War and our own standing laws, but that the design of those who promote the passing of this Act is to have a trade directly with France. 'Tis known that Scots ships are already loading wines at Bordeaux for this kingdom, and that a French factor is already arrived in this city." Indeed a Scottish ship, pretending to be a Dane, and loaded with French wines, was at that moment lying in Queensferry Road, not eight miles from Edinburgh. And another ship, similarly laden, had been brought into the Clyde, "in contempt of the law and the authority of Parliament". The Administration "seem not to think it their business to take notice of such practices. . . . Since the executive part of the Government is arrived to that state that hardly any law is put in execution, the Parliament, according to the many precedents we have in our Acts, will give order for a better administration in time to come, and take effectual care that those who are placed in the highest trusts shall see the laws duly executed. . . . 'Tis pretended that the Customs arising from the importation of French wines must serve to pay the Civil List, because the former duties are fallen one half of the usual value. A very cogent argument indeed! when we know that the Customs have been taken from the farmers, only in order to bestow the collectors' places upon Parliament men. Shall we make good such funds as are exhausted by bribing men to betray our liberty? If any justice were to be found in this nation, the advisers of these things had long since been brought to a scaffold. But as there is no crime under Heaven more enormous, more treacherous, and more destructive to the very nature of our government, than that of bribing Parliaments, so there is nothing more common and barefaced."

None of his speeches reveal more clearly than these, Fletcher's passion for the unchallengeable supremacy of Parliament, for the jealous supervision of the acts of the Executive, and for its maintenance of a standard of austere honour. That he was well aware of gross breaches of that standard being matters of common occurrence, did not in the least cause him to condone such practices; on the contrary, as may be seen by the vigour of his language, they made his condemnation of them all the more uncompromisingly merciless.

The plea of the Administration was that money must be found somehow. "You refuse us supplies; we must find the money by increased Customs dues:" such, in effect, was the plea. And so the Act was passed on 16th September, 1703, with the help of the burgh representatives, who had their farming interests to consider. But for once Fletcher and the English Ministers found themselves in agreement, inasmuch as the passing of the Act was (not unreasonably) regarded in London with the greatest concern, and its touch by the Commissioner was the first of a series of blunders by Queensberry which led ultimately to his temporary dismissal from office.

The storms of the Session did not cease with the touching of the Peace and War Act, and the Wine Act. Its close saw perhaps the most turbulent scenes of all. The feeling of the House showed itself in a marked manner on the presentation of an Act one day by the Earl of Marchmont, for settling the Succession on the House of Hanover. "It was treated with such contempt", says Lockhart, "that some proposed it might be burnt, and others that he might be sent to the Castle, and was at last thrown out of the House by a plurality of fifty-seven voices" (10). But the stormiest episode of all occurred when, in a final attempt to get a money grant, the

Treasurer-Depute moved for a first reading of the Act of Supply, which had lain on the table since the first month of the Session. At once "Parliament flew in the face of it", demanding the Royal Assent to the Act of Security before members would vote a penny. Was Parliament for no other purpose than "to drain the nation of money to support those that were betraying and enslaving it"? they indignantly cried. . . . "And the House being crowded with a vast number of people, nothing for nearly two hours could be heard but voices of members and others (it being late and candles lighted), requiring 'Liberty and No Subsidy'" (11).

The cry of Liberty and No Subsidy sounded the knell of the Government's hopes. And amid the scene of disorder ("the Throne being confounded with this vigorous appearance on behalf of the country"), the voice of the young Earl of Roxburgh could be heard declaring that "if there was no other way of obtaining so natural and undeniable a privilege of the House as a vote, they would demand it with their swords in their hands" (12).

Queensberry had evidently anticipated trouble, for the Foot Guards were ordered to be in readiness. Indeed, a drunken officer had been heard to say that ways would be found to make the "Parliament calm enough". But Queensberry thought it prudent to bow to the storm, and instructed the Chancellor to announce that the Act of Supply would continue to lie on the table. On the following day, he touched the Acts which he had been empowered to legalize, and adjourned Parliament to the following October.

Fletcher continued to be the leading debating figure in the closing days of the Session. It was only by a narrow majority that a motion to address the Queen about touching the Act of Security, had been rejected by the House. And before the Act of Supply was finally shelved, further attempts were made to secure the Royal Assent to the Act of Security. Fletcher tried once more to tighten up the issues of Security in exchange for Supplies. He returned to his scheme of limitations, but in an amended form. He reduced his demands from twelve to three, namely, (i) Civil and military places and pensions to be conferred by Parliament; (ii) Annual Parliaments; (iii) and during Parliamentary intervals a Committee of thirty-six members to administer the government, with power on extraordinary occasions to call the Parliament to-

gether. He prepared two drafts of an Act embodying these conditions, one draft naming the conditions as limitations on the
Successor, but without naming the Successor; and the other draft
leaving a blank to be filled in with the name of the Successor. He
did not care which draft was accepted, if the limitations were
enacted. In supporting his proposals, he made what was perhaps
the greatest and most impassioned of all his speeches. In his preliminary remarks, he charged each of his fellow-members solemnly
to "act according to his knowledge and conscience. . . . I say every
man in this place is obliged by the oath he has taken, to give such
advice as he thinks most expedient for the good of his country. . . .
Therefore I, who have never made court to any Prince, and I hope
never shall, at the rate of the least prejudice to my country, think
myself obliged, in discharge of my conscience and the duty of my
oath in Parliament, to offer such limitations as may answer the
general clause in the Act for the Security of the Kingdom."

He concentrated upon the first of his limitations, for he saw
clearly that, to effect his object, the necessity for the control of
places and pensions by the Scottish Parliament was essentially the
crux of the situation. Given domestic control, English pressure on
Scottish policy would be removed, and Scotland would then be
free to work out her national problems independently of external
interests.

"The regret of every wise and good man", he said, "must needs
be extraordinary, when he sees the liberty and happiness of his
country not only obstructed but utterly extinguished by the
private and transitory interests of self-designing men, who, indeed,
very often meet their own ruin but most certainly bring destruction upon their posterity by such courses. . . . The question we
have now before us is whether we will be free men or slaves for
ever? Whether we will continue to depend, or break the yoke of
our dependence? Whether we will choose to live poor and miserable, or rich and happy? . . . This limitation will undoubtedly en-
rich the nation by stopping that perpetual issue of money to
England, which has reduced this country to extreme poverty.
This limitation does not flatter us with the hopes of riches by an
uncertain project; does not require so much as the conditions of
our own industry; but by saving great sums to the country, will

every year furnish a stock sufficient to carry on a considerable trade, or to establish some useful manufacture at home, with the highest probability of success; because our Ministers by this rule of government would be freed from the influence of English Councils; and our trade be entirely in our own hands and not under the power of the Court as it was in the affair of Darien. If we do not observe this limitation, our attendance at London will continue to drain this nation of all those sums which should be a stock for trade. Besides, by frequenting that Court, we not only spend our money, but learn the expensive modes and ways of living of a rich and luxurious nation. We lay out yearly great sums in furniture and equipage, to the unspeakable prejudice of the trade and manufactures of our own country. Not that I think it amiss to travel into England, in order to see and learn their industry in trade and husbandry. But at Court, what can we learn except a horrid corruption of manners, and an expensive way of living that we may for ever after be both poor and profligate?"

It was only to be expected that their Kings in London should prefer an English interest before that of Scotland. And it should occasion no surprise "that English Ministers should advise and procure the advancement of such persons to the Ministry of Scotland as will comply with their measures and the King's orders; and, to surmount the difficulties they may meet with from a true Scots interest, that places and pensions should be bestowed upon Parliament men and others". If domestic control of these were secured, "rewards and punishments will be in the hands of those who live among us and consequently best know the merit of men. . . . Having thus shown some of the great advantages this limitation will bring to the nation (to which every one of you will be able to add many more), that 'tis not only consistent with monarchy but even with an absolute monarchy" (he had cited China as an example), "having demonstrated the necessity of such a condition in all Empires which contain several kingdoms; and that without it we must for ever continue in a dependence upon the Court of England; in the name of God, what hinders us from embracing so great a blessing?"

If the Queen refused her Assent to the Act, it would be on the advice of English counsellors; and that fact would show the necessity for having a Successor other than the Successor to the English Crown. Let them put the matter to the test, and then await the result. Haply the Queen, even by English advice, might be persuaded to give her Assent "unless her Counsellors shall think fit to incur the heavy imputation, and run the dangerous risk, of dividing these nations for ever".

"If, therefore" (so he perorated), "either reason, honour, or conscience have any influence upon us; if we have any regard either to ourselves or posterity; if there be any such thing as virtue, happiness, or reputation in this world, or felicity in a future state; let me adjure you by all these not to draw upon your heads everlasting infamy, attended with the eternal reproaches and anguish of an evil conscience, by making yourselves and your posterity miserable."

It was the speech of a man desperately in earnest, and if anything could have moved his audience to adopt his views, they would surely have been persuaded by his eloquence and sincerity. But the attitude of most of his hearers, patriotically ebullient though it might be, when it did not commit them to the precise phrasing of definite conditions, was still cynically suspicious of enthusiasm such as Fletcher's, and the courageous acceptance of risks which was his also. Besides, to the members of the nobility, the fleshpots of Egypt were sweet; they preferred, on the whole, life in London to life in Edinburgh: they had learned to like "the expensive modes and ways of living of a rich and luxurious nation".

The Ministers, on their part, made what proved to be a maladroit move to profit by Fletcher's motion for the adoption of his limitations. They were seeking to pass their Act of Supply, and it seemed to them that if they could get the House to vote whether Supply or Limitations should be discussed, there would probably be a majority against Fletcher. But Fletcher saw their game, and neatly countered by withdrawing his motion, while adhering to the necessity for his proposals in the interests of the country. The Ministers and their Supply were thus left "in the air". They were well aware that Supply had no chance against the vague call for the preservation of liberties, to which the House was so ready to respond. Lamely they were compelled to promise, in consideration of a first reading of their Act, not to trouble the House again with it for the next three sittings. But Fletcher would have none of this, for he foresaw that if the Act of Supply were read for the first time, the vote for which the Ministers were angling would inevitably be secured four days later, and then—adjournment. "Those about the throne", he said, could not expect the House to agree to their proposal. Nor did the House agree to it, for, as we have seen, its fate was sealed amid scenes of great excitement. A final attempt, in which Fletcher was implicated, to secure Annual Parliaments and the regulation of Parliamentary sittings, in exchange for Supply, was to have been made; but Queensberry was afraid to take the risk of agreement, preferring the prorogation of Parliament as the safer course.

Lockhart remarks on the "many strange and unprecedented speeches" which were made in the Session of 1703, "inveighing against and exposing the Government; especially by that worthy and never-enough-to-be-praised patriot, Andrew Fletcher of Salton" (13). Nominally a Whig—though he disowned any party label—Fletcher formed much closer contacts during this Parliament with unbending Tories such as Lockhart, than he did with impeccable Whigs such as Queensberry. In the Session of 1703 he achieved his greatest Parliamentary triumph, and shaped its legislation more than any other individual member. And yet the pathetic fact remains that he failed to achieve what he had set out to accomplish. But he had attempted something that was beyond the capabilities of any statesman of his time: he had attempted to convert an assembly of timid realists into a Parliament of courageous idealists (14).

Chapter XV

A CONVERSATION IN LONDON

SOON after the storm of Parliamentary disputation came the calm of reflective authorship. At the end of the year 1703 Fletcher again took up his pen, to write what is perhaps the most attractive of his political essays, and the most enduring excursion into literature, in form and matter, that Scotland produced during his period. It was written in the form of a letter addressed to his young political associates, the Marquis of Montrose, the Earl of Rothes, the Earl of Roxburgh, and the Earl of Haddington, and was entitled *An Account of a Conversation concerning a right regulation of Governments for the common Good of Mankind*, a formidable title which is scarcely suggestive of the liveliness of the contents. It is dated 1st December, 1703, and was published in Edinburgh in 1704. It purported to be a conversation between two Scotsmen, Tarbat, now the Earl of Cromarty, and himself, and two Englishmen, Sir Christopher Musgrave (1) and Sir Edward Seymour (2). In selecting his participants in this imaginary conversation—for it can scarcely have been other than imaginary—Fletcher chose for his purpose representative types which, for violent disagreement of opinion, could not well have been bettered. Lord Cromarty represented Scottish Toryism, and also the negligible minority outside the Whigs who favoured an incorporating union with England, while Fletcher represented—Fletcher. Of the two Englishmen, Musgrave was an excellent example of the broadminded, intelligent, and moderate English politician; while no better selection than Seymour could have been made of John Bull in his aspect as a virulent hater of foreigners in general, and of Scots in particular, and as a stout upholder of the principle, "My country right or wrong".

The form of the essay is an adaptation of the conversational convention, of which a classic example is Plato's *Republic*. It was a convention that was soon to be used to good effect in the pages of the *Spectator* and the *Tatler*; and it is not too much to say that, for purity of style, Fletcher's essay will bear favourable comparison with the English examples of Augustan literature. The matter is characterized by boldness of speculation, ingeniousness of argument, and cogency of reasoning. It was easy, of course, for Fletcher to catch his opponents tripping in their objections to his notions, for any author of ordinary ingenuity can set up Aunt Sallies to be knocked down at his pleasure. But, as in everything else that he wrote, so in this essay, Fletcher never treads the beaten path. Impracticable his opponents might call his ideas (as indeed some of them were), but the novelty and independence of his views could never be questioned. The theory of government here advanced, and the philosophy of politics and economics which it embodies, are well worth more than passing attention even at the present time. It is remarkable how closely some of the subjects discussed have a bearing upon the politics and economics of today.

He commences the "conversation" by telling how he met by chance Cromarty and Musgrave, when walking in the Mall; and how the Earl asked him to dine at his lodgings in Whitehall, from which they had a good view of "the Thames and City of London". The view gave an excuse for a discussion on the natural advantages possessed by London as a capital city.

The Thames, "this most gentle and navigable river", in combination with "the excellent genius and industrious inclinations of the English people", had raised "this glorious city" to an unequalled height, said Lord Cromarty.

"You are in the right, my Lord," replied Sir Christopher, who then developed the theme from the standpoint of the city's geographical situation.

"That which is to be admired", remarked Fletcher, "is the perfect peace and tranquillity in which the inhabitants live. . . . But that which charms me most is the liberty and rights they are possessed of in matters civil and religious." They have many advantages, such as the transactions of Parliament; the judgments in Westminster Hall; the business of "the Exchange, Navigation, and Commerce"; the affairs and diversions of the Court; "together with the recreations and pleasures of the town".

"These last words", said Sir Christopher, "have spoiled all."

The "corruption of manners . . . has infected the whole nation, and must at length bring both the city and nation to ruin . . . Experience has taught us that no human prudence can preserve the manners of men living in great cities from extraordinary corruption, and that where great power, riches, and numbers of men are brought together, they not only introduce an universal depravation of manners, but destroy all good government and bring ruin and desolation upon a people."

"What great corruptions do you find in this place?" asked the Earl.

So vast a city, was the reply, affords innumerable opportunities for the indulgence of vice. "Even the poorest sort of both sexes are daily tempted to all manner of lewdness, by infamous ballads sung in every corner of the streets."

"One would think", said the Earl, "these last were of no consequence."

"I knew a very wise man," remarked Fletcher, meaning himself, "so much of Sir Christopher's sentiment that he believed if a man were permitted to make all the ballads, he need not care who should make the laws of a nation."

"In this city", resumed Sir Christopher, "gamesters, stockjobbers, jockies and wagerers" make now "the most considerable figure. . . . In the summer they infest all the places of diversion throughout England, and may be justly called the missionaries of the city."

"Sure," said the Earl, "remedies may be found for many of these abuses." And he went on to explain what might be done.

"But who is to do this?" asked Sir Christopher. "It would be dangerous to forbid gaming, which consumes so much of the time and takes up the thoughts of a great number of men, who, if they had not that diversion, might probably employ their leisure in thinking too much upon affairs of State."

"Might not we play, like the Turks, only to pass the time?" asked the Earl.

"No," was the reply, "for you have to deal with Christians who have a Christian liberty to play for money, provided they do not abuse it." And the contagion spreads even to their representatives in Parliament.

"Sir Christopher's observations", said Fletcher, "are very impartial."

"The Justices of the Peace will inform you," went on Sir Christopher, "of a thousand evils which wholly proceed from the great number of the inhabitants and vast extent of our buildings, where all manner of crimes are easily concealed. Besides, the poor and indigent are so numerous in this place, that the ill practices to which men are tempted by poverty are but too frequent. And the luxury of all other ranks and orders of men makes every one hasten to grow rich, and consequently leads them to betray all kind of trust reposed in them. In a word, this city abounds with all manners of temptations to evil: extreme poverty, excessive riches, great pleasures, infinite bad examples of unpunished and successful crimes."

Here Sir Edward Seymour joined the company, and the Earl presented Fletcher as "his countryman and old acquaintance", adding, with a smile, that Fletcher was one of those who, in the last Session of the Scots Parliament, had "opposed the interest of the Court"; which fact, Fletcher suggested, could hardly recommend him to Sir Edward Seymour.

"It seems", said Sir Edward, addressing Fletcher, "you are one who signalized yourself in the late Session of your Parliament, by framing Utopias and new models of government, under the name of 'limitations', in which you have the honour to be seconded and assisted by several men of quality of about two or three and twenty years of age" (the young men, in fact, to whom Fletcher's "letter" was addressed), "whose long experience and consummate prudence in publick affairs" (note the heavy irony attributed to Seymour) "could not but produce wonderful schemes of government."

This attack on the young nobles who had formed the backbone of the Country party in the last Session of the Scottish Parliament, initiated a discussion on the merits and demerits of young men generally, in the conduct of public affairs, Fletcher vigorously defending youth, and Seymour charging it with ignorance and arrogance.

Are not the talents of young men, Fletcher asked, better employed in Parliament than they would be if they were wasted in a

Court with all its temptations? The only temptation in Parliament is bribery, "or the ambition of getting a place by arts they are unacquainted with". And if they are good speakers, it is not to be imagined "how much their pleading for justice with that sincerity and unaffected eloquence so natural to youth, does inflame the minds of men to all kind of virtue".

"You begin to declaim," sneered Seymour, "as if they overheard you. But you must not think such stuff will have any influence upon me, or that I am so credulous (as) to believe that boys of those years can have any right notions of government, an art which demands the longest experience and greatest practice."

This statement Fletcher rebutted, on the ground that if young men are capable of understanding mathematics, natural philosophy, the art of reasoning, and metaphysical speculations, they are surely capable of understanding the less difficult study of the art of government. It is true that by the existing system of education, young men are addicted to these abstruse studies when their time might be better employed in acquiring moral and civil knowledge. But that is due to the fact that the art of government has been regarded as a kind of knowledge "dangerous to be learnt except by those who are advanced in years". It is an advantage for young men to find out for themselves what is right, or what is amiss, in government, because they themselves have never been engaged in the ill administration of affairs, nor habituated to bad customs and indirect practices, nor biased by selfish ends. Also, in their zeal for doing things that need doing, they are undoubtedly superior to older men. And if they despise the "ridiculous vanity of great titles which is the peculiar folly of this age", think how useful they can be to their friends or to their country, to which they have thus early devoted their talents! These are the men whose experience later in their lives will be valued, rather than the experience of those "who are only skilled in the pernicious practices that tend to destroy the public liberty".

"Still declaiming!" here broke in Sir Edward, "and what does it all amount to? Nothing more than a claim for lack of experience and the violent disposition of youth."

"But", said Fletcher, "when these are corrected by the advice, and controlled by the votes, of men of riper years, do you still think them dangerous?"

" I do."

"Would they not be more dangerous if the old men had only the power of advising, and that, for example, in the Senate of a Commonwealth, all things were to be determined by the votes of the young men?"

"Certainly."

"Would there not be yet greater danger, if the young men had the disposal of all power and advantages", and the old men, in order to get these places, had to flatter the young men and give advice which they knew would please them, and at the same time be pernicious to the State?

"Who can doubt it?"

And then Fletcher, by supposing that these young men decided to choose one of their own number, and give him unlimited power, led up to the situation created by a young Prince in a monarchical system, as being as great a menace to the well-being of the State as the young men in power whom the old men flattered. But (continued Fletcher) what was it in the conduct of the young Scottish noblemen and the proceedings of the Parliament in general that, in Sir Edward's opinion, gave grounds for censure?

"Why", said Seymour, the talk about such limitations on a Successor "as tend to take away that dependence which your nation ought always to have upon us, as a much greater and more powerful people".

This naturally gave Fletcher the opportunity he sought, to define the true relations between the two countries.

"We are an independent nation," he declared. The mistake of Scotsmen since the Union of the Crowns had been to neglect making such conditions with their Kings as to preserve the power and reputation of Scotland. They were now at last seeking to repair the omission, and thus secure "the honour and sovereignty of our Crown and Kingdom, the freedom, frequency, and power of our Parliament, together with our religion, liberty, and trade, from either English or foreign influence" (a declaration which succinctly embodies Fletcher's ideals, and a phrase which, as we have seen, was frequently used in the 1703 Session of the Scots Parliament).

"Heyday!" exclaimed Sir Edward, "all in a fret". "Here is a fine cant indeed. Independent nation! Honour of our Crown and what not! Do you consider what proportion you bear to England? Not one to forty in rents of land. Besides, our greatest riches arise from trade and manufactures, which you want."

"True," allowed Fletcher. But consider certain indisputable facts. Then follows a lengthy recital of Scotland's grievances: how the loss of trade had ruined Scottish agriculture; how the Union of the Crowns had destroyed the flourishing commerce which Scotland had previously enjoyed with the Continent; how Scottish money that had previously been spent at home was now spent in England; how the country was totally neglected "like a farm managed by servants"; how the disorders of the Civil War had given the finishing blow to her resources ("since that time we have had neither spirit nor liberty, nor trade, nor money, among us"); how, during the time of "the Usurper, Cromwell", there was certainly money in the country derived from the upkeep of "those forces that kept us in subjection", but that "this was a deceitful substance, not unlike a plumpness in the natural body proceeding from disease"; how the business of a Scots Minister is now to get as much money as he can from an impoverished nation during his term of office, for well he knows that schemes for enriching the nation take time for their maturity, and, for that reason, are of no interest to him during the term of his administration.

"I take all this freedom", he went on, "before the Earl of Cromarty, tho' he be a Scots Minister of State, because 'tis well known, avarice is none of his faults, and that no person in our Government is more ready to promote any new and solid project of improvement."

"I am obliged for the good character you give me," said the Earl, "but very sorry I can promote none of your projects. They are, I fear, too great for our nation, and seem rather contrived to take place in a Platonic Commonwealth than in the present corruption of things."

Fletcher agreed that little could be done in the age in which they lived. But though this was the result partly of ignorance, it was due mainly to a "meanness of spirit" which prevented them from applying the true remedies, if they were the least difficult or dangerous. And nothing showed this lack of courage more than the attempt to "prosecute any considerable end by ineffectual and disproportionate means". For example, look at the condition of Scotland. The causes of her distresses were obvious, and the remedy was equally obvious, namely, to place real, instead of nominal power, in the hands of her Parliament.

"But", rejoined the Earl, "if this remedy is granted, what power or authority is left to the Prince?"

"As great power", said Fletcher, "as Princes formerly enjoyed in most of the limited monarchies of Europe."

This did not satisfy the Earl, who pointed out that the withdrawal from the Prince of the nomination of military officers and the distribution of pensions, would be an encroachment upon his power, and would lessen the grandeur of his Court.

And reasonably so, urged Fletcher. Besides, where no Court is, no lessening of its grandeur can occur.

And so the argument proceeded between the two until Sir Edward Seymour intervened. "And what hopes", he asked scornfully, "can you have of enjoying" the limitations that may be placed upon your Prince, when he may be assisted by the power and riches "of a far greater nation which is highly concerned to take them away?"

"I cannot think", replied Fletcher, "that the people of England are obliged by their interest to oppose these limitations, unless they think themselves concerned in interest to make us at all times their secret enemies, and ready to embrace every opportunity of declaring ourselves openly for such."

"We shall run a great risk, indeed," said Sir Edward sarcastically, "in doing so."

"Sir," was the reply, "no man is more fully persuaded than I am of the great disproportion there is between the power of the one and the other nation, especially in the present way of making war." But what if we are driven to the necessity of taking by the hand any Power that will assist us? And the only way to avoid that danger is to do justice both to yourselves and to us, "by not opposing any conditions we may make with the Successor to our Crown."

"In my opinion", said Lord Cromarty, "the only remedy is a union of the two nations."

To this Fletcher replied by recounting the different occasions upon which union had been attempted, only to fail owing to the disinclination of the English nation to unite with Scotland, except when danger threatened or policy dictated union; and when the danger passed, or the policy matured, England invariably retired from the negotiations. The Scots had now come to the conclusion that union would prove no remedy for their ills, but would instead increase the poverty of their country.

"How, I pray?" asked the Earl.

"I am of opinion", replied Fletcher, "that by an incorporating union, as they call it, of the two nations, Scotland will become more poor than ever."

"Why so?"

"Because—" and here Fletcher recapitulated his well-known views about London, by its superior attractions, drawing like a loadstone his countrymen who had good estates, from their native land. "No Scotsman who expects any public employment will ever set his foot in Scotland; and every man that makes his fortune in England will purchase lands in that Kingdom; our trade, which is the bait that covers the hook, will be only an inconsiderable retail in a poor, remote, and barren country, where the richest of our nobility and gentry will no longer reside."

"A fallacy", declared the Earl, for "you do not reflect that we shall then be a part of Britain: England will be increased by the accession of Scotland, and both those names lost in that of Britain." And Scotsmen will then be qualified for any office or employment in Britain, "and may trade or purchase in any port of the island."

But you forget, argued Fletcher, that it is the interest of the northern part of the island that we have mainly to consider, if a bargain is made on its behalf. And the union of several countries under one Government will inevitably result in those more remote from the seat of government being neglected, and made subservient to the interests of the others, unless "the prosperity and happiness of the different nations" are considered "as well as of the whole united body". But a "distinct sovereignty" always enables a people to retain some of their natural wealth (e.g., the Scottish fisheries), and leaves them without excuse if they do not turn their resources to good account. So that, if provision can be made for preventing the exhaustion of our money by the attendance of Scotsmen at Court, and to "take away the influence of English Ministers upon our affairs", why, then, "no condition of men will be more happy. For we shall then be possessed of liberty; shall administer our own affairs and be free from the corruptions of the Court. Also, we shall be closely allied with England, and all enemies by sea and land will find it in their interest to maintain friendly relations with us. Surely this would be a much happier condition than can be secured by the projects of union that have hitherto been proposed."

And so the argument proceeded between the advocate and the opponent of union, without either succeeding in convincing the other that he was mistaken. On the question of trading advantages, Fletcher remarked, "I cannot see what advantage a free trade to the English plantations would bring us except a further exhausting of our people, and the utter ruin of all our merchants who should vainly pretend to carry that trade from the English:" a statement which the Earl was unable to rebut.

But, Lord Cromarty argued, the internal trade of the whole island would be greatly stimulated, especially in view of the wealth of the North and the West of England.

Purely "accidental causes", said Fletcher, for the North possesses lead and coal mines, and the West tin and lead. "Consider", he went on, "that Wales, the only country that had ever united with England . . . is still the only place of that Kingdom which has no considerable commerce, tho' possessed of one of the best ports in the whole island; a sufficient demonstration that trade is not a necessary consequence of an union with England." And he added, "Trade is now become the golden ball, for which all nations of the world are contending." Every nation was trying to get the trade of the world, and every city to draw trade to itself. And the English were no less guilty of these attempts than any other trading nation.

"How so?" asked Sir Christopher Musgrave. For his part, he thought the English "the frankest dealers and the justest traders in the world".

To this Fletcher replied by citing the English treatment of Scotland over the Darien business, and her general policy towards her "own colony" in Ireland, as instances to the contrary. And he recounted certain historical incidents in the relations between England and Ireland, as proof of the unfairness of the English attitude towards Ireland in the regulation of trade. All this went to show that a small nation which united with a greater, can have no real security for the observance of the conditions unless these are guaranteed by a third nation. And Sir Christopher would surely prefer to hear nothing further about a union between England and Scotland, if it had to be guaranteed by, for example, Holland or France.

"True," said Sir Christopher, but guarantees in treaties of peace are only proper between nations that are not united, for unions of nations, especially incorporating unions, "suppose no breach of conditions". . . . It will certainly be our interest to "observe the conditions on which we unite with Scotland".

"Do you think", asked Fletcher, "that you always follow your interests?"

"I must acknowledge we do not."

"Then if, at any time, you should depart from your true interest in this matter, we shall want a guarantee and find none. . . . How your colonies in America are treated is well known to all men. You never could unite with Normandy, which has conquered you, nor with any part of France that you had conquered. . . . You could not unite with the States of Holland when England was likewise a Republic. And since the time of the late Revolution, which was effected by the assistance of the States and saved these nations from utter ruin, you can hardly endure the name of a Dutchman, and have treated them on all occasions with such scurrilous expressions as are peculiar to the generality of your people." Their hatred of all foreigners "and inveterate malice against the Scots" would be unbelievable if it were not so notorious. "I know very well that men of gravity and good breeding among you are not guilty of scurrilous reflections on any nation.

But when we consider the case in question, we must have a just regard to the temper and general disposition of the people."

"All in a flame", Sir Edward Seymour, at these words, broke out, "What a pother is here about an union with Scotland, of which all the advantages we shall have will be no more than what a man gets by marrying a beggar, with a louse for her portion!"

"If Sir Edward Seymour had spoken these words in the House of Commons" (he had as a matter of fact), said Fletcher, turning to the Earl and Sir Christopher, "I might not take notice of them, or question his freedom of speech in that place, but since he is pleased to express himself after this manner in a private conversation, I shall likewise take the liberty to say that I wonder he is not afraid such language should make us suspect him not to be descended of the noble family whose name he bears" (that, in short, he was "no gentleman").

"What account", blustered Sir Edward, "should we make of Scotland, so often trampled under foot by our armies? . . . Of late did not the very scum of our nation conquer you?"

"Yes," said Fletcher quietly, "after they had, with our assistance, conquered the King and the nobility and gentry of England. And yet that which you call a conquest was a dispute between parties and not a national quarrel."

"'Twas inseparable from the fortune of our Edwards", sneered Seymour, "to triumph over your nation."

"Do you mean Edward of Carnarvon, and his victory at Bannockburn?" asked Fletcher ironically.

"No, I mean Edward the First and Third whose heroic actions no princes have ever equalled."

Fletcher had his answer ready. But at this stage Sir Christopher Musgrave intervened to stop the bickering, and to resume the serious discussions about union. He wished Fletcher to develop further his opinions about Ireland. His own viewpoint was that, by her geographical situation and her commodious harbours, Ireland had trading advantages over England which might have serious consequences for England under free trade and equal privileges.

"Ay," remarked Fletcher, "trade is the constant stumbling block and ball of contention". He proceeded to argue that on

Sir Christopher's assumptions, it would be better to exclude Ireland altogether from trade. Why not, indeed, bring all Irishmen over to England? England would then rid herself of one unprofitable and troublesome country. But in that case, the French might take possession of the uninhabited country. A port in Munster would be useful to Louis, and could be easily held by him. And what then? And, pursuing that solution of the difficulty further, suppose we consider Ireland sunk in the sea? Then you will cease to fear "either that they may set up for themselves or carry away the trade from England".

"Similarly, would it not be in the interest of England to bring the inhabitants of the six northern counties of England into the South, and then sink those counties in the sea also? For trade will certainly increase, and be more easily managed, when brought within a less compass." "Besides," he added humorously, "you would then have so broad a ditch to secure you against the Scots, that you would be rid of any trouble from them also."

"If nature," retorted Sir Christopher, with equal humour, "had made such a ditch from the beginning, the happiness of England would have been complete."

The Welsh people, too, went on Fletcher, in the same bantering strain, might be much more advantageously employed in trading in England "than in keeping goats at home, and your union with them become much stricter by bringing them nearer London, and then I think that country might likewise be sunk with advantage."

Going a step still further, would it not, by parity of reasoning, be a good thing to bring all the important trade of the world into one city, and for all mankind to live within and about that place?

By this *reductio ad absurdum* Fletcher presses home his argument against centralization of government. "For what end", he asks, "did God create such vast tracts of land capable of producing so great variety and abundance of all things necessary and useful to men, except for the good of mankind? . . . Trade is not the only thing to be considered in the government of nations. And justice is due even in point of trade from one nation to another. For every good Government has always encouraged industry, because all mankind have a right to the fruits of their own labour. And on that account, all Governments which put discouragements on the industry of their subjects are not upon a right foot, but violent and consequently unjust."

"Soft and fair," interrupted Sir Christopher; "the consequences of these maxims reach further than perhaps you imagine. We must not rely too much upon our own speculations, or think the world can ever be rightly governed; but must take things as they are, and consider the interest of the society in which we live. And if any profitable trade be in the possession of our neighbours, we may endeavour to dispossess them of that advantage for the good of our own society."

"Tho' this should be granted," said Fletcher, "yet you ought not to deny to a people, who, like Ireland, live under your Government, the fruits of their industry."

"Not at all," was Sir Christopher's reply, "for as I told you, they may break with us and set up a distinct Government in opposition to our right, and perhaps with the ruin of this nation" (prophetic words except for the "ruin"!).

"What can tempt and provoke them so much to do so as unjust usage?"

"But the surest way", persisted Sir Christopher, "is to put it out of their power to separate from us. We have a right to use them at discretion because we have conquered them."

"Then you have a right to do injustice?"

"It's not injustice because 'tis our right. . . . These communities which are most remote from the seat of government, ought not to expect an equal participation of liberty and immunities with those that lie at less distance." And Sir Christopher proceeded to cite ancient Rome, in support of his thesis that the Imperial City should have greater privileges than the provinces.

"Very proper," was Fletcher's comment, for retaining the dominion of the world, but not for the happiness of the subject nations. And then he quoted Sir Christopher against himself, in proof of the argument that good manners are corrupted by bringing together large numbers of men and immense riches into one city. "Rome, the greatest of all, incessantly disturbed her neighbours for seven hundred years; and after the conquest of almost all the known world, was corrupted by excess of riches and power, and spread the infection over all the parts of that Empire," which at length brought in the barbarians and deluged the world in blood.

Yet it was necessary to have a strong central Government. How, then, were the two conceptions to be reconciled? That was Sir Christopher's poser, and Fletcher replied by sketching for him the division of Europe that seemed to him to accord with natural boundaries, and thus tended to reconcile decentralization with safety.

"What all this tends to," said Sir Christopher, "I cannot imagine."

Fletcher then enlarged upon his theme, by showing that in his division of Europe into ten parts, geographical boundaries coincided with differences of language, and with differences of "temper" and "dispositions".

"Sir," interrupted Sir Edward Seymour impatiently, "are you undertaking to teach us geography? For what else can you mean by such a division of Europe?"

Lord Cromarty, too, confessed himself to be in a "maze", and desired that these speculations might be pursued further.

If Governments so equal in strength as is suggested, were established, argued Fletcher, "mankind might certainly live in greater peace than they do: especially if these Governments were by mutual alliances obliged to preserve the common tranquillity".

"But", remarked Sir Christopher, "what is there to prevent one half of them combining against the other half?"

"A perpetual peace", said Fletcher, "is not to be preserved among men; yet, certainly, some constitutions of government are better fitted to maintain the public tranquillity than others". But the most frequent causes of wars, such as the Succession of Princes, and "their ambitious designs", would be fewer, and if wars were unavoidable, at least they would be shorter and less bloody.

"If you can show", retorted Sir Christopher, "how so happy a state of things may be introduced into the world, you will do the greatest service imaginable to mankind. For matters are now brought to such a pass that in every war, almost all Europe and America, with a great part of Asia and Africa, become engaged."

"You are in the right," agreed Fletcher. For these "universal" wars were said to have caused during the past thirty years a reduc-

[*199*]

tion of no less than a fifth in the " value " of Europe. "For wars, besides that they are become universal, are now wholly managed by the force and power of money, and by that means most grievously oppress and affect, not only the places that are the theatres of action, but even the remotest village and most solitary cottage".... "I think mankind might be best preserved from such convulsions and misery if, instead of framing Governments with regard only to a single society, as I believe legislators have hitherto done, we should constitute such as would be no less advantageous to our neighbours than ourselves."

"You talk strangely," said Sir Christopher, "as if our advantage were not frequently inconsistent with that of our neighbours."

"I am of opinion," was the reply, "that the true interest and good of any nation is the same with that of any other. I do not say that one society ought not to repel the injuries of another; but that no people ever did any injustice to a neighbouring nation except by mistaking their own interest."

"You talk", retorted Sir Christopher, "of justice, but I speak of advantage."

"If you go about", said Fletcher, "to take away by force any advantage that belongs to a neighbouring people, you not only do injustice to them, but injure yourself by the example."

But this was a novel doctrine, to which Sir Christopher Musgrave (and the type for which he stood) could not subscribe: that justice towards neighbouring countries and advantage to one's own country were in the long run as cause is to effect. "A citizen in the service of his country", he urged, "is not obliged to the same scruples as in his private affairs, and must be true to his public trust and take care that the Commonwealth suffers no prejudice."

"Then", asked Fletcher, "no man can be a good citizen of a particular Commonwealth, and a citizen of the world: no man can be a true friend to his country and to mankind at the same time?"

"I confess", admitted Sir Christopher, "this conclusion naturally follows, but we may not dispense with the interest of our country as with our own; and you know the precepts contained in the Sermon on the Mount relate to the actions of private men."

"Do you think then," asked Fletcher, "that one nation cannot do injustice to another?"

"Yes, when that which is done is to the prejudice of both."

"And do you not also think that one nation may make an unjust war against another?"

"Yes."

"Then—" and Fletcher goes on to entangle his opponent in admissions tending to destroy his argument. But, turning to another aspect of the question, they now discuss the more practical means of abolishing wars.

"The most effectual way", said Fletcher, is "that all such Governments as are of a sufficient force to defend themselves, should be rendered either incapable or unfit to make conquests."

"Impossible!" exclaimed Sir Edward Seymour, to take away the tendency to be found in "the best of men to extend the empire of their country".

And now Fletcher returns to his conception of the division of Europe into ten portions, and suggests that if each of these portions had "ten or twelve sovereign cities, well fortified within its territories, each city possessing and governing the adjacent districts", such a Government, "strengthened with forts in passes and other convenient places, might be very capable to defend itself" and yet be "altogether unfit for conquest".

"Why so?"

Elaborating his theme, he argues that "a conquest divided into twelve parts would be of little account, since they could not be made adjacent to the several cities to which they ought to belong".

"But", urged Sir Edward, "such conquered places could be governed in common to the advantage of the whole union."

"That would be like a possession in common, for which no man has any particular affection, and on that account lies always neglected."

"But you talk of sovereign cities. I fancy you mean republics, which is nothing to us who live under the benign influence of monarchy."

"You may suppose these cities", said Fletcher, "to be the capitals of sovereign and independent kingdoms or countries. For of such sovereignties, united under one monarch, we have many examples. The Prince could keep his Court in each of them successively, or, what would be better, he could reside in the country." This would obviate the necessity of harbouring "a crew of lazy, profligate, and vicious wretches, fit only to render his Court a mere sink of corruption, and a seminary to propagate all measures of vice thro' the whole nation".

Proceeding to reason "concerning the excellency of those Governments which consist of divers sovereignties, united for their common defence, whether cities or kingdoms: whether independent already or to be made so, in order to put such a design in execution; whether governed by a Prince or by a great Council of Delegates", he undertakes to argue from the particular to the general, and to show how all such schemes for united action might be extended for the common good of mankind. "One would think that politicians, who ought to be the best of all moral philosophers, should have considered what a citizen of the world is." Certainly, among the ancients, the Achaian League contained the germ of this idea, but it was nipped in the bud by "the mighty power of the Roman Commonwealth." Even in Constitutions less framed for conquest than others, there were insufficient safeguards for restraining the lust for territorial acquisitions, "as the examples of Venice and Sparta demonstrate". . . . . "This I think should have been obvious to all legislators: that whatever contrives to make people very rich and great, lays the foundation of their misery and destruction, which in a short time will necessarily overtake them. . . . No condition of men or public societies is durable and lasting except such as are established in mediocrity. . . . In small governments, laws may be duly executed, and the manners of men in a great measure preserved from corruption; but because such governments are not of force sufficient to defend themselves, a considerable number of them should be united together for the common safety; by which union, they will be enabled to resist a powerful invasion and yet remain incapable of conquest."

Take, for example, the three Kingdoms of England, Scotland, and Ireland. If a great army of enemies could be landed near London, they would be exposed to "the fate of a single battle". But if good forts were erected "in the most considerable passes, and twelve cities with all the seaports well fortified, the loss of many battles would not determine the matter". And with the navy

intercepting the supplies of the enemy, "we might defend ourselves against all our neighbours". Moreover, our militias might
be usefully employed in assisting our neighbours to form similar
leagues on the Continent, "and a gradual propagation of such
excellent governments would become easy when mankind should
be convinced of the great happiness and security they would enjoy
by living under them". There was always the possibility that these
leagues might make war upon one another, "on occasion of a
sudden pique, or to take revenge for some unneighbourly action;
yet such wars could not be lasting, because nothing but hopes of
making acquisition and conquests can make them so".

Turning to the advantage of having his "twelve cities governing themselves happily and virtuously, instead of one great vicious
and ungovernable city", Fletcher again argues for decentralization.

"But", said Sir Christopher, "to reduce London within the
compass of the old walls seems a thing impracticable."

"Not", was the reply, "if London were made the capital of the
neighbouring counties only."

That would be an injustice, commented Sir Christopher.

It has been a greater injustice, retorted Fletcher, for one city to
have retained so long, privileges that "ought to have been divided
among the considerable cities of the nation". Besides the danger
from invasion, owing to the lack of fortified cities, think of the
corruption of manners which this vicious and profligate city dif-
fuses in every part!

"I did not foresee", said Sir Christopher, "what use you would
make of my complaint against the depravation of manners that
reigns in this town, but acknowledge the consequences you draw
to be just, and that if we design to diminish the corruption, we
must lessen the city."

"What visions have we here!" broke in Sir Edward Seymour.
"Destroy the greatest and most glorious city of the world to prosecute a whimsical project!"

"Sir," was the reply, "you have heard what I have answered to
Sir Christopher, and, besides, do you not think the remoter parts
of England injured by being obliged to have recourse to London
for almost everything, and particularly for justice? Do you not

think them wronged in that almost all the treasure of England is yearly laid out in this place, and by that means the substance of the other parts exhausted, and their rents and revenues diminished?"

The national welfare is not thereby affected, argued Seymour, to which argument Fletcher demurred. "This vast city", he said, "is like the head of a rickety child, which by drawing to itself the nourishment that should be distributed in due proportion to the rest of the languishing body, becomes so overcharged, that frenzy and death unavoidably ensue. . . . That London should draw the riches and government of the three Kingdoms to the south-east corner of this island, is in some degree as unnatural as for one city to possess the riches and government of the world."

In support of his case for decentralization, Fletcher goes on to enumerate its various advantages. "So many different seats of government will highly encourage virtue. . . . So many different seats of government will highly tend to the improvement of all arts and sciences." Unlike a centralized Government which little values any interest but its own, "studying rather how to weaken" the other parts, "in order to make sure of their subjection", and which has more business to transact "than any one man can rightly execute", the offices of these lesser governments, extending only over a moderate number of people, "will be duly executed, and many men have occasions put into their hands of doing good to their fellow-citizens."

"I perceive now", said Sir Edward, "the tendency of all this discourse. On my conscience, he has contrived the whole scheme to no other end than to set his own country on an equal foot with England and the rest of the world."

"To tell you the truth," was the reply, "the insuperable difficulty I found of making my country happy by any other way led me insensibly to the discovery of these things which, if I mistake not, have no other tendency than to render not only my own country but all mankind as happy as the imperfections of human nature will admit." A state of separation from England would involve bloody and destructive wars. And if united in any manner which involved government from London, "we must of necessity fall under the miserable and languishing condition of all places that depend upon a remote seat of government." But where lies the prejudice, if the three Kingdoms were united "in so equal a foot as for ever to take away all suspicion and jealousy of separation?" (2) Every part would bear its due proportion towards the security and defence of the union, "which will preserve us so effectually from those two great calamities, war and corruption of manners. This is the only just and rational kind of union. All other conditions are but the unjust subjection of one people to another."

The announcement that dinner was served brought the "conversation" to an end, and "I", says Fletcher, "returned to my lodgings, having promised to meet them again at another time to discourse further on the same subject."

Such, in substance, is Fletcher's best-known and most attractively written essay, which, in form and matter, must be ranked high in the domain of literature and political speculation. It is a cleverly contrived means of publishing his views on political problems, against a background of conventional objections, which he demolishes as they arise. It will be observed that his method is Scottish, that is, deductive, and the cleverness with which he manœuvres his opponents into damaging admissions, is noteworthy. They are forced to admit his premises, and are compelled to accept the conclusions to which they lead. He is thus enabled to make out a good case for his speculations, fantastic as these appeared to most of his contemporaries. Yet, once more, he was only ahead of his time; in some, at any rate, of his suggestions. His brain was teeming with ideas which had entered the minds of few, if any, of his political associates, whether in England or Scotland. Unlike most of them—and it may without injustice be said unlike most politicians of the present day—he had laid the foundations of his political aspirations in an intensive study of the history of ancient Greece and Rome, and he had not hesitated to draw from classic examples the lessons which he sought to apply to the conditions prevailing in his time. For he never forgot that first principles are constant, however varied their expression. Their application to circumstances of greater complexity then ever engaged the attention of the City States of the ancient world, such as those which are now troubling the world, does not alter their fundamental character.

There is nothing insular in Fletcher's viewpoint, for his ultimate goal is the happiness of mankind, which, he conceives, would certainly follow the abolition of war, the reformation of morals, and what is more fully understood only to-day, the recognition in political and economic affairs of the interdependence of nations. And all these objects, he speculates, might be achieved by his plan of decentralization, whereby the incentive for offensive wars would be removed, while the capacity for defence would be powerfully increased. Also, in view of the fact that the concentration of population in one centre and its accumulation of wealth give rise to evils which corrupt the whole Commonwealth, his scheme for local self-government would, he thought, save the nation from social decay, and preserve for the self-governing units the springs of justice and the stimulus for progress in the arts and commerce: the preservation, in short, of their soul. And it need scarcely be remarked that, since his day, in this country, at any rate, his plan of district government, as opposed to centralization, has taken shape in concrete forms, which differ from his plans only as the widely different conditions have necessarily dictated. His extension of the principle to nations has become familiar to English ears by the term "self-determination", of American origin but European application. Only, his plan certainly did not connote the political exclusiveness and the economic self-sufficiency which have accompanied this "self-determination" with such disastrous consequences for all nations alike.

His speeches in the Scottish Parliament emphasize one aspect of Scottish nationalism; his views, as expressed in the London *Conversation,* lay stress upon other and less parochial considerations. Separation between England and Scotland he regarded as a calamity. An incorporating union he esteemed to be only a perpetuation, perhaps in an aggravated form, of the political subjugation of which he complained. Nothing, in his opinion, could give abiding satisfaction to Scotland, and, by implication, in the long run, to England as well, but a union which embodied the principles, at once of complete self-government in national affairs, and no less complete co-operation in matters, such as defence, trade, and other affairs in which the common interests of both nations were involved (3).

Chapter XVI

THE INTERLUDE

THE prorogation of the Scottish Parliament was followed by a strange spectacle. Scottish statesmen were seen scampering —the word fits, for it was an undignified proceeding—to London, to look after their own interests: some to make sure of their places and pensions, others to see whether places and pensions were likely to come their way.

"All parties", says the disgusted Lockhart, "strove who should outdo one another in paying their respect and shewing their sub-mission to the goodwill and pleasure of the Duke of Marlborough and Lord Godolphin. The Queen, indeed, for fashion sake, was sometimes addressed too; but such application was made to these two lords, that it was obvious to all the world how much the Scots affairs depended on them. I myself, out of curiosity, went once to their levies, where I saw the Commissioner, Chancellor, Secretary, and other great men of Scotland hang on near an hour, and when admitted, treated with no more civility than one gentleman pays another's *valet de chambre*, and for which the Scots have none to blame but themselves; for had they valued them-selves as they ought to have done, and not so meanly and sneak-ingly prostituted their honour and country to the will and pleasure of the English Ministry, they'd never have presumed to usurp such a dominion over Scotland, as openly and avowedly to consult upon and determine in Scots affairs " (1).

That was just, in effect, what Fletcher had been saying, and continued to say, all the time he was in Parliament. The events that followed the break-up of the Scottish Parliament drove home, by illustrations, the text upon which he had been preaching during the Session of 1703. No one knew what was now going to happen. The fate of the Act of Security, and equally the fate of those who had supported it, and those who had opposed it, hung in the balance. They were all (like Queen Anne herself) in the hands of Godolphin and Marlborough. Crow they ever so loudly on their own perches in Edinburgh, the Scottish nobles spoke with bated breath in the sacred precincts of the Court. It was, indeed, a humiliating situation. Some of them were men whose lineage made the ancestry of many of their English compeers a thing of yesterday by comparison. And they could boast of cultural acquirements and political capacity which placed them on, at least, an equal footing with the English courtiers who held the disposal of their careers in the hollow of their hands. It was really futile to pretend that a nation whose leading statesmen were compelled to hang around foreign ante-chambers, like clerks seeking a job, was an independent nation.

The taciturn and, therefore, trusted servant of four Sovereigns and, in his earlier years, the object of the romantic love of the last of the four, Godolphin wished to shape Scottish policy in the way that did greatest service to his country and to his Queen. Nor was it to be expected that Marlborough, his Scottish sub-title notwithstanding, would be any the less patriotic than Godolphin in his handling of the Scottish problem. Both were shrewd statesmen, and both were greatly concerned, at the moment, with the embarrassing complications which the proceedings in the Scottish Parliament had caused in relation to the question of the Succession. The Act of Security could not be conceded, because it left Scotland too much liberty of action for England's safety. Agreement on the Succession must be found in some other way. And the avenue that seemed to open up the best prospect of success was by a change of Ministers in Scotland.

Events had occurred which clearly pointed to that solution of the difficulty. Atholl, Seafield, and Tarbat, all men of Tory inclinations, had openly seceded from Queensberry, who was thus left to bear the brunt of English displeasure with his comparative lack of success. As if to accentuate Queensberry's isolation, Atholl had received his dukedom; Tarbat was now created Earl of Cromarty; and Seafield was left with a feeling of gratitude, if that is to be cynically interpreted as a lively sense of favours to come. These three noblemen had, indeed, made a pact with the Cavaliers; and when, with the Earl of Eglinton, they followed the pack to London, it was with the benison of the Cavaliers, and after the establishment of a common understanding. The defection of his colleagues naturally irritated Queensberry; and Atholl, with whom his relations during the last Session had been uniformly uneasy, became the particular target of his indignation. At this juncture he was provided with the means, as he thought, of damaging, by one stroke, Atholl's reputation, and dealing a deadly blow at the whole of the Cavalier party.

Simon Fraser of Lovat, a past-master in the arts of intrigue, and a maker of history in the first half of the eighteenth century, was about this time busily employed in fomenting a Jacobite conspiracy, in which he had adroitly managed to engage the interest of Louis of France, whither he had fled to escape the arm of the law. In pursuance of his designs, he came over to England, bearing with him three important letters from Mary of Modena, the widow of James II: one for the Duke of Hamilton, to be delivered by James Murray of Stanhope; one for the Duke of Gordon, which was delivered by John Murray of Abercairney; and the third, which he had "found the way to be master of", for the Duke of Atholl. The last was the letter that had a bearing on the important political issues that flowed from its delivery. It was addressed to "L. M——y", which, Lovat declared, signified "Lord Murray", the name by which Atholl was known at St. Germains. Armed with this letter, and actuated by vindictive hatred of his life-long enemy, Atholl, Lovat presented himself before Queensberry, and offered him the means, for a consideration, of being revenged upon Atholl. The direction of the letter was in a different handwriting from the text, and it seems probable, though the facts are uncertain, that, while the letter itself was genuine, the address was left blank, the intention being that it was to be directed, at the bearer's discretion, to any desirable magnate in Scotland who had Jacobite leanings. It was, in fact, directed to "L. M——y" by Lovat himself, with the double object of getting Atholl into trouble, and of reaping some substantial personal advantage.

Queensberry fell into the trap. Doubtful though he was of Lovat's good faith, he was convinced, or professed to be convinced, that the proof which the letter afforded of Atholl's trafficking with St. Germains was indisputable. He sent the letter at once to the Queen, without breaking the seal (her father's); and that was the genesis of what became known as the "Scotch Plot", or the "Scottish Conspiracy", which had a direct bearing upon the events that led straight to the union of the two Parliaments (2).

Atholl, an innocent and injured man, was, however, soon placed in a position to rebut the charges made against him. The facts of the case were wormed out of Lovat by Ferguson, the spy, whom we last met as Monmouth's chaplain, and whose mercenary hand had not lost its cunning in the intervening years; and Atholl was placed on his guard by Ferguson. Inevitably, the disclosures which followed led to Queensberry's discomfiture and disgrace; a new Commissioner and a new Ministry had to be found for Scotland. But how was this Ministry to be composed? The issues of the so-called " Scotch Plot" supplied the answer.

For the House of Lords had given their attention to what they professed to be the potential danger of a Jacobite attempt to foment an armed rising. Moreover, the whole of the supporters of the Act of Security lay under the suspicion of encouraging a rebellion by their demands. The Lords appointed a Committee to inquire into the circumstances of the "Plot". The Committee reported that, on the evidence placed before them, the proof of a dangerous conspiracy had been established; and further, that the conspiracy had been rendered possible by the fact that the Succession was still an unsettled question in Scotland. Also, they presented an address to the Queen, representing to her the urgency of a settlement of the Succession, and advocating towards that end a scheme of "union between the two nations."

The House of Commons, with a Tory majority, resented, or professed to resent, the initiative taken by the Lords, as an infringement of the rights inherent in the Crown alone. So a pretty quarrel ensued between the two Houses, the originator of the whole trouble meanwhile lurking in the easy hiding-places afforded by London, while Ministers were asking querulously where he was to be found.

All this time Atholl was in London, battling against his political opponents. Finding his strength unequal to the task, he appealed for assistance from his friends in Scotland. This was provided by the despatch of three leaders of the Country party—Roxburgh, Rothes, and Baillie of Jerviswood—in concert with the Cavaliers.

The main object of the mission (as conceived, at any rate, by the Cavaliers, some of whom, however, suspected the three Countrymen of going to London to promote their own interests) was to free the supporters of the Act of Security from the misrepresentations that had been made concerning them. The Countrymen, being untainted by Jacobitism, were better able to show clean hands than the Cavaliers, and to give convincing proofs that the so-called "Scotch Plot", which implied the indictment of a nation, had no existence in fact, except as a manifestation of individual disloyalty (3).

The disturbing news had reached Scotland that a proposal, attributed to the Earl of Stair, had been made to the Queen, to send troops to Scotland, and to suspend Parliamentary government in that country for the rest of Her Majesty's reign. The fact—or what appears to have been the fact—that the actual proposal was to meet the arrears of pay due to the army in Scotland out of the English Treasury, and to continue to maintain the army "upon foreign pay", sounds less alarming than the Jacobite (Lockhart's) version. But either of these plans was sufficiently prophetic of bitter trouble to cause grave concern to the Cavaliers and the Countrymen. Nor, indeed, could the Scottish Whigs view such an obvious declaration of dictatorship, to be followed perhaps by a mutiny of the soldiers, without serious misgivings. The proposal, however, was no sooner made than it was rejected as being palpably inexpedient. And on the question of suspending the Parliament, the Queen herself, at the audience she gave to the three members of the mission, declared that, on the contrary, the Parliament would sit "very soon". Moreover, she designed that it should settle the Succession without further delay. On which question, the three Countrymen, when asked their opinion, replied with characteristically Scottish caution (4).

The Queen was charmed with the young politicians from Scotland. Instead of the rough Caledonians whom she had expected to see, she gave audience to three cultured gentlemen with pleasing manners, and obviously endowed with political sagacity. The interview was the beginning of a better understanding on the Queen's part of Scottish politics, and possibly of a more exact appreciation of the Queen's difficulties by the Country party. Clearly, the

[*211*]

Ministers whom she and Godolphin were seeking to find, were those who would carry the Succession policy with as little friction in the Scottish Parliament as practicable. Could the Country party do it? They favoured the Hanoverian Succession for Scotland because it meant a Protestant Succession. But what of the inevitable price to be paid? What of the limitations laid down by the Act of Security? How was that stile to be cleared? Queensberry was ready to undertake the task once more, and the triumvirate thought that he would be "the man employed in all probability". . . . "There is no other to undertake it, because they know not upon what terms, for it is said they will be very insignificant ones." And the Country party knew well that "very insignificant" terms would never do for the Scottish Parliament in its existing mood. Many of the Country party would go into the Succession upon reasonable terms, "but not under Queenberry's direction" (5).

But Godolphin had, for the moment, no intention of employing Queensberry again, for his ill-success as Commissioner had weakened his position, and his reputation as a statesman had been damaged by the "Plot". He was indeed the last man who, at that juncture, was capable of swaying the unruly spirits in Edinburgh. Why not give a trial to a composite party, embracing elements which, while favourable to the Succession, would command the confidence of the patriots?

An adjustment of opposing views was not easy. Ultimately, however, a basis of agreement was reached, mainly through the instrumentality of James Johnston, whose zeal in procuring the Act in favour of the Company of Scotland had cost him his place, and the chance of further employment since his dismissal from office. He was a younger son of the Lord Warriston who was executed in the reign of Charles II, and for that reason, if for no other, the son was in favour with the Presbyterians. By Lockhart he is described as a "vile and execrable wretch" (Swift goes one better by calling him "one of the greatest knaves even in Scotland"), and by Macky as "a very honest man", who "would not tell a lie for the world"; from which clash of opinions the impartial historian may reasonably deduce the conclusion that Johnston was a good Whig, a zealous Presbyterian, and a strong anti-Jacobite. Certainly he was an ardent supporter of the Protestant Succession, and a shrewd negotiator in reconciling the differences of those who agreed in favouring Hanover, while disagreeing on other points.

The agreement made in London was kept secret until events in the Scottish Parliament disclosed their substance. The first manifestation was the appointment of the Marquis of Tweeddale to succeed Queensberry as Commissioner, while the Earl of Cromarty remained as sole Secretary, and Johnston was rewarded for his efforts with the post of Lord Register, replacing Sir James Murray, a Queensberry man. Roxburgh, Rothes, and Baillie remained in the background until the time came for them to show their hand; when, in company with other members, both of the Cavalier and the Country parties, they gave their support to the new Government's policy. Seafield, as might have been expected, "worshipped the rising sun", and the newly created Earl of Glasgow, Queensberry's evil genius (according to Lockhart), was dismissed from his post as Treasurer-Depute, to make way for someone who should, later on, merit the post by helping the Government (6).

Broadly speaking, the task which the new Government had undertaken was to settle the Succession, in exchange for certain concessions to Scottish feeling, to which Godolphin had signified his assent in advance. What was essentially a compromise ran on the same lines as the concession by Charles I in 1641, by which the bestowal of offices had to receive the consent of the Scottish Parliament, or of the Scottish Privy Council, when Parliament was not sitting. Compared with Fletcher's drastic limitations, this was a milk-and-water form of restricting the prerogative, for it involved the obvious risk that means would soon be found to nullify the restriction in effect, if not, indeed, to abolish it altogether. But it was something as a *quid pro quo* for the Succession, and so this "motley" Ministry, as it was sarcastically called in England, proceeded to try out their plan.

It was made clear, soon after the Parliament met on 6th July, 1704, that their policy had no hope of success. The usual formalities over—the Queen's letter declaring her earnest desire for a settlement of the Succession, with the speeches of the Commissioner and the Chancellor, Seafield—the main business of the Session, after a discussion on controverted elections, was at once proceeded with, and the floodgates of debate were opened afresh.

A week after the House met, the Duke of Hamilton presented as a resolution "that this Parliament will not proceed to the nomination of a Successor to the Crown until we have a previous treaty with England in relation to our commerce and other concerns with that nation". Then came a proposal by the Duke of Atholl demanding an inquiry into the "Plot", and calling for the papers and persons concerned; to which demand the Commissioner promptly acceded.

Fletcher was quickly on his feet in support of Hamilton's resolution. Lockhart says that Fletcher did "elegantly and pathetically set forth the hardships and miseries to which we have been exposed since the Union of the two Crowns of Scotland and England in one and the same Sovereign, and the impossibility of amending and bettering our condition if we did not take care to prevent any design that tended to continue the same without other terms and better security than we have hitherto had". Also, he made "a long speech" on Atholl's proposal, "reflecting on the House of Peers on their proceedings in the Plot, and commending the House of Commons".

The Earl of Rothes was put up by the Government to move a resolution designed to evade the Hamilton proposal. This resolution proposed the consideration of such conditions as might be thought necessary for rectifying the Constitution, having as their object the security of the sovereignty and independence of the nation: "and then the Parliament will take into consideration the other resolve offered for a treaty, previous to the nomination of a Successor to the Crown".

"Whereupon brisk speeches and sharp repartees were made by both parties, and great heats arose which continued a long time." Sir James Falconer sarcastically remarked that he was glad to see "such an emulation" in the House for the nation's security. Why not, he asked, conjoin the two resolutions? And he moved accordingly, the motion receiving the support of the whole of the Cavaliers and meeting the opposition of the Courtiers, who saw that the conjunction would ruin their plans. The Cavaliers pressed the motion to a vote, which was evaded as long as possible by Ministers. Roxburgh supported the Courtiers in their evasion, and was twitted by a later speaker with his famous rhetorical outburst in the last Session, demanding a vote "with sword in hand". Finally the vote for the motion, conjoining the two resolutions, was taken, and was carried by a large majority. The result caused much jubilation in the camp of the Cavaliers. The Duke of Hamilton was "caressed and huzza'd" in the streets, and "nothing was to be seen or heard that night but jollity, mirth, and an universal satisfaction and approbation of what was done, and that by people of all ranks and degrees". After making due allowance for the language of partisanship, it must be conceded that this ebullition of feeling showed clearly the popularity of the policy of standing up to the "auld enemy", and, conversely, the unpopularity of any sign of eating humble pie baked by England (7).

The unfortunate Ministers who had to bear the brunt of this unpopularity, were at their wits' end to know how to compass the purpose for which they had been selected by the Queen and Godolphin. An understanding had now been reached between the Cavaliers and the Queensberry Whigs for mutual support in opposing the Ministers, the Cavaliers undertaking not to press the awkward "Plot" inquiry demanded by Atholl; and the voting power of this coalition proved a formidable obstacle to the success of the Government's policy. A crisis arrived when Hamilton proposed to tack an Act for granting Supplies to the Act of Security, as the condition of providing the money which the Government so sorely needed. Johnston, the Lord Register, at once protested. Tacking might be a reasonable proposition in England, where there were two Houses of Parliament, and where the Commons might find it necessary to coerce the Lords by tacking a Money Bill to a Bill which the Lords would not otherwise pass. But in Scotland, where there was only one Chamber, the voting on both measures so tacked might be obstructed. Besides, it was a "straitening of the Queen, who might possibly consent to one and not to the other" (8).

And then ensued a "scene" between Johnston and Fletcher. The latter charged the Lord Register with carrying out the orders of the English Court. "Now it appears", he said, "that there must be a bargain, and unless the Parliament go on to the measures laid down in England, nothing must be done; and he who spoke last has undertaken to obtain these measures, to be performed here in prosecution of the House of Lords' address." The charge was indignantly denied by Johnston. For, he said, long before the address of the House of Lords was drawn up, the Queen had declared that she would recommend her servants to have the Protestant Succession settled in Scotland.

Fletcher asserted that he knew, and could prove, that Johnston had undertaken to further the English designs, "for promotion to himself". "There could be no influence", retorted Johnston, "but the place he had, and it was known he had lost a higher place for his concern for his country."

Confusion followed these charges and replies. "To the Bar with him!" shouted some of the supporters of the Register, furious with Fletcher. "The letter by the Queen to the Parliament", persisted Fletcher, ignoring the interruption, "was written when no Scotsman was about her, and so behoved to be by English influence;" and in that assertion he was "backed by Duke Hamilton". "No," was Johnston's reply, "it came up to the Queen from Scotland:" he believed, indeed, "there was no Englishman would be at the pains to draw a letter". " Salton still insisting, Sir James Hackett said he was impertinent." This remark irritated Fletcher intensely. "He that would call him impertinent was a rascal," he flung out passionately. Such unparliamentary language made the House "alarmed", and a member moved that both Hackett and Fletcher should be sent to prison. The Chancellor sharply rebuked both of the offenders. They immediately apologised to the House, and "promised upon their word of honour they should not take any notice of it elsewhere" (9).

Fletcher was clearly in the wrong by not accepting Johnston's denial of his charges (the Register "would not tell a lie for the world"), and showed a sad lack of restraint by his exhibition of temper. His irritability increased with the passing years, and with the growing intensity of his feeling against any semblance of English dictation. Yet although Johnston was probably telling the literal truth, when he declared that the Queen's letter recommending the settlement of the Succession emanated from Scotland, Fletcher was correct in his general charge that its substance, which was all he cared about, had been prearranged in London, and that Johnston had been an active promoter of the policy which it embodied. Clearly, as the Earl of Mar told his Countess, "Salton was as ill-pleased with our new Courtiers as he was with our old" (10).

But Fletcher was soon to show his mettle more agreeably as a constructive statesman than as a Parliamentary wrangler. He had prepared an Act bearing upon the proposed treaty with England, and in August it was carried by five votes, and ordered to receive a first reading. The essential feature of this Act was that eight members of each Estate should meet the English Commissioners "on the Borders" (11). What he really feared was their subjection to Court influence.

The Ministers were reduced to sorry shifts to meet the threatened collapse of their policy. Lord Belhaven, at no time a strong party man, and now definitely associated with the Courtiers, endeavoured to divert the impending decision of the House into a channel through which it was hoped might flow some solace for his friends. Was the "Plot" not a providential issue for the salvation of the Ministers and the confusion of their foes? Before any nomination of Commissioners was made, "he thought there was an accursed thing searched out to put out of the way, which he had found out, namely, the Scots Plot where many of the members were tainted, and until they were cleared, it would be unfit to name them for Commissioners". Hamilton, who was one of the implicated people named by Belhaven, at once agreed that it was necessary to clear the nation of the "Plot". Not only, so he reminded the House, those named by Belhaven, but all who voted last Session for the Act of Security, were accused by Queensberry, in a letter to the Queen, of being implicated.

"The fountain of our evil", then declared Fletcher, after rebuking Belhaven for interrupting the treaty debate, "was the House of Peers' undue intermeddling in our affairs," and after some "discourse to that purpose" (he) "gave in a Resolve" to that effect. His resolution declared that the interference of the peers with Scottish affairs was "an encroachment upon the sovereignty and independence of Scotland", and that the behaviour of the House of Commons in the matter "was like good subjects of our Queen and as neighbourly friends of this nation".

His resolution occasioned "much discourse". Ultimately it was divided into two clauses, the first affecting the House of Lords and the second the House of Commons. The motion on the Lords was carried "by very many"; the motion on the Commons, moved by Hamilton, was rejected by fifty votes (12). It was not to be expected that a Scottish Whig majority would approve of anything done by an English Tory majority. The circumstance throws a sidelight on Fletcher's complete freedom from party ties: he welcomed any action which he thought right, no matter from what quarter it emanated.

During August 1704 we find him active in the House in promoting measures of reform. He gave in the draft of an Act on "The Fund of Hearth-money: that all who have misapplied or shall misapply funds appropriate, be liable". That measure dealt with corruption. Another measure dealt with electoral reform. It asked for the addition of eleven to the number of shire representatives, and for the addition of one shire representative for every fresh addition to the nobility. This measure was read and marked for a first reading.

On the second reading of this Act, Fletcher had a clash with the Duke of Hamilton, who was more jealous of preserving the privileges of his order than careful of maintaining a just balance in his country's representation. On Fletcher moving for a second reading of his Act, Hamilton moved for a second reading of the Act for free voting in Parliament. "The member who spoke last", declared Fletcher, "did contradict himself, for he had been for the Act in favour of the barons." Hamilton at once expostulated. "He had been reflected on by the member who spoke last . . . and he offered to go to the Bar if he had said anything amiss". . . . "Such reckoning", said Fletcher defiantly, "is for another place". . . . "I refuse not that either," retorted Hamilton.

Seafield, an ideal Speaker of an unruly Parliament, here intervened with the soothing suggestion that both men should beg the pardon of the House, which, "after a long struggle", Fletcher was persuaded to do; and Hamilton followed his example. Also, they promised not to fight a duel afterwards (14). Fletcher's pugnacity, both inside and outside the House, was amazing. He hit out right and left at noble or commoner alike if they came athwart him, and he was ready to fight anyone: in the House with the formidable weapon of his debating power, and outside the House with sword or pistol at his adversary's option.

By this time the Act of Security, which, with the complementary Act of Supply, had lain on the table after the first reading, was the law of the land. Godolphin had realized that the stubbornness of the Scottish Parliament was unbendable. The army—which consisted of only 3000 men, but, being "double or treble officered", was really the nucleus of a much larger force—remained unpaid, and money could not be supplied by England for paying it without making matters worse. The Jacobite threat of a rising, with French help, remained. No way out of the impasse could be seen. There was only one thing to do: and that was to yield to the balanced advice of the Scottish Ministers, and make the Act law. So the Queen was advised by Godolphin to instruct her Commissioner to touch the Act. That done, Supply for six months was readily granted. But a week after the Act became law, the victory of Blenheim found England in so truculent a mood against the Scots, and in such a state of indignation against Godolphin for advising the Queen to legalize the Act, that had it not been for the exercise of Marlborough's prestige in favour of his colleague, Godolphin would have been forced to resign.

Their Scottish policy had certainly made the English Ministers vulnerable to the attacks of the Opposition, who sedulously made the most of the Act of Security to undermine the position of Godolphin. Copies of the Act were circulated freely. Scotland, it was declared, was now indeed completely independent; she was arming menacingly and drilling continuously; and Godolphin was a traitor who ought to be hanged for his complacency towards these troublesome Scots. But Godolphin was secure in the support of the Queen and Marlborough: his excuse that he had deliberately incurred one danger in order to avoid a greater, was essentially sound. Besides, the Act of Security to which the Queen's Assent had been given, did not contain the trade communication embodied in the Act, for that clause had been omitted. And how was the money to be obtained for the maintenance of the troops? So he argued in Parliament; and not without success. There was a "remedy", he hinted, for what had occurred; and it soon appeared what that remedy was (15).

Before the Act of Security was touched (on 5th August, 1704), Godolphin had kept himself well informed by more or less independent correspondents in Scotland, whose opinions he valued. The Duke of Atholl's opinion was that "nine parts" of the Scottish nation were against the Succession without terms from England. An adjusting treaty should precede the acceptance of the Succession, without which the settlement "could never be lasting nor secure". The Parliament would never accept the settlement without a previous treaty. Atholl himself had "no hand in the management of this business", which left him free to say in Parliament what he thought fit (16). On the other hand, Harley, the Speaker of the House of Commons, told Godolphin that he feared the division of the Scottish Parliament into two parties was imminent: though they might be called Whigs and Tories, they would be more correctly called "Kirkmen and Episcopalians". The opponents of the Ministers were "insolent" in their demands, and the aim of some of them was to see the "present managers in Scotland miscarry". The most effective means of bringing "that nation" to reason, was to show them that "the Queen doth not fear them". He welcomed the Queen's resolution to "dispatch" that nation, and to show her resentment towards those who had disserved her there (17).

These conflicting views, among others, were before Godolphin when he advised the Queen to give her Assent to the Act of Security. And Atholl's statement that a treaty must precede an Act of Succession, accorded with the "remedy" which was now in the Lord Treasurer's mind. England did not want a treaty. Scotland would not accept the Succession without one; and her Parliament had declared that view by means of a separate resolution, though not insisting upon its incorporation as a clause in the Act of Security. Godolphin was now gradually feeling his way towards a fresh solution of an extraordinarily difficult problem.

The English Parliament met on 25th October, 1704. A month later, an attack on the Government's Scottish policy was launched by Lord Haversham in the Upper House. He emphasized the fact that in Scotland there existed "two matters of all troubles: much discontent and great poverty". He eulogised the Scots as a nation: no braver people could be found than the Scots, nobles, gentlemen, and common people alike; but all alike were poor and discontented.

The Act of Security gave them the power to elect their own King on the death of the Queen. And who could tell what dangers might befall England if, in alliance with France, the Scots chose to declare war. He warned the House against neglecting the troubles that threatened: "no man can forbid the sparks that may set all on fire" (18).

On 29th November the House went into Committee to consider the relations of the country with Scotland. Godolphin defended with vigour and point his advice to the Queen on the Act of Security, and took occasion to warn the House that the irritation of the Scots was mainly due to the constant interference of English Parliaments in their affairs. If they would only cease from worrying the Scots, everything would come right in the end. A sensible speech, though suggestive, perhaps, of Satan rebuking sin! But there is little room for doubt that had Godolphin been an entirely free agent, the friction with Scotland would have been much less pronounced than it was, if, indeed, it might not have been eliminated altogether. Burnet gave his hearty support to Godolphin in the House of Lords, and indulged in some plain speaking on the injustices which his native country had consistently suffered at the hands of England. Unpalatable as these views may have been to his hearers, they were, at any rate, the views of a man who knew the facts, and who did not forget that although he was a bishop of the Church of England, he was born a Scot.

How was England to meet the situation? The Tory lords, and especially the Tory bishops, would have liked to condemn the Act of Security offhand by a vote of the House. But the Whig lords, anxious for a settlement of the Succession, and wishful not to exacerbate Scottish feeling, already sufficiently inflamed, favoured a different course. They agreed that England must do something to protect herself against the consequences of the Act. But what?

When the adjourned debate was resumed on 6th December (the Queen being in the House), Lord Somers made the suggestion that the proper method to adopt was to pass an Act throwing upon the Scottish people the responsibility of rejecting the Succession as settled in England, rejection to involve the imposition of such disabilities as would make them see their mistake. Lord Halifax,

[221]

on 7th December, pooh-poohed the "bad humour" of the Scotch, and attacked Johnston: "the same hand that had begun all that humour by the Act of Darien had now finished it by the Act of Security" (19): surely a misstatement of the facts. The result of these discussions was the passing, by both Houses, of the Alien Act, which received the Royal Assent on 14th March, 1705. The Bill provided for the nomination of Commissioners to treat for a union of Parliaments, if the Scottish Parliament could be persuaded to pass a similar measure. But the sting of the Bill lay in the clause which enacted that unless by 25th December, 1705, the Succession was settled in Scotland, as it had already been settled in England, all natives of Scotland, except those who were resident in England, Ireland, or the Colonies, or who were serving in the army or navy, were to be treated as aliens, with all the implications involved by the change of status. The trading disabilities, too, were serious. Scottish coals, linen, and cattle were to be excluded from England. No English horses, arms, or ammunition, were to be sent into Scotland: an obvious precaution (20).

It was a drastic step, which was intended to drive Scotland, by economic pressure, into acquiescence with the English settlement of the Succession. As if to accentuate the threat of compulsion, the Lords addressed the Queen, desiring her to provide for the defence of certain named towns in the North of England; to place regulars on the Border; and to call out the militia of the four northern shires. All this sounded very alarming, and it was meant to be alarming. But at first it did not alarm the Scots so much as it infuriated them.

There were Scotsmen who liked the notion of union, but who heartily disliked the rough manner of wooing by the prospective partner. Wooing? Did it not resemble more closely the attitude of an angry schoolmaster threatening naughty schoolboys with a cane? It was scarcely the way to placate an irritated and high-spirited nation. But the trouble was that both nations were irritated, each by the other: Scotland by England, for a succession of unneighbourly acts, and England by Scotland, for a stubborn assertion of national sovereignty which, to the average member of both Houses of Parliament, was incomprehensible on the part of a country that was only a "province" of England. At bottom, indeed, the "provincial" idea, ineradicable from the unimaginative mind of the contemporary English politician, was at the root of all the quarrels between the two countries just before the Union. If the English politician had only realized, however faintly, that, as a national boundary, the Tweed separated his nation from another nation, with all the connotations of the word, just as surely as the Channel separated England from France, he would, with his innate sense of fairness, have been more considerate towards the national feeling of his northern neighbour. But it is just this lack of historical perspective, and this imperfection of imagination in the evaluation of what is loosely termed "nationalism", that have been the main causes of all the political blunders committed in the political relations between England and her near neighbours, which history records only to deplore.

These were the considerations that were ever present to the mind of Andrew Fletcher. Nationalism implied a difference: there was no getting away from that fundamental fact. And a difference implied the freedom to realize all the implications of that difference. That, too, was, in his view, fundamental. And being completely imbued by that conviction, he worked for the ideal of nationalism during the whole of his life. It need scarcely be added that his disapproval of the Alien Act, passed by the English Parliament, was wholehearted, as being a deliberate attempt by a stronger nation to browbeat a nation less strong.

He was not alone in that view, even among thinking Englishmen. Defoe, the man who by his skilful propaganda did so much, a little later on, to promote the Union, writes:

"The English Parliament sitting soon after, viz., 1704, the Scots Act of Security came to be considered, and, however influenced by a precipitate party, God only knows, they passed an Act, in my opinion the most impolitic, I had almost said unjust, that ever passed that great Assembly." Defoe stresses the fact that tempers in both countries were at this time so frayed, that unless a change had come, it would have been "impossible" to avoid war between the two nations (21).

On such uncertain things as temper do the frightful issues of war and peace often hang!

Chapter XVII

UNION IN SIGHT

THE usual migration of the Courtiers over the Border followed the close of the Session of 1704. In London there was a shuffling of the Scottish Ministry. Tweeddale became Chancellor; Seafield and Roxburgh Secretaries; Rothes, Privy Seal; Baillie of Jerviswood, Treasurer-Depute; and the Earl of Cromarty, Justice-General.

During the debates on the Alien Act the Scottish Ministers in London followed the proceedings with anxious interest. The conclusion which Roxburgh correctly reached was that the English Whigs intended "to force us in to the Succession". He adds: "For my part, I don't well know what to say, for unless our cattle and linen can be otherwise disposed of, we are utterly ruined should those laws take effect. . . . If they cannot, I shall think a treaty necessary, and the dangers of that, too, are innumerable" (1).

"The Alien Act", said Johnston, was "very different from what any of us ever heard it to be." For the preamble mentioned the necessity for "a nearer and more complete union" between the two countries. But "no man", he declared, "will be either for the Succession or an absolute union till he has first tried what can be got by a federal union" (2). Such a thing as an incorporating union was, at that stage, a solution of the difficulty which no responsible Scottish statesman would think of proposing to his countrymen.

The truth was that at that time, as before and afterwards, the Scottish policy of the English Ministers had one thing, and one thing only, as its primary aim: and that was the settlement of the Succession. They had tried latterly, by the grant of trumpery concessions to Scottish feeling, and by the agency of Ministers who thought they could effect the wishes of the Court, to carry that policy in the Scottish Parliament in two successive Sessions. Now they were preparing to try it in a third Session, and were arming their prospective Ministers in Scotland with the bludgeon of the Alien Act. But they were well aware that they could not carry their measure by a bludgeon alone. The hand that wielded the bludgeon must wear a velvet glove. In the long run, persuasiveness was likely to be more effective than force when dealing with so stubborn a people as the Scots. If the Act of Security was to be countered, a treaty of some sort might have to be conceded as the price of a settlement, and, if necessary, a Parliamentary union on terms arranged by Commissioners appointed by the Queen.

A great deal depended upon a choice of the right men—"the right tools", as Roxburgh neatly phrased it—for carrying out the English policy. And gradually it began to appear that, to achieve that end, another shuffle of Ministers was desirable. Interviews with Godolphin and Marlborough revealed the views of those statesmen on the suitability for their purpose, or otherwise, of the numerous aspirants for office ("We have few places and many pretenders," as Seafield aptly remarked on another occasion); and the usual scramble for the spoils, with the usual intrigues in obtaining them, inevitably followed. One of the chief negotiators was the Secretary, Roxburgh, who, for so young a man, displayed a nice talent for the game of bluff. The two main protagonists were Queensberry and Hamilton, both of whom were in London waiting on events, each of them with a strong following in the Scottish Parliament. At first, Queensberry, who had cut so sorry a figure in the "Plot", was distinctly out of favour; but it soon appeared that he was a factor that could not be ignored. Hamilton, as the leader of the Cavaliers, was a big fish to catch, for if he could be induced to support, or at any rate, abstain from opposing, the policy of the Court, the rest would be plain sailing for the Government. But Hamilton proved to be as coy and as impenetrable as ever. Roxburgh's aim was to "exasperate" Queensberry with Hamilton. Queensberry's aim was to get Roxburgh "to be for his business". The Castle Tavern in Fleet Street, where the two men met, was the scene of an interesting conversation between them. Roxburgh was very confident, as the result of this conversation, that Hamilton would "fall of his price". He had it on excellent authority that the Duke, "vain and necessitous" as he was, would succumb to a good offer if the Queen had "a mind for the business" (3). Meanwhile he suspected Hamilton of "tampering"

P

with Godolphin, through Harley, the Speaker of the House of Commons, whose ignorance of Scottish affairs—symptomatic of the House over which he presided—was frankly acknowledged by himself when he declared in the House that "he was ready to take his oath on it that he knows no more of Scottish business than of Japan". Also, he declared that "he avoided even the conversation of Scotsmen" (4). Efforts were continued to secure Hamilton, but all to no purpose: "he tampers on but never concludes". What his terms were, if he ever disclosed them, we do not know. The probabilities are that he never stated them; nor does it appear that he ever received a definite offer, though it was thought that an offer should be made, with the intimation that if he did not accept it, others would. There seems to have been general agreement that his debts would have to be paid; but that was only one item in his probable demands. Had he agreed to support the Ministry, he would have lost his popularity in Scotland.

Failing Hamilton, the Ministry-makers had to turn their attention to Queensberry, whose stock was gradually appreciating in value. Seafield, ever with his face to the rising sun, was "striking up" with him. "To my certain knowledge", writes Roxburgh, his colleague in the Secretaryship, "he is impatient to be Chancellor again." His conduct gave Roxburgh "the spleen": he was, Roxburgh roundly declares, "without doubt the greatest villain in the world"! (5).

The patriotic Roxburgh himself seemed to be veering round to the idea of union. "I do believe", he says, "that an union were the best thing for Scotland:" (6) an odd statement for the champion of Succession with limitations, and indicative, perhaps, of a changed view, which ultimately found full expression in his party voting for an incorporating union when the time came.

Union, indeed, appeared to become more and more in the eyes of the English Whigs the most likely solution of the Scottish problem. In any event, they believed that the safest Ministry for Scotland would be one composed entirely, or predominantly, of Old or Revolution Whigs; and Godolphin, weary of a task the accomplishment of which eluded him whichever way he turned, acceded to their wishes. Consequently the formation of a Government on that basis aroused renewed activity among the office-mongers. Tweeddale, the Chancellor, had to go: that much was clear even to his own party, the members of which do not seem to have rated his ability over highly. Equally clearly, Seafield had to step into his shoes, though the Marquis of Annandale was also an aspirant for that desirable office. But the post of Commissioner, the most important of all? Who was to sit on the throne? The answer was soon forthcoming: it was the young Duke of Argyll, the head of the greatest Whig House in Scotland, and the traditional champion of the Presbyterian body. With Argyll on the throne, and Seafield in the Chancellor's chair, where alone he was comfortable, the formation of the new Government made an auspicious commencement (7).

John, second Duke of Argyll, had a head "which ran more upon the Camp than the Court". But it was not the first time that a fine soldier had also proved to be a capable statesman: the English Ministers had no need to look further afield than their own Marlborough for an example. Even his political opponents had to acknowledge Argyll's straightforwardness and reliability, though they doubted his intellectual capacity. He was a young man to have the responsible post of Commissioner. But Annandale, who became one of the Secretaries—his colleague, to his disgust, being the Earl of Loudoun, a Campbell—was charged by the Queen to give the benefit of his riper experience to the Duke, "whose youth and warmth may possibly have need of your lordship's temper and prudence" (8). But Argyll soon showed that he declined to be in the leading-strings of Annandale or anybody else.

The "New Party", as a majority of the Country party now called themselves, had quite expected to share the sweets of office with the new men. Indeed, that sagacious, if time-serving, old campaigner, Seafield, was doubtful how the Government could manage without them. But Argyll would have none of them. He insisted upon dropping them incontinently; otherwise he would not act as Commissioner. "His High and Mighty Grace", as Lockhart calls him, issued his orders as if he were still an army officer, instead of a Commissioner who had to study the views of his colleagues. He "neither knew nor proposed any way of loosing the Gordian knots but, like Alexander the Great, he cut them with his sword" (9). More than that: he refused to assume his duties until nominees of his own had been provided with snug billets. And he insisted, too, upon being made a peer of England (10). He was not, in fact, over-anxious for the Commissionership, and did not care much whether he sat on the throne or not. This attitude of independence and indifference to office gave him a strong position among his place-hunting colleagues, as they were forced to realize. But they knew where they were with Argyll; while for his part, he knew what he wanted, and saw that he got it.

Meanwhile Seafield continued to look around him for allies, seeing that the new Government was to be deprived of the dependable co-operation of the New Party. He did not give up hope of Hamilton, until a visit to that peer's country seat convinced him, as he told Godolphin, that it was very doubtful whether "anything can be expected of him". He took the liberty of giving Hamilton a piece of advice. If the Duke wanted to get employment, "suitable to his quality and merit", the best way to obtain it was to "concur" with the Courtiers: a gratuitous piece of advice which Hamilton probably remembered (11).

It is doubtful if Godolphin approved of Argyll's decision to scrap the New Party, though the result was to give greater homogeneity to the Administration, and consequently, in all likelihood, greater stability. But the Commissioner had now practically a free hand, and, moreover, possessed the full confidence of the English Whigs. About this time an incident occurred which revealed the administrative weakness of the New Party, and definitely lost them whatever credit they may have possessed in London. It was what became known as the "Green" incident.

Captain Green was the master of an English vessel called the *Worcester* (erroneously believed to belong to the East India Company), which entered the Firth of Forth for repairs. A ship belonging to the Company of Scotland, the *Annandale*, had shortly before been seized in the Thames at the instance of the East India Company, and adjudged forfeit on the ground of an alleged infringement of that Company's trading privileges. The Company of Scotland petitioned the Scottish Government to seize the *Worcester* as a reprisal, and, on the Government's refusal to comply with the request, a band of men led by Roderick Mackenzie ("African Rorie"), the Secretary of the Company, forcibly took possession of her on the Company's behalf. But worse was to follow. A member of the crew of he *Worcester*, when off his guard, made certain dark statements which led to the suspicion, ripening into a fixed belief, that the *Worcester* had had something to do with the disappearance of the *Speedy Return*, a vessel belonging to the Company of Scotland which, after returning from Darien, sailed on a voyage to the East, and was never heard of again, Thereupon Captain Green and fourteen of his men were compelled to stand their trial on the charge of having made away with the *Speedy Return* and her crew, and were condemned to death on evidence which failed to establish any responsibility on their part for the fate of the missing ship, though it was made reasonably clear that they had been guilty of pirating some vessel. The Privy Council, at the Queen's command, granted a short reprieve to the five men who formed the first batch ordained for execution. The Council, however, intimidated by the Edinburgh mob, and in spite of further representations from London, lacked the courage to grant a further reprieve, and Captain Green, with two of his companions, was duly executed. It was proved later on that the *Speedy Return* had, in fact, been seized, with a cargo of slaves, by Madagascar pirates, and the crew sent off to Arabia (12).

The importance of the Green incident lay in its disclosure of the strong and dangerous feeling which existed, at any rate in Edinburgh, against anybody of English nationality. Also, it demonstrated the criminal feebleness of the Scottish Administration, when faced by the choice of doing their obvious duty, and incurring the resentment of the mob. In his report to Godolphin, Seafield describes how some members of the Privy Council, summoned to decide upon the question of a further reprieve for Green and his companions, "went out of town" rather than vote one way or the other. There were murmurs in the city that Englishmen would be protected by the Administration, "though they should murder, rob, or pillage Scotsmen either by land or sea". The members of the Privy Council were fearful of going against this irrational sentiment. They were more careful of their popularity than of doing what they believed to be just. An excellent illustration of this degrading subserviency is provided by Seafield's own account of his experience with an Edinburgh crowd, when on his way to and from a meeting of the Council which was to discuss the question of the Green reprieve.

"As we went along the streets," he writes, "the whole people and mob were crying for justice and desired we might grant no reprieve. After we were some time in Council, we came to be convinced that there was no possibility of preserving the public peace without allowing some that were thought most guilty to be executed, and therefore Captain Green, Captain Mader, and Simpson the gunner, were condescended upon and the rest were reprieved to 19th April.

"As I was returning home, the people that heard some were to be executed did give huzzas, but at a further distance the mob, being informed that a reprieve was passed, did first ask me what was done with those murderers. I told them they would have satisfaction very soon, but, some of them not believing, they stopped my coach, and those at a little further distance threw stones. At last I was forced to come out and expose myself entirely to their fury, but when they saw me they fell immediately calm, for I did not in the least seem discomposed; and they separated to each hand, and I went in to a friend's house, and none of them offered to follow. The General" (the Earl of Leven, the Commander-in-Chief) "convened some of the regiment of Guards and secured the port of the town, and then the mob went and attended the prisoners to the place of execution. Many of the nobility and gentry came and waited on me home to my house, and now all is quiet, and there is no disturbance" (13).

The execution of the three men had, in fact, sobered the mob and satisfied its lust for a sacrifice to its passions. Also, by this time, Argyll had arrived in Scotland, and his fearless sense of justice soon made itself manifest by the release of the rest of the prisoners. The incident had aroused much indignation in England. Johnston reveals the strength of the feeling by a phrase. "It's now", he says, "no more conquer or unite, but reduce and annex". Also, the incident gave its death-blow to the tottering Scottish Administration. "This business of Green is the devil and all," wrote Johnston. "It has spoiled all business." It disposed finally of the question of including members of the New Party in the Ministry then in course of formation (14).

Probably the three men deserved hanging, but not for the crime with which they were charged. They were executed to propitiate the crowd; and the crowd was inflamed by strong national prejudice. The reaction to this prejudice in England was immediate, and had not the full report of the trial, "from which it was evident that they were little but pirates", allayed English indignation, the consequences might have been incalculably serious. The mutual dislike of both nations was intense, because their ignorance of one another was profound.

The Green incident served a useful purpose, inasmuch as it directed closer attention to the malady of which the Green affair was but a symptom; for it was a rowdy expression of a popular sentiment. The malady from which the Scottish people were suffering was a malady which was at the root of many international embroilments before and after the beginning of the eighteenth century: the canker produced by a sense of injustice. The Scots believed that their neighbours had wilfully inflicted upon them, as a nation, a succession of slights, culminating in the stab of the Darien dagger, and crowned by the hectoring clauses of the Alien Act. The Edinburgh rabble who demanded the blood of the five Englishmen, could not be expected to understand that to the English statesmen who were at that very moment deeply concerned with, and participating in, events which were destined to shape the destinies of Europe for a generation or more, Scotland was merely a pawn in the European game of preserving the balance of power. But they knew something about fair play; and they knew that they belonged to a nation which had once exercised the rights of an independent community by insisting upon their recognition. Their sense of unjust treatment had aroused their worst passions, and invited the spirit of retaliation that such feelings are bound to evoke. And the manifestations of resentment had inevitably provoked counter-manifestations of ill-will in England. There was, in fact, no finality to these periodical outbursts of national animosity. The roots of it called for examination. A radical distemper needed a radical cure. And statesmen in both countries were now beginning to believe that the only cure was union, partial or complete.

What was Fletcher doing all this time? It may be assumed that he was well aware of the comedy (or tragedy) in London, by which Scottish Ministries were being made, unmade, and remade, to shape English ends. But Parliament was soon to meet again, and he had not yet composed his quarrel with Hamilton. There was every likelihood that the exigencies of the coming Session would demand common action on their part: and common action between two statesmen who had quarrelled, and neither of whom would confess himself in the wrong, was obviously not easy. Fletcher may have suspected Hamilton of intriguing for his personal advantage in London. But he can scarcely have known of the length to which these intrigues had gone. At any rate, Hamilton was now back in Scotland, preparing to lead the Opposition against any overtures in Parliament conflicting with his stern sense of patriotic duty. So Fletcher was quite ready for a reconciliation.

The rôle of mediator was undertaken by Lockhart of Carnwath, who earnestly pressed Hamilton, in the interest of "Patrick Steel's Club" (the tavern which was the political headquarters of his party), to make up his quarrel with Fletcher. "Nobody will pretend", conceded Lockhart, "to justify all his actions and manner of proceedings, but yet he is so useful a member of a party, take him altogether, that your Grace cannot but perceive how great a disadvantage it would be not to have him in concert at this time. The means and ways how to bring this reconciliation about must be left on your Grace's part to yourself, but that it were effected is the hearty wish of all your Grace's friends, and I have reason to believe Salton is very far from being averse to it, but on the contrary, very desirous of it" (16).

All this shows how potent was Fletcher's influence in the House, and how high his prestige. One looks in vain, however, for any attempt, at this or any other time, on the part of the Courtiers, to attract him to their ranks by the means to which all potential Ministers were more or less accustomed. He would have been a tower of strength to the Court, could the Courtiers but have seduced him from his principles. But to attempt to attract the Scottish Cato, by the recognized methods, to any political cause of which he did not approve, or to any political party which restricted his complete liberty of action, would have been as futile a proceeding as an attempt to bribe an intelligently wary watch-dog

by offering it a suspicious-looking bone. And if he had been persuaded to join himself as a party man to any party, he would have
been like a restive warhorse harnessed to a ramshackle donkey-cart.

Fletcher was willing to be reconciled to the Duke of Hamilton.
But not, apparently, to the leading members of the New (late the
majority of the Country) Party, his former political pupils, who
had, in his opinion, betrayed their principles, and were now in the
market for personal advantages like their neighbours. When
Parliament opened on 28th June, 1705, with a completely new
Ministry, Tweeddale, Rothes, Roxburgh, Baillie, Johnston, the
Earl of Selkirk, and Lord Belhaven (like Selkirk, a Lord of the
Treasury) having been all "cashiered", one of the first things that
happened was an attempt made by Fletcher to get Baillie excluded
from the House on a technical point (17). But it was on Roxburgh,
whom he rightly regarded as the moving spirit in the New Party,
that the vials of his wrath were poured forth most abundantly. His
resentment against Roxburgh was shown during a discussion on
finance about a fortnight after Parliament met.

There were two rival schemes, both based on the security of
landed property, before the House "for supplying the national
money by a paper credit". The author of one of these was Dr.
Hugh Chamberlain, whose Land Bank had been a failure in England. The other scheme came from the fertile brain of John Law
of Lauriston, the son of an Edinburgh goldsmith, afterwards
world-famous as the originator of the Mississippi scheme, and
the financial dictator of France. Law was high in favour both with
the Ministers and the New Party. In the course of the discussion on
these schemes, Fletcher, who described Law's plan as "a contribution to enslave the nation", suggested that the two financiers
should be confronted with one another in the House, and there
debate their rival schemes in order to enable the members to form
a just opinion of their respective merits. In reply to this suggestion, Roxburgh got up to say that he thought it was unfair to ask
Law to come to the Bar of the House in such a public manner,
especially as he had not dedicated the book he had written on the
subject to the Estates, nor put his name to it. "Mr. Law or any
gentleman that had employed his time and thoughts for the good
of his country ought to be treated with good manners."

Such a remark aimed at to Fletcher was like applying a match to peculiarly combustible material. Whether Fletcher held the same opinion of Law as did Lockhart, who calls him "a cunning fellow of bad character", or whether he simply wanted to understand the intricacies of the two schemes more clearly, it was quite certain that he was not going to allow Roxburgh or anyone else to accuse him of bad manners. "If anybody taxed him with ill manners," he retorted hotly, it was they who "were unmannerly and not me". To which Roxburgh replied that he had not intended to tax any individual member with bad manners, but to appeal to the sense of justice of the whole House. "But that since that worthy member fancied himself struck at, he might, if he pleased, take it so." If the cap fitted, Fletcher could wear it.

"I take it as I ought," was the indignant reply. That meant a challenge and a duel.

Foreseeing trouble, the Commissioner gave orders that as soon as the House rose, both men were to be placed under arrest. Roxburgh willingly agreed to stay in his room. But Fletcher, who had sent a challenge to Roxburgh by Lord Charles Carr as soon as he left the House, evaded detention by an artifice, and, with his second, took coach to Leith. On finding what had occurred, Roxburgh persuaded his friends to obtain the Commissioner's consent to his release, and, with Baillie of Jerviswood as his second, reached Leith about six in the evening. He found Fletcher waiting for him at the appointed place of meeting.

The seconds were for making up the quarrel. But Fletcher insisted upon obtaining satisfaction. Roxburgh's second explained that his principal had a great weakness in his right leg, and would therefore be at an obvious disadvantage if the quarrel were decided by the sword. Whereupon Fletcher, who had anticipated this difficulty, "produced a pair of pistols, desiring very cavalierment his Lordship to take his choice". Then Baillie, who was determined to prevent the duel if he could, raised fresh difficulties, saying that Roxburgh's weakness would "equally disable him from firing a-foot as from pushing". Just then a party of Horse Guards, who had been sent by the Commissioner to prevent or stop the duel, appeared on the scene. The seconds, "glad of this handle to save the honour of their principals" (according to another account,

they had made up the quarrel before the Guards arrived), joyfully
fired the pistols in the air and returned home. His party could ill
spare the leadership of Roxburgh at this juncture, and emphatically his country could spare still less the services of his opponent.
Roxburgh was one of Fletcher's young men to whom, with a
fatherly hand, he had addressed his *Account of a conversation in
London.* How sadly since then had his "children" fallen from
grace! (18).

The sequel to the Law-Chamberlain proposals, it may be added,
was that the House passed a resolution, "that the establishing any
kind of paper credit so as to oblige it to pass, was an improper
expedient for the nation". The Scottish legislators were too wise
to sanction any scheme that involved inflation (19).

The plan of the new Ministry, prearranged with Godolphin,
was to take the Succession first, and, failing success, to proceed
with a treaty for union. Seafield believed that it would have been
better to take union first, because he foresaw that without a treaty
there was no hope for the Succession, which was Godolphin's
main objective. But Queensberry, the new Privy Seal, and an
ardent advocate of union, had not yet arrived in Edinburgh, and
meantime his followers were co-operating with the Cavaliers, as they
had done during the last Session. Lockhart thinks that the Cavaliers made a tactical mistake in not pressing their advantage more
than they did at the commencement of the Session, when, according to his observations, a Scots Parliament was always at its best:
"in a little time the zeal and fervour of the members goes off" (20).
If that theory was correct, the Ministers were perhaps wise in
waiting for Queensberry. In the meantime they took the edge off
their opponents' attacks, by arranging for the discussion of dry
subjects like trade and finance (in the course of which, on one
occasion, Fletcher told the Chancellor that he had "put the plough
before the oxen" in his management of the debate), before coming
to close grips with the business on which the thoughts of Parliament were centred. Queensberry, pleading illness, was lagging behind in London: he had delayed his coming, says Lockhart, in
order to use Argyll "as the monkey did the cat in pulling out the
hot roasted chestnuts". But when he did arrive, in great pomp and
circumstance, and had taken his seat, it was a grateful Commis-

sioner who welcomed him. For one of Argyll's colleagues, Annandale, the man whom the Queen had designed as his mentor, was being "found out" as a Minister who, said the Commissioner, only studied his own ends, and, with that aim, was deliberately causing things "to miscarry" (21). Annandale did not see eye to eye with the majority of his colleagues on the question of union, though he was all for the Succession. Queensberry was just the man to smooth away Ministerial dissensions of this sort, and a crisis was averted. But at the end of the Session, Annandale, who had been the most active maker of the Ministry, found himself in the ranks of the unemployed, and the Earl of Mar took his place as Joint Secretary with Loudoun. On one important occasion, at least, whether clumsily or on purpose, Annandale (wrote Argyll) had managed Parliamentary business "most abominably": and, on the whole, his departure from the Ministry must have been a source of relief to his colleagues, as, indeed, he professed that it was to himself to get away from "the set I was yoked with and the measures they were prosecuting". The political differences which had arisen between Argyll and his old friend and colleague were fundamental.

As the Session advanced, the Ministerial line of approach gradually unfolded itself. The feeling of the House on the main business was tested by Hamilton on 17th July, when he reintroduced his resolution of the previous Session. With the assistance of the Queensberry men, it was carried by a large majority. Thus the hope of carrying the Succession by a direct measure had to be abandoned or postponed, and next day the alternative Act for a Treaty of Union was tabled.

The forces for and against union were now arrayed for the clash from which was to issue the political future of Scotland. On the one side were the Ministers, with a predominantly Whig following, now that Queensberry had taken command of his cohorts and directed their votes. On the other side were the official Opposition, namely, the Cavaliers, composed mainly of Jacobites and Episcopalians, whose object was to stave off the Succession by insisting upon limitations which they knew the Court would never accept. Associated with them in general tactics was a small band of which Fletcher was the outstanding member, if it could be said that he identified himself with any Parliamentary group at all. They were the residue of the once powerful Country party, whose unvarying policy was nationalism of a pronounced type. Holding the balance of voting power—some thirty votes—was the New Party, led by the dismissed Ministers, who had hived off from the Country party, and were now free lances. They were known as the *Squadrone Volante* (22), a name which Fletcher, with his Italian proclivities, may have invented. The policy of the Flying Squadron was frankly opportunist, but they nominally stood for the Succession with limitations. They voted against Hamilton's resolution. But when, on 31st July, the Government put up the Marquis of Lothian to propose their Act for a Treaty of Union, and pressed for a first reading, the Squadron voted with the Opposition. "The New Party, as they are pleased to call themselves," complained Argyll to Godolphin, "joined violently in with the opposing party" (23).

This was an important debate, and a despatch from Seafield to Godolphin on 1st August gives a graphic account of it. Godolphin had told Argyll and Seafield that seeing the Succession had been postponed, they should now try to get "such an Act of treaty as the Queen would accept". They did their best. "We did," says Seafield, "in conjunction with the Duke of Queensberry, use our utmost endeavour to prepare the members of Parliament for this, and I spoke to above fourscore of them myself that had been for the resolve (Hamilton's resolution), and found a great many of them well inclined to a treaty. . . . The Duke of Queensberry was mighty diligent in this measure, and did effectually prevail with many of his friends. The high Cavalier party and New Party finding this, did reconcile upon this point, to prefer limitations to a treaty." In spite of the persuasiveness of Queensberry and Seafield, which was considerable, the Government at first failed completely to win the House (24).

Seafield himself recites the four reasons which he gave to the House for "conjoining with England on good terms", namely: (i) security for their religion, England being a Protestant country; (ii) trade advantages superior to those that could be offered by any other nation; (iii) security for the freedom and liberty possessed by England; and (iv) the absence of any other means of securing

[237]

peace between the two nations, while foreign assistance was dangerous to both nations alike (25). The opposition was led by Fletcher, whose resolution (to which an addition was made by Hamilton) is given *verbatim* by Seafield for Godolphin's information. It may be worth quoting, as illustrating the downright character of Fletcher's motions in Parliament:

"In pursuance of a resolution made last Session, and again confirmed in this, the Parliament, notwithstanding the unneighbourly and injurious usage received by an Act lately passed in the Parliament by England entitled 'An Act for the effectual securing of the Kingdom of England', is still willing, in order to a good understanding between the two nations, to enter into a treaty with England, but that it is not consistent with the honour and interest of this independent Kingdom to make any Act, or appoint Commissioners for that end, until the Parliament of England do propose the same in a more neighbourly and friendly manner" (26).

That was a nice dish to set before Her Majesty's Commissioner, spiced as it was by a long speech. It was a defiant gesture not in the least likely to be effective. In view of that expectation, the debate was switched by the Opposition to the old subject of limitations before a treaty: a useful hare, in the circumstances, to start. Put baldly, the alternatives before the House were: a treaty for union, or no treaty without previous limitations. In the result, the Government were outmanoeuvred and outvoted, but only by a majority of three.

Limitations were once more in the Parliamentary limelight. "What limitations did the Opposition require?" asked the Earl of Glasgow. If their intention was to enact them without settling the Succession, was it not better to have a treaty? Did they, or did they not, want to name the Successor? "To which the Duke of Hamilton answered with a loud, No!" (28). Obviously the nomination of a Successor would not suit the Jacobites. And equally obviously, for personal reasons, it would not suit the nobleman who shouted so emphatically that the answer was in the negative. But the majority of the members would gladly have nominated the Protestant Successor if they were assured beforehand of the security of their liberties. That applied to Whigs, Countrymen, and Squadron alike, though there was a section of extreme Whigs who would have plumped for Hanover and taken the risk. What really divided the pro-Hanoverians was the measure of the "liberties" they demanded, and that measure ranged from the tepid restrictions of the Whigs on the one hand, to the robust radicalism of Fletcher on the other.

But the proposed limitations were, after all, discussed in detail, and finally an Act embodying them was passed. They related mainly to Parliamentary control over the appointment of officers of State. Also, farmers of revenue were to be ineligible for Parliament (which ruled out the burghs). An Act for Triennial Parliaments was passed; also, an Act appointing Scots Ambassadors for treaties with foreign States, the Ambassadors to be paid out of the Scottish Exchequer and to be responsible to the Scottish Parliament. Also (a Fletcher addition which was not carried) it was proposed that no Ambassador should be appointed who was not a Scottish landowner. But for excellent reasons, as will presently appear, none of these measures received the Royal Assent.

Fletcher regarded all this legislation that needed the Royal Assent as a mere waste of time. He was convinced that the Court would either disallow it, or find the means of evading it. On 15th August he produced his twelve limitations (Seafield says "eleven") once more—they were by this time called by scoffers "the Twelve Tables of the Law"—and proposed their adoption by the House, not by an Act of Parliament, but by Claim of Right ("Petition of Right", Seafield styles it), which did not need the Royal Assent to make their adoption effective. These limitations, with some slight verbal alterations, were the same as those he first proposed in 1703. And he must have known that there was less chance now than ever of their acceptance. That conviction, however, did not deter him from expounding them once more at length. An Act of Parliament, he said, was "no manner of security to the people's fundamental liberties, but was only leaning upon a shadow and cheating the nation": whereas if the limitations he proposed were turned into a Claim of Right, no subsequent Parliament could annul or repeal them. It was pointed out to him that a Claim of Right was impracticable during the Queen's lifetime. But he stuck to his point with all the greater tenacity, and appealed to Magna Carta, "the basis and foundation of English liberties", which, he said, "the people had forced from a King then actually upon the throne" (29).

The debate lasted four hours, and at length the decision was reached that proceeding by Claim of Right was not feasible. "Which Fletcher perceiving", (says an eye-witness,) "resolved to turn the mouth of the cannon upon his own party, and in my hearing said, 'Well, is it so? I'll serve them a trick for it.'" Whereupon he withdrew his limitations in favour of an Act for regulating the Constitution, which was brought in by Lord Belhaven, and subsequently replaced by a similar measure proposed by the Earl of Rothes.

Fletcher's speech on his limitations, says this narrator, was received in profound silence by a House that was taken aback by his bold propositions. He remarked on their cold reception, and asserted that many of the members had declared to him that it was "their earnest wish and desire" that he should reintroduce his measure. It was the last that was heard of his *Duodecem Tabulæ*. He made a final desperate effort to stave off an Act of treaty by giving in an address which he proposed should be made to the Queen. That too, after "some hot debates", failed to carry (30).

In the course of the debate on Fletcher's Overture, the Earl of Stair, "who is allowed to be the best spokesman in the House", jeered at the limitations, saying that "Mr. Fletcher was resolved to do by his limitations as the ape used to do by her young ones which she grasped so fast as to stifle them". "Which comparison", says the narrator, "did so throw him off the hooks that he rose up and recriminated upon the Earl thus: 'That his Lordship stretched the prerogative' (in King William's reign) 'till it cracked when he passed the declaration for arbitrary power'." He had already told Stair, in reply to a sneer at the tenth limitation, that it was lucky for him no such law existed in previous reigns, or he would have been hanged for his share in the Glencoe massacre, and for other abuses of power. The Earl of Stair had no need to be reminded of his past, for he was painfully aware of its results upon his career. He had been excluded from office ever since the Glencoe tragedy. But he was still a power behind the Throne, and was believed, probably correctly, to have a strong influence over Argyll's political views, especially in the direction of union (31).

In his despatch to Godolphin, Seafield gives reasons why a Claim of Right could not be entertained, mainly because it touched the prerogative too closely. But, according to Argyll, Fletcher's proposal was favoured both by Hamilton and Atholl, who said that however many Acts of Parliament they might have, "English influence and English bribery would take them off": a sentiment borrowed from Fletcher, and coming less appropriately from the ducal benches. Seafield describes Fletcher's proposals as "plainly constituting a Republic after Her Majesty's death". He adds that "several joined him", (which Argyll confirms), so the "silence" with which Fletcher's proposals were received was not so profound after all (32).

A new factor now revealed itself. Ministers were beginning to fear that a tendency was showing itself to make the limitations take effect, not as hitherto proposed, after the Queen's death, but during her lifetime. That tendency had to be resisted and, if necessary, removed by timely concessions. But in spite of the resistance of Ministers, some of the reforms of the Constitution, such as Triennial Parliaments and the exclusion of revenue farmers from Parliament, were carried to take effect during the Queen's lifetime.

Seafield had been informed (so he told Godolphin) that it was Fletcher's intention to reintroduce the Act read last Session for an addition to the number of shire members, "and that any limitations which had been proposed for the Successor might take place in Her Majesty's own reign". But it appeared that the representatives of the shires were not inclined to concur with him for an addition to their number, until the limitations on the Successor had been considered. "So Mr. Fletcher proposed that my Lord Rothes's Act might be a limitation on Her Majesty. But this proposition of his was very warmly received in the House." Stair and Belhaven both spoke against it, and Fletcher's only seconder was the Earl of Home, a consistently firm opponent of union (he died in the following year). "At which", says Seafield, "Mr. Fletcher was so angry that he went out of the House. But I know he will return to our next meeting" (33).

During the debates on the limitations, there was a great deal said on the subject of the Royal prerogative, Seafield, particularly, arguing for its retention as being conducive to the good of the country. His subject led him into an historical excursus, from which he concluded that Scotland had no reason to expect any advantage from overturning the monarchy, "nor had we reason to think that a republic would ever suit with our temper and inclinations, where we have so many nobility, superiorities, and jurisdictions, and, in short, that our whole Constitution was contrary to parity". What was now proposed was "plainly a Commonwealth". These arguments notwithstanding, the Ministers were compelled, against their will, to agree to the paring of the prerogative during the Queen's lifetime. But, of course, it was one thing to pass laws, and another to get them touched.

The Ministers had to rely largely upon the New Party for their majority; and the New Party sometimes proved a sore disappointment. "Yet", remarks Seafield hopefully, "I do not discourage them to expect a share of Her Majesty's favours"—if they would be good and obedient voters. He wished to give them every encouragement "till all is ended". His "only" concern was for "success". He dared not keep "a close correspondence" with the New Party "for fear of giving jealousy". There were "so many divisions" among them that it was difficult to know what to say, and "more difficult to know whom to trust". Probably Argyll was not very far wrong when he told Godolphin, about this time, that "most people here are stark mad and do not themselves know what they would be at". In the House there was a revulsion of feeling at hand in favour of some form of union with England (34).

Before the end of the Session, the Ministers finally prevailed in carrying their great measure. The angling of Seafield for the vote of the Squadron had met with success. The plausible and persistent arguments of Seafield and Queensberry, inside and outside the House, had detached waverers from the ranks of the limitationists. The idea of union was in the air. Nationalists like Fletcher had been silenced. Opportunists like Hamilton had seized their opportunity. Even the attempt by Atholl and Hamilton to revive interest in the Queensberry "Plot", a popular theme in the last Session, had a languid reception, and the affair was finally buried with Seafield's "let sleeping dogs lie" as its burial service. But what proved decisive in determining the ultimate issue of union, and incidentally shaping the whole of Scotland's political future, was a fortuitous loss of votes on two vital questions.

Something had to be done before the Session closed. The economic clauses of the Alien Act were pressing severely on the country, and the political disabilities would come into operation at Christmas. "To whom", asked Hamilton, plaintively, "would his allegiance be due" after Christmas? But that difficulty solved itself by the sequence of events. For on 24th August, the Government's Act for a treaty received its first reading. Next day there was a lively debate, in which Fletcher reiterated his demand not to proceed with any treaty until the Alien clause in the English Act had been repealed; and he was backed up by Belhaven, Hamilton, and Atholl. The demand was ultimately met by Ministers agreeing to petition the Queen to use her influence to secure its repeal. Fletcher even went so far as to propose, as a retaliatory measure for the economic clauses of the Alien Act, that the importation of all sorts of commodities from England should be prohibited. But the Ministers, with the support of the burgh representatives, who feared the trade reactions, easily obtained a majority against so far-reaching a proposal (35).

Equally unsuccessful was the attempt by Hamilton to add a clause to the Act of Treaty designed to preserve the fundamental laws, ancient privileges, offices, rights, liberties, and dignities of the nation. This clause, if carried, would have prevented, as it was meant to prevent, the Scottish Commissioners who were to be appointed for the treaty, from agreeing to an incorporating union; and the specious reasons given by Ministers for their resistance to the clause showed that they were plainly resolved that the Commissioners should have a completely free hand. The clause was lost by two votes only, seven or eight members being absent who would have voted for it. Thus, by a wholly fortuitous event, the Commissioners were endowed with powers to which a majority of the members were violently opposed. But worse was to follow (36).

The nomination of the Commissioners came to be considered. To the utter consternation of his followers, Hamilton moved that the appointment should be left in the hands of the Queen. The implications of this proposal were obvious to all his hearers. For

if the Queen appointed the Commissioners, or, to be precise, if
the appointments were made by the English Court, it was certain
that the Commissioners selected would be men who might be
trusted, in advance, to carry out the wishes of the Court. Fletcher,
who had struggled desperately against the Act throughout the
Session, and had finally proposed to substitute for it an address to
the Queen, was on his feet at once to oppose Hamilton's proposal
"most bitterly". But it was all of no avail. Hamilton's motion was
carried. An incorporating union was now as good as settled, unless before its ratification popular feeling in Scotland, or other
untoward circumstances, should prevent it. For no one seriously
expected that England would agree to anything short of a "complete" union.

On 2nd September Seafield wrote Godolphin that he was sure
the Treasurer would be very pleased with the news of their "succeeding in the Act of treaty". On the following day he tells him of
his ceaseless efforts to secure a majority against Hamilton's clause
for the preservation of the nation's fundamental laws. He had
several friends whom he could not at first entirely influence, "but
in the end I prevailed with them". The Cavaliers had proposed that
the Commissioners might be restricted by the Act from treating of
"anything but a federal union, and spoke much against an incorporating union": and they were supported, after some hesitation,
by the New Party. The Earl of Marchmont "joined with us on the
matter and left the New Party". On Hamilton's subsequent *volte
face* Seafield has some interesting things to say. The Duke "called
to be heard and made a very handsome speech" . . . His party was
surprised, as was also the New Party, and they proposed delay in
coming to a decision. "Some of the Cavaliers had pretty sharp
speeches against the Duke, but he said very boldly that he had
told his opinion and saw no reason to retract. . . . The leaders of
the Squadron spoke. Roxburgh said he would have to vote against
the whole Act." . . . He and Tweeddale did not vote. But most of
the New Party voted for the appointment of the Commissioners to
be in the hands of the Parliament (37).

. . . "The Cavaliers and New Party shew a great inclination to
have the Act thrown out." But in the end it was approved "by a
considerable majority". And Seafield was able also to tell Godol-

phin that "I am very hopeful, if rightly managed", that the Act "may
be the foundation of a lasting settlement between the two nations".
He warns Godolphin, however, that in order to produce a favourable atmosphere for union, the objectionable clause about aliens
in the Alien Act must be rescinded. He adds that he is persuaded
that the Treasurer will now "have the honour of completing what
you have been sincerely endeavouring these several years past":
an allusion, it may be supposed, to the Succession rather than to
the Union. On 21st September, when announcing the adjournment of Parliament, he tells Godolphin quite accurately that they
had had a success "very far beyond" what they could reasonably
have hoped for at the beginning of the Session (38).

Thus Argyll's Administration of 1705 got its Act, unhampered
by restrictions, and with the help of the New Party, it got its
cess (39). What more could it desire? The Duke had brought a
difficult Session to a successful conclusion. But the men who had
done the spade-work were Seafield and Queensberry.

The incalculable Hamilton has been pilloried by Lockhart for
his amazing action in the Commission appointments. He says that
"twelve or fifteen of the Duke's party ran out of the House in rage
and despair, saying aloud, 'twas to no purpose to stay any longer
since the Duke of Hamilton had deserted and so basely betrayed
them." And he goes on to relate how the absence of these members
from the House turned the voting scale in the Ministers' favour.
Lockhart discusses at length Hamilton's reasons for his change of
front, and comes to the conclusion that he had "a true mind to be
one of the treaty himself", and hoped to recommend himself for
the appointment to the Queen by his forwardness in proposing
her as nominator (40).

Conceivably Lockhart's astonishment might have been less pronounced had he known what had happened in connexion with a
council of another kind. During the Session, a Council of Trade
was appointed for the purpose of determining all complaints
against contravention of the trading laws, and putting into execution the prohibitory laws of the country: an appointment that was
apparently a direct result of the Alien Act passed in England.
The Ministers were extremely anxious to obtain control of this
Council, for its actions would have their repercussions on

the position of the Government. The Ministers failed in their effort to have the nominations left to the Queen. It was decided that the Council was to be composed of seven representatives from each Estate. Seafield expected to get, and the Government actually did get, a majority for the Court of the representatives of the nobility and burghs, and although the shires (the most independent of the Estates) did not give them a majority, the shire men elected were "very moderate".

The Duke of Hamilton showed "a great concern" to be chosen as a member of this Council. He was extraordinarily earnest in the matter with Seafield and others, and said he would take it as an "affront" if he were not elected. But Seafield told him that "he took such measures that I could not be useful to him". Had he helped the Government in procuring the nomination for the Queen, "I should very readily have concurred in recommending him to be named. He was very dissatisfied, and we have not spoken together since that time". Argyll and Queensberry were both opposed to Hamilton's election, and, as a fact, he was not elected. From which circumstance Ministers deduced the conclusion that those who had not sufficient "interest" to be elected for a Council of Trade would not insist upon having the nomination of the Commissioners for Union (41).

It was a shrewd conclusion which events justified. When the time came to decide who should nominate Commissioners for the treaty, the Queen or Parliament, Hamilton was determined that he would not be "affronted" a second time. And yet he was chosen neither for the Council of Trade nor—a much more serious "affront"—was he chosen as a Commissioner for Union. He was compelled to rest satisfied with the reflection that his virtuous action in proposing the Queen as nominator brought its own reward. But it was not the kind of reward that he had sought.

Hamilton having turned tail, Fletcher reduced to silence, the New Party an uncertain factor, and some, at any rate, of the Ministers with their supporters contemplating complete union, the end of the Session left the Cavaliers in a despairing condition, as expressed by Lockhart's gloomy remark that from the passing of the Act of Treaty dates "the commencement of Scotland's ruin". For all parties alike were under no illusion as to the outcome of the Act. Indeed, Seafield directly encouraged Godolphin to hold for an incorporating union. He hoped the Act might be the means of settling "an entire correspondence betwixt the two nations". The Queen having the nomination, "much depends upon this, and I am very hopeful that the English will make a right use of this opportunity, and that your Lordship, under Her Majesty, will have the honour to establish what hath been so much desired and difficult to obtain" (42).

Chapter XVIII

THE END OF AN AULD SANG

"The end of an auld sang". The phrase was Seafield's, and the "sang" was Scotland's Parliament. The destruction of the outward and visible sign of national sovereignty was made the subject of a cynical quip by the last Lord High Chancellor of Scotland. Was it a symptom of national insensibility to irreparable loss, or was it a timely precaution against irremediable national ruin? It was neither the one nor the other. For the act of destruction was not national at all. The only means of declaring the national will (so far as that was possible) was by fresh elections in the counties and burghs to a Parliament summoned for the express purpose of considering and deciding the question of union. That a nation's Constitution could be abolished by a Parliamentary majority, secured by tortuous methods, without the concurrence of the nation itself, was the most glaring anomaly of what was itself an anomalous act: the act of self-immolation preceding absorption. The Union of Parliaments may have been wise, or it may have been unwise. But it was certainly not an expression of the national will. It was secured by the preponderance, partly by its vote, and partly by its influence, of the non-elective Estate; possibly, at that time, the least national in spirit of the three groups of members.

Fletcher, a shire member, and thus belonging to the Estate that was probably the most national of the three in its outlook, protested vehemently against so cynical a disregard of public feeling on an issue that was to determine, for good or for ill, the whole political and economic future of the country. "I'm told", wrote Jerviswood to Roxburgh, on 19th April, 1706, "that Salton is writing against the Union till at least a new Parliament be called, instructed for that effect; and I have ground to think he has the Advocate's assistance". The "Advocate" was Sir James Stewart, an elderly West of Scotland man, endowed with "great natural parts", whose manners were "plain, affable, and familiar", and who affected "want of ceremony" as a passport to the confidence of his colleagues. As Queen's Advocate, it might have been supposed that he would have been in favour of union. Not so, however. He opposed it when it was discussed by his fellow-Ministers. He "did not like it", says the Earl of Mar, the Secretary, "and argued against it to us all together". He offered to resign, but his colleagues were against his resignation. "His main arguments against it are the losing of our sovereignty, and that a toleration (to the Episcopalians) will ruin Presbytery": arguments which Mar regarded as "waik". But, while opposed to union, Stewart thought that separation would mean ruin to Scotland (1).

Fletcher disliked Stewart, whether personally or politically, or both, is uncertain, and until 1706 nothing in the world would have induced him "so much as speak" to him. In August 1706, however, James Erskine (afterwards Lord Grange), Mar's brother, states that the two were friendly, their common bond being dislike of the Union. According to Erskine, Stewart was making things difficult for his colleagues, in order to get the next vacancy on the Bench! Erskine reports (also in August 1706) a conversation with Fletcher, in which the latter declared that the Parliament could not constitutionally ratify the Union unless called expressly for that purpose. When Erskine showed him a copy of the proclamation summoning Parliament, and stating that ratification of the Union would be the principal business, "he turned angry and said no more, but he concluded in his ordinary strain that it was a damned villainous union, and so much the more, because those who pretended to carry it were certainly against it in their minds". On which Erskine reminded him that he had been equally positive on other occasions, but had been proved to be mistaken. "Ay, but I'm sure of this," was his rejoinder. "Then we ended as to the Union and fell a-talking of books and the building of houses:" subjects on which they could disagree without getting angry (2).

Fletcher, it would appear, had intended in April 1706 (when the Commissioners were sitting) to write, with Stewart's assistance, against union, and demand an *ad hoc* election (his tract, if written, does not seem to have been printed), and when Parliament was actually summoned, it seems likely that the Government had his objection in view in preparing the proclamation.

[249]

Erskine was amazed (and with some justification) when he discovered that Fletcher had not read the proclamation. A fresh election, as the Government were well aware, would ruin any project of an incorporating union. Probably they held the same view as the Earl of Stair, who said that a new Parliament "would raise a new ferment, whereas our humours rather cool" (3).

On another occasion, in June 1706, Erskine tells his brother of a conversation he had had with the laird of Saltoun as they supped together in Edinburgh. "I do not believe", roundly declared Fletcher, "that any of them" (i.e., the Scottish Commissioners) "are cordially for it" (the Union), "except the Dalrymples" (the Earl of Stair, Sir Hugh Dalrymple, President of the Session, and Sir David Dalrymple, one of the Queen's Solicitors, all of them members of the Commission), "and for their pains, they ought all to be dragged at horses' tails." Fletcher, however, believed the nation to be so much averse to union that "it will not stand out one sederunt in Parliament, and that the promoters will think themselves happy if they can get it quickly smothered". He and his friends would encourage the full debating of the proposals, in order to be able to expose their weaknesses, and get rid of them "for ever". He doubted, indeed, whether the English Parliament would pass the Articles of treaty even if ratified by the Scottish Parliament. And—a significant sidelight—"he" (i.e., Fletcher) "is as angry at the Squadrone and at the Duke of Hamilton as ever" (4).

But we must now see what had been happening to cause these petulant outbursts by Fletcher, in the interval between the two Sessions (1705-6) of the Scottish Parliament. During that interval, and before the Treaty of Union then drafted had become enshrined in an Act and passed by the House, much water had flowed beneath the bridges of the Forth. Indeed, at one time, it seemed likely that Fletcher's prognostication that the treaty would be ignominiously thrown out of Parliament, as the outcome of popular resentment, might be fulfilled. It was late in the Session of 1706 before the patriotic "sang" changed from a major to a minor key, ultimately becoming merged in the clatter of Westminster, where it altered its accent when it lost its individuality.

The passing of the Act of Treaty in the previous Session by

the Scottish Parliament had given great satisfaction to the Court. As a sign of that satisfaction, and a symbol of reconciliation, if not of repentance, the English Parliament, in November 1705, unanimously rescinded, against the wishes of a portion of the English public (though to the relief of the Tynesiders), the obnoxious clause in its Alien Act; and, moreover, removed the trade disabilities imposed by the Act. That was a graceful gesture, designed to create a favourable atmosphere for the conference on union with the Scottish delegates which was soon to take place.

The selection of the Scottish Commissioners was completed in February 1706, and the English appointments were made in April. The composition of both sets of Commissioners (all the nominations having been made by the Queen's Ministers) was such as to make agreement on an incorporating union a foregone conclusion. Of the thirty-one Scottish Commissioners, only one, Lockhart of Carnwath, was a known opponent of union, and he owed his election to the fact that he was a nephew of Lord Wharton, a member of the English Commission. Lockhart explains laboriously what he was doing in that galley, and makes it clear that he was there neither to help nor to obstruct, but to observe and to report. His account of the proceedings of the Commissioners may be accepted as accurate in substance, if anti-Whig in colour. There were two notable omissions from the list of Scottish nominations: the Duke of Hamilton and the Duke of Argyll. The latter refused to be nominated, because Hamilton, to whom he had promised election, was rejected (5).

When the two sets of Commissioners met in London on 16th April 1706, it might have been thought that negotiations of such extreme importance to both countries might probably be protracted. But agreement is not difficult to secure between negotiators, when one side knows in advance what the other wants, and is prepared, in need, to concede it. The Scottish Commissioners did, indeed, for home consumption, make a feeble show of pitting a federal basis against the incorporating union required by England. The Earl of Stair, who "firmly believed" that an incorporating union was the "best for both nations", was nevertheless hoping, in January 1706, that the English would not insist too peremptorily "upon an entire union at present". But that was just what the English did. Federalism, which represented the true Scottish feeling where that feeling existed at all, was rejected by the other side with something like derision, and nine days after the conference opened, the principle of incorporation, as the basis of union, was provisionally accepted by the Scots. Once that principle was accepted, the details were of relatively minor importance. But what was Scotland to get in compensation for the loss of her Parliament?

The English Commissioners throughout the proceedings showed themselves the better bargainers. It is true that as one of the Scottish representatives, the Earl of Mar, afterwards said, they had to make "the best we could". The same Commissioner hoped that Parliament would ratify the treaty, and so put an end "to all our divisions, and honest people would get leave to live at peace and ease, and mind their affairs and the improvement of their country: a much better employment than politics" (6). And, incidentally, it was the same Commissioner of 1706, who in 1715 headed an insurrection which had for its objects the restoration of the Stewarts and the abrogation of the Union.

The English Commissioners displayed a sound business instinct, making concessions in non-essentials and being immovable in the things that really mattered. And for England the essential condition of union with Scotland was that the dependence of the latter country upon her neighbour, which, in the past, Parliament House in Edinburgh had decently obscured with a façade of sham sovereignty, should continue, not merely undiminished, but under more direct surveillance, and with less power to kick. There was no pretence of altruism in the English stipulations for union. In the English view the proposals did not admit of federalism, because a federal union, though it would presumably close the back door in the North just as effectively as incorporation, would give Scotland a free Parliament. Federalism was esteemed to be too low a price to pay for the communication of trade which England conceded. For England it was to be incorporation or nothing; just as, for St. Augustine, the Celtic Church had to submit to absorption or ostracism.

That the Scottish Commissioners ("the bonny blewcaps", as Harley facetiously called them) had decided beforehand to accept, if necessary, an incorporating union, would seem to be suggested by a letter from the Earl of Cromarty to the Earl of Mar, written on New Year's Day, 1706. He wishes Mar and his family "a happy New Year", and "as that which I think Scotland's chief politic good", an "entire union with England. Unless we be a part of each other, the Union will be as a blood pudding to bind a cat, and till one or the other be hungry, and then the pudding flies." He goes on to express a sentiment which must have as ill accorded with the feelings of patriotic Englishmen and Scotsmen in 1706 as in 1935. "God give all of you prudence, wisdom and honesty—and British minds. May we be Brittains, and down go the old ignominious names of Scotland (and) of England. Scot or Scotland are words not known in our native language (Gaelic). England is a dishonourable name imposed on Brittains by Jutland pirates and mercenaries. . . . Brittains is our true, our honourable denomination" (7).

Cromarty had plumped for union, and had given the measure his hearty support in Parliament. But his plea for the adoption of the name of "Britons" by Englishmen and Scotsmen alike, based upon the original homogeneity of the two peoples, carried as little conviction then as it does now, though, to be sure, as an expression of a common heritage, it is for other reasons as convenient a denomination as can be found.

The financial and fiscal arrangements embodied in the Articles of Union may have been reasonable and fair to both countries. Indeed, that would seem to be a just conclusion to draw from the opinions expressed by two eminent Scotsmen, Bishop Burnet and Lockhart of Carnwath, who were intimately interested in the measure. Lockhart thought that the financial and fiscal clauses were as thoroughly bad for Scotland, as the Bishop thought they were surprisingly good: so good, in fact, that, in his view, "nothing but the consideration of the safety" which the Union secured for England "could have brought the English to agree to a project that in every branch of it was much more favourable to the Scotch nation" (8). Taking a middle line between these extreme views, coloured as they were by political prejudice, the inference suggests a deal that comprehensively was not inequitable for either side. The Equivalent of £398,085 10s. od. (one must not overlook the ten shillings) may or may not have been computed on a reasonable basis, as compensation for Scotland shouldering her share of the English Public Debt. The adjustment of taxation as between the two countries may or may not have pressed with unfair incidence upon certain commodities of greater relative importance to Scotland than to England. The communication of internal trade may or may not have been hedged with onerous restrictions, and participation in Colonial commerce hampered by the pre-existing privileges of English Chartered Companies. The limitation of Scottish membership of the British Parliament to forty-five Commoners, and sixteen elected Peers may or may not have been niggardly in its calculations. But at any rate, the English concessions might well have been on a less generous scale, for the Scottish Commissioners were handicapped in their bargaining equipment by what would nowadays be called an inferiority complex; and they obtained what all of them, with one exception, honestly desired: a definite settlement of the Protestant Succession, and the opening of a front door to England in exchange for the closing of a back door. Also, what was more important than anything else, the fear of a war with England, a real and not ill-grounded fear, which was haunting the minds of thoughtful men in both countries alike, was by an incorporating union removed decisively and finally.

Had either side paid too high a price for the privileges secured from the other? That remained for the respective Parliaments of the two countries to say, by ratifying or rejecting the treaty. The Scottish Commissioners can scarcely have anticipated, for their complacency, other than a hostile reception in Parliament House at Edinburgh. The Articles—there were twenty-five in all—were to be kept secret until the Scottish Parliament met, for it was in Edinburgh that opposition was expected to be fiercest, and it was there that the first clash had to be encountered. Long before the Scottish Parliament met, however, the fact that an incorporating union had been settled leaked out, and, as we have seen, Fletcher knew months before the opening of the Session that the Scottish Commissioners had agreed to union on that basis.

The Equivalent (also monies arising from future Equivalents) was to be spent on liquidating "Scotland's public debt; in refunding the losses sustained by the shareholders of the Company of Scotland, which was to be dissolved forthwith; in promoting and encouraging the manufactures and fisheries of Scotland; and in assimilating the coin of that country with the standard and value of the coin of England." Also, Scotland was to retain her Courts of Judicature, and (for the present) her Privy Council. Also, thorny ecclesiastical questions were avoided, for they had been placed outside the purview of the Union Commissioners. "All they aimed at", says Cunningham, "was that laying aside all enmity, each nation should have its own modes of worship left inviolate and entire" (9).

How the Equivalent was actually spent is another story. According to the Earl of Haddington, a facetious young man (a member of the Squadron), who wrote bad verses, and unpardonably inflicted them on his friends, there were "some upon the Commission of Equivalent that are by much the greatest fools in the United Kingdom". This was written in July 1707, by which time other Scottish noblemen besides Haddington were finding that "Hide Park, St. James, the Opera, and Holburn are never out of my head"; some of them, perhaps, who were not precisely "fools", spending on the Opera money from the Equivalent Fund that should have gone to pay for the development of their country's resources. The shareholders of the Company of Scotland were naturally gratified by getting their capital back with accrued interest. But the directors of the Corporation were not satisfied with the settlement. Having secured an Act of Parliament which ratified the original privileges of the Company, with the addition of other valuable rights, they were now compelled to relinquish everything for the benefit of the English East and West Indian Companies. So hard is it to please everybody when international treaties have to be negotiated! Probably the English Commissioners, perhaps not unreasonably, held the view, quite firmly, that in a poor country like Scotland "siller" would heal all manner of wounds: whether of angry Darien shareholders, or of greedy noblemen shorn of their privileges, or of the disgruntled Commons in Parliament, deprived alike of their legislature and their birthright of independence, nominal though the latter had been, owing to English control.

The Scottish Parliament met on 3rd October, 1706. Once more the throne was occupied by Queensberry, in whose suavity and tact for guiding the affairs of what was certain to prove a turbulent Session Godolphin placed complete confidence. The choice of Commissioner was wise. With Queensberry on the throne, and Seafield again in the Chancellor's chair, Godolphin had at his disposal the two men in Scotland who were best suited to carry through a measure which was intended at once to place the relations between the two countries on a permanently stable footing, and to protect the Treasurer against the attacks of his opponents for his share in giving effect to the Scottish Act of Security.

The Government were weakened by the replacement of the Marquis of Annandale by the Earl of Mar, who contributed less to the debating power of the Ministers than they lost by the departure of Annandale. The latter was offered, but refused, the post of President of the Privy Council, which was not filled up until it was given to the Marquis of Montrose, who was nominally a member of the Squadron (10). Annandale proved to be a thorn in the side of the Government during the debates, for, like the Queen's Advocate, he was no friend of the Union (11).

It was soon made manifest that the ultimate fate of the treaty would depend upon the vote of the Squadron. They had never been in favour of an incorporating union, and unless they could be induced to change their views, the Government could not escape defeat. The destination of their vote was complicated by the fact that they were unreconciled to Queensberry, and the task that rested upon the shoulders of Seafield was consequently a heavy one. It is true that Roxburgh had on one occasion called Seafield a "villain", but in party politics a man may easily be a "villain" one day and the saviour of his country the next. At any rate, Seafield concentrated upon securing the Squadron's vote, and plied Roxburgh, the real leader of the party, with insinuating attentions. Nor was he alone in his courtship of the Squadron. If Lockhart is to be believed, the Duchess of Marlborough tried to sap Roxburgh's political virtue by holding out hopes of putting the Squadron in office if they would support the Union. When taxed with the intention of turning his coat, Roxburgh—again according to Lockhart—declared that he was indifferent to the execrations of posterity, so long as he could attain his present ends, and be revenged upon Queensberry. But it was a queer kind of revenge, or a remarkable exhibition of the Christian virtue of for-giving one's enemies, to promote, as Roxburgh and his colleagues ultimately did, the very measure that was bound to make or mar the fortunes of their political bugbear. Motives in politics are frequently so complex that to unravel them is a task which had better be left unattempted. The reason why the Squadron carried the Union by their vote is perhaps incapable of analysis. They may have become so completely convinced that the Union was in the best interests of their country, that neither their aversion from Queensberry nor the anathemas of their anti-Unionist fellow-Scotsmen were allowed to weigh with them. Or (what was freely suggested by the opponents of the Union), they may have been seduced by the usual methods from their former allegiance to an independent Parliament. The most charitable view to take of the Squadron's action is that it was dictated by what one of their number, Baillie of Jerviswood, had said of union in the previous December, namely, that "wise men will be forced to drink the potion to prevent greater evils" (12).

It is difficult, indeed, to discover among the leading public men in Scotland any instances of complete political consistency during the Parliament that commenced its life in 1703 and was ended in 1707. "Among the faithless faithful only he", Andrew Fletcher never swerved from the course which he had mapped out for him-self: from the time that he entered Parliament as member for Haddingtonshire until he shook the dust off his feet on the scene of what he regarded as Scotland's betrayal. Was this consistency a sign of weakness or of strength? Was it a hidebound conservatism that shut its eyes to what was happening around him, and obstin-ately refused to acknowledge that he had been pursuing a political will-o'-the-wisp? Or, was what some of his contemporaries chose to regard as his pedantic and conceited stubbornness, the expres-sion of matured ideas which, as they were not easily reached, so they were not lightly abandoned? Self-opinionated he certainly was. But that is an attribute which is not rare in men of strong character. It is only weak men who are blown about by every wind of doctrine. Fletcher was so completely convinced of the inherent

R

rightness of his attitude towards Scottish politics, and so passionately devoted to the cause which he believed in his soul would be benefited by the application of his political ideas, that his tenacity of purpose was not merely excusable but completely consistent with his character. Throughout his political career he acted without any regard to his personal interests. While his fellows were busy looking for posts and pensions, he was busy fighting every form of political corruption with all the power at his command.

The mainsprings of his politics were simple enough. They were two in number; and the whole of his political philosophy can be interpreted in terms of them. He believed in the supremacy of Parliamentary government as the safest ultimate repository of power for any people and the most reliable guardian of the personal and political liberty that he prized so highly. Dictatorships, whether by the medium of anointed monarchs or of talented demagogues, were, in his view, full of danger. Human nature, as seen by him, was not proof against the abuse of power when vested in any individual, untrammelled in his policy by the shackles imposed by public opinion. Essentially, therefore, the basis of his politics was democratic, though in view of the limited electorate then existing, it was not democracy as we understand it to-day. The other element in his political philosophy was the sacredness of complete liberty for any social organism lying within the bounds of nationality. And for him a nation was an aggregate of individuals having a community of interests, historical, traditional, economic, and social. Thus his unceasing efforts to resist equally the exercise of arbitrary power emanating from the Throne, and the control by English Courtiers of Scottish Ministries, flowed naturally and logically from the same fountain whose name is freedom.

During the Parliamentary Sessions of 1703-5 he had, as we have seen, battled unceasingly for these dominating principles, and we shall see how, in the closing phases of the long struggle, he maintained his unflinching opposition to what had now become a winning cause. Never was there a greater foe of compromise. The flowing tide swept over him and his limitations, but he remained to the end, standing where he had stood ever since the fight began.

Before the Articles of Union were made public by the Ministry, there had been considerable speculation how the proposal of an incorporating union would be received by the country. We have seen what Fletcher's view was. James Erskine, however, believed or professed to believe that there were very many who were "in a kind of suspense about it", including the clergy whose influence over the people no one was inclined to underrate. Even "some of the Episcopal blades pretend to favour it and others the contrary". Erskine stated also that "the most part of the trading people talk pretty favourably of it". But when Parliament met, and the full particulars were disclosed, there was not much room for "suspense". The shires and the burghs, being disabled from expressing their views by means of an election, could only intimate their opinion by means of addresses to Parliament, which were supplemented by a protest from the Kirk. These addresses poured in to the House in a volume which showed how strongly feeling had been stirred throughout the country by the terms accepted by the Scottish Commissioners. And the flow was all in one direction, for not a solitary address in favour of the Union was received, though it need scarcely be said that this was no proof of complete unanimity in the country. These addresses, which Argyll flippantly advised should be "made kites of", and which the Earl of Marchmont regarded as seditious, were, in fact, representative of the views of the solid elements in the community. The opinions of the mob mattered little, and their ebullitions of wrath hindered rather than helped the opponents of the Union. Still, they were sufficiently alarming to cause considerable uneasiness, for they threatened developments which, had they occurred, might well have sent the Government packing. Probably Lockhart was not overstating the case, when he declared that "the Union was crammed down Scotland's throat" (13).

Street riots occurred both in Glasgow and Edinburgh. In Glasgow, where the Provost and Town Council (probably scenting in advance a lucrative trade in sugar and tobacco) opposed the presentation of an address to Parliament against the Union, the "tradespeople marched through the town with this inscription on their hats: 'No incorporating union'. " For "two or three days" an armed mob "rambled about in the city and had to be dispersed by a detachment of dragoons from Edinburgh, who captured two of their chief leaders, both mean artificers". "The Provost", says Seafield, "was in hazard of his life." The mob broke the windows of his house. In Edinburgh the rabble were equally demonstrative and no less dangerous. Hamilton was their hero. They "huzza'ed" him when he appeared in the streets, and escorted his chair from the House to his rooms in the Abbey. The Ministers of the Crown, and especially the Union Commissioners, were the targets for their rage. As the former passed through the streets, they were greeted with cries of "villains", "rascals"; and among those who had to submit to this fusillade of anathemas were Argyll, Mar (both of whom have given an account of the matter), Loudoun, and Montrose. Also, the mob "went up and down the city and got a drum or two and beat to arms", while some of them went to the house of Sir Patrick Johnston, Lord Provost (or ex-Provost) of Edinburgh (he was a Union Commissioner), and broke open his door, "threatening to murder him for betraying his country by being for the Union". According to Lockhart, the mob would have torn him "in a thousand pieces", had he not managed to make a timely escape, and Mar confirms that opinion, adding that having failed to get hold of the Provost himself, they "riffled" his house.

When, however, the rabble threatened to break in the doors of Parliament House, a pass was reached at which the services of the Earl of Errol, the Hereditary High Constable of Scotland, had to be requisitioned for the protection of the members. But even the soldiers could not be trusted, for there were ominous patriotic mutterings in their ranks. Finally there came a time when the life of the Commissioner himself was in danger; stones were thrown at his coach, some "from windows"; and one of his servants was maltreated in the dark. Matters looked extremely threatening (14).

The greatest potential danger, however, came from an unexpected quarter.

The Cameronians were the austerest sect of the Presbyterians and the dourest fighters in the South-west. They were haters of Popery, Episcopacy, and Jacobitism. Yet so strong was their aversion from the Union that they composed their differences with the Cavaliers, and having formed themselves into regiments, chosen their officers, and supplied themselves with arms, they offered to place themselves under the direction of the Duke of Hamilton for resisting the menace of subjection to England, which they believed was threatening their country. What, precisely, they thought that menace consisted of, apart from danger to the Church, and how they proposed to harmonize their rigid views with the ultimate aim of the Jacobites, their strange bedfellows, is not quite clear. But as a visible sign of their political faith, they burnt the Articles of Union at the market-cross of Dumfries. Their intentions, whether to overawe the Parliament and nothing more, or to declare for St. Germains, were not put to the test. Their chief organizer was Major Cunningham of Eckett, a Darien adventurer, and an adventurer in a wider sense, whose fidelity was, with good reason, not above suspicion, though Lockhart believed that he was innocent of spying for the Government. That was certainly more than could be said for Mr. Hepburn, a "mountain Cameronian Minister", who had "roared as much as any against the Union", or for Ker of Kersland, a plausible scoundrel. The Duke of Atholl, according to the plans made, was to secure the pass of Stirling with his Highlanders, and the Cameronians— some seven or eight thousand well-armed men—were to meet at Hamilton on an appointed day, thence march on Edinburgh, and do what Cromwell and his troopers did to the House of Commons. But unfortunately for the Cameronians, the Duke of Hamilton who was to head the movement for the suppression of that Parliament, was too much like his grandfather whom Cromwell had beaten at Preston, to undertake a rôle which Cromwell would have found easy. Whatever the reason, whether his failing was that of an Earl of Argyll who declared that "dubiety plays upon me like a flute", or whether he really feared a clash with the English troops who were believed to be concentrating on the Border, the Duke countermanded the rendezvous at Hamilton; and the Government were saved. They seem to have used their escape with skill by spreading dissensions among their potential destroyers: a task which was not difficult to accomplish, with so many itching palms, such as those of their spy, Ker of Kersland, stretched out to grasp their wages for deluding the credulous peasantry (15).

Turning our attention now from the external evidences of opposition to the Union to the proceedings inside the House, we find, from Lockhart's narrative, that on the failure of the Cameronian adventure, the Duke of Atholl and Fletcher (there is no evidence of Fletcher being associated in any way with the Cameronian fiasco), with Hamilton's concurrence, planned to present a national address to the Queen, describing "the almost universal aversion" to the treaty and praying her to set it aside. It is to be remarked that this address describes the principle of incorporation, not merely as destructive of the nation's sovereignty, but as calculated to " sink the rents, destroy the trade, and subject the people of this Kingdom to intolerable taxes". The address likewise prays for the calling of a new Parliament, "according to our Claim of Right by which we are entitled to frequent Parliaments".

It was held, indeed, both inside and outside the House, that "it was high treason to treat of an entire union", as being opposed to the Claim of Right by which William and Mary succeeded to the Scottish Crown. That objection was stressed by Annandale in Parliament. The Earl of Stair replied to it by stating that the objection was rendered invalid by the fact that when the Convention of Estates framed the Claim of Right, they appointed Commissioners to treat for an entire and complete union. In view of subsequent events, however, the Earl's argument does not seem conclusive. Fletcher was one of those who strongly supported the opinion that the Claim of Right ruled out a settlement such as that contemplated by the Treaty of Union, unless it was confirmed by a new Parliament (16).

The Duke of Atholl and Fletcher might have saved themselves the trouble of organizing a national address to the Queen. For any plan needing the concurrence of the Duke of Hamilton seemed to be foredoomed to ultimate failure. Five hundred country gentlemen had actually arrived in Edinburgh, and many more were coming to take part in the national protest. The intention was to wait upon Queensberry, and by a prolocutor beg of him to "lay aside the designed Union", or, at any rate, "grant a recess" until the Queen had been informed of the state of feeling in the country and, whatever the Commissioner's reply, to send the address to the Queen. Lockhart has a marginal note on the design: "broke by the Duke of Hamilton". On the day before the

[*262*]

appointed date for putting the plan into execution, Hamilton announced that he would take no part in the project, unless a clause was added to the address, intimating the willingness of the petitioners to settle the Succession on the House of Hanover. His excuse for blocking the scheme was too specious to be convincing. Was dubiety once more playing on him like a flute? Clearly he was hedging as usual. Tired of waiting in Edinburgh for an adjustment of this eleventh-hour difficulty, many of the country gentlemen went home, and one more opportunity of making an effective protest was lost. Also, warned of their danger, the Government took steps to prevent any recurrence of similar meetings in Edinburgh (17).

The Government were more concerned with building up their majority than with answering their critics inside the House, or answering addresses from country gentlemen and the Convention of Burghs outside the House. They were bent upon winning individual waverers, and, most of all, two such dissimilar bodies as the Squadron and the Kirk. It is instructive to observe how they set about that business.

"All our treaters", says Seafield, "continue fixed to what they did, but we believe Mr. Lockhart of Carnwath will be against us." Those who had agreed to the Articles of Union could not well do otherwise than support them in Parliament. But some of the Whigs in the House were uneasy. Among them were men like the Duke of Argyll, who probably resented having been passed over in favour of Queensberry for the Commissionership. He was certainly annoyed that the Duke of Hamilton had not been nominated as a member of the Commission for Union. If Argyll declared against the Government, the effect would be far-reaching. He must be kept in a good humour at all costs. He wanted an earldom for his brother Archibald. "They will not be pleased", said Seafield, "unless it is granted, and it is certainly necessary to keep them right at present." This was on 14th October, and a few days later we find that Argyll, whose support on the earlier date seemed a little doubtful, was now "so useful that we at once agreed that he might exped his brother's patent when he pleased, so he has sent it to the Seals, and he obliged the Commissioner also to exped his son, my Lord Charles's patent". At the same time it was "probable" that vacancies in the Session and Justiciary Courts would not be filled up "till after the Parliament"; in other words, the offices would be kept dangling in front of candidates who were ready to support the Government in payment for them. The commissions for the new appointments were to be sent "blank" to Queensberry, who would fill them up in his discretion (18).

Money, too, played an important part in this game of indirect bribery. During his Commissionership Argyll had drawn Godolphin's attention to the fact that the Government had lost "above twenty votes" by not meeting arrears of pensions. This danger had to be carefully avoided by the Union Ministry. On 4th October the Earl of Glasgow, Treasurer-Depute, writes that Queensberry had ordered him to ask the Treasurer, Godolphin, to pay "as soon as possible" the sum of £10,000 to Sir David Nairne, the Under-Secretary of State in London, whereof Nairne was to retain £4,500 on Queensberry's account and remit the balance to Scotland. The money was needed "in regard that many of our nobility who are come to Parliament that want their bygone pensions, are calling for some money, and it is for her Majesty's service that they have a part at this juncture".

Tweeddale, Montrose, and Roxburgh were among those who received payment of the arrears of pensions due to them. And the £5,500 was followed by a further remittance to Scotland of £10,000, to be used for a like purpose. The money was undoubtedly intended to grease the wheels of Union, though the crude methods of bribery, popularly believed to have been employed, cannot be proved (19).

Even those who had been selected to calculate the Equivalent (one, at least, of whom had grumbled that Scotland should have had to pay any share of England's debts), had to be kept quiet by a proposal that Parliament should recommend the gift of a "gratification" for their services. "By this", adds Mar significantly, "they are kept in dependence" (20).

But all these devices would have failed to overcome the opposition to the Union, had it not been for the change in the attitude of the Kirk, and, more immediately, the deflection of the Squadron's vote. The Kirk, guided in its counsels largely by Carstares, one of the statesmen-parsons that Scotland has a way of producing at critical periods in the history of her Church, had at first feared that, as the result of the Union, she might be "swallowed up", as Burnet puts it, by the Church of England. The clergy were encouraged in that belief, suggests Burnet, by the Duchess Dowager of Hamilton, who had great influence with the Presbyterian body, and who, moreover, had to consider her son's interest in preventing the Union at any cost. But an Act, safeguarding the interests of the Church, which was passed by Parliament in November 1706, altered the situation so radically that the Government were completely relieved from the fear of the Kirk's opposition, which, if persisted in, would certainly have proved fatal to the Union proposals. That the cautious attitude of the Kirk, encouraged as it was by the wily wire-puller who had been the trusted adviser of William of Orange before he became the protector of Presbyterianism under Queen Anne, was superfluous, can scarcely be urged by anyone who has followed the debate in the House of Lords when the Treaty of Union was before that Assembly. But the Church of Scotland was reassured, and thenceforward its opposition to Union became lukewarm or, at any rate, entirely passive. The Government had now only one more deal to negotiate: the vote of the New Party, as they called themselves, or the Squadron, as they were called by others.

Seafield's reports to Godolphin at different stages of the Session on the wooing of the Squadron are illuminating. On 14th October he had taken "all the methods" he was capable of using, to keep the Squadron from joining with "our Torie Pairtie", and he doubts not but that they will "concur" with the Government, "which I think will make the carrying the Union certain". He thinks the New Party "deserves all encouragement if they continue to do as they have begun". Two days later he repeats that he is doing all he can to "encourage" the New Party, for it is "of great consequence to have a considerable majority". On 3rd November he reports that the New Party continues to act "very zealously in conjunction with us". Great efforts were being made "to incense the gentry, towns, and common people against us. . . . If we can but please the ministers in the security of the Church, our greatest difficulty will be over." On 7th November, when reporting that the first (and fundamental) Article of the treaty had been carried by a majority of thirty-two votes, he says that the New Party had given them all the "assistance we can desire". And on 11th November he informs Godolphin that the New Party had been with him last night "and are as right in this matter as I am myself". Indeed, the adhesion of the Squadron to the Government's proposals seems to have been well assured before the vote was taken on the fundamental Article. According to a letter of 25th October, from Viscount Dupplin, the Squadron by that time were "now all as one man for the Union". The same letter gives the following reasons why, in the opinion of the writer, conversions to Union were taking place: "the great success abroad" (Ramillies); "the extreme poverty of the nation; the power and influence of the advanced Equivalent; with the arguments that have prevailed with the Marquis of Tweeddale's party" (the Squadron). Seafield's arguments had indeed prevailed (21).

All was now apparently plain sailing for the Ministers and for Union. The Kirk had cooled down; waverers had been secured; and the Squadron captured. What need was there, then, for Seafield to do anything but smile expansively at the fury of the Opposition, or for Queensberry to do anything but listen unmoved to their vigorous protests? But one more desperate contrivance was to be tried by the anti-Unionists before they finally threw in their hand.

We have seen how the plan to present an address to the Queen was baulked by the indecision (or whatever else it may have been) of Hamilton. Atholl was furious with his fellow-duke, and so, too, were the country gentlemen as they returned home. But the Nationalists were to have another Hamiltonian experience. The Government had got as far as the discussion of the twenty-second Article of the treaty, when Hamilton proposed to his colleagues another and a "final plan" to do something to save the nation "just come to the brink of ruin". The plan was for the anti-Unionists to enter a formal protest against the Article providing for the representation of Scotland in the British Parliament, and then leave the House in a body "not to return again". It was believed that the protest was drafted by Sir James Stewart, the Queen's Advocate, who was so bitterly opposed to the Union that when he perceived the probability of the measure being passed, he ceased attending the House. It will be remembered that in the previous Parliament a similar proceeding—a protest and a march out of the House—had been followed, under Hamilton's leadership, and, as a consequence, had vitiated the negotiations for union by the "Rump". It was hoped that the same result would follow on this occasion; and, indeed, Seafield afterwards told Lockhart that had the plan not miscarried, the Government would have abandoned the measure for union altogether. How, then, did the plan miscarry? Once more Lockhart has a marginal note: "the measure broke by the Duke of Hamilton". Truly, the Duke was a record-breaker, for this was the third time he had thrown his party over at the last moment. It is scarcely surprising to find Atholl declaring (in 1708) that "his (Hamilton's) politics have been most unaccountable for some years, but especially at the last Scots Parliament, since which time, I have had no manner of correspondence with him".

What happened was that when the time came for the protest to be presented in Parliament, and for the protestors to walk out, Hamilton was detained at home with—toothache. And when dragged, figuratively speaking, by his friends to the House, he positively refused to present the protest, a distinction which, throughout, had been reserved for him. So that was the end of one more abortive attempt to impede the Union, for without their leader the protesters refused to proceed further. It was believed, probably with some justification for the belief, that the night before the protest was to be handed in, Queensberry, either personally or by an agent, had given Hamilton a pretty plain hint that if the protest was not abandoned, he would be held responsible in London for the consequences. So this final opportunity was lost, and afterwards the opponents of Union had no heart to persevere in their opposition: they accepted the inevitable with passive resignation (22).

We must now see what part Fletcher had taken in the Union discussions, and his general attitude towards the great questions that were involved. He spoke frequently and always effectively in the House in 1706, but his speeches have not been printed, and we are unable therefore to judge of their quality, as we can of those delivered in the stirring Session of 1703. Nor does he seem to have joined the host of tract-mongers for and against the Union, who sought to influence public opinion in favour of their views. But he commended to the consideration of James Erskine one of the most effective of the anti-Union treatises, namely that of James Hodges, who took the line that the loss of Scotland's independence would be dearly bought, if bartered for "some hogsheads of sugar, indigo, and stinking tobacco". That was precisely Fletcher's position. As we have seen, no one was more alive than himself to the national advantages of profitable trading. But if the whole wealth of the Indies had been offered to him in exchange for the independence of his native country, he would have unhesitatingly rejected the offer with scorn. To him her independence was literally priceless: a possession upon which no valuation could possibly be placed. It was an attitude of mind, a thing of the spirit, that few in that Scottish Parliament of realistic placemen could have understood; or, if understood, could have sympathized with. Fletcher, in the view of many of them, was a man of one idea: a fantastic builder of Utopias, in an age and in a country where there was small room for sentimental dreamers.

Hodges argued that an incorporation which retained mutual obligations was an absurdity, since it implies that what has become one is still two. And logically it is, as he says, an absurdity. But there are many theoretical absurdities in practical politics. The Union of Parliaments was, in a sense, like the union between Jonah and the whale. Something like the argument used by Hodges appears in a tract which Dalrymple, in his *Memoirs of Great Britain*, attributes to Fletcher. It was found among his papers, and though not in his handwriting, one sees no real reason to doubt that he was the author, since matter and manner alike seem to point to that conclusion. The paper is entitled *The present State of the Controversy betwixt United and Separate Parliaments*, and it puts in a strong plea for a federal union. Incorporation, it is argued, would be ruinous for Scotland, whereas a federal union would aggrandize both countries if the power of the Crown were kept within proper limitations: that is, the Fletcher limitations. Dalrymple ventures the opinion that Fletcher's proposals, if made effective, would have led to a war between England and Scotland. "Fletcher saw it," he goes on to say, "and is reported to have laid his account with it, and his writings show that he despised it" (23). Dalrymple may be right. For after the victory of Ramillies England was in no mood to be trifled with, and France, sadly licking her cruel wounds, was certainly in no position to reinforce, either with men or money, Scottish resistance to an English attack. On the other hand, no responsible statesman in England could have contemplated without the gravest misgiving the prospect of holding Scotland as a conquest, even if the subjugation of that country proved feasible. But the issue in all likelihood would have been one of war, or separation, or both. These were evils varying in magnitude, and offering alternatives which no statesman in either country could view with equanimity. It is highly probable that Fletcher, who was cast in a heroic mould, would have been ready to pick up the gauntlet if it had been thrown down; certainly not in any light or defiant spirit, but in a spirit of sacrifice. He was a man who would never have flinched from offering himself on any sacrificial altar for what he conceived to be the permanent good of his country, or as the logical expression of his ideals.

He held a gloomy view of the outlook in mid-October. "The whole nation are become rogues," he declared despairingly. "I believe", remarks Mar, "before the Parliament ends he will go out of it. But he has not spoken much. He reserves himself until we come to determine:" in other words, just before the vote on the first and fundamental Article of the treaty. For the Articles were being discussed separately, and it was not until 1st November that a proposal was made (by the Earl of Marchmont, whom we have met before as Sir Patrick Hume) to take a vote on the first Article, providing for the two Kingdoms to be united under the name of Great Britain. The debate, lasting for three days, which preceded the vote, marked the climax in intensity of the speeches for and against the Union, and Fletcher reserved his main attack for that occasion. For the result of the vote on the vital Article number one was going to determine the question of union one way or the other; and all the other Articles were to Fletcher, and those who thought with him, of relatively small importance.

But before the beginning of November Fletcher figures in two more "scenes" in the House. The first clash was with certain members who were also members of the Standing Committee of the General Assembly of the Kirk. The General Assembly had taken a hand in the question that was agitating the country, by appointing "a day of prayer for direction to the Parliament", and later recommended the observance of a "fast-day" throughout the land in accentuation of that laudable object. As if to stress its necessity still further, the Duke of Atholl proposed that sermons might be preached in the House on the "fast-day". During the discussion, Fletcher attacked the "carriage" of the above-mentioned members, of whom he said that if it were "not to rip up a sore he could make them blush". The attack was strongly resented by the members concerned, and with such success that Fletcher and his friends were forced "to let the Duke of Atholl's proposal fall, to bring himself off this undertaking of his" (24). An example of this sort, among others, seems to justify the opinion expressed by a friendly critic that he did much injury to his cause in the House by the hastiness of his temper leading to reckless charges which he failed to substantiate.

An incident which occurred on the following day showed that his temper was getting frayed beyond endurance, by what he saw to be the growing and imminent prospect of the Union being passed by the House. "To-day" (29th October), so Mar tells Nairne, "Fletcher in passion said that the treaters had betrayed their trust:" the treaters had, in fact, been traitors. To tell honourable members to their faces that they were traitors argued a courage that had no regard at all for consequences. It is not surprising that there was an immediate demand that he be sent to the Bar of the House for his audacity. But he was not alone in the expression of his opinion, though his supporters made use of more discreet language. "We had pity on Fletcher," says Mar magnanimously, "and upon his begging pardon let it fall:" but not before (according to another account) he had refused to withdraw his charge, alleging that "he could not get softer words" (25). Certainly he was a man who called a spade a spade, and not an agricultural implement. But his cause might have been better served, had he applied to his personal charges the same degree of exactitude that he was careful to observe in his speeches intended for publication. Yet the members of the Scottish House of Parliament seemed to have illimitable patience with the petulant outbursts of the representative of Haddingtonshire. No matter how frequently he offended against the etiquette of the House, he was always forgiven on his offering an apology, which, to do him justice, was invariably forthcoming. The fact seems to be that, however violently the majority of the members disagreed with his views, they were all proud of him, as, in some respects, the greatest ornament of the House: "the ablest" of the Scots of his time, as Dalrymple asserts. They respected a personality in their midst that was unique; and they paid willing tribute to a sincerity of purpose to which some of them must have uneasily felt that they themselves could lay small claim.

Then came the great three days of the Session, when the speeches which were to determine the vital vote were delivered. One of these is historic, and if it is a fair sample of the others, the old oak roof of Parliament House must have echoed to the ringing tones of rhetorical oratory such as had never been equalled in the Scottish Parliament, or excelled in the Parliament of any other country. Lord Belhaven's moving, if theatrical speech can still be read by all. But, besides that speech, what of the eloquence of Stair, the charm of Roxburgh, the elegance of Argyll, and the persuasiveness of Queensberry and Seafield, all in the cause of Union? And, on the other side, what of the compelling rhetoric of Hamilton and the incisive logic of Fletcher? On 1st November, Mar tells Nairne that Fletcher "gave us two of his studied speeches which certainly we'll have ere long in print" (he was mistaken), "as also Belhaven's. My Lord Roxburgh spoke very handsomely for the Union, and gave Belhaven his payment particularly." It was on the following day that Belhaven made his famous oration which is popularly, if possibly mistakenly, believed to have been the greatest of all the Union speeches. He was a natural orator, endowed with all the arts, dangerous, if seductive, of the rhetorician who appeals mainly to the emotions. Fletcher, on the other hand, was not a ready speaker. His speeches had to be carefully prepared beforehand, for (as he told Wodrow in 1712), owing to his defective memory, he had to write everything he said in Parliament. He memorized his speeches "every day as ever a school-boy did his grammar and directly repeated some of them ten or twenty times; and being uncertain what matters were to come before them, he was obliged sometimes to have six or ten speeches upon distinct heads in readiness at once" (26). The care taken over his speeches, and the "incredible fatigue" which their preparation entailed, testify to the tremendous seriousness with which he took his politics, and, some would add, himself. He was thorough in his work, as in his likes and dislikes; and similarly, his political ideas were thoroughness itself in their radicalism.

Probably the two "studied speeches" to which Mar alludes did not produce the same effect as Belhaven's more turgid oratory. According to William Paterson, one of them was a historical review, citing apt instances to show that "the fate of all weaker States after an union with greater kingdoms was to be at length swallowed up and enslaved by them". But Belhaven's appeal was to the public: a speech contrived "to incense the common people", says Seafield, who adds, "It had no great influence in the House." Cunningham describes it as "rough and unpolished" (27). It may be doubted, indeed, whether votes were influenced by any of the three days' speeches. Theoretically, speeches are made in Parliament to secure votes, though practically they may be delivered for quite other purposes. The question of uniting the two Parliaments had been so thoroughly examined at every angle, and the Government had been so unremitting in its canvassing, that by 1st November every Whig in the House must have made up his mind on which side his vote was to be cast on such a fundamental issue; and no subsequent speeches, however eloquent, can very well have altered the destination of a single vote. Thunder as he might in his loudest tones, as he demanded "Where are the Douglases and the Campbells?" the Duke of Hamilton addressed an unmoved Douglas on the throne, and a disdainful Campbell on the benches of the peers. Belhaven might apostrophize "Mother Caledonia", only to be scoffed at by Marchmont as a sentimental dreamer, and to be "refuted" by Roxburgh "in substance much more than in words". Appeal and apostrophe were alike in vain. In vain, too, was Annandale's proposal for a federal union. "Very few concurred with him." And it was equally in vain that Fletcher "reproached and inveighed against the Queen's Ministers, without any regard to his own fortune, though very large" (28).

"I pray God", said Seafield, in his report to Godolphin of 3rd November, "we may carry the Union in Parliament so it may be approved in England." It was with keen satisfaction that Godolphin heard from him a few days later, that Article number one had been passed by a majority of thirty-two votes, of which twenty-two were contributed by the Squadron, whose total voting strength was then twenty-four. Had these twenty-two votes gone to the other side, Article number one would have been rejected by a majority of twelve, and the measure for union would have been abandoned (29).

The opponents of the Union did not entirely give up the struggle in the House. Some of them were determined to fight to the end, until the final and comprehensive vote was taken. On 15th November Fletcher made a speech on the second Article of the treaty, recognizing the Princess Sophia as Queen Anne's successor; and on the following day he supported a proposal by Annandale that in view of the state of public feeling against the Union, "the Articles might be laid aside", and that Parliament should proceed to a settlement of the Succession on limitations. This was the old proposal dished up afresh, and things had now gone so far that it had no possible chance of acceptance. Indeed, the Nationalists as a party seemed to recognize that fact, for the approval of Annandale's motion was "lukewarm". Apparently the Government interpreted the motion as a mere device for obstruction: so they refused to listen to it. "We would hear none of them speak, and so with their bawling to be heard and ours to stop them, the House came in a great confusion." Hamilton and Belhaven then suggested an adjournment, in order that an address might be drawn up to the Queen, stating that they were willing to settle the Succession on limitations. They had the full support of the Nationalists for an address to the Throne. But the Government refused to agree, stating that the conditions of union had been misrepresented to the people. Now that the Church had received satisfaction, it only remained to explain to the public, by free discussion in Parliament, the trade advantages conferred by the treaty. It would then be recognized that the Union was in the country's interest.

Annandale, who had taken an active part in opposition, rather inconsistently voted for the second Article, which he had opposed. According to Mar, he had "pulled off the mask entirely" and kept company with the Jacobites only. "The Register" (the Earl of Glasgow) "carried me", says Mar, "to a tavern as I came from the Abbey to-night, and after we had drunk a bottle of wine, we were coming away, and at the door we met with some of that set who had been with Annandale to-night and last night too. They were very drunk, and would have us turn in again to drink one bottle, which we were forced to do." They said they regretted having been forced to take up with Annandale, whom they ridiculed. A good deal of political business seems to have been transacted in the Edinburgh taverns (30).

To the third Article, providing for the United Kingdom to be represented in one and the same Parliament, the Duke of Atholl proposed to add that the Parliament of Great Britain should sit, once every three years, "within that place of Brittane now called Scotland": a proposal which received no support from the Ministers. It would certainly not have been "approved in England". But it was on the fourth Article, relating to the communication of trade, that Fletcher made one of the most remarkable speeches of the Session. Contrary to the boast of the Government, that the benefits of trade communication, when explained in Parliament, would satisfy the public, Fletcher argued in "a long discourse" that free trade with England would be positively disadvantageous to Scotland. Another member moved that all the trade matters in the treaty should be remitted to a committee for consideration and report. But the Government would have none of this, alleging that there was "an evident design to protract and delay business". Fletcher was so angry when the vote went against him, that he "ran out of the House" (31).

And so the business went on, one Article after another being carried, until the fourteenth was reached, when Fletcher moved an amendment that exemption from the duty on malt should be "for ever". But it was carried against him that it should be free during the War only. Another amendment to the same Article was moved by Fletcher, stipulating "that the nation of Scotland be for ever free of all burdens but what is agreed to by these Articles". To this others added, "for payment of the English debt". But once more, this was a proposal which clearly would not "be approved in England", and it was consequently resisted by the Government. On the following day Fletcher moved an amendment to Article fifteen, "that they should not be subject to the English debts": a hopeless proposition, as he must have known. But these radical amendments were obviously intended by him as protests, rather than as practical proposals for serious consideration. On 10th December a noisy discussion, in which Fletcher participated, occurred on the report of a committee on Article six. "Some of them spoke so often" that the Duke of Argyll moved "that the orders of the House ought to be kept" (32).

A week later another "scene" took place in the House, this time between Fletcher and the Earl of Stair. The two men seemed to be mutually antipathetic; at any rate, Fletcher obviously disliked Stair's politics. It will be remembered that he had previously attacked Stair in the House, and, since then, the part taken by Stair—a very real part behind the scenes—in promoting the Union had probably increased Fletcher's antipathy. He accused Stair of having said what was not true about the Minutes, apparently of the last sitting. "My Lord Stair desired the House to take notice of what Salton had said; otherwise he would be obliged to say what he had said was a lie. After near an hour's discourse about this, and some having moved that both should crave the House's pardon, Salton craved the House's pardon, but slighted craving Stair's pardon." Eventually a formula was suggested by the tactful Chancellor, to which Fletcher subscribed, "and both of them gave their word of honour not to resent it without doors". (33). These Parliamentary tiffs would be scarcely worth recording, were it not that they illustrate the tenseness of the feeling that was displayed during the Union debates; and they illustrate, also, the irritable pugnacity that was such a blemish on Fletcher's character. His sensitiveness to moral slips was such that he sometimes made rash personal accusations on grounds that were shown to be flimsy. His temper was explosive rather than bad, and he possessed the commendable quality of telling a man to his face what he thought of him, instead of making charges behind his back to which the other had no opportunity of replying.

His last speech in Parliament seems to have been delivered on

27th January, 1707, when he made a motion disabling noblemen
or their eldest sons from election to the House of Commons by the
shires or the burghs of Scotland, "which was agreed upon by the
barons and burrows". But this motion was rejected by thirteen
votes in favour of another, providing that for the elections to the
House of Commons, the elections by the shires and burghs
"should continue as is now by law established" (34).

On 16th January, 1707, the treaty with the amendments (none
of them fundamental), made by Parliament, was finally approved
(35), and the Act of approval, when touched by the sceptre, was
sent up to London, where, after a debate in both Houses of Parliament, it was, in turn, approved without amendment. But not
entirely without opposition. There was, for example, the Arch-
bishop of York. "God forbid", said His Grace, "that I should
give assent to an union with a people who are not so much as
initiated in Christianity, and are even averse to the English cere-
monies, vestments, prayers, and primitive liturgies" (36). Judged
by these tests, the Scots were indeed a hopeless set of barbarians!

There was a time in November when the popular opposition
in Scotland wore such an alarming aspect that the Government
suspended the arming provisions of the Act of Security; when the
Commissioner (as Burnet admits) "despaired" of succeeding; and
when the Earl of Cromarty, the Justice-General, actually urged
upon Godolphin the advisability of adjourning Parliament. But
Godolphin replied that this course would mean the total abandon-
ment of the treaty, and hinted that if the troops were in danger of
being overpowered by the mob, English soldiers would be available to keep order. For Godolphin it was then or never; and
Queensberry was heartened to persevere. Civil war may have been
prevented by his perseverance, and by his ultimate success (37).
But Fletcher would have replied that the price of peace was too
high.

Chapter XIX

A MARRIAGE HAS BEEN ARRANGED

"A MARRIAGE has been arranged and will shortly take place: the contracting parties being a bridegroom who is masterful and wealthy, and has no love for the bride, but has insisted upon the match owing to certain advantages which he expects to derive from it; the other party to the contract being a lady of good birth and ancient lineage, but impoverished estate, who dislikes the prospective bridegroom, and is indignant at the manner of his wooing, but has been coaxed to the altar by her friends, some of whom have an eye on the wealth of the bridegroom, others on his political and social favours, and all on the maxim that out of evil might come forth good. The least self-interested of the bride's friends believe that the match is the best that she can hope for, and optimistically visualize a time when husband and wife will probably endure one another, and possibly even love one another. And, incidental to this marriage of convenience: it had not lasted more than six years before a divorce was prevented only by the merest tip of the scale: already there had been a breach by the husband of the marriage contract."

That was the union between England and Scotland.

On 28th January, 1707, the Queen announced to both Houses of Parliament that the Treaty of Union had been ratified by the Scottish Estates. It was an announcement that betokened the end of one epoch in Scottish history, and the commencement of another. On 19th March a copy of the English Act of Union which, after perfunctory criticism, had passed both Houses of Parliament in London without any alteration in the Articles, was presented in Edinburgh by Queensberry, who, six days later, singing the swan-song of the dying Parliament, announced its "adjournment", a curious word to express a final dissolution.

The Thanksgiving Service which was held in St. Paul's Cathedral on 1st May, and the *Te Deum* which was sung to the accompaniment of the thunder of the guns at the Tower and St. James's

Park, expressed the relief of the English nation that the back door in the North had at long last been closed, barred, and bolted. That belief, as events proved, was rather premature; but, at any rate, the Union disposed once for all of the Succession question; and had there been no Succession question, there would have been no Union. But from the standpoint of the average Englishman, there was little significance in the Union, other than the insurance against political trouble which it connoted. It was hardly more than if Yorkshire, or any other district in England, had transferred to Westminster delegates from a local council that had hitherto managed its own concerns; except, indeed, that the provincial newcomers in this case hailed from that side of the Tweed which had for centuries made things unpleasant for the other side, and spoke a dialect of English which was regarded as quaint (1).

"All that passed away", said Mr. J. R. Green, the historian, writing of the Union, "was the jealousy which had parted, since the days of Edward the First, two peoples whom a common blood and common speech proclaimed to be one" (2). And Sir Richard Lodge writes, "The population of Southern Scotland, as thoroughly English as their neighbours across the Border, acquired ascendency over the Celtic people of the Highlands, and colonised the eastern district from the Forth to Inverness. In language, in law, in municipal institutions, in architecture, and in social life, the English and the Lowlanders were to all intents and purposes identical. The Gaels were as alien to both peoples as the Welsh were to the English" (3). Nothing (it would appear) had happened, except the happy reunion of two branches of the same family which had long been estranged from one another.

Had that been a fact, instead of a fiction, there could have been nothing but mutual congratulations for the healing of a wound which had festered for four hundred years, and nothing but astonishment that brothers by blood could have maintained a family feud so long. Unhappily for the facile theory of this school of historians (to which Freeman and Lang also belonged), it is based upon a conception which is entirely at variance with ethnological facts. For Green's "two peoples" and Lodge's "identical" races were (and are) really two peoples and two races, and not "one", as they supposed. Apart from Mr. Green's contemptuous ignoring of the Highlands, and Professor Lodge's racial differentiation, which the thesis implies, it is completely fallacious in its application to the Lowlands. The speech in the Lowlands may be English (with dialectical variations), but the race is mainly Celtic. That speech and race are not synonymous terms needs no stressing. And with the exception of the Lothians (long subject to Northumbria, before being finally annexed to the Scottish Crown, though even in the Lothians Celtic toponomy shows itself), it is an historical fact, conclusively proved by the incidence of place-names, that the whole of Scotland, north, south, east, and west, was at one time occupied by a predominantly Celtic population. The ancestors of the present population, who gave these Celtic names to rivers and streams, hills and dales, farms and fields, can scarcely have been Anglo-Saxons speaking a Celtic tongue. Clearly they were Celts, mainly of the Gaelic and (an older stratum) partly of the British branch of that race (4).

Thus racialism, a fundamental fact in nationhood, has tended throughout the history of both nations to keep them apart; and it is futile to ignore that factor in the assessment of national values, and in its effect upon political adjustments. Alike in England and Scotland there is, of course, a mixture of races, but the predominant strain in Scotland to-day is of as indubitably a Celtic ancestry as the predominant strain in England is of Anglo-Saxon origin. We have seen how that genial ethnologist, the Earl of Cromarty, welcomed the Union, because he hoped it would do away with the terms "Englishman" and "Scotsman" which connoted racial differences. He would substitute for both the "glorious" name of "Brittains", which implied unity based upon the common possession of an island home. For a national name to embrace the whole of the inhabitants of the island, he would go back, in fact, to pre-Roman times, when from John o' Groats to Lands End the island was inhabited by a homogeneous race (excluding its prehistoric elements). But since then, this homogeneity (he lamented) had been broken into by "Jutland pirats and mercinaries" who had given England its name, and by rovers from Ireland, who had given Scotland its present title. After the Union a feeble effort was made, not indeed to attach to England the name of "South Britain", but to make the term "North Britain" synonymous with

Scotland. Logical as was Lord Cromarty's argument, it could not, however, successfully stand against the spirit of separate nationalities, which demanded that the distinctive and historic name pertaining to each country should remain. There was always the sense of "two peoples", not one; of two races, not one. If Scotland to-day resents the label of "North Britain", she might accept it as a geographical expression, if England were willing to be called "South Britain". But to apply the name "Englishmen" to Scotsmen (as is frequently done), is plainly an expression of the "provincial" idea.

It was only natural that unity between two peoples living on the same island in close propinquity (only separated by boundaries that are essentially artificial), and having a common literary language (though each vernacular differs widely from the other),— it was natural that the desirability of uniting two countries so situated should never have been far absent from the minds of the statesmen of both nations. We find Edward IV writing to the Pope in 1482, "We would that these two nations should be so united in heart and soul as they are by neighbourhood, soil and language" (5) (i.e. the literary language). And the same aspiration was ever before the minds of his predecessors and his successors. Force had been tried by the stronger nation to bend the weaker to her will, but it had been revealed over and over again that neither by the victories which she won, nor by the defeats which she suffered in the field of battle, could the smaller nation be induced to accept absorption, and relinquish the sense of separateness as a nation to which she jealously clung throughout the centuries.

At the time of the Union this sense of separateness was particularly strong in Scotland, stimulated, as it had been, by unneighbourly acts on the part of England. This awareness of difference in race, temperament, history, traditions, culture, and even speech (in short, the spirit of nationalism) made a wide difference in the standpoint of contemporary Scotland and England respectively on the implications of the Union. England (so the anti-Unionists contended in Scotland) was giving up nothing except a trade monopoly, a share in which might be of doubtful advantage to her neighbour. But Scotland was parting with the last shred of her national independence, as embodied in a Constitution which was now to be dissolved (6).

That was the standpoint of Fletcher. He differed both from the ignorant mob in its furiously anti-English attitude, and from the cultured classes in their nicely balanced reasons for or against the Union. His character was simple in its essence, and direct in its expression. He had two absorbing passions: love of country and love of liberty. He was master of his soul, and never allowed himself to be seduced from these twin ideals by considerations of expediency or by the lure of sophism. His patriotism was of the kind that every country needs and most countries lack. It was based upon no narrow self-sufficiency; it expressed itself in no blatant arrogance. He believed, with Cardinal Mercier, that "there can be no perfect Christian who is not a perfect patriot". And probably he would also have agreed with Amiel, that "there is not one (nation) in which the good is not counterbalanced by evil. Each is a caricature of man, a proof that no one among them deserves to crush the others and that all have something to learn from all." There is a selfish nationalism and an unselfish nationalism; and Fletcher was careful to distinguish between the two. He fully recognized what was, in his time, a novel doctrine, the doctrine of the interdependence of nations. That all civilized nations are economically interlocked; that what hits one hits all: and what makes one prosperous makes all prosperous; that an injustice inflicted upon one nation by another reacts as cause and effect upon the offender; that all wars of oppression are ultimately disastrous for victors and vanquished alike; and that it is the duty of every nation to defend itself with all its power against foreign attack from any quarter whatsoever: these, for Fletcher, were first principles with which few of his contemporaries were in agreement. But for him they were also logically compatible with a passionate preference for the country of his birth over any other country, and with no less a passionate determination that, so far as in him lay, he would defend her birthright of complete liberty as he would defend his own life. In his view Scotland must be free or she must be conquered: there was no middle way, either by means of an incorporating union or any other method that shackled her complete liberty. And in furthering that view with all his strength,

[*281*]

he could not be bought and he could not be silenced. He was born at a time when his native country lay under the iron heel of Cromwell. It was a memory of childhood that left its ineffaceable mark on his conceptions of nationality. No one knew better than he did that the rule of the Englishmen was accompanied by an exposition of impartial justice to which his country had previously been a stranger. But that fact, when placed in the scales against her loss of liberty, the infringement of her national independence, had relatively little weight. He was, indeed, one of those who preferred bad government by their own people to good government by foreigners. For while one of these régimes touched material interests only, the other, in his view, corroded the national soul. And to him this was not merely an academic doctrine, but something that affected the deepest-seated emotions; not a stupid prejudice that could be bought off by tangible advantages, but a compelling conviction to be lived for, and, if necessary, to die for.

He was not even convinced of the tangibility of the commercial advantages that were to accrue to Scotland by the Union, either in the domestic or the foreign field, for in his opinion these were largely illusory. His writings show that he feared an emigration of Scottish capital to London and an emigration of Scottish settlers to the Colonies, both of which would, in their incidence, cripple a country that was already in the throes of economic distress. In the competition that would ensue between the trading interests of the two countries, the Scottish merchants would be bound, in his opinion, to get the worst of it. And free trade between the two countries was more likely to injure than to benefit Scotland's industries (7).

Before the Union, the Scots had surreptitiously found the means of getting a share of Colonial trade, and their aptitude as settlers had received full recognition at English hands. About 1703 a proposal was made for settling Jamaica by raising "two or three thousand Scotchmen to have free passages and £3,000 amongst them on arrival and to be settled on some 50,000 acres . . . each man to have 7 or 8 acres allotted to him". Papers of the same date show how, in the American Colonies, the local influence of the Scottish settlers was out of proportion to their number. The English settlers, indeed, were afraid of "Barbadoes becoming a

Scotch island". And in 1705 complaints were made to the Home Authorities of unnaturalized Scots trading and fishing in Newfoundland: "their men working cheaper and provisions etc being cheap in Scotland, they will be able to undersell us" (8).

At the beginning of 1707, when an attack on Martinique was contemplated, the Governor of the Leeward Islands, Daniel Parke, wrote home asking for the despatch of "ten thousand Scotch with oatmeal enough to keep them for three or four months. Let them be well provided with arms. . . . Let us try our fortune; if we take it (Martinique) we will have the plunder; the Scotch shall have the land. In time the warm sun will exhale all those crudities that makes them so troublesome, and 'tis not impossible that it may have the effect to make them of a more sociable religion. If we have not success; if you choose out those that are so zealous to maintain the Kirk and against the Union; if I get them all knocked on the head, I am of the opinion the English nation will be no great losers by it".

And he goes on to say that if the Martinique project should prove impracticable, they should try their luck with Porto Rico "the finest island in America. . . . I will dispose of the Scotch for you there: 'twill be a better settlement for them than their beloved Darien" (9).

That was the sort of mentality which was ranged against the Scots in their Darien venture.

The Earl of Sunderland, writing on 28th March, 1707, replied that the Government "does wholly reject" the Parke proposal. "Perhaps", he adds drily, "the sentiments of those (10,000 prospective settlers) may differ from yours as to religious matters. Yet Her Majesty looks upon them as good subjects and good Christians—too good to be knocked on the head upon so wild a project." "I am glad", he remarks significantly, "your scheme did not appear before the Union was finished, for if it had, possibly it might have occasioned some delay to that which all well-wishers to Great Britain think so great an advantage to Her Majesty's interest and the people of both nations" (10).

A very proper rebuke to a masterpiece of national arrogance.

All English Governors, however, were not of the Parke stamp, for in March 1708 we find one of them warmly advocating the settlement of certain eastern parts of America, "and humbly conceive nothing better than by the Scotch" (11).

So Fletcher's fear of the further depopulation of Scotland by emigration, or deportation, to the Colonies, cannot be said to have been groundless. Nor was his fear altogether without foundation that, while in isolated instances commercial advantages to his country might be reaped by free trade with the Colonies, her internal trade might decline. Glasgow might (from Fletcher's standpoint) sell her soul for sugar and her birthright for "stinking tobacco"; but what of Edinburgh and Dundee and Aberdeen and Inverness, which had not the same geographical advantage in relation to America?

Writing exactly twenty years after the Union, Defoe, who did so much by his work as a propagandist to effect its accomplishment, remarks upon the poverty of the Scots nation, and says, "As the people have no hands (that is, no stock) to work, so the gentry have no genius to trade: tis a mechanism which they scorn. Tho' their estates are not able to feed them, they will not turn their hands to business or improvement. They had rather see their sons made foot-soldiers (than which as officers treat them now, there is not a more abject thing on earth), than see them apply to trade, nay, to merchandize or to the sea, because those things are not (forsooth) fit for gentlemen" (12).

So the Union had not stimulated afresh the enthusiasm for trade which was damped down by Darien. There was a difference of opinion at the beginning of the eighteenth century whether the national business of Scotland was soldiering or theology; and in Defoe's view, twenty years after the Union, neither of these Scottish accomplishments had been displaced in the national esteem by the profession of huckstering. Except, perhaps, as travelling pedlars in England, and on the Continent, where the spice of adventure sweetened the dullness of commerce, the Scots had not yet recovered in Europe that expertness in making a bargain to their advantage which at one time apparently they possessed, and by which, in the centuries after the eighteenth, they have been distinguished, equally, indeed, with soldiering and theological disputation.

Another of Fletcher's prognostications of the effect of the

Union is exemplified by what Defoe writes concerning "the decay of all these sea-port towns", first by the Union of the Crowns and then by the Union of the Parliaments. "For it is most certain", he remarks, that "when the Court was at home they had a confluence of strangers, residence of foreign Ministers, being of armies, etc., and consequently the nobility dwelt at home, spent the income of their estates and the product of their country among their neighbours". . . . The surplus wool of the country "went to France and returned ready money; their lead went to Holland; and their cattle and sheep to England; and brought back in that one article above £100,000 sterling per annum". Now, however, "the Union opens the door to all English manufactures and suppresses their own, prohibits their wool going abroad, and yet scarcely takes it off at home. If the cattle goes to England, the money is spent there too. The troops raised there are in English service, and Scotland receives no *premio* for the levies as she might have done abroad, and as the Swiss and other nations do at this time" (13).

Was Saul also among the prophets?

It is true (as Defoe goes on to say) that there was another side to the question, such as the cessation of the wasting wars between the two countries, the easier and fixed taxation in Scotland, and her participation in the West India trade. But "why might not the wool which they send to England be manufactured in Scotland?" he asks. And why should not her own nobility take a hand in improving their own country with "the large sums they get in England", and instruct their stewards to employ the poor people to spin the wool into yarn, and send the yarn to England, instead of allowing themselves to become the victims of "thieves and cheats", who have "teased and hanged about them to draw them into manufacturing, only to bubble them of their wool and money"? (14). Why not indeed?

No; the Union did not, within a generation, bring to Scotland the economic advantages which had been so confidently predicted. It is true that fifty years after the Union an era of prosperity set in, which transformed the industrial and commercial life of the country. But although this prosperity has been generally, and even enthusiastically, ascribed entirely to the Union, it is doubtful how far that attribution is correct; or how far the prosperity may have been attributable, as already suggested, to the vastly improved machinery for the education of the people; or, indeed, how much of it was due to the backwash of improved prosperity in Europe. A federal union, if it had been agreeable to England (which it was not), might conceivably have achieved similar or even superior economic results, while retaining for the smaller country the independence which she cherished so highly, combined with the complete co-operation in common economic and foreign interests which the federalists desired. The incorporating union may have been, from both the English and the Scottish standpoints, a political necessity, but it was a necessity which was imposed by one side on the other in unequal conditions of bargaining.

Fletcher was not, of course, to be found in the ranks of the necessitarians. He did not mince his words in describing their weak-kneed compliance with the terms of the Treaty of Union. Here are two pictures illustrative of the moods, on their departure from Scotland, of two statesmen, one of whom had done more than any other man (with the possible exception of the Earls of Seafield and Stair) to bring the Union to pass, while the other was its most formidable opponent.

It is related of Fletcher that immediately after the House rose, he left Edinburgh. "On the day of his departure his friends crowded around him, entreating him to stay. Even after his foot was in the stirrup, they continued their solicitations anxiously crying, 'Will you forsake your country?' He reversed his head and darting on them a look of indignation, keenly replied: 'It is only fit for the slaves who sold it': then leaped upon the saddle and put spurs to his horse, leaving the whole company struck with a momentary humiliation and (blind to the extravagance of his conduct) at a loss which most to admire, the pride of his virtue, or the elevation of his spirit" (15).

This picture, which is certainly true in essence, if not in detail, may be contrasted with another. The Duke of Queensberry left Edinburgh on 2nd April for London. He was received at Berwick "with great pomp and solemnity", and at every town on his route he was honoured by the magistrates and country magnates as if he had been a royal personage. When he reached Barnet, he was met by Ministers and nobles, and made a public entry into London on

16th April, attended by forty-six coaches and several hundred horsemen: the same evening he was waited upon by Godolphin and all the other members of the Government. He was given an annual pension of £3,000, and in 1708 was created Duke of Dover, Marquis of Beverley, and Baron Ripon in the British peerage (16). The ambition and avarice which (with some justification) have been attributed to him were thus fully satisfied. It may be added that a dukedom, in the Scots peerage, also awaited the Earl of Roxburgh, Queensberry's quondam enemy, of whom political necessity had forced him to become an ally. These rewards were bestowed upon the Scottish noblemen for their outstanding services in promoting the Union. But it would be unjust to say that the element of barter entered into the transaction. They had served the Court well, and perhaps believed that they had also served their country well. But dukedoms came from the Court, and curses came from the country: they were, at any rate, heaped with abundance on Queensberry's head. Seafield, somehow, missed a dukedom, though he became the Earl of Findlater in succession to his father. Stair, perhaps the ablest and possibly the sincerest of the Unionists, died of apoplexy in January 1707, on the day after the delivery of an extraordinarily telling speech in Parliament.

In the tract entitled *State of the Controversy betwixt United and Separate Parliaments*, published in 1706 (referred to in the last chapter), Fletcher discusses at length, for the last time, the question that was so near to his heart.

He assumes in this tract that all well-meaning men desired a closer union between the two countries, as the only effectual means of bringing them to a peaceable state at home and making them formidable abroad. The great question was that of security, and whether that could be attained better under separate Parliaments than by an incorporating union. "There is no necessity", he says, "of giving a child its name before it is brought forth." A Government "ought to be adapted to the nature of the things to be governed, and not the things to it."

If all manner of things of both countries were to be incorporated, it was no doubt reasonable that the whole parts of the government of both kingdoms should likewise have been incorporated with those things. But seeing the treaters in their wisdom

had seen fit to reserve some things of value, as a separate property
to each nation, then it would seem a reasonable consequence that
a separate property must be managed by a Government less or
more separate, as the nature and value of that separate property
might require. The Articles of Union ought to have been first
adjusted before the character of the Union was decided upon, instead of the character of the Union being decided upon before the
Articles were framed.

It had been said that the English treaters positively declared that
they would only consider an incorporating union. That was not
the way to treat men who were free, or Commissioners called together by one and the same Authority. The form of government
should be subservient to the union of interests.

A Government may be divided into two branches: the executive and the legislative. The first properly belongs to the Prince;
the other has its rise from the people, with the sanction of the
Prince. The ends of government may also be divided into two
parts: one for defending the united property of the whole of the
subjects from foreign aggression; the other for protecting the
individual against domestic injuries. As to the first end of government, "nature seems to have pointed out a necessity that England
and Scotland shall be governed by one Prince. Their situation is
so contiguous that one cannot be invaded but the other must be in
danger"; and if they were under two Princes, they might be in
danger of invading one another. But as to the other end of
government, a united Parliament is a most improper Power to
protect the subjects in the several parts of the island in their united
properties, and far more so in those which are to be reserved
distinct and separate.

He feared legislation that would injure specifically Scottish
trade while benefiting English trade. A united Parliament makes
us one and not two, and what is done in that Parliament, is done
for the British and by the British. There are two ways only by
which the Scots can secure themselves against the unequal power
of the English. One is to purchase their affection; the other is to
avoid their influence. There was no honourable way of compassing
the first but by uniting the nations. But the Scots will only have
themselves to blame if they voluntarily surrender their united and

separate interests to the mercy of a united Parliament where the English will have so vast a majority. The English can always find ways, if they so desire, of injuring the Scots in their trade and other concerns, either by their influence upon a Scots Parliament (as in the past) or by laws passed in an English Parliament. But it is much easier to corrupt forty-five Scots in London than to corrupt three hundred in Edinburgh. And there will be no need to corrupt them when Scotsmen become North Britons and Englishmen South Britons; for the North Britons can be outvoted without being corrupted.

Then he comments sarcastically on "this dream of being one and not two". With an incorporating union there is no such thing as Scots or English: they are all British: they are one and not two. In the case of a new law, if it hurts, it hurts the British, of whom the English are a part. And the only way to know whether it hurts or does good to the British, is to put it to the vote of a British Parliament. "This will be the issue of that darling plea of being one and not two: it will be turned upon the Scots with a vengeance, and their forty-five members may dance round to all eternity in this trap of their own making."

The peerage proposals, too, are subjected to scornful criticism. He calls the sixteen, "the new species of mongrel peerage . . . the new set of diminutive peers". It was, he said, a "degrading" of the Estate of peers. . . . "It is plain that in process of time, an united Parliament would mumble this spurious race of Scots peers into nothing, for very obvious reasons." He is conscious that the peerage representation in the Scots Parliament, especially of late, had been swollen to a very overgrown bulk, and hopes the nation will keep its eye on those responsible for some recent scandalous promotions. But the fundamental settlements of a Constitution are like so many links in a chain: when one is broken, the whole chain is broken. There had been some talk of dismembering the Estate of peers in the Scots Parliament; but let them beware of the effects of such a course. He was in favour of "mending" and not "ending" the peerage representation.

He was for separate Parliaments in both countries. He was met by the argument that they had better run into an incorporating union, otherwise the English would never hear of treating again, and the result would be ruin and desolation for Scotland. Shall the Scots, he asks plaintively, never find themselves in the position of treating as free men? Their Commissioners had been hurried into the Articles of Union, and now their nation is to be bullied into their acceptance.

Three objections had been made to the Scottish Constitution: (1) the expense and constituents of Parliament; (2) the exorbitant number of the nobility; and (3) the corruption of the judicature. Well, the remedy lay in the hands of the Scots themselves. For years there had been laws before Parliament for dealing with the first two of these grievances.

The solution of the whole problem was to rectify their own Constitution instead of uniting their Parliament with that of England. He makes suggestions as to how this might be done, and concludes by saying that it lay in the power of England to do them justice, and not to oppose their constitutional reformation. "It is not to be imagined," he says, "that so wise and so generous a nation will endanger their own and their neighbours' peace when they can find so easy and so just a remedy" (17).

This moderately worded and reasonably argued statement in favour of separate Parliaments had a weight of logic behind it which, from the theoretical side, was unanswerable. But the advocates of union in both countries were not concerned with abstract principles of justice and constitutional law. They were concerned, from their different standpoints, with the immediately practical question of escaping from an impasse. Fletcher's was conceivably the long view and theirs the short one, but that was a problem for future generations to solve. And the generations which came after him have seen his ridicule of the "one-not-two" theory justified on many occasions at Westminster, when conflicting national claims have proved the falsity of the premises.

The constitution of the first Scottish representation in the British Parliament is described in the vigorous but not unjust language of Lockhart, whose bitterness as an anti-Unionist was not exceeded by that of Fletcher himself.

"The Courtiers being conscious to themselves that the nation was so displeased with them that they could not expect any of their stamp would be returned from the shires or burroughs, were

resolved not to swallow a cow and stick at the tail ... picked out
sixteen peers", (Hamilton was among the number), "thirty barons
and fifteen burgesses that were thorough-paced and altogether at
their becks; whereby it came to pass that some shires had their
whole number of representatives, as in the Scots Parliament, such
as Argyleshire etc.; some had two, some one, and some of the
chief shires, such as Edinburgh, Fife, Stirling etc., none at all" (18).

That was scarcely a hopeful beginning for Scottish representative government in its new sphere. It must have been difficult,
indeed, for the sixty-one members to know precisely what or
whom they actually did represent in the first British Parliament.
For, compared with their English fellow-members, sixteen were
elected peers without an equality of privileges, and forty-five were
pocket-commoners without a mandate from their constituencies.

Chapter XX

MY POOR COUNTRY

THE first British Parliament had not been long in existence before the Privy Council of Scotland was abolished. Although its history since the Union of the Crowns had been mainly that of a body whose direct function was to carry out the wishes of the Court, with occasional manifestations of an independent spirit, still it was a national institution and, as such, was sentimentally esteemed in some quarters as a historic link with the past. Its abolition was certainly not regretted by disinterested people who were intimately acquainted with its history; and the whole of the administrative affairs relating to Scotland being now vested in a Secretary resident in London, its continued existence, without a Scottish Parliament to watch its proceedings, was not only unnecessary but undesirable.

That its proposed abolition was unpopular would appear to have been the view, actual or assumed, of certain alarmists in Scotland. Writing to his brother, the Earl of Mar, on 9th December, 1707, James Erskine tells him of the consternation and surprise caused by the proposal to abolish the Council, and by certain other proceedings (in relation, probably, to the militia and the administration of justice), which had been taken, it was stated, at the instigation of the Squadron. "Salton, the Marquis of Annandale, and some of that kidney", says Erskine, "are rejoicing at them, but they tell people at the same time that these are the effects of the happy Union. . . . All sorts of people, Unionists and anti-Unionists, Episcopal, and Presbyterian, are thunderstruck with these news, and I pray God they don't exasperate to the highest degree if these proceedings be not stopt . . . . I think the Union more prejudiced by this than anything that ever happened" (1).

Two days later David Erskine tells Mar that the Squadron has turned "most odious to this country", being regarded apparently as the source of these measures. The Squadron, in fact, saw eye to eye with reformers like Fletcher in their desire to abolish an institution like the Privy Council, which had been an engine of tyranny in the past, and contained potentialities for mischief in the future. In accusing Fletcher of blaming the Union for the abolition of the Council, while rejoicing in the decision itself, and in reporting, with the emphasis of exaggeration, the feeling aroused in Scotland, James Erskine was speaking the language of the disappointed place-man, and not declaring the sentiment of the outraged patriot (2).

The Court was in favour of retaining a separate Council for Scotland, hoping, as some of its Scottish advisers gave reason for hoping, that it would be a useful mechanism for controlling elections in North Britain. For an election was now looming in the near future, which, in relation to Scotland, was bound to affect, one way or other, the fruits of the Union. In appointing the Duke of Queensberry, now a British peer, as a Secretary whose special function was to "manage" Scotland, the Government believed, and rightly believed, that they were appointing the right man for controlling the Scottish elections in their interest. The Privy Council for Scotland was abolished by Parliament in February 1708 in the teeth of the opposition of the Court. The effort to delay its dissolution from 1st May until 1st October (by which time the elections would be over), was unsuccessful. But private intrigue under Queensberry's management might prove an effective substitute for the pliancy of a subservient body like the Council. True, Queensberry had to reckon with the hostility of the Squadron, led by the Duke of Roxburgh, and the Duke of Montrose (for he, too, had been promoted), and when the Duke of Hamilton joined his interest to theirs, the combination looked formidable. But at this juncture of affairs an event occurred which favoured the Ministry, though its initial menace was sufficiently alarming.

The time was considered propitious by France for striking a blow at England, by utilizing the intense dissatisfaction with the Union which continued in Scotland without abatement. Louis' stalking-horse was the Chevalier de St. George, known to the Scottish Jacobites as James the Eighth, in whose interest Louis decided to equip an expedition, having as its object the restoration of James to the throne of his ancestors. The leaders of the Jacobites had been sounded by Colonel Hooke, an emissary of

St. Germains and Versailles. Atholl, and particularly Hamilton, the two biggest fish to be landed by Hooke, had shown extraordinary wariness, but Hooke's report of the prevailing conditions had been deemed sufficiently encouraging to warrant the attempt. The circumstances were indubitably favourable. "The standing forces were few;" says Defoe, "the militia in a state of transition between the old and the new models; the fortifications were out of repair; the magazines were empty; the new Government was unformed; the people were divided. Never was nation in such a condition to be invaded" (3).

But the intelligence service of Great Britain was not at fault, and precautionary legislation was hurriedly passed providing against the emergency. What was of more practical value, a fleet was quickly equipped to deal with the expeditionary force, and transports were hired to convey troops from Ostend.

With the Chevalier on board one of the ships, the French squadron sailed from Dunkirk on 17th March, under Forbin's command, and arrived at the Firth of Forth, just too late to avoid the vigilance of Sir George Byng, who chased the easily scared enemy away, and, capturing one of his ships, forced him, with the help of bad weather, to abandon the half-hearted enterprise and return to Dunkirk with nothing accomplished. Bad weather had delayed the expedition initially, and bad weather prevented a landing on the north-east coast of Scotland, which, had it been effected, would have formed the rallying-point of the well-prepared Jacobites, and led, conceivably, to a serious rebellion.

The issue of the expedition, had the original plan been achieved and the Castle of Edinburgh seized (the main objective) (4), is doubtful. "Mr. Melancholy" was too honest a man for his times: he would not change his religious faith; and that was the main obstacle to a successful restoration. His ancestor, Henry the Fourth, thought the Kingdom of France worth a mass; James thought the Kingdoms of Great Britain and Ireland not worth a recantation.

The winds blew and they were scattered. It is really remarkable how, time and again, the elements refused to accommodate themselves to the Jacobite plans. The tempestuous weather which intervened to save England from invasion on several occasions in the history of the country, was regarded by Englishmen as a manifestation of Divine favour towards their nation. Providence was clearly their ally; and the fruitfulness of the alliance was proclaimed by the raging seas that confounded the politics and frustrated the knavish tricks of their enemies. The Channel that divided France from England was rightly named the English Channel.

The attempted invasion of 1708 had a strange sequel in Scotland. On 29th March the Earl of Mar told his brother that he hoped the fears of the invasion were now over. Several people in Scotland, he said, had behaved so foolishly that they had got themselves into trouble. "There are more people ordered to be taken up, and amongst the rest, your friend Mr. Fletcher, who, I'm sure will be very angry. But if he is innocent, as I hope he is, his friend the Highland duke (Atholl) is the occasion of it, and there was no saying against it. Say nothing of this until it be public."

The laird of Saltoun under arrest as a Jacobite! Mar might well say that he would be angry, if indeed his anger was not overcome by his sense of humour. For he had avoided "the very appearance of evil", by refusing to visit the Earl of Errol, lest the visit should give rise to the suspicion that he, too, was involved in the Jacobite conspiracy. He told Errol that he had always warned him of the danger of keeping "ill company and that now he (Errol) was seeing the fruits of it" (5).

The arrest of a number of leading men in Scotland had been ordered by the Privy Council in London, on the ground of their supposed complicity in the late Jacobite fiasco. With the exception of Fletcher, who was sent to Stirling Castle, they were placed in Edinburgh Castle. There those of them who were really engaged in the enterprise could contemplate at leisure their proximity to the "Equivalent" instalment of upwards of £20,000, which the Jacobites had planned to seize; also the jewels with which they had intended to crown the Chevalier. But although it would not have been difficult to prove the Jacobite sympathies of certain of the prisoners, the only evidence against others was contained in certain intercepted letters addressed to them by the Duke of Atholl. As for the Duke himself, a guard was placed over him in Blair Castle, and this "garrison", as Atholl called it, kept him a close prisoner until his case could be considered. Fletcher was among those who were alleged to be incriminated by the ducal correspondence; but it was soon made quite clear that there was no case against him.

He found himself in comfortable quarters in Stirling Castle; as, indeed, it was intended that he should. In a letter dated 14th April to the Earl of Mar, the hereditary Governor of the Castle, he thanks the Earl for showing his friendship "by effects not words". Lady Mar, the Earl's mother, had put herself to much trouble on his account. "But my greatest mortification was from the civilities I received from Colonel Erskine" (Mar's deputy), to whom he had never shown even common civility. "All that I could say for myself was that my prejudices were never personal."

"You see", he goes on to say, "what uneasiness one falls under by imprisonment, when even kind things done him turn to be of a different nature, especially to a man who sees himself in no capacity to return them. You may tell my Lord Colvin we are not locked up here at night, and that we drank all yesternight of the Colonel's good wine, and continued till this morning; that he can find no such company in Scotland; and that for his excuse we shall persuade the Colonel to say that he is confined" (6). Saltonian humour!

It would certainly appear that Fletcher was treated at Stirling Castle as an honoured guest rather than a traitorous prisoner.

On the day after this letter was written, a fresh order came from London. All the prisoners, with the exception of Fletcher, were to be sent to London for examination. This order by the Privy Council aroused much indignation in Scotland. Queensberry was blamed for it; so was Mar. But Mar's explanation that the initiative came from the Ministry in London, because the Privy Council in Scotland, whose function it should have been to examine the prisoners, was in the throes of dissolution, seems reasonable enough. Among those ordered to London were the Duke of Hamilton, the Duke of Gordon, the Marquis of Huntly, and nineteen other peers of Scotland, including Belhaven, who died soon afterwards, after a most vigorous protest against his arrest. Some well-known commoners were also among the number sent under guard to London. The first batch of prisoners (there were three batches) were to have been taken through the City of London under guard. But Sir David Nairne told the Queen that this would be a "mortifying experience" for them, and he suggested that the guards should be dismissed at Barnet; so the prisoners were spared the crowning humiliation of being made a public spectacle (7).

Meanwhile what of Fletcher, the distinction between whose case and that of the other prisoners was so marked? On 22nd April he wrote the Earl of Leven, the Commander-in-Chief in Scotland, to whom the warrants had been sent by the Privy Council, that he was grateful for an obliging letter which he had just received from him. "All I fear", he said, "is that so inconsiderable a man as I am may be forgot, and no further orders given about me." He urged Leven, therefore, to mention his affair the next time he was writing to London. "For I doubt not that having before this time examined Straloch (? Gordon of) and Mr. Scot, they will see there is nothing can touch me in these letters" (Atholl's) (8).

James Erskine seems to have exerted himself to procure the release of Fletcher, but Mar told him to inform Saltoun that he could not be set at liberty just yet, "because those who were taken up upon the same account (I mean the Duke of Atholl's letters) are ordered up here with the rest. But as soon as they are gone, he'll be set at liberty, though he would" (should) "not speak of this. I know not what he'll think of it, but here 'tis thought a mighty favour, and I assure you I bestirred myself for him, tho' I fancy I'll hardly get thanks" (9).

It is quite certain that the laird of Saltoun did not consider it a "mighty favour" to be released from prison (though a more comfortable "prison" can scarcely be imagined), simply because the absurd charge made against him could not possibly be substantiated. But when the order for his release came, as it did soon afterwards, he had the satisfaction of knowing that his fellow-countrymen never doubted, from first to last, that his conduct throughout the recent happenings had been entirely consistent with the political sympathies which he had never sought to hide.

The Duke of Atholl, his protests notwithstanding, had to suffer yet awhile the ignominy of being kept under close guard in his own house. He was ill, but his illness did not move the Privy Council, who had their own reasons for keeping him out of the way, and he was not admitted to bail until July. Atholl, perhaps a more patriotic man than Hamilton, was less skilful in covering up his tracks. On one occasion, when interviewed by Colonel Hooke, Hamilton conducted the conversation literally in the dark, so that he could truthfully declare that he had never seen the Colonel's face! That was an idea which could never have occurred to his rival. The latter, in June 1708, was not surprised that Hamilton had joined the Squadron, for as he truly said, his politics had been unaccountable for years.

Gradually it became clear that the arrest of the Scottish notabilities, and the subsequent proceedings in London, must have formed part of a plan for controlling the coming elections. The arrests, it would appear, were made in order to prevent the men arrested from either standing as candidates for Parliament, or assisting those who did. Having the men they feared in their hands, the Ministers applied the political pressure which the circumstances favoured. Writing to Mar on 1st May, the Earl of Glasgow tells him that the Cavalier party will be as "one man" for the Ministerial measures. Four of the party had already "qualified", including (it is scarcely believable) Lord Belhaven. "This last", remarks Glasgow, "sounds damnably with me, tho' he has been at great pains against the Squadrone. All the rest will universally qualify and give their proxies to our friends. My dear pupils, the Duke of Montrose, Earls of Rothes and Haddington, are mightily enraged against my Lord Leven and me." They accused Queensberry, he said, of having instigated the imprisonment and bringing up to London of his political opponents. "It takes no great impression, but I do verily believe such a set never was upon the earth." (10). Hamilton, as usual, was "unaccountable". Mar thought his party had secured him, but then the Squadron and "the Juncto" (the English Whig lords) "fell a-tampering with him". Meanwhile Hamilton's imprisonment was easy—only a messenger sitting in his outer room—and he was finally admitted to bail by the influence of "the Juncto", who also tampered with the other prisoners and influenced their proxies. Hamilton was finally allowed to give bail to go to Scotland; and afterwards declared openly that he had obtained his liberty by the "influence of these called the Juncto lords". Also, Lockhart gives him the credit for effecting the release on bail of his fellow-prisoners. The bail was soon remitted, and the whole business was seen in its true light as an election dodge. There were some Stirlingshire lairds who had to stand their trial for treason in Scotland, but they too were ultimately acquitted (11).

Such being the condition of affairs, it was only to be expected that the elections in Scotland, thus manipulated, should have favoured the English Whigs, and that there was no visible sign in the results of the strong feeling that persisted in the country against the Union. Atholl was tardily released, but only apparently because it was feared that if he were not set at liberty, the Court interest might suffer (12). Everything, in fact, was made subservient to election results, and no method of cajolery or intimidation was left untried to secure a party triumph. In the new Parliament, which assembled in November 1708, the Whig interest continued to predominate. But the Scottish membership was in no way representative of Scottish political opinion. Fletcher was in London in October 1708, for in that month, writes a correspondent to Harley, he "kissed the Queen's hand". The interview must have been interesting (13).

Before the elections took place, Fletcher's name was associated with a curious attempt on Hamilton's part to revive concerted action by the Cavaliers, to promote presumably the interests of his new friends. James Erskine tells Mar on 24th December, 1708, that it was reported that Hamilton had written to "his slaves", asking them to meet for consultation. But there was no meeting. The Duke of Atholl, who confessed to Erskine that he "hated" Hamilton "and cannot hide it", pretended he was sick; Strathmore and Salton "refused to join them"; and so did the Stirlingshire lairds who had been recently released. Erskine was amply justified in remarking that "those we call Cavaliers here seem to be a set of discontented, weak people" (14).

On one thing the wire-pullers in London of the pending elections in Scotland were apparently resolved: that Andrew Fletcher should not be a member of the House of Commons. They knew what to expect if he were elected to the British Parliament, and they were determined to keep him out. It was probably with that end in view that he had been arrested as a Jacobite. He himself was quite ready to fight at Westminster, as he had fought in Edinburgh, in his country's cause; and he stood as a candidate for the sole membership of East Lothian. The Ministers—to be more precise, Queensberry—put up against him Morison of Prestongrange, a local magnate and a wealthy man; and they worked the constituency so skilfully that Fletcher received only nine votes. This is recorded by the Reverend Alexander (Jupiter) Carlyle of Inveresk, who voices the informed opinion of the generation that followed Fletcher when he refers to him as "the celebrated Andrew Fletcher" and "the famous patriot". The successful candidate for East Lothian was an opponent who was not worthy of Fletcher's steel. He fell a victim to a notorious gambler, one Colonel Charteris, who was popularly believed to be a wizard, and who stripped the member of Parliament of the whole of his wealth, thereby apparently justifying his reputation for wizardry. But, indeed, it does not seem to have needed much wizardry to pluck this witless pigeon bare; he was such a simple Simon that he believed that "close by his creek of Morison's Haven was the place where St. John wrote the Apocalypse, because some old vaults had been discovered in digging a race-mill for a mill that went by sea-water." And that was the man who was sent to Westminster instead of Andrew Fletcher (15).

The subject of this biography was now fifty-five years of age, the last five of which had fulfilled the promise of the previous fifty. His public work was done. During those five years he had striven with all the energy at his command, by eloquent speech and by persuasive pen, to strike off the fetters which, in his view, were binding the liberties of his native country. He had failed to make his views prevail in the end. By a paradox, indeed, he was unwittingly one of the main instruments of the incorporating union which he detested. For he, more than any other man in the Scots Parliament, was responsible for the Act of Security, which was touched by a strongly reluctant sceptre, and which had now, with the Act of Peace and War, been repealed by a British Parliament. The reluctance to pass the Act of Security was an expression of the alarm felt in London at the implications of the Act; and the alarm undoubtedly stimulated the English feeling for a complete union, which was believed to be a political necessity, to secure at once the nullification of the Act, the settlement of the Succession, and peace between the two countries.

He must have felt the bitterness of defeat. But there was nothing now that he could do to help his native country consistently with his principles. Like so many other malcontents, he might have engaged in Jacobite intrigues to embarrass the Government. But he was not, and never could be, a Jacobite, and his leanings were not and never could be, towards intrigue (16). So his only recourse was to retire into private life. The Scots Parliament, which, when tempted by James II to legalize the toleration of Catholics in exchange for Free Trade, had replied with indignation, "Shall we sell our God?" had now, in his opinion, in exchange for the same bribe, sold their country.

He seems to have spent his later years in visits to London and the Continent, when he was not at home in Saltoun. One can well believe from his writings that the management of a Scottish estate on lines that were in advance of those on which his contemporaries worked was, for him, a congenial task. There is early evidence of his interest in the smallest details of practical farming. As far back as 1691 we find him writing to his friend Sir George Mackenzie, Viscount Tarbat (later the Earl of Cromarty), suggesting that Tarbat should inform himself on "the new improvements in husbandry", and that he should buy books on the subject for the use of both of them. Particularly he would like to be informed how land should be used when converted from arable to grass for the first three or four years, and what grain should be sown for the last year of ploughing. If barley, he will perhaps remember that "we sow ours in summer and the English theirs in winter". Also, he asks him certain questions about new methods of dealing with trees intended for timber.

A sidelight on the versatility of the two men is shown by a post-script to this letter; the incongruity of subjects is violent. "I cannot think", he tells Tarbat, "but that you might have some satisfaction to look after the late progress of Arian opinion" (17). Clearly theology was included in the list of Saltonian studies; but there is nothing to show what Fletcher's own views were on the "Arian opinion". His views on farming were definite enough, for one of his *Discourses* (the second) makes his position clear, particularly on the necessity for the legal enforcement of his dictum that no man should be allowed to possess more land than he could cultivate by his own servants. On his own estate there was a barley-mill which was the last word in efficiency as then understood. Of this mill the tenant was Henry Fletcher, his younger brother, and the husband of a remarkable woman, Margaret, the eldest daughter of Sir David Carnegie of Pitarrow.

The laird of Saltoun had long been a friend of the Carnegie family. In 1689 he helped Archibald, a son of Sir David, by securing for him his pay for his company, of which his colonel had tried to deprive him. Young Carnegie told his father that he owed a debt of gratitude to Saltoun which he could not find words to express. But there was a particular reason why the latter should exert himself to assist a brother of Margaret Carnegie.

Andrew Fletcher never married: he was wedded to Scotland, and to Scotland only. When his friends rallied him on his celibacy, his reply was, "My brother has got the woman that should have been my wife." It was so. His, apparently, was the tragedy of the unloved lover. Probably he was not the type of man who would attract women. Macky describes him as "a low (short) thin man of brown complexion, full of fire, with a stern, sour look": though his portrait is that of neither a "stern" nor a "sour" man. These are not attributes that generally find favour in feminine eyes. True, he had intellectual attainments and a force of character such as few men of his, or any time, have possessed. But these are not often the determining factors in love-affairs. Perhaps, indeed, Andrew Fletcher had loved in silence and had never disclosed his secret. For, at the time his brother was pressing his suit, he himself was an outlaw in Holland, his estates confiscated, and his life forfeit if he ventured to cross the sea. And when at length he reached his home, and was once more the laird of Saltoun, it was to find that Margaret Carnegie was now the wife of Henry Fletcher. And Henry, judging by his portrait in Saltoun Hall, was a remarkably good-looking man.

Parental reluctance had to be overcome before the marriage took place. Eventually that obstacle was removed by the persistence of the daughter, aided by the diplomatic tactfulness of the prospective son-in-law; they were married in April 1688. Obviously it was a love-match, for Henry Fletcher's position as a younger son, with the family estate under confiscation, was not attractive to a father who naturally desired that his daughter should make a good match. The restoration of the estate to Andrew, who was thereby enabled to make provision for the young couple, marked for them a turn in the tide of material adversity. And it was not long before the tide of prosperity was flowing strongly in their favour, owing to the extraordinary capacity for business displayed by Margaret Carnegie—her portrait in Saltoun Hall is full of character—whose domestic virtues no one extolled more than the man whose wife she "should have been" (18).

She made a wonderful success of the Saltoun mill, but it was her brother-in-law who enabled her to do so. When in Holland, Andrew Fletcher had seen barley mills and fanners for winnowing corn; and he foresaw their industrial potentialities for his own country. So in 1710 he entered into a contract with an intelligent East Lothian mill-wright, James Meikle (father of Andrew Meikle, who subsequently became famous as an ingenious inventor), to construct machinery for a barley-mill at Saltoun, after the Dutch model. The two men journeyed to Holland, and while Fletcher went to the Hague, Meikle stayed in Amsterdam, and had such parts of the ironwork made there as he thought necessary. On their return to Scotland, Meikle built a barley-mill at Saltoun; also, he made fanners there.

This mill for making "pot" barley had constant employment, and "Saltoun pearl barley" became known in most of the Scottish towns. For upwards of forty years it was the only barley-mill in Great Britain or Ireland or the Colonies. The Saltoun mill was under the special charge of Henry Fletcher's wife. Writing to his son on 22nd November, 1714, Henry admitted that his wife knew more about the mill than he did himself. Your mother, he tells his son, "is now perfectly master of the making of the barley, and the mills go extraordinarily well, and we have a very good sale". The mill property had an office in Edinburgh where the business was transacted. Mrs. Fletcher occupied a room in the mill itself, where she received orders across a door "which was securely fastened by a chain to prevent strangers from entering"; so jealously did she guard the secret of the construction of the machinery.

But alas! the proprietor of a neighbouring mill in Keith at length discovered the secret by the simple method of making a Saltoun mechanic drunk, and extorting the desired information from him when in that condition. In time similar mills became common throughout Scotland, and the Saltoun monopoly disappeared (19). It must have been a profitable monopoly while it lasted. Yet Andrew Fletcher, the opponent of monopolies, would scarcely have approved, with consistency, of their exemplification on his own estate.

It was not only as a barley manufacturer that the business instinct of Margaret Carnegie showed itself. She is said to have gone over to Holland to learn the art of making "Holland cloth". She took with her, in the guise of a domestic servant, a weaver named Melchisedec—surely a nickname—who found out all that was necessary for their purpose. Soon the manufacture of Holland cloth was in active process in a field adjoining the barley-mill at Saltoun. Also, weaving and other manufactures were actively promoted by this energetic lady, who made of the village of Saltoun a hive of industry. It was only fitting that what is now a great Scottish Bank—the British Linen—should have made Saltoun its headquarters for the manufacture of linen before it became a bank (20).

Henry Fletcher, who probably shared his brother's political views (he was, it may be remembered, clapped into prison at the time of Argyll's adventure in 1685) seems to have been a worthy and a pious man, whose religion, like that of Andrew, was free from aggressive sectarianism: an unusual circumstance in Scotland at the beginning of the eighteenth century. There is in print a remarkable letter written by him to his son, Andrew, then a student at Leyden, and afterwards a Lord of Session and a Lord of Justiciary, under the title of Lord Milton (Milton being a small property adjoining the Saltoun estate). Of that son the following incident is related. When Andrew Fletcher lay dying in London, he was visited by his old friend, the Earl of Sunderland, who asked him if there was anything he could do for him. "I have a nephew", was the reply, "who has been studying the law. Make him a judge when he is fit for it." He had his doubts, for he had predicted on one occasion that his nephew would turn out "a corrupt fellow and a perfect courtier". The corruption he had in view was doubtless political corruption, which to him was the unforgivable sin. But his nephew turned out to be a credit to his name. Lord Justice-Clerk, the correspondent of four successive Dukes of Argyll, and the adviser more particularly of the third Duke in making appointments in Scotland, he wielded considerable influence, and though he may have been "a perfect courtier", there is certainly no evidence of his having ever been "a corrupt fellow". The letter from his father to which allusion has been made, enjoins upon him precepts of perfection, the strict observance of which could not have failed to make of him a pattern of morality and a model of gentility. His father's advice covered a wide field. Specific directions are given about the daily devotions to be observed by his son. But he is not to addict himself to any Church party, either Presbyterian or Episcopal. "Be free to hear them both, and censure none of them: there are sincere good men in both parties". . . . Every Lord's Day get by heart a psalm in Buchanan. . . . Fill up the rest of the day with reading the Scripture and books of devotion and with pious meditations. . . . Be always ingenuous in what you say or do. Dissimulation and lying are base, mean faults. . . . Be modest and humble with all men. . . . Beware of censuring your neighbours. . . . In conversation the best quality is to hear attentively and to answer pertinently. You must abstain altogether from cards, dice, billiards, and all house games. The half of the time betwixt dinner and supper may be employed in study and the other half in diversion, as dancing, walking, golf, conversing. Shun the tavern and all idle conversation. Endeavour to acquire a politeness in your carriage which consists in being civil to everyone and rude to nobody."

And directions are given about the correct posture of the body, keeping the head straight, sitting evenly on a chair, and so forth. He was not to cross his legs or bite his finger-nails. He was to pay attention to his clothes, and keep them whole and clean. He was to be sane in conversation, and not like some people who were in "a perpetual flyre of laughter which is very undecent".

A letter to the young man from his mother is (as might be expected) more severely practical. She feared that the air of Leyden was not good for him. He was to take no "strong physick". But he was to diet himself well, and was recommended to put "a Burgundy pick plaister betwixt your shoulders" as a relief to his eyes which had apparently been troubling him. And to this letter his father added a postscript, taking his son to task for having committed the dreadful solecism of saying in a letter that there had been "a great mortality of cattel", when he should have said "a great death of cattel"; for "mortality has a correlation to immortality, and is only used when one speaks of men" (21). If Andrew was called a pedant by some of his contemporaries, what must they have called Henry?

Incidentally we learn from one of the nephew's letters that Andrew was in Leyden in 1715. On 16th July of that year young Fletcher, then about twenty-four years of age, tells his father that "my uncle is thinking of going to Paris in two months, and Mr. Cunningham" (probably the historian) "is thinking of going to London for three weeks". (In 1709, he had "lately come from Holland", and in the following year he was at Aix-la-Chapelle.) Andrew Fletcher was as much at home on the Continent as he was in Scotland; and it is a grievous loss that his impressions of the countries he visited have not been preserved. It can scarcely be thought credible that his pen was idle after he retired from public life; and it can only be concluded that the papers which have been lost, included discussions on current questions in Europe, which coming from so acute a mind and so powerful a pen, would have been a valuable addition to our knowledge of the period.

The laird of Saltoun was not, as we have just seen, a mere theorist in his recommendations to his fellow-countrymen for their social and economic welfare. He showed them how to do things. He always held that the fisheries, more particularly, of Scotland were capable of very considerable development. The Dutch knew how to reap a rich harvest from that source of wealth. Why not the natives? One of the proposals in his *Second Discourse* was that there should be an interchange of residence between indolent and troublesome Highlanders and industrious and peace-loving Lowlanders. Probably, among other things, he had the valuable fisheries of the West Highlands and Isles in mind as a promising field for skilled enterprise. Possibly he knew that, nearly a hundred years before, his neighbours in Fife had made the experiment, with results that were disastrous for themselves. But since then a great change in manners had occurred in those far-off parts; other attempts had been made with partial success, and the time was ripe for further and well-conceived plans, as advocated by Fletcher, to be carried out for tapping a source of wealth much of which was going to waste. He seems to have been of the same opinion on the subject of economic nationalism as John Spreul, a Glasgow merchant of wide experience (and a Covenanter who had twice been put to the torture in his earlier years). In 1705, when Scotland was threatened with the effects of the English Alien Act, Spreul addressed a memorial to the Duke of Argyll, the High Commissioner, and to the Estates, with the object of showing that by restricting the import of luxuries, and particularly by manufacturing for herself articles which had previously been imported from England, and by finding new markets for her increased exporting capacity, Scotland could do without the English trade (22). At that time Scotland was faced by a crisis similar in kind to that which is now turning Europe into isolated economic camps, each striving to outdo the other in self-contained independence, and in restricting economic intercommunication to reciprocal necessities. Whether or not their "Wisdoms", as Spreul called the Estates, would have responded to his call for constructive energy in legislating for the development of internal trade and industry, if the Union had not averted the crisis, it is tolerably clear, as I have shown, that the principle which underlay his proposals was firmly held by at least one of the "Wisdoms" whom he addressed. Fletcher, who demanded in Parliament the repeal of the obnoxious Alien clause in the English Act, before treating with England, and who introduced an Act prohibiting English imports until the prohibitions in the English Act had been removed, could hardly do otherwise than welcome with eagerness any practical scheme for stimulating home industries and reducing economic dependence upon England.

Education was one of the main channels through which Fletcher hoped that material, as well as a higher form of prosperity might come to his native country. He is said to have written a treatise on education; but if so, it does not appear to have been preserved, unless, as may be possible, it is identifiable with an anonymous tract published in 1704, on *Proposals for the reformation of Schools and Universities in order to the better Education of Youth.* His views on that big question were, as might be expected, unhackneyed and stimulating. He thought that small classes were necessary for adequate instruction. Taking the faculty of theology as his theme, when discussing University education with Wodrow, the eminent Presbyterian divine and historian, he proposed that each of the Universities should have six Professors of Divinity: and that the number of students under the care of each Professor should not exceed ten or twelve: "they can intimately know no more," he said. And he had a scheme in his head for improving the pulpit supply. "He dislikes", said Wodrow, "our present way of licensing probationers." Many members of Presbytery were "no judges of a young man's fitness", and their trials of the probationers were "very overly". One of the members of Presbytery proposed a youth, "and all is taken upon his testimony". He would have a parish, when it fell vacant, apply to the Presbytery, the members of which would be intimately acquainted with the "temper" of the parishioners. Then he would have the Presbytery apply to a University for a suitable candidate, stating with the application what they knew about the place. The University would choose a youth from those recommended by the Professors, who had previously examined closely the temperaments and gifts of their students, and send him on trial to the parish. If the candidate was not liked by the parishioners, the University would send another, and continue sending probationers until the people were satisfied. A sensible and democratic method of selection, one would suppose, and vastly superior to the system of patronage which prevailed in the Church of Scotland so long.

He discussed politics, also, with Wodrow, and one would hazard a guess that he was in London about the time (1712) the conversation took place. He described how a Bill was brought into the House of Commons which involved discriminatory and excessive taxation of Scotland; how Lockhart proposed to his fellow-members from Scotland that they should "leave the House in a body and protest the Union was broke"; how this proposal, after discussion, was adopted; and how two of their number were sent to the Treasurer and two to the Queen, to inform them of their intention; and how finally the Court intervened, and several of the "gravaminouse" things in the Bill were dropped.

Also he told Wodrow that he used to say to Sunderland, Wharton, and the leading Whigs in England that they had committed three major follies: (i) by settling the Succession on the House of Hanover because they were Lutherans, for the nearer a people went to Popery, the greater was their inclination for absolute government, and the more were they for a Tory interest; (ii) by promoting and pushing the Union with Scotland, which "now they are sensible is an addition to the power of the Court and makes the Prince by far more absolute than before"; and (iii) by the unpopularity they had incurred by "pushing" the trial of Sacheverell, and thus inciting the cry of "danger of the Church", without doing themselves any good by the prosecution. The result was a reaction in favour of absolute government and non-resistance, which, Fletcher gloomily remarked, had "sadly verified" his fears (23).

It is easy to visualize the old war-horse, eager for the fray, as he watched the political proceedings in London after his retirement. But his political life was finished. When asked by Wodrow whether he had written a history of the Union, he replied that he had not kept a daily account of the proceedings, and that he had written nothing but his speeches (if he refers to the closing Session, these speeches must have been lost), "and it's impossible now for him to do anything. He complains extremely of his memory."

It was four years after this conversation with Wodrow, who describes him as "one of the brightest of our gentry", that his death took place. He fell ill in Paris, from the effects, it was said, of drinking the water of the Seine (24). His nephew and namesake, then a student at Leyden, hurried to his side, and brought him over to England. He was too ill to be taken home to Saltoun, and he died in London on 15th September, 1716. His nephew brought his body to Scotland in a leaden coffin, and in the family vault under the parish church of Saltoun, the illustrious laird of the estate was laid at rest among his own people.

At the time of his death, the rising of the "Fifteen" had been suppressed, and the victims of Mar's folly were now about to pay the penalty of his rashness as a statesman, and his incompetence as a soldier. "Poor Salton", writes Sir Hugh Paterson to the Duke (Jacobite) of Mar, from Leyden on 9th October, 1716, "who has appeared all along very much concerned for the condition of his countrymen, died last week at London, and since ever he got the accounts of these people being carried to England" (the Jacobite prisoners), "never was well. The last words he spoke were 'My poor country'. He has left the prisoners £200" (25).

"My poor country!" As throughout his life, so at its end, his thoughts were of her. In that deathbed sentiment, he anticipated Pitt.

Another letter from Edinburgh to Mar of the same date confirms the report of the legacy he had left for the prisoners at Carlisle, "and other Scots poor prisoners, which he said his brother is immediately to pay, and himself to go to Carlisle with it" (26).

These prisoners were Jacobites who were taken to Carlisle for trial (to the intense indignation of Scotsmen), because it was feared that if tried in their own country, their judges would let them off. Fletcher's gift was undoubtedly intended to pay for their defence.

What did this last recorded act of Fletcher denote? Did it mean that he had become a belated convert to the Jacobite cause, and wished to show his political sympathy with the Jacobite prisoners? That is, to say the least, a doubtful hypothesis. Far more likely, his gift was simply an expression of sympathy with his countrymen in distress, and a sign of the indignation which he felt at the flagrant act of injustice by which political prisoners who should have been tried in Scotland were sent for trial to England. He was not likely to have changed his consistently held political views at the end of his life. He cannot have had any personal respect for the first representative of the House of Hanover. But at least George the First ostensibly stood for certain principles with which Fletcher was in sympathy. He would have preferred to see a Protestant Stewart on the throne. But best of all, as he himself had said quite plainly in Parliament, he wanted a king, be he native or foreign, who would accept a crown from which the jewels of prerogative had been plucked by an all-powerful Parliament.

His political ideas were not popular. But never, during the whole of his career, did he seek easy popularity; and it does not seem to have sought him out. It was Hamilton, the Protean politician, who was the hero of the Edinburgh mob, not Fletcher the stern and unbending patriot. His aloofness did not consist with cheap popularity. Nor did his impatient and unaccommodating temper. His incapacity to see more than one side of a question impaired his usefulness in promoting the very aims which he had most at heart. Although he enjoined forgiveness for private injuries, he was completely implacable in his refusal to forgive those who, in his opinion, were acting contrary to his country's interests. Had he been more tolerant of the views of his political opponents, he might have won, as well as the respect which was always his, more of the active support which was frequently denied to him. After all, it is a strain upon human vanity to have one's opinions treated as if they were those of a fool or a knave, and that was the unpleasant impression which the intellectual arrogance imputed to Fletcher must have too frequently produced upon his duller contemporaries. He did not mean to be arrogant, but the people whom he snubbed could not be expected always to discriminate between wilful arrogance and momentary petulance.

In the eyes of some of his contemporaries, Fletcher's ideas were what Lord Beaconsfield would have called "the fantastic scheming of a presumptuous pedant". The views of his commonplace acquaintances who disagreed with him are well epitomized by Sir John Clerk, who says "he was a little untoward in his temper, and much inclined to eloquence. He made many speeches in Parliament which are all printed, but was not very dexterous in making extemporary replies. He was, however, a very honest man, and meant well in everything he said and did, except in cases where his humour, passion, or prejudice were suffered to get the better of his reason". "A worthy man", Sir John believed him to be. As Mr. Omond rightly remarks, "that excellent place-man, Sir John Clerk, patting Fletcher of Saltoun on the back, is the tame pigeon patronising the eagle." Men of Sir John's stamp were of opinion that the "eagle" would have been more profitably employed in feathering its own nest than in soaring skywards in flights which led nowhere.

It is a remarkable circumstance that in an age of political invective which produced a Swift; an age in which no man's character was safe from his enemies (or even his "friends"), the worst charges that his opponents could bring against Fletcher were those of pedantry and ill-temper. His antagonists in Parliament were often the targets of his temper. They were all afraid of the fiery little orator who had no political axe to grind, no party leaders to mollify, and who (in the words of Macky), held that Whig and Tory were names used "to cloak the knaves of both". Self-opinionated, and therefore an uncomfortable controversialist; an enemy of compromise and therefore a hopeless politician; a visionary and therefore a crank; such was the man whom his friends and his enemies alike had to put up with as best they could. Some of them, however, forgot that without vision the people perish.

The homeliness of the tame pigeon picking up corn from the ground and looking up gratefully for more, was for Fletcher's contemporaries a more comfortable, if less inspiring object to contemplate, than the soaring eagle spreading its disdainful wings on an upward flight and disappearing into the clouds. At the end of his life, one may well picture him as a man, certainly not without friends, but out of touch with those with whom he had so long been associated, and a statesman who was now outside the circumference of the activities which he had made his lifework. He was a lonely if a unique figure; a tired man conscious of having slipped into the background; forgotten, perhaps, by his political contemporaries; with his aims unaccomplished, and his ideals shattered in the march of events. But he has not been forgotten in his native land, nor will he be forgotten until his single-minded devotion to his deepest convictions ceases to stir the admiration, and evoke the gratitude, of those whose permanent welfare he passionately desired to serve. His work remains; his spirit persists; and his inspiring example is a bequest to posterity.

The apparent lack of elasticity in his character was due to his complete sincerity. And after all, his disabilities of temper, which it would be idle to conceal, were but specks on a bright and shining armour. His most discerning and friendliest contemporaries, while acknowledging these defects of character, were not slow to see them in the right perspective (27). Lockhart has paid a tribute to his sterling qualities which deserves to be written in letters of gold. "To sum up," he says at the end of a lengthy analysis, "he was a learned, gallant, honest, and every other way well-accom-

plished gentleman; and if ever a man proposes to serve and merit
well of his country, let him place his courage, zeal, and constancy as
a pattern before him, and think himself sufficiently applauded and
rewarded if he obtained the character of being like Andrew
Fletcher of Salton."

His fellow-countrymen have preserved the memory of this
gallant gentleman by enshrining it in a casket of patriotism. In
these days, when the foundations of liberty are being sapped before our eyes; when democratic ideals are scorned; when representative institutions are fighting for their existence; it is well to
turn one's eyes to the doctrines enunciated by Fletcher, and held by
him with tenacity throughout the whole of his career. How would
he answer the present-day sneers at patriotism, and the noisy
clamours for the vague thing called internationalism, and the
exaggerated nationalism that is resulting in the pernicious segre-
gation of communities? He would say (one believes), in his direct
fashion, and in incisive language, that patriotism is a natural instinct, and its repression an unnatural inhibition. But he would
make a distinction. "Show me a true patriot," he would say, "and
I will show you a lover, not merely of his own country, but of all
mankind. Show me a spurious patriot, a bombastic fire-eater, and
I will show you a rascal. Show me a man who loves other countries
equally with his own, and I will show you a man entirely deficient
in a sense of proportion. But show me a man who respects the
rights of all nations, while ready to defend the rights of his own
against them all, and I will show you a man who is both a nation-
alist and an internationalist." That, if I have interpreted it aright,
was Andrew Fletcher's patriotic creed.

His character is summed up in a few unforgettable words by
Macky, the Whig, whose estimate of his qualities may be placed
side by side with that of Lockhart, the Tory, already quoted. "He
is," says Macky, "a gentleman steady in his principles, of nice
honour, with abundance of learning, brave as the sword he wears,
and bold as a lion. He would lose his life readily to serve his
country; and would not do a base thing to save it."

"He would lose his life readily to serve his country; and would
not do a base thing to save it:" the words will bear repetition.

Could a finer tribute be paid to any man? (28).

APPENDIX

Tract printed in Edinburgh in 1699, entitled *A defence of the Settlement of the Scots on the Isthmus of Darien in America. With arguments to prove that it is in the interest of England to join with them and to protect them in that Colony.*

THE tract of which the following is an analysis, was published under the pseudonym of "Philo-Caledon". Its authorship is attributed, in a contemporary handwriting, to Andrew Fletcher (Halkett & Laing). It has also been attributed to Archibald Foyer, a clergyman, and to others.

In my opinion, the author was probably Lord Belhaven. The standpoint of the tract is similar to that upheld in the memorial presented to the English Council of Trade by the Company of Scotland, when desired to state its case against Spain; and, indeed, the tract and the memorial seem to be identical, for the tract is included in the *Collection of State Tracts* (William III, 3, pp. 494-520).

The tract has an appendix, describing Darien, and it is specifically stated that the information came from Wafer. Allusion is made to "our men" (presumably the Company's men), followed by an account by one of the colonists of their experiences with the natives.

Belhaven was a director of the Company of Scotland, and would be the most likely man to draft the memorial (possibly with Fletcher's assistance: Dalrymple hints that both Stair and Fletcher assisted the Company with their literary skill). But the main reason for my attribution of the authorship of the tract to him, is that a comparison with his printed speech in Parliament, in 1703, reveals a similarity of style (even of phrase) and of historical argument which can scarcely be fortuitous. The tract is dedicated to King William (in terms which Fletcher would scarcely have employed), and the pseudonym proves nothing, though Lord Belhaven's invocation of "Mother Caledonia" in his famous oration of 1706 may conceivably suggest a link between the two.

The dedication says, "We are Your Majesty's subjects as well as our neighbours, and have an equal right to share your protection, which it's hoped they will at last be convinced it is their interest to agree to in relation to our American settlement. . . . As it has pleased God to make you the glorious Instrument of our common deliverance, (we pray) that he would also make you the happy Instrument by an inseparable union."

The writer notes the Spanish claim, and challenges Spain to prove her right to the Isthmus by inheritance, marriage, or donation. The

Dariens, he says, are in actual possession of their liberty, and were never subdued; nor did they ever receive any "Spanish Governor" or "garrison" among them. Moreover, they hate the Spaniards heartily. He cites a case to show that in or about 1680 the English Government looked upon Darien as being in no way subject to Spain. The Darien "Princes" are now in league with the Scots, and have "joyfully" received them into their country. The Spaniards, it is true, claim that they were allowed some gold mines within some fifteen leagues of the Scottish settlement, but they were admitted as labourers only, and were finally expelled by force. The natives refuse to have anything more to do with them, for they have made themselves odious to the Dariens.

As for the Pope's general grant of America to the Spaniards, such an agreement cannot be seriously considered by Protestants, and even by Roman Catholics themselves it is regarded as a precarious contention. Spain, by her crimes and impiety, had certainly done nothing to justify such a grant as a reward.

Darien is enclosed by Spanish dominions, but there is not a Spanish post or garrison on either side of the territory in dispute. Instances are cited, both in Europe and America, to show that independent sovereignties are sometimes enclosed by the dominions of other nations.

The Spaniards should be the last to complain of treaty-breaking, for had they not committed a breach of the treaty of 1670 by detaining unlawfully Scots and English prisoners who had been forced ashore at Carthagena by shipwreck? And had they not given the King of Great Britain just reason to complain of their action by attacking his subjects by sea and land? The Scots had done them no injury, but had acquainted them that they had come to Darien peaceably, without any hostile design against them or any other people.

The Scots had as good a right to their settlement in Darien as any people in the world could have. They were acting under the authority of an Act of Parliament, and they had conformed to the requirements of that Act by taking possession of a territory with the consent of the natives, and not possessed by any other European Prince or State. They entered peacefully upon this new colony "without either Force or Fraud", after concluding with the Darien paramount chief, Andreas, "a solemn treaty and alliance", written in Spanish, "because the said Prince understands that language". Therefore they have a just and legal right, and a right, also, to the protection of their King against the attempts of the Spaniards or any other people whatsoever.

The arguments used against their settlement can be proved to be fallacious. Damage to the trade of England was feared. In the first place, "being a distinct and independent nation", they are not obliged to consider the interests of Spain or their English opponents, "more than they consider ours". But the settlement cannot damage English trade, for it consists chiefly of sugar and tobacco, neither of which has yet been discovered in New Caledonia. A complete answer to the English objections is that the English may, if they choose, become partners with the Scots in the venture, and on such conditions as will prevent any injury being done to their own commerce.

Nor is there greater substance in the argument that the greater immunities and freedom from Customs duties granted to the Scots Company will enable the latter to undersell the East India Company, forestall their markets, or reduce the Customs revenue. For the Scots have no intention of setting up an East Indian trade. Even if they entered that trade, it would be to the advantage of the English nation, by creating competition and cheapening commodities to the consumer. And once more, if the English see fit to join the Scots, they will receive their share of the advantages conferred upon the Scots Company.

Another objection had been urged, namely, that the ships of the Scottish Company must break bulk in Scotland only, and English ships would suffer by Scottish ports being made the only free ports for cargoes. The reply is that Scottish ships may break bulk where they please, and that the Scottish Parliament would, beyond doubt, give the English all the satisfaction they needed in the matter.

But what about a rupture with Spain consequent upon the Scottish occupation of Darien? The question is faced fairly and squarely. The Spaniards would never break with England. They were not able, in existing circumstances, to maintain themselves against the French; and was it likely, therefore, that in spite of their minatory language, they would throw the weight of England against them for the sake of Darien? And if once British authority were consolidated there, what an "effectual curb" it would be upon Spanish policy! A powerful colony in Darien, in the very centre of the Spanish dominions in America, and within reach of their silver and gold mines, would prevent any active hostility on the part of the Spaniards against Great Britain, or an alliance with Great Britain's enemies. In the contrary event, being masters of their money, "we shall speedily cut the sinews of their war".

Indeed, the advantages to England of this Scottish colony were conspicuous. The Scots in time would build up a navy, which would be capable of assisting England in the common defence of their island, and in maintaining "the Sovereignty of the Seas". Let the English beware of Dutch rivalry in trade, which is only kept in check during the lifetime of King William. If the English and Dutch in combination have been hard put to it, to hold their own against the French, how would the English fare without the Dutch?

A prosperous Scotland would enable her to bear a greater share of the joint burden, and thus lighten the load for England of foreign wars. The more money the Scots made, the more would they spend in England. London, particularly, would benefit "as the sun draws vapours after it". The Scots nobility and gentry spent freely in England, and

Appendix

would spend more as their prosperity increased. Complaints had been made in Parliament of the competition of Scots pedlars in England with shopkeepers and others. Scottish prosperity would relieve England from their presence. And it would prevent the emigration of "vast numbers of their youth who follow the same sort of employment, or betake themselves to the Sword in Denmark, Sweden, Poland, Muscovy, Germany, Holland, and France". As the result, the fleets and armies would be reinforced with "as good mariners and soldiers as any in the world". If they joined the Scots, the English would have their Plate brought home in their own bottoms from their own mines, "with which we are assured that country abounds". They would not have to touch at Cadiz or any foreign port, and would thus escape foreign taxations or interruptions.

And then what of the maintenance of the balance of power which England is designed "by nature and Providence" to hold? The position of Darien would prevent the junction of France and Spain, which England dreaded. It might also prevent the outbreak of a religious war, or bring it to a speedy conclusion. For the Spanish mines in the West are "Antichrist's Pouch". It is the surest method of destroying Antichrist to seize his Purse: "for if he once be deprived of Judas's Bag he will quickly drop St. Peter's Keys". It is by the charms of her gold that the "Babylonish whore" has made the world wander after her.

Also, the English would be better able to avoid the ruin of their trade in the Mediterranean and West Indies, in the event of the French possessing themselves of Spain. And they would be better able to prevent the Netherlands falling into the hands of the French. For if once the French succeeded in doing so, and occupied ports capable of holding a fleet, English trade to the Eastland would be ruined, and the liberties of Great Britain would be at an end.

England and Scotland would be united "by an inseparable tie" if the English joined in the Scots venture. The ancestors of the English would have gladly purchased this union at a much dearer rate, but they were always outbid by France, with the result that, lacking this union, the English became an easy prey to their successive conquerors and lost the large provinces they had enjoyed beyond sea.

The establishment of this Scottish colony would serve the Protestant interest, and would contribute to the advancement of Christianity. The Pope and the conclave of Rome have espoused the quarrel of the Spaniards in this affair as a cause of religion. But when the natives of Darien discover the difference between the morals and the doctrine of Protestants and Papists, and find that unlike their experience of the Spaniards, they are treated with humanity, they will be the more inclined to embrace Christianity.

Would the Scots, without the assistance of England, succeed in maintaining their footing in Darien? The writer thought they would. On

[317]

what grounds? Because, the whole kingdom of Scotland being "more jealous for it and unanimous in it than they have been in any other thing for forty or fifty years past", they will do their utmost to support themselves by their own strength, and if that prove inadequate, they will look elsewhere for assistance "with a naval force". If they have only to meet the opposition of the Spaniards, it will be easy for the nobility and gentry and the Royal burghs to raise money on their lands, and with the increase of stock, to buy ships for the protection of the colony. Indeed, all they need do is to commission buccaneers for their service, who will be more than a match for the Spaniards. But what if the French join the Spaniards to drive the Scots out of Darien? Such offers, if made, are not in the least likely to be accepted; for the Spaniards know well that if once the French got a footing in America, the Spanish grandees might protest in vain against the succession of France to the Spanish Crown: for the French would immediately seize the Spanish mines and treasures in the West Indies. Or, even supposing the King of Spain should live many years, and so keep the French out of the Spanish Succession, yet, having once got possession of Darien, they would soon show the Spaniards that they were more dangerous neighbours than the Scots. As for any danger of the Scots winning the Spanish settlements in America from their allegiance to Spain, that is inherently impossible, if for no other reason than that the Scots are zealous Protestants, and therefore hateful to the Popish clergy and laity. But there might be a real danger of the French Roman Catholics undermining the loyalty to Spain of her American colonists. In short, the Spaniards have no reason of any kind to fear the Scots, if they, on their part, forbear hostilities. On the contrary, they may find the Scots useful if attacked by the French, as in the late war, "it being the interest of the Scots as well as of the Spaniards to prevent the accession of the Crown of Spain to that of France". It is known that the French had been endeavouring to insinuate themselves into the good graces of the natives of Darien, with the view of effecting a settlement there. Surely it is more in the Spanish interest that it should be in the possession of the Scots. The French have already been tampering with both the Spaniards and the Indians, hoping to have a large share of America when the King of Spain dies.

But even if the Spaniards are foolish enough to accept the offers of the French to expel the Scots, it is not beyond the power of the Scots to find allies to assist them with a naval force if the English hold aloof. The Dutch, for example, know how useful an alliance with the Scots would be, both in the fishing privileges they would receive as a *quid pro quo*, and in other ways. The Scots and the Dutch are on good terms: they have a common trade and common religious interests. And if the Dutch fail them, the Scots can turn to the Scandinavian Protestant countries.

"We could heartily wish" (the writer proceeds) "there had never been any ground for this suggestion" (English antagonism), "and that the opposition we have met with from England had been less national than that which we had from both their Houses of Parliament after the passing an Act for an African Company etc. in ours; and it were to be wished that so many of the English had not given us such proofs of an alienated mind and aversion to our welfare as they have done since, by their Resident at Hamborough and their late Proclamation in their West India Plantations; and we could have wished, above all, that His Majesty of England had not in the least concurred or given his countenance to that opposition, for as King of Scots it is plain he could not do it. He hath confirmed what we have done by the Touch of his Sceptre, which no Private Order or Instructions can revoke. And we could wish that his English Counsellors who put him upon those things would remember that Strafford and Laud lost their heads for giving King Charles I that bad advice of oppressing and opposing the Scots."

The writer then recounts the prejudice that Scotland had suffered by the Union of the Crowns by reason of the residence of their Kings in England. Henry VIII, he remarks, matched his daughter with the King of Scots, because he foresaw that by this means, the Crown of England would fall to the King of Scots, who would remove to England; whereas, if his daughter had married the King of France, the latter would draw the English Court to Paris. The Stewart Kings, after their accession to the English Crown, had shown small concern for the interests of Scotland. And quite recently, the English Parliament had excelled itself in insulting Scotland by its bitter opposition to the Scottish Company. "If these continued slights and injuries", he concludes, "be not enough to make us weary of the Union of the Crowns, let any man judge."

From this point the tract goes on to recapitulate the circumstances at the Revolution: how Scotland had then opportunities which she did not grasp, of enforcing readjustments of co-partnership with England before agreeing to any settlement. Could the Scots have been blamed if they had stood to terms, seeing how they had been treated by Cromwell and his party, after the Scots had saved them and the Parliament of England? The ancestors of the English had treated them better. They had always considered the Scots as "denizens of England". They had even given them the three northern counties of Northumberland, Westmorland, and Cumberland, to be held in fee of the Crown of England. Surely there was every reason why the English should now show a friendlier spirit towards the sister nation. Surely they might expect the King to attend upon the Scottish administration in person *pro re nata* (as he does now upon the affairs of Holland), or lay down methods to have his pleasure signified to them at home when required, "which would save a vast deal of money annually to the Kingdom of Scotland".

It was impolitic, as well as ungrateful, for England to treat them as she did, "since we have so many open doors to get out at". She need not think that the Scots had lost their courage or their sense of national honour. The best way for England to assure themselves of the Scots was "to treat us in a friendly manner". He (the writer) had no intention of arousing animosity between the two nations, but his desire was to show their neighbours that they are bound in gratitude, duty, and interest, to support the Scots in their American settlement. They must side either with the Spaniards or the Scots. Which was it to be? The Spaniards were in no position to have a rupture with England; if, however, they deemed otherwise, they could be speedily reduced to reason.

If, in the end, owing to English discouragement, the Darien venture should fail, the results would be calamitous for Scotland, and would have serious repercussions on England. Or if Scotland, in spite of that discouragement, should manage to bear up, it will lay the foundation "of an irreconcilable feud and perhaps issue in a war betwixt the two nations". In such an event, the English "will find us unanimous as one man against them".

They, in Scotland, had never believed in the doctrine that it is unlawful to resist a king, or "any that have a commission under him", upon any pretence whatsoever. "They left that doctrine in Scythia, from whence some authors derive our origin, and think it only fit to be sent back to Turkey from whence it came". They know very well how to distinguish betwixt "a lawful power and the abuse of it". The history of Scotland furnishes examples of this distinction, one of which (in the reign of James I of Scotland) the writer cites.

Those in England who are hostile to the Scots are either disaffected to the present Constitution, or have been actuated by "a sordid principle of private interest". "It is to be hoped they will never be able so far to leaven the sound part of the English nation as to occasion a rupture betwixt them and us." It was certainly surprising to find an English Parliament regarding as a "misdemeanour" their taking subscriptions in England, when these were intended to make the English joint sharers with themselves. Also, the English press Scottish seamen in time of war, "as if they were their own subjects". Sometimes, too, they confiscate Scottish ships by reckoning Scots mariners as aliens. "So that the English have not only deprived us of our Government and the warm influence of our Court." They do all they can, also, "to prevent our application to trade". The English complain when the King goes to Holland. But let them consider what Scotland has had to suffer in this respect for nearly a hundred years. It comes to this: that "they will neither admit" the Scots people "to the privileges of fellow-subjects with themselves", nor "suffer" them to take such measures as will enable them to stand on their own feet. It is equally bad policy and bad Christianity to keep the Scots low because they are an independent and free nation, and having been formerly the enemies of England, may again be dangerous if they grow rich and powerful. The Scots have several times proposed a union which "the gentlemen of that kidney" have prevented. Let them look into their history-books and see what England has gained by her Scottish wars.

In the last resort, if the English allow the Scots in Darien to be overcome by the French (for the Scots are not afraid of the Spaniards), they may be compelled to make an honourable capitulation to the French, which would probably be followed by a renewal of the ancient alliance between France and Scotland, with a share to Scotland of the trade of Darien. What, in that event, would become of the East and West Indian trade of England, or of the English plantations, if England were confronted by an allied France and Scotland? Already the French are threatening the English plantations in America with a rival settlement on the Mississippi, which, indeed, was a greater menace to Spain than the Darien colony. And yet France is hypocritically crying out against the Scots for planting themselves in Darien! It would seem, therefore, to be in the interest of England "rather to strengthen themselves by our friendship and to look after the French, than to provoke us to look out for other allies by their opposition and neglect".

He has no ill design against the English nation. On the contrary, "a stricter union is absolutely necessary that both nations may have but one interest": a union that would render both nations "less liable to convulsions and intestine commotions", and save them against attack by enemies abroad. To the advantages already enumerated, English friendship towards the Darien scheme would add the ensuring to her of safe places of retreat for her ships, if attacked by enemies or struck by tempest; also, the Scots colony would buy from England whatever Scotland could not supply; and voyages of English ships to the East Indies would be considerably shortened.

In the reign of James I (of England) the Scots were under no more restrictions of trade than the English (except in the exportation of wool), but at the Restoration England did "very ungratefully" lay "preclusions and restrictions" upon them, contrary to the laws relating to the *Postnati*. The effect of the Navigation Act, passed in the reign of Charles II, was to place Scotland in a worse condition relatively than Ireland, "that is a conquest". This is all the more unreasonable, because the Scots have to take part in England's wars, generally with the very nations (France and Holland) with which Scotland does nearly the whole of her trade; whereas England has many other markets to fall back upon when at war with either of these countries.

Thus the Scots are forced to be sharers in the troubles of the English, "tho' they will not allow us to partake of their profit, nor suffer us to take any measures to procure such as we may call our own".

On her present footing Scotland is worse off by the Union of the

Crowns than if the Union had never taken place. "For when anything happens wherein the interest of England seems to be contrary to ours, it is certainly carried against us, and we are left without remedy." Indeed, they are worse off than foreigners: for foreigners can take their own measures when their interests are affected. But we, unhappy Scots, have no one to appeal to, "but one that is either an alien and enemy to us, as being king of a greater people who are such, or if he be inclinable to protect and do us justice, as King of Scots, he is a prisoner in England and cannot do it". In his dual capacity, as King of England and King of Scotland, if the interests of the two countries clash, he is bound to take the English view: so our Crown, "which we defended so gallantly for many ages, and which the English could never make subject to theirs by force", is now under complete subjection to that of England. But the Scots themselves are blameable for not making better terms for themselves at the Revolution. As the proverb says, "Scotsmen are wise behindhand."

The situation (he argues) is really preposterous. If we look to France or some other Power for help, "we are rebels". If we rely upon our own King, what do we get? The influence of the Crown is exerted to divide us among ourselves. See what happened in the reign of Charles II. Those in Scotland who complied with the Court were bribed with all the chief offices in the Scottish Administration, while those who were true patriots (e.g. "the late great Duke of Hamilton and our present Lord High Chancellor") were exposed to all sorts of dangers and vexations. Scotland had no reason to wish for a continuation of the Union of the Crowns, "except the interest of the nations be more closely united than ever they have been hitherto". If, indeed, the Crowns were severed, it might be fatal to England, for it would mean a renewal of the alliance between France and Scotland. In that contingency he (the writer) would not fear that religious considerations would be a fatal obstacle. For were not the persecuted Hungarians protected in their religion by the Turks, the sworn enemies of it? Besides, Louis XIV "is not immortal", and "even Julian the Apostate found it in his interest, for some time, to protect the orthodox Christians whom he mortally hated". Of course, a renewal of the ancient alliance between France and Scotland is in the highest degree unlikely. But what if it should become a fact? And what if the King of England, after a rupture with his Parliament over (say) standing armies, should betake himself to Scotland, which by law is compelled to furnish him with a force of 22,000 men?

What would England say if the Scots Parliament interfered with English affairs, as the English Parliament interfered with Scottish affairs? Is not such interference to be very much resented? Then why should they deny to Scotland the same liberty, "for we are a free nation as well as they"?

[322]

The English proclamation in the West Indies was not the act of a King of Scotland, for it is contrary to his own Act of Parliament. Plainly it is the result of force placed upon him by a nation which, in this matter, thinks it their interest so to act. If Scotland has to obtain satisfaction for the colony being starved, or if the ships should be attacked by any nation as pirates (the King of Scots having declared against us), to whom is she to apply for redress? Not to the King of England, for he is a declared enemy, having emitted these hostile declarations. He is, in point of fact, a "prisoner in England, and is compelled to act against the interests of his own ancient Crown and Kingdom".

The writer winds up his argument as follows: If, in return for the Scottish offer of co-operation with England in the Darien scheme, "we meet with neglect and contempt; have our sovereignty trampled under foot; our settlement in America by an Act of Parliament in Scotland reflected upon as unjust by proclamation from England; the world cannot blame us to complain of the violence done to our Independency and Honour, which is not to be salved by any politick consideration, whatever that our neighbours can pretend for this treatment".

Note.—In his tract, *A Defence of the Scots Abdicating Darien*, Herries ("Phil. Scot.") calls the author of the foregoing "the masked champion of your company" (the Company of Scotland).

A reply was also written by "Philo-Britan." (1699) in a tract entitled *The Defence of the Scots Settlement at Darien answered paragraph by paragraph*; a singularly unconvincing document. The writer's argument in favour of the English attitude is that every independent nation has the right to secure its commerce against the "encroachments" of its neighbours (p. 52).

It only remains to add that "Rob. Ferguson" (the "Plotter" no doubt) wrote, also in 1699, a tract consisting of a lengthy preface and a text of 214 pages, entitled *A Just and Modest Vindication of the Scots Design for the having established a Colony at Darien.*

REFERENCES AND NOTES

Chapter I

1. Lord Buchan's *Life*, pp. 5 and 6: Family MS. Andrew Fletcher's father was the fifth in lineal descent from Sir Bernard Fletcher of the county of York. Sir Bernard was a son of Fletcher of Hatton in Cumberland. Robert, his son, emigrated to Tweeddale. Andrew, the son of Robert, was a merchant in Dundee. David, the son of Andrew, purchased the estate of Innerpeffer in Angus: he married a daughter of Ogilvie of Pourie. His grandson, Andrew, succeeded to the estate of Innerpeffer, and in 1643 bought Saltoun in East Lothian; he was knighted by James I in 1620. He was one of the Senators of the College of Justice with the title of Lord Innerpeffer, and his son, Sir Robert, was the father of "the patriot". (Appendix to Lord Buchan's *Life*, pp. 65-7: Family MS.).

The Family MS. states that Sir Robert Fletcher was "learned in mathematical science and all the branches of *belles lettres*; the Holy Scriptures were familiar to his mind; he read them with facility in the original languages, and could repeat Greek and Hebrew quotations from them with as much ease and readiness as others do in their mother tongue".

He found his estates heavily encumbered (a debt of £17,000 sterling), for Lord Innerpeffer had to pay £5,000 sterling on account of his protestation against delivering up Charles I to the English army, and the "Engagement" of 1648 involved him in a much greater expense. Sir Robert was compelled to sell his estates in Angus. He never received any compensation from the Crown.

Catharine Bruce's mother was Martha Haldane, daughter of Sir John Haldane of Gleneagles, by Barbara Johnstone, daughter of the laird of Elphinstone, by a daughter of the Earl Gowrie. Sir Henry Bruce was the son of Sir Robert Bruce by Margaret Murray, daughter of the laird of Tullibardine, by Catharine Campbell, daughter of the laird of Glenorchy. Thus Andrew Fletcher had good Highland as well as Lowland blood in his veins.

It will be seen that he came from English stock on his father's side, a circumstance which one could have hardly suspected from his intensity as a Scot. In that respect he was like the descendants of the English settlers in Ireland, who became more Irish than the Irish themselves. The Family MS. states that Sir Bernard Fletcher was said to be descended from an ancestor who came over with William the Conqueror. Macaulay remarks that Andrew Fletcher was "the head of an ancient Norman house and was proud of his descent".

I have retained the usual spelling of "Saltoun", the older form of "Salton", though the latter form was more frequently used even by Andrew Fletcher's contemporaries than the former; also by himself. "Ton" (Scots "toun") originally meant a farm.

Perhaps I should say here that in the numerous direct quotations from contemporary writers which appear in the text, I have thought it desirable generally to give the modern spelling where it varies from the original. Also I have thought it desirable to give direct quotations from these writers, in many instances, in preference to paraphrasing them.

2. *History of his own Time* (1839), p. 405. *Supplement*, p. 161 (Foxcroft).

Andrew became laird of Saltoun at the age of twelve, and it is amusing to find him, at the age of thirteen, gravely reporting to the Presbytery of Haddington, that he had checked with the catalogue the books in the library of the Saltoun church, and had found that Burnet, in whose charge they were, was "taking proper care of them". Burnet did not forget the Saltoun library: he left a sum of money for its support. It is still known locally as "Bishop Burnet's Library" (Omond, p. 10).

3. *Introduction to History*, p. iv, being an extract from Burnet's *Life* by his son. Burnet was accused of having written this sermon on Sir Robert Fletcher in order to "make his court to Fletcher's widow", i.e. Andrew's mother. He (Burnet) bought up all the copies he could find (Portland MSS. 7, p. 354).

4. *History*, pp. 668-9.

5. Lord Buchan's *Life*, p. 7: Family MS. Buchan says that Fletcher "was from his infancy of a very fiery and uncontroulable temper; but his dispositions were noble and generous". Obviously the child was father of the man.

6. Omond, pp. 11-12.

7. Sir John Lauder of Fountainhall's *Historical Observes*, Appendix No. 2, pp. 270, 277; *Register of the Privy Council of Scotland*, 5 (3rd Series), pp. 480-1. In the same volume (p. 446) there is a significant entry: "License granted to Andrew Fletcher of Saltoun to goe out of the Kingdome." (1678).

8. W. C. Mackenzie's *Life and Times of John Maitland, Duke of Lauderdale*, p. 454.

9. *Ibid*, pp. 301-3. This militia had been created in 1663, and Lauderdale's Act of 1669 merely regulated its pay and other matters of detail. In England, its existence was rightly regarded as a menace to popular liberty, for it was clearly intended by Lauderdale as an expedient to strengthen the Crown in the struggle between Charles and the refractory House of Commons.

10. *Historical Notices*, i, p. 270.

11. *Ibid*, p. 281.

12. *Historical Notices*, i, p. 305; *Acts of Parliament of Scotland*, 8, p. 232; *MS. Supplementary Par. Papers*, II; Omond, p. 16.

13. *Historical Observes*, p. 209.

14. *Memoirs*, (1771) I, p. 66, Sir John Dalrymple was a Baron of Exchequer in Scotland, late in the eighteenth century.

15. *History*, p. 340.

16. Burnet, *History*, p. 340, gives an illuminating picture of the inconsistencies of the Test Act. See *Acts of Parliament of Scotland*, 8, pp. 244-5, for the detailed provisions of the Act.

17. *Acts of Parliament of Scotland*, 8, p. 245: *MS. Supp. Par. Papers*, II (addenda).

18. Burnet, pp. 341-3; MacPherson's *Original Papers*, i, pp. 125, 133.

19. *Memoirs of the Secret Services of John Macky*, p. 220. In January 1682 the "laird of Saltoun for the paroch of Salton", by an order of the Privy Council, was to fill a vacancy caused by the minister's refusal to take the test. (*Register of Privy Council of Scotland*, 7 (3rd Series), p. 308).

20. Fountainhall's *Historical Notices*, i, p. 352; *Register of Privy Council of Scotland*, 7 (3rd Series), p. 380. As far back as 1670 Fletcher was appointed Commissioner of Excise for the militia in Haddingtonshire. (*Register of Privy Council of Scotland*, 3 (3rd Series), p. 143.)

Chapter II

1. Echard's *History* (1720), pp. 1028-9. Burnet, p. 352-3. The character of Algernon Sydney, as described by Burnet, his attainments and his political ideals, all remind one strongly of Andrew Fletcher.

2. *History*, pp. 353-4.

3. Lord Buchan's *Life*, pp. 8-9: Family MS.

4. Echard, p. 1028; Burnet, p. 354.

5. Echard, p. 1028.

6. *Ibid*; Burnet, p. 355.

7. *Historical Observes*, p. 214. In 1682 "Saltone" was one of those reported as "paying court" to Shaftesbury (*Hist. MSS. Com. Buccleuch MSS.* II, p. 106).

8. Burnet, p. 370 Lord Buchan's *Life*, p. 10. "Baillie", says Buchan, "was offered his pardon on condition of his impeaching his friend Fletcher: but he persisted to the gallows in rejecting the proposal with indignation." Omond, p. 21.

9. *App. Hist. MSS. Commission*, 7th Rep., 343b.

10. Burnet, p. 404.

11. Echard, p. 1060, who incorporated in his history a MS. of Ferguson the Plotter. Assuredly Ferguson knew more intimately than most of his contemporaries the whole of the facts relating to Monmouth. But the question arises: How much of his narrative can be believed? It

is probable, however, that his evidence is trustworthy where it has no bearing upon himself or his motives.

There is a tract embodying "a letter written by a gentleman in Brussels to his friend in London" dated 10th August, 1684, which tells us that "both the gentry and commonalty respect him (Monmouth) with a sorrow compounded of love and pity. His retinue is but small, by reason he has no certain place of residence, but is therein mostly accommodated by the gentry of the country". He employed his time, it seems, in inspecting engineering works, attending race-meetings, and so forth. Burnet, incidentally, is described as "an eminent Scotch doctor student, who writes all manner of Lives and turns a Peny at very reasonable rates".

12. Burnet, p. 405, says that Fletcher . . . "did not like Argyll's scheme;" also that "Fletcher, however vehemently soever he was set on the design in general (Monmouth's) yet saw nothing in this scheme that gave any hopes; so he argued much against it. And he said to me that the Duke of Monmouth was pushed on to it against his own sense and reason; but he could not refuse to hazard his person when others were so forward". And then he relates Lord Grey's fatuous remark, with Fletcher's reply, as stated in the text. See also James Ferguson's *Ferguson the Plotter*, p. 210.

13. Burnet, p. 404.

14. Echard, pp. 1060-1.

15. Burnet, pp. 405-6.

Chapter III

1. Echard's *History of the Revolution* (1725), p. 66, states that James told Monmouth that he could "pardon everything but that unworthy scandal upon his fame, his publick declaring that he had poisoned the King his brother". . . . "And so," says Echard, he "left him to the executioner".

2. Supplement to *History*, p. 161 (Foxcroft).

3. *Memoirs*, I, p. 121.

4. *Ferguson the Plotter*, p.221.

5. *History*, p. 701. Oldmixon, who had the unpleasant habit, as a historian, of attributing unworthy motives to those with whose political views he disagreed, is the only contemporary writer of whom I have any knowledge, to impugn Fletcher's honesty of purpose. He says he had "some knowledge" (it must necessarily have been slight) of Fletcher, and that he remembers very well that he was "hot, positive, obstinate, opinionative". That much may be conceded, but when he goes out of his way to say that Fletcher turned against William of Orange because "he had not the place he had cut out for himself",

(p. 376), he makes a statement for which there is neither warrant nor probability. Also, he gives a palpably prejudiced account of the Dare incident. The secret of Oldmixon's dislike of Fletcher is revealed, by his scornful remark: "This Mr. Fletcher was the Hero of the opposition to the Union".

6. *History*, p. 160. It is difficult to say what evidence was in Lingard's possession for this confident assertion.

7. *Memoirs*, p. 220. I have made an unsuccessful attempt by inquiries in Hungary to trace Fletcher's military association with that country. Professor Szekfü, Budapest, states that Arpad Karolyi, the historian, in his book on *The Re-capture of Buda and Pest in* 1686, says that there were many English and Scottish gentlemen fighting as volunteers in the army of Charles of Lotheringia (including James FitzJames, later Duke of Berwick, illegitimate son of James II). In the storming of Buda, on 13th July, 1686, several English and Scottish "lords" took part, and it is suggested that Fletcher may have been one of them.

But this relates to the post-Monmouth period of his career, and does not touch the question of his military adventures prior to that time. In support of the statement by Macky that he had served in Hungary before he joined Monmouth, I find, under date of "*c.* January 1685-6" the following, in a letter written by the Earl of Moray, the Secretary for Scotland in London : ". . . I doe not know what kepes Mr. Fletcher hear: he ons (once) intended to goe to Hungary but that I belive was over long agoe. I shall speake to him to hast home". (*Hist. MSS. Com. Buccleuch MSS.* 2, p. 97.)

The date given, if correct, makes this letter frankly unintelligible to me, for about January 1686, London was the very last place Fletcher would desire to be in, and the very last thing he would do was to "hast home". But assuming the allusion is to the laird of Saltoun (and that, I think, can scarcely be doubted), his association with Hungary "longe agoe" is clearly indicated.

Lord Buchan, quoting from the Family MS., says (p. 22) that "Fletcher's active genius led him to serve in the Hungarian war", after the Monmouth affair.

8. *Coltness Collections* (Maitland Club), part ii, p. 166.

9. The authorities for the Dare incident are: Burnet, p. 411; *Ferguson the Plotter*, p. 220; Echard's *History*, p. 1063; Dalrymple's *Memoirs*, i, p. 120-1; Fountainhall's *Historical Observes*; Oldmixon's *History*, p. 701. The information that Dare's horse was taken from Ford Abbey comes from Roberts's *Life of Monmouth*, i, p. 272.

The details of the Dare affair vary in the telling, but the version in the text embodies the facts as nearly as I can discover. The most succinct account is given by Nathaniel Wade, who was one of the captured companions of Monmouth. "Old Dare of Taunton", so Wade's "Confession" (*Harleian MS.* 6845, p. 264) runs, "was paymaster in Holland, who was killed at Lyme by one Fletcher, a Scotchman. Fletcher gott upon Dare's horse. Dare bid him dismount. He told him he would not. Other words followed, and Fletcher shott him in yᵉ head with his pistole two days after they came into Lyme".

Dr. Hill Burton, while paying a tribute to the integrity of Fletcher's character, is querulously critical of his politics. That he was quite entitled to be. But he was not entitled to give what is a misleading account of the Dare tragedy. And he was not entitled to make such a careless statement of fact as the following: "He (Fletcher) fought at Sedgemoor" (*The Reign of Queen Anne* (1880), 8, p. 6).

Burnet's account has a peculiar value, inasmuch as it was probably given to the historian by Fletcher himself.

10. Burnet, p. 411.
11. Ralph, p. 876.
12. *Life*, pp. 18-19: Family MS. The discrepancy may be explained by the suggestion in the text, or by some other lapse of memory.
13. *History*, p. 702.
14. Echard, *History*, p. 1061.
15. Oldmixon, p. 701.
16. *History*, p. 704.
17. *Ibid*, p. 705.
18. Sir Charles Petrie's *The Jacobite Movement*, p. 296.
19. A contemporary tract states that among the papers and books found on Monmouth's person when he was captured, was a MS. of "spells, charms and conjurations, songs, receits, and prayers"; all written by himself.

Chapter IV

1. Lord Buchan's *Life*, pp. 19-21: Family MS.
2. *Ibid*, p. 22.
3. Fountainhall's *Chronological Notes*, pp. 110, 120, 146, 153-4, 158; Fountainhall's *Historical Observes*, pp. 208-9, 213; Fountainhall's *Historical Notices*, pp. 572, 600, 660, 665, 686, 688, 690, 698, 837.

Fountainhall, as a lawyer, revelled in the case, and his account of the trial (interlarded with legal phraseology) is full and precise. To the layman, the difficulty of establishing Fletcher's identity may seem overstrained, but it serves to show the punctiliousness of the judges. Some members of the jury were disposed to think that the evidence of identification was insufficient, in view of the fact that only one witness, Captain Bruce, could identify Fletcher from his personal knowledge. See Howell's *State Trials*, ii, pp. 1023-57. See also note 2, Chap. V.

4. *Life*, pp. 37-8 (Letter from Lord Hailes to the Earl of Buchan).
5. Omond, p. 39.
6. Alexander Cunningham in his *History of Great Britain*, i, p. 83

(Eng. translation), notes among those who accompanied William to England, "Mr. Fletcher"; also, "William Carstairs, an honest man", and "Ferguson, a knave".

Chapter V

1. Wodrow's *Analecta*, ii, p. 45.

2. Cunningham's *History*, i, pp. 106-7. "Mr. Fletcher", says Cunningham (a Whig and a friend of Fletcher), "a man of great probity as well as spirits, but very bigoted to his own opinion, would not return to his estate by any law but his own, and that without asking leave of Kings or Parliaments". But all the same, Fletcher had to petition the Estates (in 1689) for the restitution of his estate, while asserting that the sentence of forfeiture had proceeded on "frivolous and weak pretences and upon lame and defective probation" (Omond, p. 45). *MS. Supp. Par. Papers*, 13, give an account of the proceedings in connection with the rescission of Fletcher's forfeiture. It would appear (vol. 12) that at the meeting of the Estates on 18th March, 1689, Fletcher "being called upon, refused to give his oath to the meeting." A later entry records the issue of a warrant "to secure Mr. Fletcher not to return to the Castle" (Edinburgh). These entries appear to confirm Cunningham's statement quoted above. Fletcher must have been an extremely "difficult" rebel for the Convention of Estates to whitewash.

The Committee for Fines and Forfeitures confirming Fletcher's contention, reported to the House, on 14th May, 1690, their opinion on his case. The House decided that the "probation" against Fletcher was "lame and defective", as proceeding only upon the testimony of "one probative witness", the other "witness deponing only that he saw a man of such a stature, and in such companie, called Fletcher of Saltoun; as also, that both the witnesses were under the fear of death, have (*sic*) their remission only presented and delyvered to them in the time they are deponing. This last was proven by a member of the Justice Court and the under-keeper of the Great Seall who appended the same to the Remissiones."

Thus the majority verdict of the jury who convicted Fletcher of high treason was upset by the finding of the Convention of Estates, and the Act of Remission was voted upon and approved accordingly.

The whole case forms an interesting study in Scottish jurisprudence.

3. "Yesterday", wrote Argyll and Montgomery from London, on 12th May, 1689, "we disburdened ourselves of the Crown, which was done in the Bankueting house with great solemnitie" (*Hist. MSS. Com.*, 11th Rep. App., pt. 6, p. 82).

4. Argyll seems to have believed in the efficiency of what he called "the ready pennie" to keep the clans quiet. "I told his Majestie at London", he writes the Duke of Hamilton, "4000 p. stg. would buy all

the clans. . . . Both MacLeod ¦and Sleat (MacDonald) would be King
William's if recruited in time" (*Hist. MSS. Com.*, 11th Rep. App.,
pt. 6, p. 183).

After what Argyll called the "misfortune" of Killiecrankie, Sir
George Mackenzie (Viscount Tarbat) was imprisoned, on General
MacKay's representations that he had not used his influence with the
Highland clans to prevent them from joining Dundee. He protested to
Hamilton that he did not possess the supposed influence (*Hist. MSS.
Com.*, 11th Rep. App., pt. 6, p. 193).

Mr. J. Ramsay MacDonald (*Scottish Review*, p. 76), says that when
the Haddington horse were called out against Dundee, Fletcher declined the command, which was given to Lord Belhaven, and this is
confirmed by *MS. Supp. Par. Papers*, 12.

Incidentally, I observe that in his Preface, Mr. Omond calls Mr.
MacDonald "Mr. J. R. Donaldson", an anglicization of his name
which the Prime Minister would scarcely relish.

Mr. John Buchan (*The Massacre of Glencoe*, p. 25), departing from his
customary carefulness, permits himself to write as follows: "There was
Tarbat, handsome and genial, but slippery, *like all of the Mackenzie
blood*" (italics mine).

A parallel to this deliverance would be provided, if I were to commit
the fatuity of saying: "There was Thomas Buchan (who, superseding
Cannon, commanded the Jacobite forces after the Battle of Killiecrankie), saturnine and loyal, but thoroughly incompetent, (as indeed
he was), *like all of the Buchan blood*".

5. *Life*, p. 45. But Lord Buchan is mistaken in supposing (pp. 32-3)
that Fletcher was a member of the Convention of Estates.

6. *Memoirs*, p. 69.

7. *Life*, p. 45.

8. Lord Buchan, *Life*, p. 43, tells us a curious story about Hamilton.
He was suspected of wishing to embarrass the settlement of the Crown
(precisely as did his successor), "with a view to favour the eventual
pretensions of his own family. He went secretly on board the ship of
Van Aärfen Somelsdijke, the Dutch admiral in the road of Leith, and
proposed a union of Scotland and Holland as one Commonwealth. It
may be guessed who expected to be vice Statholder in Scotland".
(Buchan gives as his authority: "communicated by Somelsdijke to his
relation, Lord Auchenleck, one of the Senators of the College of Justice
in Scotland"). I find that this story is told by Sir David Dalrymple,
Lord Hailes, in a letter dated 26th April, 1787, (Edinburgh University
Library), to Lord Buchan, which contains some "Fletcheriana". He
asks a curious question: "What I wish to know: was he (Fletcher) a
Whig at bottom"? Also he says: "It was said of Fletcher that he wished
for a republic in which he himself might be king".

9. Dalrymple's *Memoirs* (1773), i, App., p. 208. Mr. Omond (p. 46), in

copying this letter, unaccountably inserts "not" before the word "approve".

10. *Memoirs*, p. 230.

11. *Memoirs*, pp. 71-2.

12. Fletcher's Protestantism is illustrated by the fact that in 1674 he craved the Privy Council that "his kinsman, Menzies of Pitfoddels, who has been educated abroad as a Catholic may, on his return, be placed where he may be educated in the Protestant religion" (*Register of Privy Council of Scotland*, 3, (3rd Series), p. 184).

A recent search in the unprinted portion of the Register of the Privy Council has failed to discover any material relating to Fletcher.

Chapter VI

1. This question is discussed in greater detail later in these pages.

2. The distinction between "the people of the hills" and "the people of the plains" is purely arbitrary, though convenient. What, indeed, is the true boundary between the Highlands and the Lowlands? There are, of course, hills in the Lowlands as there are plains in the Highlands. But it remains true that, relatively, the Highlands are more hilly than the Lowlands; otherwise, there would be no sense in the distinction implied by the names.

3. Fletcher's *Second Discourse*, pp. 150-1 (1732). He describes the fishings of the Highlands as "the richest . . . of any in the world". For the lack of development of Highland resources of wealth, he blames the chiefs. Comparing "the Alps which have no such advantages", with the Scottish Highlands, he says: "they are inhabited everywhere by a civilized, industrious, honest, and peaceable people: but they had no lords to hinder them from being civilized, to discourage industry, encourage thieving, and to keep them beggars that they might be the more dependent".

4. Burt, an overbearing type of man (as the Inverness people discovered), upon whose *Letters* Macaulay based his acid and misleading sketch, had not an extensive knowledge of general conditions in the Highlands outside the town of Inverness. He says truly enough (Letter XIX) that "the Highlands are but little known even to the inhabitants of the low country of Scotland . . . to the people of England . . . hardly known at all". The Highlanders on their part despised the Lowlanders, "as inferior to them in courage". They thought they had a right to plunder them because, according to their traditions, "the Lowlands in old times were the possession of their ancestors". (They confused race with language, for although the Lowlanders had lost the speech and customs of the Celt, they had not lost their Celtic descent.) As John Major wrote in the reign of James IV, "most of us spoke Irish (Gaelic) a short time ago".

Burt makes this specific statement: "I never had the least reason to

[332]

complain of the treatment towards me of any of the ordinary High-landers" (Letter XIX). Also, he had "the charity to believe" that the robberies in the Highlands, of which there were so many stories, were "uncommon". They were perpetuated by the "ill-minded people among the clans" (Letter XXIV). (Would one readily gather that impression from Macaulay?)

Defoe, another Englishman, says: "Nor are the inhabitants (of the Highlands) so wild and barbarous . . . as our writers have pretended. We see every day the gentlemen born here: such as the Mackenzies, McLeans, Dundonalds (he means MacDonalds), Gordons, Mackays, and others who are named among the clans as if they were *Barbarians*, appear at Court and in our Camps and Armies as polite and as finished Gentlemen as any from other countries, or even among our own, and if I should say outdoing our own in many things, especially in arms and gallantry, as well abroad as at Home" (*Tour through the Whole Island of Great Britain*, 1724, 1725, and 1727, p. 821, 1927). Also, he refers (p. 829) to "the extreme Courtesie of some of the Gentlemen of the Country" in the far North, who helped him on his journey.

It is true that Burt and Defoe wrote a generation after the massacre of Glencoe,* but general conditions, notwithstanding the futile Jacobite risings of 1715 and 1719, must have been fundamentally the same.

As early as 1618, still another Englishman, Taylor, the water-poet, when recording his impressions of the Highlands, had written in much the same strain as Defoe.

Of native writers, Dean Monro, writing in the sixteenth century, gives an account of the Isles which suggests agricultural and pastoral well-being, and a present-day Highland writer, Mr. Evan Barron (*The Scottish War of Independence*) shows that in social and educational con-ditions, the towns of the Highlands were well abreast of their Lowland opposites even before the Reformation.

These, then, were Macaulay's "savages". Incidentally, it may be observed that the last clan battle was fought in 1688.

It is scarcely necessary to add that conditions varied from district to district in the Highlands, as in the Lowlands, in the degrees of enlighten-ment and tranquillity.

The report of the Commission of inquiry on the Glencoe affair is given in *Collection of State Tracts published in the reign of William III*, 3, pp. 602-614. In Howell's *State Trials*, 13, p. 879, it is stated that Queen Mary pressed for the inquiry, as she was "grieved at the heart" that her husband's reputation had suffered so much.

5. Speech in the Parliamentary Session of 1705.
6. Dalrymple's *Memoirs* (1788), II, p. 95.

* Professor Trevelyan points out (*Blenheim*, p. 2, *note*), that Defoe's tours were "largely taken in the early and middle years of Anne," though his observations were not published until the reign of George I.

7. *First Discourse*, p. 82 (1732).

8. *Some Seasonable and modest thoughts partly occasioned by and partly concerning the Scots India Company, humbly offered to R. H. Esq., a member of the present Parliament, by an unfeigned and hearty Lover of England*: printed in the year 1696 and signed C. K.

9. The genesis of the Company of Scotland is well summarized by Dr. G. Pratt Insh in his *The Company of Scotland trading to Africa and the Indies*, pp. 23-8.

10. See Appendix analysing a memorial concerning the Company of Scotland, the authorship of which, sometimes ascribed to Fletcher, I have attributed to Lord Belhaven.

11. *History*, p. 618.

12. *Ibid*, p. 620; *Lords Journals* for December 1695.

13. *Ibid*, pp. 620-1.

14. *Memoirs*, II, p. 95.

Chapter VII

1. *The Company of Scotland trading to Africa and the Indies*, by G. Pratt Insh, pp. 88, 97.

2. *Ibid*, pp. 101-4.

3. *Ibid*, p. 90.

4. *History*, p. 618.

5. *Memoirs*, II, p. 95.

6. *Ibid*.

7. *Ibid*.

8. For these particulars the author is mainly indebted to Dr. Insh's informative book on the Company of Scotland, pp. 110-114; also to Herries's tract signed "Phil. Scot." and entitled *A defence of the Scots abdicating Darien*, published in 1700. A recent publication is *A new voyage and description of the Isthmus of America*, by Lionel Wafer, with Wafer's secret report (1698), and Davis's *Expedition to the Gold Mines* (1704), edited by L. E. Elliott Joyce, published for the Hakluyt Society. From this book it would appear that the Cuna Indians, who inhabited Darien, and who gave every encouragement to the Scots against the Spaniards, closed Darien to all comers soon after 1700.

Dampier is also the subject of a recent book, *Captain William Dampier, Buccaneer-Author*, by William Hallam Bonner, who shows how flagrantly Dampier's material was pilfered by other authors, including Defoe and Swift.

Chapter VIII

1. The "farming" of the Customs by the burghs, and the opportunities it gave for bribing Parliament, seems to have inflamed the prejudices of an anti-monopolist and a shire representative like Fletcher against the burghs, and to have caused him in one of his speeches to question their right, in view of this monopoly, to send delegates to

Parliament at all. According to Burnet, the farmers of the Customs were "the creatures of the Ministry, some of whom, as was believed, were sharers with them" (*History*, p. 803).

2. Events vindicated the prescience of Fletcher in the Darien business. If he had been a member of Parliament at the time, his speeches might conceivably have effected to the advantage of the colony, what his written views could not be expected to accomplish.

3. For a full discussion of the conditions, see Mr. Henry Grey Graham's *Social Life of Scotland in the Eighteenth Century*, pp. 146-152. The author questions (p. 229) the accuracy of Fletcher's estimate of 200,000 beggars. He states (*note*) that when Fletcher wrote his *First Discourse*, in which he put the population of Scotland at a million and a half, the actual population was about 1,100,000. Mr. Graham does not give his authority for the latter figures, though (p. 536) he quotes Chalmer's *Domestic Economy of Great Britain and Ireland* (1812), p. 387, for the population in 1755, as being 1,255,663. On that basis, his estimate for, say, 1700, would appear to be nearer the mark than Fletcher's. Assuming its correctness, a total of 200,000 unemployed persons would certainly seem at first sight to be an incredibly large proportion (nearly a fifth of the whole). But according to Dr. P. Colquhoun, who in 1806 discussed the problem of indigence, there were in that year in England and Wales, out of a total population of nine millions, no fewer than 1,320,716 "indigent persons, mendicants, and vagrants, idle and immoral persons, rogues and vagabonds, and criminal offenders". That makes (roughly) one in seven of the population; so it is not so very much better than Fletcher's estimate of one in five for Scotland a hundred years earlier. Normally, as stated in the text, there were in Scotland (according to Fletcher) about 100,000 of "these vagabonds who have lived without any regard or subjection either to the laws of the land or even those of God and nature". Probably Fletcher's figures were more or less guesswork, for it is difficult to see how exact statistics could be obtained in those days.*

4. It is interesting to compare Fletcher's reading of this passage (1 Corinthians, chap. vii, ver. 20-4) with that of the Authorized Version and Dr. Moffatt's translation. All agree in their rendering of the injunction for slaves to remain in the condition of life in which they were "called". The essential difference consists in the words in v. 21. Fletcher's translation is: "But even if thou mightest be free, chuse to continue in it" (the condition of a slave). The A.V. has it: "But if thou mayest be made free, use it rather". Dr. Moffatt's translation is: "Of course, if you do find it possible to get free, you had better avail yourself of the opportunity". The decision as to the truest rendering must be left to Biblical commentators.

* It may seem a paradox that in Scotland at this very time, there were, it has been estimated, over ten thousand titled Houses, and about half of the population regarded themselves as members of the aristocracy.

5. Fletcher's proposals for compulsory servitude and compulsory employment of the idle, were not so revolutionary in the Scotland of his own time as they seem to us to-day. By Acts of Parliament passed in 1579 and in 1597, compulsory servitude, first for a term of years, and then for lifetime, was legalized in Scotland, and subsequent legislation showed the same trend. A proclamation of 1692 embodied the substance of these Acts for dealing with idle beggars. Fletcher's proposals only sought, in effect, to give shape, by concrete and radical methods, to the prevailing ideas among Scottish statesmen about the problem of unemployment. Even Hutcheson the philosopher, who was like Fletcher, a friend of freedom, advocated compulsory labour as a punishment for the incorrigibly lazy.

Transportation to the plantations for a term of slavery was, of course, a frequent punishment for criminals.

As late as 1774, an advertisement appeared in the *New York Gazetteer* (April 18), announcing the arrival from Scotland of a number of tradesmen and spinsters "to be sold on board the ship *Commerce*. For terms apply to Henry White or said Master on board". (Copied by the *Morning Post* of May 12th, 1774).

Fletcher's aphorism: "I regard not names but things" finds a curious reflection in a passage from Burke (*A Vindication of Natural Society*) in which, when seeking to vindicate the excesses of party in Britain, he remarks that "I could show how vehemently they have contended for names, and how silently they have passed over things of the last importance".

6. Mr. Macfie has kindly sent me a unique tract in his possession. It is a collection of certain of Fletcher's works published in Edinburgh in 1698, and this copy is inscribed by "David Fletcher", with a note in his handwriting that the written corrections inserted in the book "are copied from the author". So this copy contains Andrew Fletcher's latest thoughts on his subject-matter.

Some of the corrections in the *Second Discourse* are verbal only, but there are others of greater importance. However, they all get down to the broad principle of Fletcher's proposals for the improvement of land, the payment of good wages, and the provision of capital for trade. The fundamental argument in his *Discourse* is, that no man shall own more land than he can cultivate by his own servants, and should be compelled by law to sell any land over the annual value of £200 sterling which he failed so to cultivate. Also, holdings of less than £200 value should be discouraged, by means of holders being compelled to sell half the annual rent at twenty years' purchase to holders of land over £200 in annual value. The tendency would then be for the land to get into the hands of the comparatively wealthy, who were obviously expected by Fletcher to make the best use of it for the benefit of the general community.

7. Fletcher's views in the *Second Discourse* simply invite criticism: and it has not been withheld. See McCulloch's *Literature of Political Economy* and the article in the *Retrospective Review* published in 1821. The writer of the latter is a warm admirer of Fletcher's politics, but shakes his head at his economics.

Mr. J. Ramsay MacDonald (*Scottish Review*, p. 63) declares that in his view, Fletcher's proposals for getting rid of unemployment were "humane" and "almost enlightened", when considered in relation to his general teaching on economics.

Chapter IX

1. The Italian title is *Discorso delle cose di Spagna* and the place of publication is given as Naples. Mr. Macfie, however, believes from internal evidence that it was really published in Edinburgh. He states that Fletcher's Italian is not free from errors (Lord Hailes comments upon its inadequacy, and says, also, that like the elder Cato and the elder Scaliger, he went late to the study of Greek), but that most of them may be attributed to the carelessness of a compositor who was ignorant of the language. He quotes a criticism by Mr. Eduardo Tortora Brayda of the Royal Library, Naples, who stated that he was "inclined to believe" that the tract had been "edited by an Italian hand". He was also of opinion that "it is not a Neapolitan edition, by the quality of the paper and the brilliancy of the type; far superior to those used among us by the end of the seventeenth century".

According to Lord Buchan (pp. 1-2) Fletcher could not speak Italian, though he could write it well. He says that on one occasion, when Fletcher was having an interview with Prince Eugene of Savoy and was addressed in that language by the Prince, "he could not utter a syllable to be understood".

An English translation of the *Discorso* is given in the 1749 edition of Fletcher's works, from which the analysis in the text is taken.

There are four editions of Fletcher's collected works, dated respectively 1732, 1737, 1749 and 1798.

2. In the corrected copy (see Note 6, Chap. VIII) the title of "*A speech upon the State of the Nation*" is altered to "*A Speech supposed to be spoke in ye House of Commons*" *upon the Partition Treaty*, and commences with "Mr. Speaker", instead of "Gentlemen". Throughout the "speech", the wording is altered to accord with the change in the address. The written emendations seem to prove conclusively that Fletcher was the author of the tract.

3. In this speech Fletcher gives play to his powers of sarcasm. There seems to be no reason to doubt that he had turned completely against King William, owing partly to the King's attitude towards the Glencoe

Y   [337]

and Darien affairs, and partly to his conviction that the King was secretly aiming at autocracy. A contemporary report (*Rawlinson MS.* and Hearne's *Diary*) says that on his death-bed, one of his chief regrets was that he had been "base enough to have kissed the hand of . . . the insulting tyrant"—a conventional phrase, intended apparently to apply to William of Orange.

Lockhart (*Memoirs*, p. 69) asserts that Fletcher "saw his (William's) designs, and left him, and ever thereafter hated and appeared as much against him as any in the Kingdom".

Chapter X

1. The memorial was addressed to the King. Its concluding paragraph had a minatory tone: "His Majesty (of Spain) will take such measures as he thinks convenient".

2. The report of the Council of Trade and Plantations is endorsed 26th May, 1699. (*Cal. of State Papers, Colonial Series, America and W. Indies* (1699), pp. 250-1.) See also Appendix.

Macaulay's analogy to the Scottish occupation of Darien (1914), 6, p. 2919, does not seem a particularly happy one. He argues that it would have been just as reasonable for the King of Spain to take possession of Appin and Lochaber, as it was for the Scots to seize Darien.

3. F. Cundall (New York, 1926), *The Darien Venture*, p. 26-7; F. H. Hart, *The Disaster of Darien*, p. 147; *Cal. of State Papers, Col. Ser.* (1699), pp. 250-1.

4. A proclamation was issued on 15th May, 1699, by the Governor of New York, forbidding any assistance to be given to, or correspondence with, the Darien colonists (*Cal. of State Papers, Col. Ser.* (1699), p. 221.)

5. See Cundall, pp. 37-9, and pp. 44-5, for the citation in the text.

6. Cundall, p. 30.

7. *Cal. of State Papers, Col. Ser.* (1699), pp. 251, 277. The Governor of Jamaica, writing to the Governor of New York, remarks (p. 278) on the "scandal" of privateers and pirates, under which the island lay. They ought, he says, "to be dangled up like pole-cats and weasels in a warren". Cundall (p. 61) shows the opinion held by the Spanish governors, that the French were only "seeking a way, be it under the pretext" of driving the Scots from Darien.

8. The Rev. Alexander Shields (or Shiels) the author of a famous Covenanting tract, *A Hind Let Loose*, was one of four ministers (one of them died in the colony) who sailed in the last fleet to Darien. They formed themselves into a Presbytery, of which Shields was Moderator. The report quoted in the text was addressed to "The Presbytery of St. Andrews, Caledonia Bay, Feb. 2. 1700". Shields had more pluck than some of the laymen: he favoured Captain Drummond's proposal to

attack Portobello, in order to forestall the Spanish attack on themselves which was preparing. Also, after the capitulation to the Spaniards, he interceded with the Spanish commander (in Latin) for the natives, while the Council left them to their fate. See Supplement to the *Memoirs of William Veitch* (who was one of the Colony's Councillors) pp. 236-7, 240, 248-251.

It was this William Veitch (he had led a most adventurous career) who, when minister of Dumfries, gave the following advice to the Marquis of Annandale, when he was appointed in 1701 Commissioner to the General Assembly. "Take abundance of patience along with you, and when you speak, suggar your words well." (*The Annandale Family Book*, 2, p. 210, by Sir W. Fraser.)

9. When, in 1701, Paterson urged a new expedition to Darien, "he recorded his conviction that a canal" (through the Isthmus) "was practical" (Cundall, p. 28).

10. Cundall, p. 101. Mr. Cundall has embodied in his narrative valuable matter from letters in the archives of Sevilla. These letters show the alarm aroused by the arrival of the Scots, and the preparations made for an armed expedition against them (pp. 57-79). Mr. Cundall sums up the causes of the Scottish failures (p. 85), and his opinion, as an impartial American who has studied the best sources for his information, is interesting. The causes were: (1) Jealousy among the Councillors with whom the sailors had too big a say; (2) too much drinking; (3) lack of trading sloops; (4) unsuitability of goods; (5) lack of provisions; (6) hostility of the Spaniards; and (7) the hostile English proclamation.

In a letter to the Earl of Seafield, the Earl of Marchmont, (Sir Patrick Hume) says that the delay in sending assistance to the colonists "has in all probability occasioned what has happened" (*Marchmont Papers*, ii, p. 179). See *Collection of State Tracts published in the reign of William III*, 3, for the following:

(1) *An inquiry into the causes of the miscarriage of the Scots Colony at Darien*, pp. 530-565. This was a reply to the tract published by Herries, the ex-surgeon, approving of the abdication of the venture. The tract by Herries was itself a reply to the statement of the case for the Company (see Appendix).

(2) *Scotland's Grievance relating to Darien, etc.*, presented to Parliament, pp. 565-598.

Chapter XI

1. Mr. Macfie remarks that the first edition of this work was written for *English* readers. Such words as "England", "the Nation" and "Parliament" are replaced in the later editions by "Britain", "these Nations" and "Parliaments". "England or elsewhere" is rendered by "Scotland", "England" or "Ireland". Also, some twenty-seven of the

sixty-four pages which the tract contains are, in the later editions, new matter. In the first edition Fletcher declared that proposals for a national militia formed a task "for which only Parliament was qualified".

2. A curious blunder, for at Naseby the Parliament had more than twice as many men as the King.

As for Fletcher's statement about the Gordons, one thinks that the MacDonalds would have something to say on the subject.

3. This seems incredible, seeing that the whole army consisted of only about 7500 men. But see Mr. Buchan's *Oliver Cromwell* (p. 138), where it is stated that the King's army "was full of colonels commanding handfuls". Losses were supplied by the raising of new regiments and the lavish granting of commissions, instead of by the Parliamentary plan of merging a regiment in another when it fell below strength.

4. The corrected copy (see Note 6, Chapter VIII), makes a number of alterations, but there is only one that affects importantly the printed scheme. It appears on page 51. For the "two years" service laid down in the uncorrected copies, the written notes on the margin substitute two "months in that time of the summer (which according to the several countries) shall be freest from any necessary labour. And this every year for 9 years. The next nine years, having entered into the 27 years of their age, they shall be obliged to come and remain in the camp only the last month of the two". And for nine "years thereafter, having entered into the 36 years of their age, (they) shall be obliged to remain in the camp only the last half of the last month". Apparently either the first "9" should read "5", or "36" should read "40". Possibly Mr. David Fletcher may have made an error in copying the figures.

5. As Mr. Macfie points out, there has been a variety of opinion about Fletcher's militia proposals. Hill Burton called the tract "a harsh ungenial pamphlet with its unvarnished nomenclature". Sir John Dalrymple describes the tract as "one of the finest compositions in the English language". The author of *Militia Reformed* (1698) refers to "the ingenious author of the unanswerable argument against a standing army".

Defoe (who apparently did not know that Fletcher was the author of the tract) criticises the discourse in his *An argument showing that a standing Army, with consent of Parliament, is not inconsistent with a free Government* (written in reply to a tract seeking to prove the contrary). He points out the omission of the writer to consider the propriety of a standing army under the control of Parliament; and that was certainly a standpoint which one might have expected Fletcher, the champion of Parliamentary authority, to have discussed. But evidently he had a rooted objection to standing armies, and probably had in view the risk, under exceptional circumstances, of a transfer of their control from Parliament to the Crown.

There are other scattered references to Fletcher's tract.

Chapter XII

1. *Memoirs*, II, p. 189.

2. *Ibid.* A tract entitled *A Speech without doors concerning toleration* (? 1703) is sometimes attributed to Fletcher, but there are no substantial grounds for the ascription.

3. Fletcher would have been untrue to his principles if he had not been in favour of liberty of conscience. He was, of course, brought up as an Episcopalian, but his attachment to that or any religious body seems to have been slight. In his *Second Discourse*, when urging the Presbyterian members of the Convention not to be cajoled into supporting the intention to continue the Army, against which he had argued in his writings, he tells them that "all those who love their country tho' they be not of that" (the Presbyterian) "persuasion" will stand by them in future Parliaments: but if the Presbyterians "abandon and betray their country, they will fall unpitied". "They must not tell me that their Church can never fall since it is the true Church of God. If it be the true Church of God, it needs no crooked arts to support it". Obviously Fletcher was not "of that persuasion".

The *Scotch Patriot unmasked*, a tract published by Mr. W. Atwood, Chief Justice of New York, in 1705, mainly against George Ridpath, remarks (p. 26) that both Ridpath and Fletcher "inveigh bitterly against the best of the clergy of Scotland, and since it cannot be supposed that they are for the Church of England, it need be no great question what religion they serve". The suggestion apparently is that they were Roman Catholics.

4. *Memoirs*, pp. 69-71.

5. It would be difficult for party venom to betray itself more openly than in the following estimate of the character of the first Duke of Queensberry, given by the Earl of Perth to James II in the first year of his reign: "An atheist in religion; a villain in friendship; a knave in business; and a traitor in his carriage to him (the King)." (*Hist. MSS. Com.*, 11th Rep., pt. vi, p. 171.) Yet Lockhart (*Memoirs*, p. 9) says that the same Duke was "highly in favour with both King Charles and King James": but his son, the second Duke, "was the first statesman that deserted over to the Prince of Orange, and from thence acquired the epithet (amongst honest men"—i.e. Jacobites) "of Proto-Rebel".

6. See *The Scottish Parliament: its constitution and procedure*, 1603-1707, by C. Stanford Terry.

7. *Ramillies and the Union with Scotland*, p. 235.

8. Macaulay's *History* (1914), 2, p. 535, and 4, p. 1582. The author pays a fine tribute to Fletcher. But was he quite accurate in saying that "he hated monarchy; he hated democracy: his favourite project was to make Scotland an oligarchical republic"?

Chapter XIII

1. George Ridpath was a Whig journalist, who went to London and there conducted the *Flying Post*, established in 1695. He was continually in hot water for the bold advocacy of his views, and served a term of imprisonment in Newgate for libel. The *Flying Post* was a valuable property and sold well. Ridpath was said to have "one of the best pens in England"; which one can well believe, judging by his output of political tracts. Swift (of course) described him as "a Scotch rogue", and Pope sneered at him in his "Dunciad".

2. Macky, p. 184. Macky (or Mackay; Gaelic: *MacAodh*) was the captain of a packet-boat, who delineated his characters for the information of Princess Sophia (how he obtained such an intimate knowledge of English and Scottish statesmen is a puzzle). His humour was of what Mr. Fowler called the "flood-of-tears-and-sedan-chair" type. Of Queen Anne's husband (e.g.) he said that he loved "news, his bottle, and his Queen". The "bottle" figures in more than one of his Scottish characters. (I find that in my *Life* of Lord Lovat I inadvertently made one of Macky's bottle-huggers the Duke of Gordon [The Cock of the North] instead of the Marquis of Lothian.)

3. Lockhart's *Memoirs*, p. 24.

4. There were two methods by which public business could be introduced to the House, namely, by resolution or by overture, the latter being the draft of an Act. In 1703, overtures were printed and distributed to members. A resolution to proceed "by way of overture" meant giving leave to introduce a Bill (Scottish "Act"), the provisions of which had already been made available to members. The Bill was read, but that did not constitute a technical reading. An order that a Bill should lie on the table meant either that the members wished to have further time to consider it, or had no wish to proceed with it. See chapter on legislative procedure (p. 142-154) in Terry's *Scottish Parliament*.

5. *Godolphin MS.* 28055, p. 25.

6. *The Earls of Cromartie* (Fraser), i, p. 185.

7. *Memoirs*, p. 49.

8. *An account of the proceedings of the Parliament of Scotland which met at Edinburgh, May 6, 1703*, p. 132.

9. *Ibid*, pp. 136-8. Hill Burton (*The Reign of Queen Anne*, i, p. 155) quotes a correspondent of Nottingham, who tells the latter that in the Dutch *Courants* the proceedings of the Parliament were published at length, special attention being directed to Fletcher's Overtures, which some admired and others laughed at. Hill Burton cites *MS. Mus. Brit.*, 89, f. 79, for this statement, which goes on to comment on Fletcher's "extravagances". "He is enheaded, as the French phrase is, with the

notion of a republic, and has an inveterate pique at all sovereignty"·
These commentators all seem to overlook the fact that the sovereignty
of *Parliament* was Fletcher's aim.

On 6th July, 1703, Fletcher presented to Parliament a form of oath
which bound members to "defend and mentaine the trew Reformed
Religion"; also the Claim of Right contained in the Declaration of the
Estates of 11th April, 1689 (*MS. Supp. Par. Papers*, 18, No. 49).

On 20th July, he lodged a protest against the "illegal adjournment
of the House on the 16th" (*Ibid*, 18, No. 52).

Chapter XIV

1. I have thought it desirable to give in this chapter selected
examples of Fletcher's Parliamentary oratory, which serve also as
vehicles for the purpose of narrative.

The writer of the article in the *Retrospective Review*, 4, part i (1821),
devotes some space to an analysis of Fletcher's speeches. "He was as
argumentive", he says, "as Fox, whose eloquence it has been justly said
was his logic; and as fiery and impetuous as Lord Chatham. Every sentence is an argument, and every argument an impeachment. His words
are blows. . . . He never played or seemed to play either with his subject or upon his hearers. He went steadily to his object, and used the
most direct, honourable and efficient means for the accomplishment of
his purpose". That seems to me to be fair and judicious comment. ·

2. *An Historical Account of the Antient rights and power of the Parliament of Scotland.*

Ridpath argues in his dedication of the book to the Estates, that
there had been a conspiracy for over a century to lessen their authority,
and says that for the remarkable statements he makes in the text about
the former power of Parliament, "my vouchers are the printed Acts of
your own Illustrious Court", and "not only those which our late
Princes thought fit should appear to the view of the Publick, but those
upon which they had passed an Index Expurgatorius" (pp. v-vi).

Ridpath's arguments are ingenious, but the supremacy of Parliament
is not so clear as he would seek to make out.

3. For a full discussion of the history of Parliamentary representation
see Sir Robert Rait's informing contribution in *The Union of* 1707,
pp. 10-22.

4. A copy of the Act of Security is given in *An Account of the Proceedings of the Parliament of Scotland* (1703), pp. 242-9.

5. Sir David Hume's *Diary*, p. 115.

6. *Ibid.*

7. *Ibid*, p. 118.

8. *An Account of the proceedings of the Parliament of* 1703, pp. 185-6.

In a letter to Godolphin, Seafield explains as the reason for the adjournment, that "the point under consideration was of great importance . . . it was then past eight, so we were most of us much fatigued". (*Pub. of Scottish History Society*, 11 (2nd Ser.), p. 9, (Addl. MSS. 28055).

He is very emphatic in declaring that the Lord Privy Seal and himself did what was in their power over the matter of the adjournment (*Ibid*, p. 11). Indeed, the two persons who were mainly responsible for blocking Fletcher's "limitations" were Atholl and Seafield, the former by bringing the Tory cohorts to the help of the Government.

In a letter to Godolphin dated 18th September, 1703 (Addl. MSS., 6420, p. 58) Atholl makes pointed reference to the "very unreasonable limitations which were first given in by Mr. Fletcher of Salton, and afterwards proposed by the Marquis of Montrose".

9. *An Account of the proceedings of the Parliament of* 1703, p. 190. Sir David Hume of Crossrigg (*Diary*, p. 120) gives an account of a "breeze" in the House on 21st July, when Fletcher was taken to task for sitting in the area of the throne. He had to remove to another part of the House when so desired by the Earl Marischal, as directed by the Lord Commissioner, on the ground that he was not privileged to take his seat on the steps of the throne, where the Officers of State sat. He pleaded that he had occupied the same seat since the beginning of the Session, but "there having been a change in the form of the House, he knew not where to sit", and so with characteristic obstinacy he declined to move without a vote of the House. Ultimately he gave way, declaring that he did so in obedience to the Earl Marischal, and not to the order of the Commissioner.

In *The Stair Annals*, by John Murray Graham, i, pp. 203-8, Stair gives Godolphin an account of the Session of 1703. Stair had not been in office since the Glencoe affair (though he was, with difficulty, dissuaded from taking part in the proceedings of the Convention of Estates), but his views on contemporary Scottish politics were always received with respect, for he was a man of outstanding political ability, and considerable charm of manner. He told Godolphin that Hamilton, in trying to please both the Presbyterians and the Episcopalians on toleration, had succeeded in estranging both. He shows, too, how wary the Presbyterians had to be in "these encroachments on the monarchy: for everybody will lay it at their door, because in former times Presbyterians did such things".

10. *Memoirs*, p. 60.

11. *Ibid*, p. 57.

12. *Ibid*.

13. *Ibid*, pp. 61-2.

For other accounts of the Session of 1703 see Hume's *Diary*; *Portland MSS.*, 4; Boyer's *Annals*, 2; and Cunningham's *History*, i.

Cunningham (pp. 411,414) remarks on Fletcher's "great eloquence" in supporting the Act of Security. He was, he says, "inflamed with an incredible zeal in his country's cause".

14. Two memorials sent to the Queen by the Earl of Cromarty (then Viscount Tarbat) give a shrewd estimate of the political situation in Scotland in 1703. Cromarty defines the terms "Whig" and "Tory" as used in Scotland, and as understood by him. The Whigs were mainly for "parity in Church Government by Presbytery. They were not anti-monarchist, but monarchy has but the second place in their esteem". The Tories might be divided into two classes: (1) the Jacobites who were for the Prince of Wales, "by whatsomever method or assistance", and (2) those Tories who were equally attached to the monarchy and "the true line", but in the Protestant religion. The Tories of both classes were "three to one among the vulgar", and "four to one among the nobility and gentry" (surely a party-coloured statement). The Tories will "beare with Presbytery"; the Whigs cannot "beare with prelacy". Most of Scotland's misfortunes, Cromarty averred, were due to "the fanaticks". One of his general conclusions was, that it is always dangerous for a prince to put the government in the hands of a party. There may be good men in all parties, "yet all parties, as such, are odious in, and to, Government". He thinks the Queen would be safer in Tory hands, but that it would be well to "keepe the affections" of both Whigs and Tories, in order to avoid danger either from a Jacobite or a Republican party.

Also, he gives an account of the leading Scottish magnates and their political attachments. Hamilton was the representative of the greatest family in Scotland, "chiefly by its alliance". Argyll was "deepe in the fanatick principle." The "fanatick Government" had brought a great part of the other Highland clans under the Campbells: "a wrong politick", for they should have been employed to balance the Campbells. Then there was the Duke of Buccleuch, "of an old family as gentlemen"; the Duke of Gordon, "great but remote"; the Earl (or Marquis) of Seaforth (he was a Jacobite Marquis), the head of his own (Mackenzie) clan: "of very considerable power in the Highlands", and the only Highlander who, in conjunction with the MacDonalds, MacLeods, and the lesser clans, could be set up to balance Argyll. The Marquis of Atholl was very considerable in his own power, and by his situation in the midst of the Highlands, nearer to Edinburgh than other Highlanders; of a loyal family, and now allied with Hamilton. There were also the Duke of Queensberry, the Duke of Lennox, the Earl of Breadalbane, "much sunke by Argyl's being his chiefe"; and Lord Lovat, "one of the antientest of the nobility", and of "a very considerable power" in the Highlands.

The annual distribution of £2,000 yearly, to be discreetly divided among those who have "neither pension nor offices" would make the Government safe "against all insurrection and mobs", for that sum would secure the services of 2000 men, together with about 2000 more, whom Atholl, Mar, Breadalbane, and Lord Reay (all of whom were supposed to be obliged to the Queen "by other tyes") could supply.

This summary of Cromarty's views and proposals gives a fair indication of the political principles (and clan attachments) of that wily, if genial, old man. Whatever else Cromarty may have been, he was certainly not a "fanatick". (*Scott. Hist. Soc.*, (2nd Ser.), 11, pp. 118, 123, 132.)

Chapter XV

1. Sir Christopher Musgrave, says Burnet (*History*, p. 589), "was a gentleman of a noble family in Cumberland whose life has been regular and his deportment grave". He was "a high Tory", who came to be considered as the head of the party. He was "a man of good judgment and of great experience".

2. Sir Edward Seymour was a prominent member of the House of Commons. He was Speaker during the reign of Charles II, and was afterwards Treasurer of the Navy. The last official appointment he enjoyed was that of Comptroller of the Household to Queen Anne, from which post he was dismissed in 1704. He was "feared more than loved, and respected more than esteemed". He was too haughty to be popular. But for the share he took in getting the Habeas Corpus Act passed, he deserves to be remembered (Burnet, *History*, p. 235, *note*).

He was a rabid anti-Scot, and a book by a Dr. Drake attacking the independence of Scotland was dedicated to him. The book was ordered by the Parliament in Edinburgh to be "burnt by the hand of the common executioner". (*Scott. Hist. Soc.*, 11, (2nd Ser.), p. 8 (Addl. MSS. 28055); Defoe's *History of the Union* (1786), p. 75).

Fletcher obviously had in view the contemptuous language used by Seymour in the House of Commons about the Scots, when he quoted him as described in the text ("a beggar—a louse for a portion").

Hill Burton (*The Reign of Queen Anne*, 8, p. 10, *note*) quotes Vernon's *Letters* (2, p. 408) as his authority for stating that the words were used by Seymour in the House. The Scots were "very angry" about it.

3. In 1888, in connection with the discussions then proceeding on Home Rule for Ireland, the "Conversation in London" was reprinted in the London *Morning Leader*, and was subsequently issued, in pamphlet form, under the auspices of the Scottish Home Rule Society, who described Fletcher as "our first Home Rule Statesman".

Writing on the literary revival in Scotland (embodied in *The Union of* 1707 by various writers), Mr. J. H. Millar remarks upon the dearth of literary figures in Scotland during Fletcher's period. He names Sir George Mackenzie of Rosehough as "the most accomplished Scotsman of his time". His prose, he says, was of the "more stately and old-fashioned type". Sir George was certainly a distinguished author, though his style can scarcely be called attractive.

Mr. Millar does not mention Fletcher, who, of course, did not commence to write until after Mackenzie's death in 1691. But, Fletcher was never a professional man of letters.

It will be observed how closely Fletcher's ideas approximated that of the Greek political unit of the City State. Also, his sentiments on the study of politics are similar to those of Pericles, whose picture of an ideal Athens was as follows: "We alone regard a man who takes no interest in public affairs, not as a harmless, but as a useless character." (Bury's *History of Greece* (1922), p. 405.)

Chapter XVI

1. *Memoirs*, pp. 73-4.
2. Full details of the plot are given in W. C. Mackenzie's *Life and Times of Simon Fraser Lord Lovat*, pp. 112-152. Lockhart, by the way, although a Jacobite, had a particularly bad opinion of Lovat. He says he was a person "with whom no honest man in Scotland would converse": an exaggerated but significant statement. He gives an account of the Lovat-Queensberry episode (*Memoirs*, pp. 76-93).
3. Lockhart's *Memoirs*, pp. 102-6.
4. *Marchmont Papers*, 3, pp. 263-5.
5. *Ibid*, pp. 266-7.
6. Lockhart's *Memoirs*, pp. 109-115. Cunningham's *History* (i, pp. 359-366) gives an interesting account of the proceedings in Scotland and in London after the 1703 Session.
7. Lockhart's *Memoirs*, pp. 115-121; Hume's *Diary*, pp. 137-8.
8. Hume's *Diary*, p. 146.
9. *Ibid*, pp. 146-7. See Burnet's account: *History*, pp. 761-6, of the Session of 1704, and its repercussions in England. See also Somers' *Tracts*, 12, p. 505; *Lockhart Papers*, pp. 99-107; and *Portland MSS.*, 4, p. 121. Addl. MSS. 6420, endorsed "Proceedings of the Marquis of Tweeddale's Parliament", animadverts upon the unhappy choice of Johnston to have managed the Succession business: a man who had neither "interest nor residence here, and who was brought into business, as is notoriously known, by English influence to bring our Parliament into the English Succession. It's remarked what a brave champion he has been on the matter, for tho' he promised to many to demonstrate the necessity of it when the case should be brought into Parliament, yet when it was agitated through several days, he never opened his mouth on the head. And on the contrary, when some time after he was taxed by Salton for having undertaken that measure, he denied it", and blamed

Queensberry and others for having "engaged the Queen in that measure four months before he came into business. . . . Whether the Queen will trust him again or not, time will tell". Johnston was in an invidious position: he had to do his duty and yet not forfeit his claim to be a patriot. That accounts for his weakness in Parliament. But his contention that he was not the person who was responsible for the arrangement in London, may be in accordance with the fact.

In a letter from Johnston, dated 26th July, 1704 (Addl. MSS. 6420, p. 109) he says that his silence had been "misconstrued as if I was so guilty of I know not what that I durst not speak". And he then refers to his quarrel with Fletcher, congratulating himself that he had "put an end" to the "heats" as to himself.

The "heats" were all the more "violent" that they were "amongst friends".

The Old Party (Revolution Whigs) "except my Ld. Argyle only lookt on". The Marquis of Montrose and his friends joined with the New Party (Tweeddale and his friends) in supporting the Government. They were positive that if the Act of Security were passed, it would not be in the power of "the three Dukes" (Atholl, Hamilton, and Queensberry) "to spoil matters in another Session".

Lord Rosse (Addl. MSS. 6420, p. 113) gives his version of the support he had given the Government, which was nullified by Fletcher's intervention, just when "there appeared a general consent" for both the Act for cess and the tacking clause to lie on the table until London had been consulted.

In a letter endorsed "to Mr. Harley" (Addl. MSS. 6420, p. 121) dated 27th July, 1704, the writer confirms the bad impression created by Johnston's silence in the House. He was (he says), "assaulted with a direct attack by his old friend, Mr. Fletcher, who speaks liberalls't enough of all persons who are not exactls't of his mould". The writer then quotes the defence made by Johnston as stated in the text.

In a letter to Godolphin dated 6th September, 1704, the Earl of Leven refers to "the misterious management of our Statesmen", and says he hears that they are called to Court and are thereby "in great expectations to have all employments at their own disposal, and if you will take their own testimony, no doubt they and their friends will be the most deserving persons in the nation". (*Scott. Hist. Soc.*, 11, (2nd Ser.), p. 156 (MS. 28055).)

10. *Hist. MSS. Com., Mar and Kellie Papers*, p. 228.

11. Hume's *Diary*, p. 144; Boyer's *Annals*, iii, p. 34.

12. Hume's *Diary*, pp. 151-2. See also *Lockhart Papers*, p. 103. "Fletcher", says Lockhart, "gave the Court a Rowland for their Oliver."

13. Hume's *Diary*, pp. 157-8.

14. *Ibid*, p. 160.

15. Burnet's *History*, pp. 763, 765-6.

See *An Account of the Proceedings of the Parliament of* 1703, pp. 193-214, for a description of the cross-currents which influenced the Estates on the question of the communication of trade.

16. *Scott. Hist. Soc.*, 11, (2nd Ser.), pp. 137-9 (Addl. MSS. 28055).

17. *Ibid*, pp. 143-4. Harley seemed to think that the Scots opposed the Succession just because the English had proposed it. The Queen was willing to compensate the Darien sufferers. What more could the Scots want? (*Carstares State Papers*, p. 728).

18. Boyer's *Annals*, 3, pp. 159-162.

19. *Jerviswood Correspondence*, p. 16. Lord Somers was at the back of the Alien Act, as he was of the movement for union.

20. Lockhart (*Memoirs*, p. 134) is very severe on the Statute. It was "so imperious and haughty that the like treatment was never given by one nation to another". He says he had been assured "by a pretty good Hand" that the Alien Act had been suggested by "our own statesmen" to frighten Scotland. And he calls these statesmen "vile, ungrateful, rapacious vultures, thus to tear their own vitals" (pp. 135-6).

21. *History of the Union*, p. 86.

MS. Supp. Par. Papers, 19, No. 68, give particulars of a Fletcher Overture for an address to the Queen. It attributes the misunderstandings between the two countries to the "intermeddling" of English peers in Scottish affairs. It deals with the Succession, and asks that the papers and persons concerned in "that which was called a Scottish plot" be sent to Scotland for examination.

Chapter XVII

1. *Jerviswood Correspondence*, p. 18.

2. *Ibid*, p. 47.

3. *Ibid*, pp. 20, 35.

4. *Ibid*, p. 27.

5. *Ibid*, p. 42.

6. *Ibid*, p. 44. This was in February 1705, but in January 1705, Roxburgh had declared, after a meeting between himself and Seafield with Godolphin and Marlborough, when they were desired to give their views in writing, that "for my part I am persuaded that an union is impossible, and that if the Succession be brought about, it will be out of fear of an union" (p. 31).

7. *Jerviswood Correspondence* gives an illuminating account of the intrigues that went on in London for office in the new Session of the Scottish Parliament. Adam Cockburn of Ormistoun, who got the post of Justice-Clerk in the new Government (Fletcher's three colleagues in the representation of Haddingtonshire were Sir John Lauder of Fountainhall, William Nisbet of Dirleton, and John Cockburn of

Ormistoun the younger) was the target of reproaches. Roxburgh says that he was "bragging and puffing himself up" for "a very great man". Johnston says that "he has behaved himself as if he had all Scotland at his command" (pp. 32-3). It will be observed that Haddingtonshire had now four representatives against only two when Fletcher entered public life (*Acts of Par. of Scot.*, 8, p. 232.)

8. *The Annandale Family Book*, 2, p. 222.

9. *Hist. MSS. Com., Hamilton Papers*, p. 201; Lockhart's *Memoirs*, pp. 132-3). Lockhart gives a "mixed" character to Argyll (*Memoirs*, pp. 132-3), but he acknowledges his possession of wit, valour, and an independent spirit. Cunningham (*History*, i, p. 366) has an odd note about him. He says that no sooner had the Duke taken possession of his estate, than "he turned all his father's mistresses out of doors, and seized their ill-gotten goods by his own authority, according to the Highland custom". And yet according to Lockhart (*Memoirs*, p. 45) the first Duke was "the darling of the Presbyterians", because he was descended from, and the representative of, "a family that suffered for the Cause".

10. *Jerviswood Correspondence*, p. 60; *Seafield Correspondence with Godolphin* (*Scott. Hist. Soc.*, 11, 2nd Series), pp. 23, 46.) Argyll (reports Seafield) was "of great consequence to the Revolution Pairtie" (p. 44), i.e., the Old Whigs, composed of true-blue Presbyterians. Their policy, declared Seafield in April 1705 (p. 32) was for a treaty for "ane intire union". But the New Party did not get so far as that for some time longer. Seafield's problem (p. 32), was to create a good understanding between the two, "for without that I see little hopes of success".

11. *Ibid*, p. 46.

12. See W. L. Mathieson's *Scotland and the Union*, pp. 103-4.

13. *Seafield Correspondence*, p. 29.

14. *Jerviswood Correspondence*, pp. 70, 85.

15. Argyll ("Original Letters of the Duke of Argyll to Lord Godolphin", *Edinburgh Review*, October 1892) refers to the "unmerciful violence in the unlucky affair of Captain Green and his crew", which might lead to consequences to the two nations greatly to be regretted. These men, wrote Johnston, will be reckoned "martyrs, and the New Party must atone for it" (*Jerviswood Correspondence*, p. 71). They did.

16. *Hist. MSS. Com., Hamilton Papers*, p. 201.

17. Hume's *Diary*, p. 162. The true cause of Fletcher's objection to Baillie (writes Greg to Harley) was his (Baillie's) "apostacy from the Country to the Court party" (*Portland MSS.*, 4, p. 199).

18. MS. 28055 (Letter to Harley from Greg), p. 248. *Seafield Correspondence*, p. 58; *Mar and Kellie Papers*, p. 234; *Portland MSS*, 4, pp. 207-8 (embodying Greg's letter to Harley).

19. Lockhart's *Memoirs*, pp. 144-5.

20. *Ibid*, pp. 142-3.

21. *Original Letters*, p. 515.

22. Ridpath (*An Account of the Proceedings of the Parliament of* 1703, p. 237) applied the term in 1704 to the Jacobites. He suggested that the "Flying Squadron" might have to take a "flight" over to France.

23. *Original Letters*, p. 515.

24. *Seafield Correspondence*, p. 62. Had it not been for Queensberry and Seafield, it is very doubtful whether the New Party could have been won over to the Government policy. Argyll had no use for them.

25. *Seafield Correspondence*, p. 63.

26. *Ibid*, p. 65. Even Stair, as well as Fletcher and Hamilton, was for "clogging" the treaty, and "spoke warmly of the Act passed in England" (*Scot. Hist. Soc.*, 11, (2nd Ser.), p. 162). See also *MS. Supp. Par. Papers*, 19, No. 97.

27. Hume's *Diary*, p. 167. Hume says that in his speech Fletcher "spoke of the King of Prussia to be named" (as King of Scotland?) and Greg, a Scottish correspondent of Harley, tells him that Fletcher had "made a speech in favour of the Prince of Prussia" (*Portland MSS.*, 4, p. 214). He never made any suggestion to do without a king altogether.

28. *Original Letters*, p. 515.

29. Addl. MSS. 28055, p. 278. This letter to Godolphin (the writer is unknown) is dated Edinburgh, Aug. 16th, 1705; Hume's *Diary*, pp. 169-170.

30. Hume's *Diary*, p. 170; *Portland MSS.*, 4, pp. 223-4, 232-5. Greg tells Harley on 21st August of an attack made by Fletcher on the Synod of Merse and Teviotdale for imposing new oaths and bonds as terms of commission on ministers and probationers, without permission from Parliament or the General Assembly. Annandale, late Commissioner to the Assembly, replied to the attack, and (says Greg) "gravelled" Fletcher, whom the Chancellor dubbed *Athanasius contra totum mundum* (*Portland MSS.*, 4, pp. 226-7).

31. Addl. MSS. 28055, p. 278.

32. *Seafield Correspondence*, p. 74. Seafield's attribution of "Republican" ideas to his opponents is paralleled by a similar attribution, at the present day, of "Socialist" ideas to respectable Conservatives who venture out of the beaten track.
Original Letters, p. 516.

33. *Seafield Correspondence*, p. 74.

34. *Ibid*, pp. 76-7; *Original Letters*, p. 516. In the course of the debate there was a good deal said about the nobility and gentry going to London to seek places "which did mine our private estates and fortunes". Hume Brown reckoned the cost of a journey to London and a month's residence there at £600, and it was stated that only one Scottish peer could meet the expense out of his own pocket. *Seafield Correspondence* (Note, p. 75).

35. Addl. MSS. 28055, p. 304 (Letter to Harley dated Sept. 8th, 1705).

The attempt to place an embargo upon English imports is called by Harley's correspondent "Fletcher's freak".

36. Lockhart's *Memoirs*, pp. 161-6. Lockhart (*Memoirs*, pp. 150-3) gives an account of the various abortive measures that were approved for limiting the prerogative.

37. Lockhart's *Memoirs*, pp. 170-7; *Portland MSS.*, 4, pp. 238-9, 242. Greg tells Harley how Fletcher tried to limit the numbers of Commissioners, and nearly succeeded in doing so; how he insisted upon their not going beyond the Border; and how, on the Queen's nomination, he boldly told the House that, in effect, this meant that the appointment of the Scots Commissioners would be in the hands of Godolphin. For this "the madman" (as Greg, following Harley's example, called him), was "snubbed" by the Chancellor. Yet he only said openly what all his hearers knew to be the truth. *Seafield Correspondence*, p. 87.

38. *Seafield Correspondence*, p. 80.

39. Seafield was greatly concerned about Supply. He told Godolphin on 28th August, that if the Act of Supply were not passed, the Army must be disbanded, and it was with a sense of relief that he reported the first reading of the Act (*Seafield Correspondence*, pp. 80-1). Parliament granted six months' Supply in September, but with "great difficulty" (*Scott. Hist. Soc.*, 11, (2nd Ser.), p. 181).

40. *Memoirs*, pp. 170, 176. Lockhart's disgust with Hamilton was profound. His final comment on the incident is *"that sitting between two chairs often occasions a fall,* which was the Duke of Hamilton's case at this time" (p. 177).

41. *Seafield Correspondence*, pp. 71-2; Hume (*Diary*, p. 169) relates a curious incident in connexion with the appointment of the Councillors for trade; whether they should be chosen by "billots" or not. This was "pressed by Salton", among others, and was objected to on the ground that it was expressly prohibited by Act of Parliament of 1663 (see the present writer's *Lauderdale*), and "branded" as "pernicious and dangerous". It was "voicing". Salton said, "very far from voicing, which is to do a thing audibly and avowedly, and voicing and voting are the same thing". The debate was "let fall". This is another instance of Fletcher's passion for members voting in accordance with their convictions.

42. *Ibid*, p. 90; Cunningham, *History*, i, pp. 425-428. After the Session Argyll returned to London "loaded with praises and rewards". Godolphin granted him "many things", but when Argyll demanded more, Godolphin found at length his "rapacity" to be "insatiable" (p. 428).

For once in a way, during the Session of 1705, Fletcher concurred with the Court party. Greg reports to Harley as a "paradox" (*Portland MSS.*, 4, pp. 238, 240) that he had "turned Courtier" by giving in the draft of an address to the Queen, to use her endeavours with the English Parliament to have the Alien clause in their Act repealed. This (says

Greg) was "so little expected from a professed enemy", and it was so contrary to his "usual fierce and violent manner", that the surprised members actually thought the tone to be "too humble or rather too mean". Fletcher could, of course, be suave enough when occasion demanded suavity. His proposed address to the Queen is copied in *MS. Supp. Par. Papers*, 19, No. 125.

Chapter XVIII

1. *Scott. Hist. Soc.*, Letters from Mar, 11, (2nd Ser.), p. 175.

2. *Mar and Kellie Papers*, pp. 272-3.

3. *The Stair Annals*, i, p. 214.

4. *Mar and Kellie Papers*, p. 267.

5. Lockhart's *Memoirs*, pp. 176-7, 186-191. It is worthy of notice that Lockhart here describes himself as a member of the "Country" party. Latterly, this appears to have been a fairly elastic designation.

6. *Mar and Kellie Papers*, pp. 268-9. The attitude of the English Commissioners is well illustrated by a letter from Harley to Newcastle. "We have stretched our consciences (he says) to forty-five and *no more*" (Scottish members of the House of Commons) "and sixteen for the Lords, and expect the Scots answer on Tuesday, who are certainly in the right to take an (? all) they can" (*Portland MSS.*, 2, App. 2, p. 193).

7. *Ibid, p.* 242.

8. Burnet's *History*, p. 799. Burnet gives Lord Somers the credit of having had "the chief hand in projecting the scheme of the Union". This view is confirmed by others. Lockhart's *Memoirs*, pp. 268-272.

9. *History*, i, p. 430.

10. One cannot but admire the public spirit shown by Montrose, who, when appointed High Admiral in 1705, refused to accept the salary of £1,000 attached to the office, "because the Treasury is in a very low condition" (*Seafield Correspondence*, p. 22).

11. In May 1705, Roxburgh had suggested that there was "no harm in trying Annandale with some 'suggar plums' ", after he had broken with Argyll (*Jerviswood Correspondence*, p. 95). The "suggar plums" had not succeeded in sweetening him.

For other aspirants to office, "green ribbons" (the "Thistle") were suggested.

12. What the precise motives of the Squadron were in voting for the Union, must necessarily be impossible to determine. Dr. W. L. Mathieson (*Scotland and the Union*, pp. 172-3) thinks they were patriotic, and he has a particularly good word to say for Roxburgh (pp. 174-6). While paying a high tribute to Fletcher's character, as he could not fail to do, he is inclined to agree with Swift's opinion of his pedantry. Also, he alludes to his "intellectual deficiency" (p. 166), a view which, possibly, he does not now hold.

Dr. James Mackinnon (*The Union of 1707*, p. 283), thinks that "the element of party and personal advantage was by no means omitted from the calculation of Roxburgh and his colleagues".

He describes (pp. 16-17) Fletcher as a "pure-minded and fervent patriot" . . . "emphatically a man of genius and towers in intellectual and moral strength above the ordinary level of the political leaders or party satellites of his time" (p. 104). "Posterity has endorsed many, if not all, of his contentions in favour of a Parliamentary republic, of which the sovereign, if he is to be retained, is merely the highest official" (p. 106). See also Dr. Mackinnon's views in *The Union of England and Scotland* (1907) about Fletcher and his politics, and about Roxburgh (p. 354).

But Dr. Mackinnon is in error in stating (p. 337) that Fletcher suffered "the humiliation of being carried in custody to London" (in 1708).

One does not, of course, go to the Tory Lockhart for his violently Jacobite opinions of the Squadron. But here is the view of Cunningham, the Whig contemporary historian, about Roxburgh and his friends. The Squadron, he says (*History*, 2, p. 60) "made a specious pretence of the public good, yet had an eye, in the midst of the public affairs, to their private interest".

As I have shown in the text, if they were not seduced by Seafield's "encouragements", it was not for want of the plausible Seafield trying, and trying successfully, to overcome their scruples.

13. Lockhart's *Memoirs*, pp. 222 *et seq.*; Boyer's *Annals*, 4, pp. 345-6; *Seafield Correspondence*, p. 101; *Mar and Kellie Papers*, p. 309.

14. *Seafield Correspondence*, p. 107; *Mar and Kellie Papers*, pp. 313, 325-7; *Original Letters*, pp. 517-8; Hume's *Diary*, p. 176. To the resentful Edinburgh mob, the Duke of Argyll was now "the Earl of Greenwich".

15. Lockhart's *Memoirs*, pp. 277-285; Mr. G. M. Thomson (*Rediscovery of Scotland*, p. 154) remarks on "Fletcher's undoubtedly being in the plot" (the Cameronian affair). I doubt it. In any case, there is no evidence at all of his complicity.

16. *Mar and Kellie Papers*, p. 304; *Marchmont Papers*, 3, p. 304.

17. Lockhart's *Memoirs*, pp. 285-293.

18. *Seafield Correspondence*, pp. 96, 98. Argyll's brother, Lord Archibald, was made Earl of Ilay. He succeeded his brother as Duke of Argyll.

Scott. Hist. Soc., *Letters from the Earl of Loudoun*, 11, (2nd Ser.), p. 171. Loudoun (a Campbell) says that Argyll "desires to have one of his familie amongst our peers".

19. *Scott. Hist. Soc.*, *Letters of the Earl of Glasgow*, 11, (2nd Ser.), p. 182; Lockhart's *Memoirs*, pp. 409-412.

There is a strongly held popular belief that the Union was secured by bribery. As stated in the text, bribery to that end, in the sense of money having been paid directly to buy votes, cannot be proved, and is, on the face of it, unlikely. But as everyone knows, there are subtle, indirect, and no less effective means of bribery. These were certainly employed to secure the passing of the Treaty of Union.

In the Appendix to Lockhart's *Memoirs* (pp. 405-420) an account is given of the whole transaction, so far as the facts could be ascertained by the Commissioners (of whom Lockhart himself was one), appointed in 1711 for examining the Public Accounts of the United Kingdom. From this statement, it appears that, in 1706, the Queen (or rather her Ministers) was "prevailed upon" to lend the (empty) Scots Treasury the sum of £20,000, "to be employed for payment of part of" arrears of salaries and pensions, lest (Lockhart says), some of the persons to whom these arrears were due might prove "humorous" (not in the modern sense) "and ungovernable".

The money was to be disposed of "in such manner as you shall find most fit for our service". This letter of authority was kept secret by the Scottish Ministers, in order not "to obstruct the Union", but the money was duly sent and expended. Lockhart gives a list (pp. 414-5) of the recipients, the principal item (£12,325) being the payment to Queensberry "for equipage and daily allowance". Among the recipients was the Duke of Atholl (£1,000) a violent anti-Unionist; a fact that has been more than once stressed as showing the falsity of the charge of bribery. But as Lockhart remarks, "one swallow does not make a summer", and he adds: "who knows what the managers did expect, and with what intentions they gave it". As against this payment, he cites instances where payment was made to persons who had "no manner of claims", any money due to them having been paid long before the distribution of the £20,000. It may be added that the leaders of the Squadron figure among the recipients; also, Major Cunningham of Eckett (£100) whose dubious conduct in connexion with the Cameronians has been mentioned in the text. Cunningham (*History*, 2, p. 62) asserts that Eckett "received his instructions from Queensberry and his payment from the Court".

Lockhart declares that Queensberry's allowance as High Commissioner was settled in full, after the Union, out of the "Equivalent", and that it was believed that the Queen had made a present to Queensberry, Godolphin, and Glasgow (as a reward for their services to the Union), of the sums already paid for Queensberry's account before the Union.

Cunningham (p. 60) says "there were Scotsmen of both parties of unquestionable probity, who never received a penny for their support of the Union; wherefore, out of twenty thousand pounds which were remitted to him out of the English Treasury, the Lord Commissioner ordered £12,000 to be laid up in the Treasury, after the business of the Union was completed, since he had nobody to give it to". Which version is correct: Lockhart's or Cunningham's?

But Cunningham had "no doubt" that Queensberry had dealt with the members, "by courtship, promises, solicitations, hopes, threatenings, and even with rewards and money". These are rather vague allegations. Yet they are probably in the main quite true.

Hill Burton (*The Reign of Queen Anne*, 8, p. 179) alludes sarcastically to the story that the Earl of Marchmont had so nicely balanced the value "of his conscience as to give back 5d. in copper on receiving £1,104 16s." He alludes also in the same strain to Lord Banff having "agreed to dispose of himself" for £11 2s.

20. *Mar and Kellie Papers*, p. 350.

21. *Seafield Correspondence*, pp. 94-103; *Scott. Hist. Soc.*, 11, (2nd Ser.), p. 173. It is significant that Lord Dupplin says (p. 174): "The merchants who everybody thought would have been the first that would have grasped at the Union" were afraid that "the little trade they have will suffer". That was also Fletcher's view, for which he has been derided by some historians.

22. Lockhart's *Memoirs*, pp. 293-326; *Mar and Kellie Papers*, p. 443

23. *Memoirs*, II, Appendix 2, p. 39.

24. Hume's *Diary*, p. 177; *Mar and Kellie Papers*, p. 304. Argyll intervened in defence of the treaters and rebuked Fletcher, but hoped for the sake of their "old friendship" that the House would accept his submission (*Portland MSS.*, 8, p. 259).

25. *Mar and Kellie Papers*, p. 306.

26. Wodrow's *Analecta*, 2, p. 46.

27. Lord Belhaven's speech could be read with advantage to-day by any member of Parliament who may wish to avoid the perils of turgid oratory. It was too much even for some of Belhaven's contemporaries, who were well accustomed to rhetorical flights.

The last of thirteen paragraphs (each commencing with the words "I think I see"), is the famous "Mother Caledonia" invocation, in which the speaker pictures a vision of Caledonia "sitting in the midst of our Senate, ruefully looking round about her, covering herself with her royal garment, attending the fatal blow, and breathing out her last with a *et tu quoque mi fili* . . ." Yet "some ram will be caught in the thicket when the bloody knife is at our mother's throat . . ." Let his fellow-members, then, for her salvation, bruise "the hydra of division", and crush "the cockatrice's egg . . ." "Hannibal, my lord", he declaimed, addressing the Chancellor, "is at our gates". But the impending arrival of Hannibal did not in the least perturb the cynical Seafield, who entirely failed to respond to Belhaven's impassioned appeal, when on his bended knees he implored the Chancellor to receive his proposals for a healing of their divisions. And Belhaven, strongly moved, broke off his speech, "that I may drop a tear on the prelude to so sad a story". The Earl of Marchmont's comment on Belhaven's performance was: "Behold he dreamed, but lo! when he awoke, he found it was a dream."

This famous speech produced a sarcastic retort in *The Vision*, a poem, attributed to the Earl of Haddington, in which the "dreamer" is held up to ridicule. "I have sent you a song on Belhaven", writes Mar, "but it's not in print which is a pittie" (*Mar and Kellie Papers*, p. 351). Yet extravagant though Belhaven's similes were, they probably represented, not merely the phrases of a rhetorician striving for effect, but the emotional expressions of a genuine patriot.

The speech presents a vivid contrast to that of Seton of Pitmedden on the other side, solid but dull.

William Paterson of Darien fame, now acting as a correspondent for Harley, remarks that, in the great debate, Fletcher spoke " . . . with all the rhetoric, art, and force of argument the subject could bear, and (which is not his ordinary) with great calmness too" (*Portland MSS.*, 8, p. 261). Defoe (*Portland MSS.*, 4, pp. 345, 356), in his reports to Harley also alludes to Fletcher's speeches.

28. Cunningham's *History*, 2, pp. 59, 65. This historian says of the Union that it is "very remarkable that the nobility should have been the first who failed their country", and that "not only the lowest of the people" but the traders were "the first that made a brisk stand for the name of liberty and sovereignty" (p. 58). Also, he makes what may seem to be the striking statement that "the multitude " were above all against the Union, not so much for material reasons, as for the fact that "the very name and antiquity of the Kingdom was of great weight with them " (p. 59). That is a point of view which is seldom stressed. *Seafield Correspondence*, pp. 101-2.

29. *Seafield Correspondence*, p. 101. Seafield told Godolphin (p. 99) that the debate on the first Article was of "the greatest importance", as indeed it was, for all the other Articles depended upon it. The debate continued until eight at night, after the House had sat for nine hours. The Opposition (says Seafield) tried obstructive tactics to ensure delay. It was on this Article that the great speeches were made.

30. *Mar and Kellie Papers*, pp. 325, 330. "The British Parliament", wrote Mar to Nairne, "is what frights most of our Scottish members that we are forced to manage. So, for God's sake, set this matter in a true light when the memorial comes" (the address to the Throne). Nairne, on his part (pp. 315, 326), was bothered by Ridpath's articles in the *Flying Post* : "that fellow Ridpath", as he called him (who, by the way, had been receiving subsidies from his Scottish patrons) (*Jerviswood Correspondence*, p. 143). The *Flying Post* had stated that far from Fletcher having begged the House's pardon for calling the treaters "traitors", he had actually used the treaters "worse". And a few days later Ridpath was telling a story in the *Post* about guarding the passes "to prevent a descent of the Highlanders". Quite a newspaper "stunt". *Mar and Kellie Papers*, p. 330.

31. Boyer's *Annals*, 4, p. 347. Boyer (pp. 341-2) relates an incident

illustrating Fletcher's regard for the freedom of the press. He had been informed that the Edinburgh printers had been warned, under penalty of a fine, that nothing must be printed until it had been censored by the magistrates. Fletcher warmly protested. Hume's *Diary*, p. 184; *Mar and Kellie Papers*, p. 330.

32. Hume's *Diary*, pp. 189-190.

33. *Ibid*, p. 192. Lord Buchan (p. 59) gives still another instance of Fletcher quarrelling with Stair when the latter was Secretary of State. Fletcher "seized Stair by the robe in his place, and gave him the reply valiant. Stair had to ask his pardon publicly."

34. Hume's *Diary*, p. 197.

35. "Upon the great question", says the Earl of Marchmont, "Approve of the Union or not", 21 of the Squadron being present, "the yeas besides them were 88, the noes 69, to whom, if the Squadron had joined, the vote had been lost by 2. If any of these questions had miscarried, the Union would have been stopped" (*Marchmont Papers*, 3, p. 330).

36. Cunningham's *History*, 2, p. 68.

37. *Marchmont Papers*, 1, p. 431; Burnet's *History*, p. 801.

Chapter XIX

1. This view is plainly set forth by the author (W. Atwood, Chief Justice of New York) of *The Scottish Patriot Unmasked*, who says (p. 137), "Scotland's becoming by its own consent a province, or part of England, is indeed the consequence of being in earnest for a compleat union of the Kingdoms".

2. *Short History of the English People* (1892), 4, p. 1562.

3. *The Union of* 1707, p. 160.

4. As one who has written a book on Scottish place-names, I may perhaps be disposed to attach excessive importance to the teaching of ethnology and history through the medium of toponomy. But it is a means of revealing the past which has certainly, so far, been undervalued. The students of place-names are few in number, and not infrequently they disagree in their interpretations. But if historians were to pay more attention than they do to the established facts in this department of science, they would find material that might assist them in the formation of sounder conclusions than are otherwise possible.

Perhaps I may be allowed to say that in my *Scottish Place-names* (pp. 255-296) there is a discussion, from various angles, of the ethnological factors to which allusion is made in the text. As showing the wide permeation in former times of the Lowlands by a Celtic-speaking population, three citations may be given. John Major (1521) mentions Welsh as one of the languages of Scotland. Sir Thomas Craig (1605) writes, "I myself remember the time when the inhabitants of the shires of Stirling and Dumbarton spoke pure Gaelic". And Burt (Letter XVIII) declares (soon after the close of the first quarter of the eighteenth century) that he had been told in Edinburgh, that the Irish (Gaelic) tongue, before the Union, "was the language of the Shire of Fife"; and that after the Union, "it became one condition of an indenture, when a youth of either sex came to be bound on the Edinburgh side of the water" (the Firth of Forth), "that the apprentice should be taught the English tongue". That may well have been true of some of the districts in Fife, outside the direct influence of the burghs.

5. *Cal. of State Papers* (*Venetian*), 1, p. 146. The King refers to "the royal city of Edinburgh", and comments upon the fact that it had been given up to the Duke of Gloucester without resistance.

6. Professor Hume Brown (*The Union of* 1707, p. 2) asserts that the reattachment of Scotland to the European movement was "the supreme compensation for the surrender of her legislative independence: which had been severed by the Union of the Crowns". This reattachment, could, of course, have been equally secured by a federal union.

7. Mr. W. R. Scott (*The Union of* 1707, pp. 101-5) shows how Scotland was hit in those commodities where she had an advantage over England. Free trade with England meant the collapse of highly-protected industries, founded under the Act of 1681, such as textiles, foundry, wool-card, glass, paper, leather, and others. When the Union arrived, "most of the factories for fine cloth were closed down or reconstituted". But the cattle trade benefited considerably, and the benefit had its reaction on agriculture. Taking the results as a whole, can it be argued that Fletcher's forebodings were unjustified?

8. *Cal. of State Papers*, 22, pp. 639-640.

9. *Ibid*, p. 358. Parke suggested that "if they chuse out all zealous Kirkmen, I promise they shall never trouble the Queen's affairs more. If they do not take Martinique, I will get them disposed of, and I think that will be some service" (p. 35).

10. *Ibid*, 23, p. 411.

11. *Ibid*, p. 707.

12. *Tour through Great Britain*, 1724-7 (1927), 2, p. 734.

13. *Ibid*, pp. 781-2.

14. *Ibid*, p. 786. Defoe does not deny the advantages derived from the Union by Glasgow, for "they have the greatest addition to their trade by it imaginable" (p. 745), but (as Lockhart would say), "one swallow does not make a summer". Defoe is obviously dubious about that portion of the Equivalent which was designed for the promotion of industry: "how much of the money has been so employed", he remarks, "I desire not to examine. I leave it to them whose proper business it is" (p. 762).

15. Omond, p. 139, who has a foot-note : "The author of the

History of Modern Europe, in a series of letters from a nobleman to his son,
who tells this story, says, 'This anecdote the author had from the late
Patrick, Lord Elibank'."

16. Sir John Clerk, Queensberry's henchman, and a member of his
retinue, gives with great gusto this account in his *Memoirs*, of the
Duke's journey (*Scott. Hist. Soc.* 13, p. 67).

17. This tract is copied by Sir John Dalrymple in Appendix III of his
Memoirs, II, pp. 55-84.

There is the same measure of support for the belief that the style and
matter of this tract point clearly to Fletcher as the author, as for the
belief that, for the same reason, the author of *A Discourse upon Union*
(1702) cannot be Fletcher. Similarly, both the matter and the style of
the tracts, *A Speech without doors concerning toleration* (? 1703), and *Scotland's Interest in the great benefit and necessity of a communication of trade with
England* (1704) show that they must have come from a pen other than
Fletcher's. All three are occasionally attributed to him.

Mr. Macfie agrees in ascribing these three tracts to pens other than
Fletcher's. But he thinks that the following tracts may "possibly" be by
Fletcher:

(1) *A Letter to a Member of the Convention of States in Scotland* by "a
Lover of his religion and country" (1689). It was reprinted in
1707 as *A Speech made by a Member of the Convention of States in
Scotland*. Fletcher was not, of course, a member of the Convention of Estates.

(2) *Some thoughts concerning the Affairs of this Session of Parliament*
(1700).

18. *Memoirs*, p. 338.

Chapter XX

1. *Mar and Kellie Papers*, p. 421.

2. James Erskine was the second son of Charles, tenth Earl of Mar.
He was appointed to the Bench in 1706, and in 1710 became Lord
Justice-Clerk with the title of Lord Grange. He was an extraordinary
combination of professed piety and loose living. It is said that a casual
talk with a barber's boy who was shaving him led to the boy's conver-
sion. But this pious individual had an unsavoury record. In his latter
days, a poor man, he lived in London, where it is believed he married
the keeper of a coffee-house who had formerly been his mistress.

The abduction, with his connivance, of his virago wife who was
carried off to the Hebrides, where she died after years of hardship, is
one of the Scottish historical problems of which a complete solution
has not yet been found. Whether the abduction was for private reasons,
or to prevent the disclosure of dangerous political secrets (or for both
reasons), has not been satisfactorily determined.

3. *History of the Union*, p. 8. See also *Harleian Miscellany*, 7, pp. 577-585.

4. Boyer's *Annals*, 6, p. 350.

5. *Mar and Kellie Papers*, p. 435; *The Spalding Club Miscellany*, 2, p. 302.

6. *Ibid*, p. 436.

7. *Mar and Kellie Papers*, p. 442.

8. *Correspondence of the Melvilles*, by Sir W. Fraser, 2, p. 222.

9. *Mar and Kellie Papers*, p. 437.

10. *Ibid*, pp. 438-9.

11. *Ibid*, pp. 445, 450. Mar tells Nairne (p. 448), that there had been a mob in the Edinburgh streets "drinking the Pretender's health". The Town Guard tried to disperse them, but Mar and some friends were forced to sit at General Maitland's until one o'clock before they could venture out.

The Earl of Sunderland (p. 448) tells Roxburgh that he hears of "violent means to influence the Scottish elections". He adds: "they will find they will not now come so well off here as they used to do in a Scots Parliament, managed by a Scots Minister".

12. *Ibid*, p. 74; *Portland MSS.*, 4, p. 507.

13. *Mar and Kellie Papers*, p. 458.

14. *Ibid*, p. 476.

15. *Autobiography of Dr. Alexander Carlyle* (1860), pp. 5-7. I have not seen in previous notices of Fletcher's career ("the famous patriot" as Carlyle calls him) any allusion to the fact that he was a candidate for the British Parliament. But there can be no reason to doubt Carlyle's accuracy. He knew Lord Milton's family intimately. (Also, he knew Lord Grange and Lovat, and tells some interesting stories about them.)

It is impossible to tell how many electors Haddingtonshire had in 1708. In 1788 the number was seventy-five (Porritt, *The Unreformed House of Commons*, p. 171). This author details (p. 145) the qualifications at the Union for the county franchise in Scotland. He shows (pp. 170-2) how the electors were "thirled" to the magnates. In 1681 the commission in favour of Fletcher and Cockburn who were elected for Haddingtonshire, was signed by "twentie heretors" (*MS. Supp. Par. Papers*, II).

16. The author of *The Scotch Patriot Unmasked* suggests, spitefully enough, that "Mr. Fletcher owned he was for humouring them who may favour the Court of St. Germains, by giving them a chance for their pretensions". There is no discoverable ground for any such assertion. The author alludes sarcastically to those of Fletcher's views as "Fletcherians" (p. 43). But there is stronger evidence for Fletcher having expressed definite views on the Hanoverian dynasty. "Fletcher of Salton", says an acquaintance in 1706, "though he owns himself of republican principles" (he must have known that a Scottish Republic was an impossibility), "always opposes the Court with vigour, speaks boldly and well, and has often said to myself that he will oppose union and Hanover still, as thinking both destructive of the nation".

(MacPherson's *Original Papers*, p. 10). The text shows that he would have accepted an emasculated Hanover, but not with unimpaired prerogatives.

17. *The Earls of Cromartie*, by Sir. W. Fraser, p. 77.

18. *History of the Carnegies, Earls of Southesk, and of their Kindred*, by Sir W. Fraser, pp. 275-6, 287.

19. *Ibid*, pp. 278-9. *General view of the agriculture and rural economy of East Lothian*, by George Buchan-Hepburn, pp. 145-6. The first authority gives the credit to Mrs. Fletcher, the latter to Andrew, of going over to Holland, and obtaining there the plans for the barley-mill. The Carnegie version is obviously a mistake. The plans for the barley-mill appear to have been confused with those for the "Holland" cloth.

20. *History of the Carnegies*, p. 279.

21. *Ibid*, pp. 280-4.

22. *Miscellaneous Writings of John Spreull* (1646-1722), pp. 3-72. Fletcher's Act was introduced on 3rd August, 1705; it had a first reading on 5th September (*MS. Supp. Par. Papers*, 19, No. 127).

23. Wodrow's *Analecta*, 2, pp. 44-7. This conversation, as reported by Wodrow, offers some support to the view that the tract on *Proposals for the reformation of Schools and Universities* may quite well have been written by Fletcher. Mr. Macfie is inclined to favour that view. There is nothing in the tract inconsistent with it. The Family MS. says that Fletcher declared that "the education of youth is one of the noblest objects of government", and that on this subject "he wrote a treatise".

Mr. Macfie points out that in the *Transactions of the National Association for the Promotion of Social Science*, 1851, it is stated that "when Fletcher of Salton, at the latter end of the seventeenth century, proposed to the Scotch Parliament to extend and improve the system of their parochial schools, he gave as a reason the ignorance and violence of a large part of the population".

Fletcher, not being a member of the Convention of Estates, could not have made that proposal in the House. Yet there is nothing inherently improbable, but on the contrary, in the suggestion that he was at the back of the movement which led to the passing of the Education Act: a measure of incalculable benefit to Scotland in the eighteenth century.

The Family MS. states that Fletcher, during his exile, "made a collection of books composing the best private library in Scotland", and that he "maintained a useful and extensive correspondence with the friends of liberty at home". Captain Fletcher of Saltoun was good enough to show me a catalogue of these books, and the fine family portraits in Saltoun Hall.

24. That statement is by Thomas Rawlinson, an antiquary of note.

25. *Cal. of State Papers*, 3, p. 54 (Letter from Sir Hugh Paterson to the Duke of Mar dated 9th October, 1716.) It was Paterson (he knew

Fletcher well) who recorded the opinion of the latter about the future of his nephew.

It seems curious, in view of his previous record, as related in the text, to find Mar in the capacity of a Jacobite duke. But of course, he was not alone in the violent reaction against the Union among its most prominent supporters. Seafield was a conspicuous example; so too was Argyll. In 1711, Mar told his brother, Grange, that "the English, as most of the Scots are, seem to be wearie of the Union" . . . The Scots peers would have "some comfort", if they could get rid of the Union "without a civil war, but that I'm afraid is impossible" (*Mar and Kellie Papers*, p. 491). Harley himself declared, in 1709, to Carstares, that "we have violated our treaty with Scotland" (Carstares, *State Papers*, pp. 774-6).

Mr. G. M. Thomson relates (*Rediscovery of Scotland*, p. 158) a story about George Keith, the tenth Earl Marischal, and Fletcher, which is new to me. He says that when Keith was in London, preparing secretly to join Mar for the "Fifteen" rising, Fletcher called on him and tried to dissuade him from his purpose: the people whom Keith was going to join were not so "honest or steady" as himself. On Keith declaring that he was chiefly concerned with getting rid of the Union, "which oppresses us", Fletcher replied: "It is a good thing to be young". When he was Keith's age (about twenty-two) he would have done the same thing as Keith proposed to do. "I have been sorely brought down by sickness", he added, "and I find my mind is failing with my body".

26. *Cal. of Stuart Papers*, p. 107 (Letter from H. Straton to the Duke of Mar, dated 9th October, 1716.)

27. The letter from Lord Hailes to the Earl of Buchan in the Edinburgh University Library relates a story which probably gives something like a true illustration of the quickness, but evanescence, of Fletcher's temper. It seems certain that in his private relations he never cherished resentment long. But where public interests were concerned, he was relentless in his animosities. "Fletcher of Saltoun" (says the story), "is well known to have possessed a most irritable temper. His footman desiring to be dismissed, 'Why do you leave me?' said he. 'Because, to speak the truth, I cannot bear your temper'. 'To be sure, I am passionate, but my passion is no sooner on than it is off.' 'Yes', replied the servant, 'but then it is no sooner off than it is on'."

28. With the first part of Macky's tribute, those of the school of Mr. H. G. Wells will presumably disagree as a ground for applause; and with the laudability of the second part, those who think, with the late Mr. F. S. Oliver, that, in the welfare of the nation, the end justifies the means, will find themselves equally out of sympathy. But the two parts are really complementary to a consistent whole. Fletcher's antipathy to a conception that gives to the world what is due to country, would have been as pronounced as his refusal to accept

Cavour's maxim when he said: "What scoundrels we should be if we did for ourselves the things we are prepared to do for Italy".

In the *Lockhart Papers* there is a rhymed epitaph on Fletcher. It commences:

"The brightest glory of the Scottish race
And nation, lyes interred within this place";

and ends:

"For while there does remain the name of Scot
Fletcher's great worth shall never be forgot,
Honour shall still attend the Patriot's name
Remotest ages shall respect the same
And spite of envy eternise his merit and his fame."

The quality of the sentiment is superior to that of the poetry in which it is expressed.

ADDITIONAL NOTES

Article in the Dictionary of National Biography.

Mr. Espinasse's excellent article on Fletcher contains two mis-statements of fact which need correction. It confuses George Keith, the tenth Earl Marischal (the Ambassador in Paris and Madrid of Frederick the Great, and the friend of Rousseau and Voltaire) with his father, the ninth Earl. The latter, and not the tenth Earl (born about 1693), was with Fletcher in the Parliament of 1703-7. Frederick was greatly attached to George Keith: "Your old friend till death", as he called him, when condoling with him on the death, at the battle of Hochkirch in 1758, of his brother, James, Frederick's famous Field-Marshal.

Also, the article is in error in including Fletcher in the list of prisoners who were sent to London in 1708, charged with complicity in the Jacobite affair of that year.

"As a writer", says Mr. Espinasse, "he" (Fletcher) "is superior to any Scotchman of his age."

INDEX

Index

Burnet, Gilbert, and the living of Saltoun, 1-3; his son's tribute, 3; as Fletcher's tutor, 4; on Fletcher, 17, 29, 30; on Ferguson, 19; high in Court favour, 50; and the Scottish Episcopalians, 51; supports Godolphin, 221; cited, 11-13, 71, 265, 276

Byng, Sir George, 294

Cameronians, the, and the Union, 260-1

Campbell of Finab, Captain Alexander, and Darien, 117

Campbell of Glenlyon, Captain Robert, and Glencoe, 62

Campbell, John. (*See* Argyll, 2nd Duke of.)

Carlyle, Reverend Alexander, 300

Carnegie of Pitarrow, Sir David, 302

Carnegie, Margaret (wife of Henry Fletcher), 302; and the Saltoun barley mill, 303; and Holland cloth, 304; letter to her son, 305-6

Carr, Lord Charles, Fletcher's second, 234

Carstares, Reverend William, and the Council of Six, 18; high in Court favour, 50; his statesmanship, 264-5

Cavaliers, the, and Queensberry, 157; relations with the Countrymen, 159, 210; and an Act of Security, 167; 208-9, 211, 213; and the Courtiers, 214; their victory, 215; 225; their tactical mistake, 235; their composition, 236; and Hamilton, 244; 298-9

Chamberlain, Dr. Hugh, and his scheme, 233

Charteris, Colonel, and Prestongrange, 300

Chevalier de St. George, the, and the Jacobites, 293-5; the main obstacle to a Stewart Restoration, 294

Claim of Right, and Fletcher, 50, 239; and the Union, 262

Clerk, Sir John, cited, 159; on Fletcher, 311

Club, The, formed, 45-6; Fletcher a member, 45; its principal members, 55; dissolved, 57; its main work, 57

Cochrane, Sir John, and Argyll, 24

Cockburn of Ormiston, Adam, Fletcher's colleague, 9

Cockburn of Ormiston, John (younger), Fletcher's colleague, 157

Colonial Governors and the Darien Scheme, 109-110

Colvin, Lord, 296

Company of Scotland, the, formed, 66; its capital issued, 68; incorporation

resented in England, 68-9; its trading privileges, 68; directors threatened with impeachment, 69; and the King, 70, 74; subscriptions withdrawn, 70; Fletcher subscribes, 71; national subscription, 71; Continental subscriptions blocked by England, 72; and Sir Paul Rycaut, 72-3; the Hamburg snub, 74; the Darien Scheme, 79; and Fletcher, 106; and Wafer, 106; the Spanish protest, 107; its choice of colonists, 113; directors' lack of prevision, 115; and James Johnston, 212; the *Annandale*, 228; the Equivalent, 254-5

Commissioners for Union, the, 251

Commons, House of, and the Plot, 210

Convention of Estates, at the Revolution, 148

Convention of Royal Burghs, and Colonial settlements, 67

Council of Six, the, 15; and the Rye House Plot, 16

Council of Trade, the, 245-6

Council of Trade and Plantations, the, and Darien, 107

Country Party, the, Fletcher's relations with, 144; its leading members, 153-5; and the Convention of 1702, 156; and the Claim of Right, 156-7; and the Act of Security, 167; and the Cavaliers, 210; 213

Cromarty, Earl of (Sir George Mackenzie, Viscount Tarbat), as Secretary, 150, 213; his character, 151; secedes from Queensberry, 208; as Justice-General, 224; his sentiments on Union, 253; advises adjournment, 276; and "the Brittains", 279; his correspondence with Fletcher, 301

Cunningham, Alexander, cited, 255, 272

Cunningham of Eckett, Major, and the Cameronians, 261

Dalrymple, Sir Hugh, and the Union, 250

Dalrymple, Sir James (1st Viscount Stair), 11, 12, 40, 63

Dalrymple, Sir John (successively Master of Stair, Viscount Stair, and 1st Earl of Stair), and Glencoe, 63; his eloquence, 145; 211; and Fletcher, 240, 275; and Argyll, 240; 241; and the Union, 250-1, 286, 262; 271; his death (1707), 287

Dalrymple, Sir John (Baron of the Scottish Exchequer), cited, 11, 32-4, 77-8, 138, 268

366

Index

Dampier, Captain William, 75, 112
Dare, Heywood (Alderman—? Mayor—
of Taunton), 22, 28, 31; shot by Fletcher, 32; sequel to his death, 34; 40-1
Darien Scheme, the, 106-120; and Paterson, 64, 76, 78-9; and Wafer, 78-81;
and Dampier, 78-9; Fletcher's enthusiasm for, 77; and the Spanish settlements, 78; and the Earl of Tankerville (Lord Grey), 78; and John Locke,
78; and Sir John Munro, 79; and Captain Pennycook, 79-80; Wafer visits
Saltoun Hall, 79-80; Fletcher's bargain with Wafer, 81; and Walter
Herries, 80-1; the Spanish claims, 108-
9; the English boycott, 111; Fletcher's
views, 112; ineptitude of Councillors,
116
*Defence of the Settlement of the Scots on the
Isthmus of Darien, A* (tract attributed
to Fletcher), *Appendix*, 314-323
Defoe, Daniel, and the Alien Act, 223;
on Scottish poverty, 284; on economic
effects of the Union, 285; on the threat
of invasion, 294
Discorso delle cose di Spagna (Fletcher), 82
*Discourse of Government with relation to
Militias, A* (Fletcher), 121
Discourses on the affairs of Scotland (Flet-
cher), 82
Douglas, James (*see* Queensberry, 2nd
Duke of)
Dumbarton, Earl of, and Fletcher's
estates, 42
Dupplin, Viscount, cited, 266

East India Company, Old and New, 67
Edinburgh, the mob and the Green inci-
dent, 229-230; riots against the Union,
259-260
Education, probable effect on Scottish
trade of, 285-6; Fletcher's views on,
307-8
Edward IV and the two nations, 280
Eglinton, Earl of, 208
England, and the Darien Scheme, 118;
and the Green incident, 231; and the
provincial idea, 278
England, Privy Council of, and Scottish
Jacobites, 295
Episcopal clergy, rabbling of the, 46
Equivalent, the, 253-5, 295
Errol, Earl of, and the anti-Union riots,
260; warned by Fletcher against Jaco-
bite adventures, 295
Erskine, Colonel, and Fletcher, 296
Erskine, David, 292

Erskine, James (Lord Grange), 249, 259;
and Fletcher, 250, 268, 292-3, 297,
299
Erskine, John (*see* Mar, Earl of)

Falconer, Sir John, 214
Ferguson, Robert ("the Plotter"), 16; his
character, 19; and Monmouth, 22, 28,
35-6; and Fletcher, 33-4; 39-40; and
the "Scotch Plot", 210
Fletcher of Saltoun, Andrew, his parent-
age, 1; his education, 2-5; enters public
life, 5; and Lauderdale, 6; and the militia, 8; returned for Haddingtonshire
(1681), 9; and the Test Act, 10-12;
leaves Scotland, 14; and the Council of
Six, 17; and Viscount Preston, 20;
Monmouth's adviser, 22; and Argyll,
23; refuses to desert Monmouth, 25;
with Monmouth, 28; his military reputation, 29-30; his service in Hungary, 30; the Dutch skipper, 31; the
Dare incident, 31-2; and Ferguson,
33-4; his Spanish prison, 38-9; tried in
absence, 40-42; condemned to death,
42; and hereditary monarchy, 42-3; excluded from pardon, 44; returns with
William of Orange, 44; a member of
the Club, 45; his estates restored, 45;
and the prerogative, 55-6; and Glencoe, 63; and Paterson, 64, 76-7, 272;
and the Scottish attitude to trade, 65;
and the Darien Scheme, 77, 106; and
Wafer, 79-81; his treatises, 112; and
the Company of Scotland, 114; his
draft of an Act of Security, 138; elected
to Parliament (1703), 140; his dominating principles, 141-3; Dean Swift
on, 142; George Lockhart on, 143-4;
and the Country Party, 144; his detachment from parties, 155; and Atholl,
158; his "Limitations", 160; risks of
his proposals, 164-5; a protest, 171-2;
on separation, 176-7; the Act of Peace
and War, 177; the Wine Act, 177-8;
the supremacy of Parliament, 179; re-
duces his Limitations from twelve to
three, 180; and places and pensions,
181; and annual Parliaments, 184; and
Hamilton, 214, 218, 232, 244, 299; and
the English Parliament, 214; and Johnston, 215-6; his Act for a treaty, 217;
and the New Courtiers, 217; and the
intermeddling of English peers, 217;
and political corruption, 218; and the
Alien Act, 222, 238, 243; his prestige
in Parliament, 232; and the New

367

Mackenzie, Sir George, of Rosehaugh, 40

Mackenzie, Sir George, of Tarbat (*see* Cromarty, Earl of)

Macky, John, cited, 30, 56, 154, 302, 312; his tribute to Fletcher, 313

Mar, Earl of, Secretary, 236, 249; his views on the Union, 252; 253; replaces Annandale, 256; unpopular as a Unionist, 260; 264; and Fletcher, 270, 271; 274; 292; and the attempted invasion (1708), 295; and Fletcher's imprisonment, 296; 298; 299; and the "Fifteen", 309-10

Mar Lady (mother of the Earl of), and Fletcher, 296

Marchmomt, Earl of (*see* Hume, Sir Patrick)

Marlborough, Duke of, 207, 208, 219, 225

Marlborough, Duchess of, and Roxburgh, 256

Mary of Modena, and the Jacobites, 209

Matthews, Captain, and Monmouth, 21

Meikle, James, and the Saltoun barley mill, 303

Melfort, Earl of, 48

Melville, Earl of, and the Council of Six, 18; Secretary, 52; supersedes Hamilton as Commissioner, 54

Milton, Lord (*see* Fletcher, Andrew)

Monmouth, Duke of, 15; in Holland, 20; and Fletcher, 22, 30, 32-7; leaves Amsterdam, 27; lands at Lyme, 28; his fatal manifesto, 34; his evil genius, 35; the battle of Sedgemoor, 36; compared to Bonnie Prince Charlie, 37

Montgomery, Sir James, and the Club, 52, 55-6

Montrose, Marquis of (later 1st Duke), 153; his character, 154; President of the Privy Council of Scotland, 256; unpopular as a Unionist, 260; 264; created duke, 293; 298

Morison of Prestongrange, elected for East Lothian, 300

Murray, Sir James, 213

Murray of Stanhope, James, 209

Murray, John (*see* Atholl, Marquis and Duke of)

Murray of Abercairney, John, 209

Nairne, Sir David, Under-Secretary, 264, 270, 271, 297

New Party, the (*Squadrone Volante*), its composition, 227; and Argyll, 228;

and the Green incident, 230; and Fletcher, 233, 250; 237; and Seafield, 242; Marchmont leaves, 244; their vote, 256; their motives in carrying the Union, 257; Seafield's skilful angling and success with, 265-6; vote of, deciding factor in the Union, 273; 292; their hostility to Queensberry, 293; and Hamilton, 293, 298

Ogilvie, James (*see* Seafield, Earl of)

Ormond, G. W. T., cited, 311

Parke, Daniel, his proposals, 283

Parliament, the first British, and its Scottish members, 291

Parliament, the English, and the Scottish Parliament, 218; 220-1; passes the Alien Act, 222; and the Union, 250; a graceful gesture, 251

Parliament, the Scottish, not democratic, 47; its "riding", 146-7; and the Ministry of 1703, 150; unfree, 163; its historical development, 165-6; and inflation, 235; and Seafield's quip, 248; its abolition not a national act, 248; its last Session, 256; passes Treaty of Union, 276

Paterson, Bishop, 9

Paterson, Sir Hugh, 310

Paterson, William, and Fletcher, 64, 76-7; his aim; 74-5; 78, 79-80; his enthusiasm for Darien, 112; on the Council of Seven, 114; a man of vision, 119; on a speech by Fletcher, 272

Perth, Earl of, 48

Plot, "the Scotch", 209, 211, 242

Present State of the Controversy betwixt United and Separate Parliaments, The (Fletcher), 268, 287

Presbyterianism, re-established in Scotland, 51

Proposals for the reformation of Schools and Universities (attributed to Fletcher), 308

Protestant Succession, the, 139; and the Parliamentary parties, 238-9; and the Union, 278

Queensberry, 2nd Duke of, High Commissioner, 145-6, 150; his Parliamentary difficulties, 157; 159; 170; 172; and the Act of Security, 174-5; his first blunder, 179; 180; 184; secession of his colleagues, 208; and Lovat, 209; and the Plot, 210, 217; his ill-success, 212; 213; and Roxburgh, 225, 257;

PRINTED IN GREAT BRITAIN BY ROBERT MACLEHOSE AND CO. LTD.
THE UNIVERSITY PRESS, GLASGOW